William Rothman

Hitchcock - The Murderous Gaze

HARVARD UNIVERSITY PRESS
Cambridge, Massachusetts
London, England

**Copyright © 1982 by the President and
Fellows of Harvard College**
All rights reserved
Printed in the United States of America
Sixth printing, 1997

Publication of this volume has been aided by a
grant from the Andrew W. Mellon Foundation

Library of Congress Cataloging in Publication Data

Rothman, William.
  Hitchcock—the murderous gaze.

  (Harvard film studies)
  Includes index.
    1. Hitchcock, Alfred, 1899–1980. I. Title. II. Series.
PN1998.A3H553   791.43'0233'0924   81-1700
                                          AACR2

ISBN 0-674-40411-4 (paper)

For my parents
Ruth J. Rothman and Irwin M. Rothman

and my sister
Judith R. Streisand

Acknowledgments

The friends whose words and ideas echo in these pages are too numerous to list. The names of Norton Batkin, Peter Biskind, Barry Gewen, Timo Gilmore, Timothy Gould, Tom Hopkins, Harry Hunt, Pepe Karmel, Steven Levine, Ellen Mandel, Miles Morgan, Jon Ostriker, Linda Podheiser, James Shapiro, and Paul Thomas will have to suffice.

Among the friends, colleagues, and students who have made helpful comments on drafts of the manuscript, Marian Keane has my special gratitude for the multitude of ideas that emerged from our talks and for the generosity and shrewdness with which she boosted my morale at critical moments. I also want to express my appreciation of my editor, Joyce Backman, for all she has done to make this a better book and for all her editing taught me about writing.

To Stanley Cavell, I owe a deep debt. He taught me that philosophy can be motivated and sustained by something as apparently mundane as a movie. Over the years, by his work and through his friendship, he has provided immeasurable guidance and encouragement.

I am grateful to the faculty, staff, and students of Carpenter Center for fostering an environment conducive to productive work; and to the National Endowment for the Humanities, the Luce Foundation, and the Mayer Foundation for giving the Harvard film program vital support. I also wish to thank EMI Films Limited for allowing me to reproduce frame enlargements from *The Lodger* and *Murder!*, to thank The Rank Organisation Limited for granting permission to use stills from *The Thirty-Nine Steps*, and to acknowledge MCA (Universal City Studios, Inc.), a corporation that strikes a hard bargain, for authorizing the use of illustrations from *Shadow of a Doubt* and *Psycho*.

Without the friendship and love of my wife, Kitty Morgan, and the infinite patience with which she endured this project, the book could never have been written.

Contents

Hitchcock — The Murderous Gaze

Introduction

This book follows five Hitchcock films, moment by moment, as they unfold from beginning to end. Using frame enlargements as illustration and evidence, I attempt to put into words the thinking inscribed in their successions of frames. (In transcribing dialogue and describing gestures, expressions, and movements of the camera, I relied on no scripts and checked my language only by direct observation of the films themselves.) My aim was to demonstrate something fundamental about Hitchcock and about the making and viewing of films, and to reflect on the implications of this demonstration for our understanding of the conditions and history of the art of film.

I do not claim that these five are necessarily the best or the most important of all Hitchcock's films or that, as a group, they are most representative. They are among the Hitchcock films I have come to know especially intimately over the years, for a variety of reasons. And I believe that these five are, at the very least, more than good enough and more than representative enough to enable them, individually and as a group—I believe they complement each other meaningfully—to stand in for Hitchcock's authorship as a whole.

Nonetheless, I realize that my selection will strike many readers as peculiar. For one thing, the inclusion of three British films seems to unbalance it. I must emphasize that such a distribution does not represent a critical assessment of the relative merits of the early and late Hitchcock films. However, it does reflect one of the book's major claims: that such films as *The Lodger* and *Murder!* are vastly richer than has generally been recognized and, beyond this, that they cast unexpected light on the range of Hitchcock's ambitions and on his place within film history.

More peculiar than the inclusion of three British Hitchcocks, perhaps, are the book's conspicuous omissions. None of the Hitchcock masterpieces of the 1950s, *Rear Window* and *Vertigo* in particular, have been included, and neither of the most remarkable post-*Psycho* films, *The Birds* and *Marnie*.

One relevant consideration was the desirability of selecting only films in black and white in order to keep the cost of the volume from soaring wholly out of sight. I judged that these omissions would not make the book fundamentally incomplete, as long as *Psycho* could serve double duty, representing both the unbroken series of great films it brings to an end and the "late" period it initiates. With *Rear Window* and *Vertigo* there was a further consideration. They are among a group of films—*The Trouble with Harry* and *The Man Who Knew Too Much* are the others—Hitchcock kept out of circulation during the last years of his life. Although I have had a chance to study them at the Library of Congress, I decided not to select any films not readily available for screening. I am honestly convinced that the book does not suffer from this omission.

Conceivably, each of these five readings could stand on its own. In a sense, each one puts the reader through the same experience of running through a Hitchcock film from start to finish. What justifies the repetition of this experience? The book is so written as to distribute its reflections and arguments across all five of its readings. But also it is so written as to pick up and exploit resonances from reading to reading. There is a general strategy in this regard. The opening chapter makes almost no reference to Hitchcock films other than *The Lodger*, which befits the film's status as, in effect, the original Hitchcock film. Each subsequent reading incorporates more, and more intricate, references to other Hitchcock films, as the films themselves increasingly incorporate into their texture and forms a complex system of references. And each new reading continually invokes, implicitly and explicitly, the readings that precede it in the book, playing on the resonances that the writing accumulates. This process is completed in the chapter on *Psycho*. While a reader could go right to this last chapter and follow its argument, it is also very much composed as the book's climax and conclusion. In the reading of *Psycho*, all the discoveries of the preceding readings are meant to reverberate, all their lines of thought to be brought into play and interwoven.

Yet I can imagine a sympathetic reader coming to the end of the *Psycho* chapter and wondering exactly where he or she has arrived, perhaps feeling that the book has really gone nowhere. This is because I can imagine the book's engendering in the reader the sense that Hitchcock's work ends where it began. For I demonstrate what no previous criticism has suggested, that *Psycho*'s position is already declared, indeed already worked out, in *The Lodger*.

But who does not know the experience of looking back across an artist's lifetime of work and feeling that no real distance separates the first creations from the last? The possibility of such an experience cannot be separated from what art is. And it is closely related to another, very different, experience that I can also imagine. I can imagine a reader coming to the end of the book and suddenly being overcome by the magnitude of all that separates *Psycho* from *The Lodger*. What separates these films is also what joins them: a body of work that movingly stands in for an entire human life, even as it traverses and sums up the history of an art.

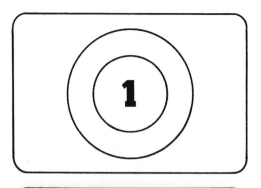

The Lodger

The *Pleasure Garden* (1925), a German–English coproduction filmed in Munich, was the first film Alfred Hitchcock completed as director. The Pleasure Garden of the title is a nightclub, and the film, which tells the backstage story of two dancers, anticipates Hitchcock's abiding interest in theater. No doubt *The Mountain Eagle* (1926) is equally worthy of study, but no prints survive. Yet however important these films may be, and however closely related to his later work, Hitchcock was not being arbitrary when he spoke of *The Lodger: A Story of the London Fog* (1926), his third directorial effort, as the first true Hitchcock film, the one that inaugurates his authorship. When he returned to England fifty years—and fifty films—later to make *Frenzy*, whose protagonist may or may not be a psychopathic killer of women, it was to *The Lodger* that he turned, closing a circle.

By 1925 the basic forms and techniques, and many of the major genres, of the movies were firmly established. A decade after D. W. Griffith's *The Birth of a Nation*, film had become a giant international industry, a powerful medium of mass communication, and a great art. Hitchcock began his career as a director at the height of what he always called the Golden Age of film. The Hollywood studios were astonishingly productive, putting out films so universally popular they were America's principal forum for dialogues on sexuality, romance, marriage, the family and other "private" matters of public concern in an era of social change. The great directors of the German cinema, such as F. W. Murnau, Fritz Lang, and G. W. Pabst, were achieving unprecedented expressive effects with camera movement, set design and lighting. Louis Delluc, Germaine Dulac, Jean Epstein, Marcel L'Herbier, Abel Gance, René Clair, and the young Jean Renoir in France were experimenting with subjective devices and other formal innovations, and referring to themselves as an avant-garde. The Scandinavians Victor Sjöström, Mauritz Stiller, and Carl Dreyer were probing dark, disquieting areas of the human psyche. In the Soviet Union, amid an atmosphere of artistic and intellectual ferment, Lev Kuleshov, Dziga Vertov, V. L. Pudovkin, Sergei Eisenstein, and others were demonstrating and debating the possibilities of editing.

Hitchcock started with a clear sense of film's traditions and a conviction that film was an art. His achievement, in part, was to create the first films that, fully embracing the medium, reflected seriously on their nature as films. Perhaps we cannot really speak of modernism in regard to an art that was not even born before the modern emerged in painting, music, poetry, and theater. If there is a modernist cinema, however, it begins with Hitchcock, in whose work film attains a modern self-consciousness.

A measure and expression of the modernity of the Hitchcock film is its call upon us to acknowledge, at every moment, not only what is on view within the frame but the camera as well. One of his deepest insights is that no moment in any film can be fully comprehended without accounting for the camera. Another is that, in the camera's tense and shifting relationships with its human subjects, the author's and viewers' roles are intimately revealed. Yet another is that the camera's presence is fundamentally ambiguous. It frames our views: the instrument of our gaze, it shares our passivity. But it also represents the author: it is the instrument of his presentation to us, his "narration," and manifests his godlike power over the world of the film, a world over which he presides. Within the world of a Hitchcock film, the nature and relationships of love, murder, sexuality, marriage, and theater are at issue; these are among Hitchcock's constant themes. His treatment of these themes, however, and his understanding of the reasons film keeps returning to them, cannot be separated from his constant concern with the nature of the camera, the act of viewing a film, and filmmaking as a calling.

Hitchcock did not gradually "find himself," as did Jean Renoir, for instance. Rather, at the outset of his career, he announced his central concerns and declared a position—at once a philosophical one on the conditions of human existence and a critical one on the powers and limits of the medium and the art of film—to which he remained faithful for over fifty-five years. *The Lodger* is not an apprentice work but a thesis, definitively establishing Hitchcock's identity as an artist. Thematically and stylistically, it is fully characteristic of his filmic writing. By "writing" I mean not what we ordinarily think of as a script but a film's construction as a succession of views, what is technically called its "continuity" and in France its "découpage." The writing of *The Lodger* in this sense is amazingly imaginative and complex. Every shot, every framing, reframing, and cut, is significant.

This is not to say that all we mean when we speak of Hitchcock can be found in *The Lodger*, or that it reveals his full stature as an artist. It is certainly not equal to his masterpieces of the fifties and early sixties, such as *Rear Window*, *The Wrong Man*, *Vertigo*, *North by Northwest*, *Psycho*, *The Birds*, and *Marnie*, or even to the classic thrillers of the thirties, such as *The Thirty-Nine Steps* and *The Lady Vanishes*. For one thing, the late films have a sensuality and visual power perhaps unmatched in all of cinema, and barely to be glimpsed in *The Lodger* or any of the other early films. Nonetheless, *The Lodger* amply repays close analysis. When film's "Golden Age" is celebrated, Hitchcock's silent films are never given their due. Yet, as I understand it, Hitchcock occupies a central place in the history of film, a place already secured by *The Lodger* and the small but remarkable body of silent films that followed.

1.1

The Lodger opens with a view of a woman screaming (1.1); then the screen fades to black. We are not shown what precedes this scream or what immediately follows it, but in a moment we will understand that this shot is a fragment of a scene of murder.[1] It is our introduction to the murderer known as "the Avenger," who has been terrorizing London, killing a golden-haired woman on the Embankment every Tuesday night. The Avenger has just stepped forward into this woman's view, provoking her scream. Yet we are given no view of this figure: we do not know who or what he has just revealed himself to be or in what spirit he has stepped forward. The shot is from the Avenger's point of view, and the woman screams in the face of the camera; this is the film's first suggestion that the camera and the murderer have a mysterious bond. The mystery of the Avenger— who and what he is—is also the mystery of what the camera really represents.

The opening shot shows us what the Avenger sees, even as it withholds all views of this figure from us (in particular, it withholds the woman's frightful vision). Within the world of the film, the Avenger is a viewer. The scene of which this shot is a fragment is rooted in our own role as viewers. We possess views of this world, while necessarily remaining unseen by the beings who dwell within it. By stepping forward to be viewed, the Avenger enacts what to us can only be a fantasy—that of entering the world of the film and presenting ourselves to be viewed. This is not merely a personal fantasy, of course; it is built into the role of the viewer of a film. Here that fantasy becomes a nightmare. We step forward to be viewed only to find that our presence engenders horror. And this nightmare is also Hitchcock's. If *The Lodger*'s opening is a viewer's fantasy, it also grows out of a fantasy intrinsic to the author's role. It is as if Hitchcock steps forward from his place behind the camera, only to find that his presence is horrifying.

After the opening shot, the words "to-night golden curls" flash three times on the black screen. Then the body of a woman, lying lifeless on the ground, fades into view. This view helps explain the film's opening: the body is that of the woman who was screaming. The next shot defines this view in turn as from the perspective of an old woman who now clutches her hands in horror and covers her eyes. When Hitchcock next cuts to a policeman taking notes, the context of the previous shot is disclosed: an eyewitness is relating her story to the police, gathering a crowd.

This passage demonstrates one of Hitchcock's characteristic strategies. Again and again, he presents a view we cannot interpret because he has withheld something about its context, or we misread because we take its context to be other than it really is. Sometimes Hitchcock makes no secret of cloaking his presentations in enigmas and sometimes withholds information without our realizing it. The process of following any Hitchcock film is one of continual rereading or rethinking. By this strategy and others, Hitchcock makes us aware that what we view is presented by an author whose intentions are enigmatic. Here, he specifically reminds us that authors are capable of deception by introducing a prankster who plays a practical joke on the old woman. As she tells her story with dramatic flourish, there is a cut to a man in the crowd who pulls his collar up, mimicking the woman's description of the murderer. When Hitchcock cuts to her point of view—an expressionistically distorted image of the man, reflected off a polished metal wall—we are not frightened as the woman is. We have been let in on this trick, which deflates her self-importance and brings home the reality of her fear. Yet if this prankster does not deceive us but reminds us of any author's capacity for deception, the passage also plants a picture of the Avenger in our minds, and furthers Hitchcock's central strategy for deceiving us. When the lodger first appears in the film, we see him cast in this image, and believe he may really be the Avenger.

A shot of a reporter telephoning the story in to his office provides a transition to a quasi-documentary account of the process by which the newspaper, the *Evening Standard*, is produced and distributed. The main point of this account is that the *Evening Standard* whets London's appetite for violence by invoking scenes Londoners desire to view yet dread viewing, and that what draws newspaper readers to stories about murder cannot be separated from what draws viewers to films.[2] The idea that the *Evening Standard*'s readers are also *The Lodger*'s viewers is underscored by three characteristic touches that punctuate this passage. First, Hitchcock personally appears as an extra in the editorial office. (He appears again at the film's climax.) Second, as a truck carrying bales of newspapers drives into the depths of the frame, two heads, visible through oval windows, swing back and forth (1.2), as though they were the newspaper van's eyes. Third, a crowd is shown looking upward, all eyes moving in unison—to all appearances, an audience viewing a

1.2

1.3

1.4

film (1.3). When Hitchcock cuts to the crowd's point of view, we realize that these people are reading a huge electric sign spelling out the *Evening Standard*'s report of the latest Avenger murder.

In one of the most remarkable sequences of the film, Hitchcock dissolves from a radio announcer reading the story of the murder to one solitary listener after another: a man who rolls his eyes, an angry woman who yowls like a cat, a man who listens taut with excitement, a woman so aroused that she runs her tongue sensually over her lips (1.4). Each listener appears less an individual than a representative of the London public. All these faces seem to collapse into one, a face with alternating male and female aspects. The series ends with a woman who gazes fearfully about her.

To begin the narrative proper, Hitchcock must effect a transition from London in general to the individual characters of his drama. In a brief scene, several women enter what we recognize as a dressing room, apparently after a performance. The camera isolates one whose blond hair marks her as a potential victim. Hitchcock cuts to her point of view, and we see a menacing, knife-wielding figure who rises without warning into the frame. The apparition is then explained: it is a stage hand in disguise, playing a practical joke. This time, however, Hitchcock did not let us in on the prank. We too were taken in. Hitchcock has declared his capacity for deceiving us. He has given us fair warning.

A title reading simply "Daisy" is followed by a view of a beauti-

1.5

ful blonde, who opens her ermine coat to reveal her elegant evening dress (1.5). We cannot help recognizing her as another potential victim of the Avenger, in part because this framing echoes the film's opening, as though our view were once again the murderer's. Our tension increases when Hitchcock cuts to a newsboy hawking the *Evening Standard* and then back to Daisy, who gives no sign that she is listening and appears indifferent to the possibility that she is in the Avenger's presence. Showing no fear, she steps toward the camera. Only then does a cut to a longer shot disclose the real setting: this is a fashion salon, and Daisy is a model making her entrance. What we took to be Daisy in the London night, going about her private affairs, is Daisy in costume, about to display her outfit—and herself—to the wealthy men and women gathered for the show. The next shot shows us this audience—the men who take pleasure in viewing models like Daisy and the women who hope to buy the ability to arouse men's desire (1.6). We do not know who Daisy really is. All we know is that modeling is her job. Perhaps it is only a way of making a living. Perhaps she models because she dreams of being the kind of sophisticated woman of the world, disdainful of those who would judge her, that we first took her to be. Or perhaps she dreams of a romantic figure who will one day step forward from within her audience to possess her.

1.6

Hitchcock next cuts to an unidentified man buying a newspaper on the street and walking into a boarding house. Then two other characters are introduced: a woman we take to be his wife and a police detective named Joe, a friend of the family. As Joe brags about how quickly he would apprehend the Avenger if he were put on the case, a second title reading "Daisy" appears on the screen. Identified as "the daughter of the house," Daisy enters.

Daisy's two introductions anticipate a conflict basic to the narrative. She appears fated for marriage to Joe, but unless there is more to him than meets the eye, such a marriage would be the denial of all dreams of wealth and freedom, of commanding an audience, and of romance. Daisy is a girl on the threshold of womanhood torn between romantic yearnings and the wish to be a good daughter. Not wishing to disobey her parents, she also does not wish to be trapped in a sexless marriage like theirs. She is the first of a long line of Hitchcock heroines faced with this predicament.[3] Indeed, Hitchcock's films characteristically take the form of dramas about a girl's growing up, and begin with the appearance, as if by magic, of a mysterious man who may have the power to make the girl's romantic dreams come true but who also may be a monster.

Hitchcock elegantly lays out Daisy's dilemma by presenting a scene "directed" by Joe, a passage that also illustrates his characteristic care in differentiating the camera's relationships with its various subjects and his interest in the ubiquity of theater in everyday interactions. Daisy is reading about the Avenger in the newspaper. Joe assumes a blustering stance—the framing exposes his unattractive self-importance—and says, "I'm keen on golden hair myself." Under the watchful eyes of her mother, who endorses Joe's courtship, Daisy can only give in to his demand that she participate in this charade. She puts on a look of disdain. He continues the performance by responding with a deflated look. But then Hitchcock presents us a privileged view, unavailable to Daisy or her mother, which discloses Joe's real feelings. In this frame, he sighs and looks

directly into the camera (1.7), revealing both his longing and his feeling of impotence. Frustrated in his desire but unwilling to declare it frankly, he is reduced to playacting that makes a joke of the idea of rejection.

Daisy ignores Joe, her display of indifference part of the charade. Joe then picks up a cookie cutter and presses out a dough heart, which he lays down on the table. When she continues to act un-

1.7   interested, he presses out a second heart

and places it beside the first. Daisy again looks disdainfully at Joe. Hitchcock once more inserts a closeup, this time of Joe's hands hanging limply by his sides. Daisy's hand reaches into this frame, picks up one of the hearts, and tosses it aside. Joe's face registers no emotion, but in yet another close insert, his hands pick up the re-

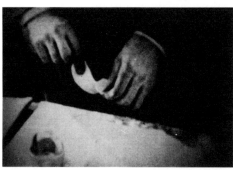

maining heart and tear it in two (1.8). Viewed in close-up, Joe directs a "puppy dog" look to Daisy; this is not the mask of the swaggering braggart but that of the lovelorn suitor. The expression is part of the charade, although the feeling it caricatures is also real. Joe here casts himself as a clown who has given his all to win his audience's love and casts Daisy as heartless for rejecting his plea.

1.8   It is important not to misunderstand

this moment. Joe has dropped his bully act and now presents himself as an innocent whose heart has been cruelly broken. But Hitchcock's camera still claims the power to see through him. The image of Joe's hand pressing down on the cookie cutter is an emblem of his capacity for violence. That of his hands tearing the heart sustains the suggestion: Joe depicts the breaking of his own heart, but the heart also stands for Daisy and Joe's gesture expresses a wish for vengeance. However, we attribute to Joe little or no consciousness of the violence in his nature that is transparent to the camera. Thanks to Hitchcock's camera, we know Joe better than he knows himself.

Like Daisy, Joe is the original of a Hitchcock type. *Blackmail's* Frank, for example, is closely related to Joe, and the story of the relationship between Frank and Alice is a variant of that between Joe and Daisy (John Londgen, who plays Frank, is a dead ringer for Malcolm Keen, who plays Joe). It is plain that Daisy does not pine for Joe as he does for her, and, indeed, she will be drawn to the romantic figure of the lodger from the moment of his appearance on the scene. But Joe irrevocably loses Daisy only through his own actions. The process by which he damns himself in her eyes, delineated with great precision, illustrates Hitchcock's recurring theme of the potentially tragic consequences of allowing wishes to influence judgments. He focuses particularly on figures like Joe—a police detective—who abuse official powers or break with the discipline of a calling.[4]

Hitchcock cuts from Joe's glance, which announces the end of the charade, to Daisy (1.9). Joe has not declared himself, and she is not called upon to accept or reject him. The look she gives expresses only a grudging admission of the cleverness of his performance, and does not reveal her deeper feelings toward him. Yet, surely, she has perceived—and resents—the way he forced her to participate in his charade by exploiting her mother's presence in a species of moral blackmail. On the other hand, for all we know he has the key to her heart and may yet win her. While Joe is no romantic figure, he has one major asset: the ability to make Daisy laugh. Some of Joe's descendants, indeed, win the respect and even the love of the heroine. It is not that Daisy hides her feelings or that the camera masks them. A girl like Daisy, in Hitchcock's films, does not yet know her own feelings. Only in the course of the film does she come to know herself, to grow up, to become a woman. That we do not know Daisy's feelings at this moment, then, reflects something about her particular identity as a character, who she is in relationship to others in her world. But, as with all Hitchcock characters, her identity is also a function of a particular relationship to the camera, who she is in relationship to Hitchcock and to us. To the camera, at this moment, she remains who she was when we first viewed her at the fashion show: a creature of beauty whose dreams and desires are

1.9

inaccessible to us. Joe does not know how Daisy would respond if he declared his love, whether she would look on him with amusement, desire, or horror. He recognizes Daisy's power of passing judgment over him, and fears it. And we do not know—nor does Hitchcock—how Daisy would respond if we—or he—stepped forward into her presence. The camera, like Joe, acknowledges Daisy's mystery and power.

Recognizing that an episode is over in what she takes to be a smoothly progressing courtship, Daisy's mother nods to her husband. But he has been oblivious of the whole scene. She expresses annoyance at his lack of awareness, then beams in condescending toleration of his foibles. He casts her a resentful look, which she gives no sign of noticing. The whole history of their marriage, with its unacknowledged bitterness and frustration, can be glimpsed in this exchange. The scene freezes into a tableau; the situation, completely laid out to our view, is at an impasse. The stage is set for a dramatic entrance.

Signaled by the mother's gaze, there is a cut to a wall lamp,

1.10

which dims mysteriously (1.10). There is a plausible explanation: it is time to put a coin in the electric meter. But the shot operates at a number of other levels as well. First, references to light and darkness and to lamps run through the whole film. Second, our view of the dimming lamp is the mother's, linking this moment with her role throughout the film. It register's the beginning of what will be, for her, a nightmare. Third, this shot draws on and parodies theatrical conventions. House lights go down as the curtain rises on a play, and darkness is associated with the villain of a melodrama. Fourth, this self-consciously melodramatic signal reminds us that our views of this world are presented by an author. The arrival of a

1.11

stranger at just this moment fulfills Daisy's wish and her mother's fears; it is self-evidently plotted.

Hitchcock cuts to the front door of the house (suggestively enough, number 13). The camera moves in as the shadow of a man appears and grows larger, and a hand enters the frame and grasps the knocker (1.11, 1.12). This camera movement—the first in the film—matches the motion of the unseen man as he approaches the door; the shot also represents his point of view. Hitchcock introduced Daisy by allowing us to view her, but the man at the door is introduced by presenting what he views and withholding the sight of his face. He appears in the frame first as a shadow, as though he were an agent of the devil (in a melodrama, the agent of the devil is the villain; in *The Lodger*, the villain is the Avenger; then is this the villainous mur-

1.12

derer at the door?). The shot suggests that he has a special bond with the camera, which has assumed his place. The forward tracking movement underscores the camera's identification with him. Whether or not he is the Avenger, he is a viewer who shares something of our relationship to this world. He is also an agent of the film's author: when his hand enters the frame and seizes the knocker, setting in motion the events of the plot, it is as if Hitchcock himself were showing his hand.

The man at the door arrives as if by magic, and his arrival cues a significant development. The mother leaves the room to see who is at the door, while the father goes to put a coin in the electric meter. Seeing that they are now alone, Joe embraces Daisy. Before she has

a chance to respond, hence with her feelings still at issue, Hitchcock cuts away to the father climbing a ladder to reach the meter, then to the mother at the door. The first clear view of the stranger is the climax of a series of shots: an extreme long shot of the mother with a staircase at the left of the frame (1.13); a much closer shot of the mother beginning to open the door; a man appearing framed in the doorway; the mother's startled, horrified reaction; and finally, the view that made the mother recoil (1.14). The man at the door, come to rent a room, is the film's star, Ivor Novello. The film's original audience would have recognized him instantly; in the twenties, Novello was a matinee idol of the stage, the romantic lead in a series of popular operettas in which no psychopathic murderers walked the boards. Yet he looks exactly like the Avenger as

1.13

1.14

Hitchcock has cued us to imagine him. Indeed, the face seen in this shot—an expressionless mask half obscured by glare—is so much the picture of mystery that the effect is comic. We do not simply identify with the mother; she is in Hitchcock's hands, and he shares the joke of his power with us. Our laugh is at the perfect appositeness of stimulus and response and at the mother's perfect obliviousness of the author's design. Hitchcock intends the viewer to recognize this apparition as an absurdly conventional vision, yet at the same time to be genuinely shocked. This apparent paradox reflects his wish for us to recognize this face as a kind of mask.[5]

Throughout the film, our views of the lodger remind us of his introduction as a figure of mystery. This is a central strategy of the narrative, which continually raises suspicions but provides no conclusive evidence either that he is the Avenger or that he is not. From the outset his expressions and actions can be accounted for by supposing that he is the Avenger; if he turned out not to be the Avenger, his appearance of guilt would need to be explained. Yet Hitchcock does not actually give us false information, as he does in *Stage Fright*'s famous "lying flashback," which presents a character's account of an event without giving any indication that it is not true. Rather, *The Lodger* continually reminds us that its author is withholding crucial information, and that his intentions cannot be taken for granted. We know that the lodger has a secret, but hold back from concluding that his secret is that he is the Avenger, for we know it is within Hitchcock's power to make the lodger's secret be something else.

At one level, the film tells the story of the lodger's revelation of his secret to Daisy, and her response. Until this occurs, he exists in a state of suspense: he does not know his own nature and dreads seeing himself reflected in the eyes of anyone who knows who he really is. He is the prototype of a recurring Hitchcock figure. Laurence Olivier in *Rebecca*, Cary Grant in *Suspicion*, Joseph Cotten in *Shadow of a Doubt*, Richard Todd in *Stage Fright*, and Anthony Perkins in *Psycho* clearly play what might be called "lodger figures." And the characters played by Robert Donat in *The Thirty-Nine Steps*, Montgomery Clift in *I Confess*, Henry Fonda in *The Wrong Man*, and Sean Connery in *Marnie* derive, in certain essential respects, from the lodger as well. But if the lodger figure represents a type of character, his identity cannot be separated from the form of narrative in which he appears, or from his particular relationship to the camera.

The Lodger is the model for the self-conscious Hitchcock narrative that acknowledges its own indirectness and its practice of withholding information. In it, the author's relationship with the viewers comes to the fore. The film's story about its lodger figure is also a story about the camera; the camera's presentation of the lodger is also its presentation of itself. At one level, *The Lodger* is an investigation of the nature of the camera.

Contrasting *The Lodger* with the Gothic novel helps us to appreciate the camera's central role. Such a novel is typically narrated from the point of view of the innocent but passionate heroine. The troubled, brooding man with whom she falls in love, but whom she alternately fears and pities until she learns his secret, is a projection of her romantic yearnings. The heroine's faith that the man she loves cannot be a monster is, by convention, rewarded.[6] Daisy, too, envisions the man of mystery who enters her life as the fulfillment of her dreams. Though *The Lodger* registers Daisy's point of view, however, the camera retains its autonomy. Nothing in the Gothic novel corresponds to the camera's enigmatic bond with the lodger and his double, the Avenger. It is the man's view of the woman, not the woman's view of the man, on which Hitchcock's film turns, but the story is not told from the lodger's point of view; the camera stands apart from him as from all its other subjects, in spite of the bond between them. In the Gothic novel, a mystery is explained away. *The Lodger*'s true mystery, which is in the succession of frames that make up the film, is never explained away. When the lodger finally tells Daisy his secret and that secret is also revealed to us, the mystery of his bond with the camera is not explained but invoked.

The Lodger is also not a conventional detective story. We cannot glean the lodger's secret by careful attention to clues strewn about the narrative. The author has planted clues to the lodger's mysterious nature, but they do not allow us to deduce his story; all they reveal is how well Hitchcock keeps a secret. Hitchcock films are not puzzles to be solved; there is more at stake than matters of observation and deduction. For Daisy, her dreams are at stake; for the lodger, his self-knowledge and salvation; for Hitchcock, his identity as an author. For us, the destinies of characters we care about are at issue, and, beyond this, what we will be called upon to view. *The Lodger* compels us to recognize film's power of showing us what we dread viewing and what we desire to view, and to acknowledge that the lodger's state of suspense is akin to our own. A Hitchcock film provokes us to imagine that our nature, like that of the Avenger, may be monstrous. It conjures this suspicion and this suspense, this anticipation and dread, into wakefulness. If Hitchcock so chooses, his narrative can settle the question of whether the lodger is the Avenger. But at the heart of *The Lodger* are matters Hitchcock cannot simply decide or settle by his own testimony. Who or what the camera's subjects really are, what his role as author makes of him and what it reveals about him, and what the film calls for from its viewers, for example, are central concerns of Hitchcock's reflections, not his secrets.

As the mother swallows her revulsion at the sight of the man at the door, the wall lamp comes back on. At this signal, Hitchcock cuts back to the man, whose face shows life for the first time. A slight, furtive movement of the eyes indicates his alertness.

The man points to a sign reading "room to let." The mother, adopting the obsequiousness of the landlady toward the potential tenant, goes upstairs to show him the room. As the lodger steps forward, there is a quick montage of shots. The father falls off the ladder; a cuckoo springs out of a clock to announce the hour; the lodger springs to attention, his eyes wide; the lodger stands with his back to the camera in the foreground, his figure completely framed by the staircase behind him (1.15); Daisy, viewed in closeup, sees something that makes her laugh; the father, seen from Daisy's point of view, lies on the ground, helpless (1.16); Daisy laughs; the lodger hears Daisy's laugh, an impenetrable expression on his face. The keystone of this passage is (1.15). It echoes (1.11) the lodger as shadow, and thus reiterates the earlier suggestion of his bond with the Avenger and with the camera. The lodger is given the camera's own position: framed within this space, he also looks in from outside, possessing it with his gaze. If he is the camera's subject, he is also its stand-in in the frame, both a passive viewer and an agent of the author. Riveted by the cuckoo's cry, the lodger stares into the depths of the frame as though a picture held him spellbound. He appears to have lost his grip on the present, as if imagining or remembering a scene we cannot view. But a real scene is taking place at this moment to which Hitchcock does give us access: Daisy discovers her father on the ground and laughs at the spectacle. The sequence suggests a connection between this scene and the one in the lodger's imagination.

1.15

1.16

The lodger is aroused by Daisy's laugh, as the Avenger surely would be. Because *The Lodger* never tells the Avenger's story, we do not know what real or imagined acts of violence by what golden-haired woman has led him to his mad acts of killing. But I take it that he calls himself "the Avenger" because he sees himself as exacting retribution in a world where women dominate men. Wouldn't the Avenger be provoked by the scene of Daisy laughing at her fallen father? The cuckoo, conventional symbol of madness and a bird that eats other birds' eggs and makes its home in their nests, is a suitable totem for the Avenger. Its cry is linked to Daisy's laugh, which the Avenger would hear as mocking the powers of men.[7]

Daisy's mother, showing the stranger the room to let, turns on the lights. The frame is illuminated, and the lodger's face shows the alertness previously triggered by the wall lamp. This echo links what he now views—a beautiful young woman with blond hair (1.17)—to his turning inward when he heard Daisy's laugh. It is only when the camera pans along the wall, following the lodger's gaze, that we realize that what we are seeing is a painting. Hitchcock cuts back to the lodger, then to a second panning shot from his point of view that ends by framing another painting of a golden-haired woman. The pattern is broken by a shot of the mother, who is looking on expectantly. Then Hitchcock cuts again to the lodger and to yet another pan across a painting of a blond woman, but this shot ends by framing a painting that depicts a scene of rape (1.18), and is followed by a quick cut to a setup that includes both the lodger and a painting of a woman within the frame (1.19). The abrupt shift from the lodger's point of view at first suggests that his spell has been broken. When the lodger next steps toward the camera, however, revealing that the painting is framed in a mirror, he appears transfixed, back to the camera, reflected in this frame (1.20). In his imagination, we take it, he has entered the painting's world.

Suddenly, with a wild look in his eyes, the lodger rushes to the window. The climax of this sequence is a shot that echoes the first view of him at the door (1.21). A shadow runs down the

1.17

1.18

1.19

1.20

1.21

1.22

center of his face, cutting it in two. His doubleness and look of anguish are emblems of his mystery. When Hitchcock cuts to a newsboy seen out the window from the lodger's point of view, the suggestion is that the Avenger's murders are linked to his suffering.

Alone for the first time, the lodger sits and thinks, a look of cold calculation on his face. He casts his eyes at something offscreen, and there is a cut to his view of the black bag he had been carrying. Its contents are a mystery to us. The next shot (1.22) contains a veiled suggestion that this mystery has an erotic aspect. In this schematic composition, the lodger is at the left; the bag is at the right; and the backlit bedroom, the bed framed by the doorway, is at the center.

When the mother comes upstairs to bring him a glass of milk and opens the door to his room, she interrupts the lodger in the act of turning the paintings toward the wall. He asks her to put them somewhere else, without explaining why he does not wish to see them. The mother leaves and calls Daisy to remove the offending pictures, thus setting up the first face-to-face encounter between Daisy and the lodger.

Hitchcock cuts from the lodger, in a prayerlike posture, to a longer view that includes the door to the hall. Daisy enters unnoticed. The sight of a painting turned to the wall makes her laugh, and, once again struck by the sound, the lodger turns toward her. Initially his face is away from the camera, and he turns a full 270 degrees before he meets the camera's gaze and then continues staring. He may be drinking deeply of his view of Daisy or waiting until this intrusion is over. What we might expect to see next is Daisy from his point of view, her reaction to his look, or perhaps the two combined. Instead Hitchcock shows us the room with the two looking at each other across the frame. Hitchcock withholds the lodger's view, leaving it a mystery how Daisy appears in his eyes. And the withholding of Daisy's reaction suggests that she has not yet formulated a response to his presence. At this charged moment, the mother appears at the door and, characteristically, pushes her daughter across the threshold, while the lodger continues to stare. That an erotic bond has been forged is underscored by what follows. The mother leaves the frame, so that Daisy and the lodger are alone on camera; exactly as the door to the bedroom is about to frame Daisy, Hitchcock cuts to the lodger, who follows her closely with his gaze.

Daisy carries the paintings downstairs. Joe opens the door for her, pinches her cheek, straightens his tie, and follows her into the room. Back upstairs, the mother leaves and the lodger closes the door behind him. Hitchcock cuts from the closed door to Joe and Daisy, now embracing. As Joe presses the kiss, however, the

door opens and the mother enters, before Daisy responds. The mother, once again chaperone and the author's unwitting agent, tells Joe about the paintings. He is amused that the lodger is not "keen on the girls." Then Hitchcock gives us a close shot of Daisy against a black backdrop (1.23), echoing our first view of her in the fashion show. When she turns to the camera, looking thoughtful, we take it that she is thinking of the man who has just entered her life. Suddenly the mother grabs Joe's arm. The three look up at the ceiling lamp, which begins to vibrate. Hitchcock cuts to the lamp, over which a view of the room above appears superimposed; the lodger paces through the frame in front of a dark curtain, yet another symbol of his mystery (1.24). The scene fades out with Joe, Daisy and her mother wrapped in their separate thoughts, ending a major part of the film. The lodger is now ensconced in this home, with consequences yet to be revealed.

The next part of the film begins as Daisy brings breakfast to the lodger's room. While she pours his tea, he looks up at her (1.25). This shot is followed not, as we might expect, by one from his point of view but instead by an objective

1.23

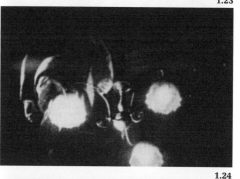

1.24

1.25

shot, from the perspective of no one in the world of the film, in which he reaches down with his hand as if for a cup. We perceive,

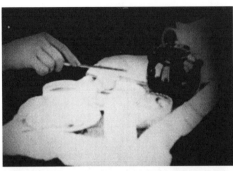

1.26

1.27

however, that he is reaching for a knife (1.26). This privileged view, available only to the camera, leads us to imagine a frightful scene. A close shot of the lodger's profile increases the tension (1.27). We cannot read his intense, absorbed expression. It is characteristic of Hitchcock to frame a figure in profile at the moment of his or her most complete abstraction and absorption in an imagined scene to which we have no access. In such a profile shot, the camera frames its subject in a way that does not allow that figure's interiority to be penetrated. Indeed, such a shot declares that impenetrability; it announces that we have come to a limit of our access to the world of the film.[8]

The lodger raises his knife to Daisy's chest, but the suspense is deflated when he flicks a speck from her dress, an innocent explanation of his apparently menacing gesture. Of course the explanation does not rule out the possibility that he had the impulse to stab her. And it is disquieting in itself, for it suggests that the speck disturbs the lodger aesthetically, that it spoils a perfect picture, reminding us of his mysterious fascination with the paintings of golden-haired women. The pivotal shot that follows underscores the suggestion that Daisy presents a picture to him. In a soft-focus medium closeup from the lodger's point of view, Hitchcock presents the view of Daisy that has been deferred (1.28). In the picture she presents to the lodger's gaze—to the camera—in this frame, Daisy could be one of the women in the paintings that held him spellbound.

Clearly this shot suggests that, at this moment, Daisy's beauty first fully awakens the lodger's desire. We, however, have beheld Daisy's beauty before; indeed, it was by such a view that we were introduced to her. The present shot echoes (1.5) and invokes the ambiguity of its perspective (was (1.5) the Avenger's view or was it only the view

1.28

of ordinary members of Daisy's audience at the fashion show?). But it differs from the earlier shot in a number of ways. First, it is clearly identified as the lodger's view. Second, within this frame, Daisy looks invitingly right into the camera: she acknowledges the lodger's gaze and invites him to view her. Third, it is veiled by soft focus. At one level, the soft focus is a conventional indication that the lodger's gaze is animated by desire—a desire that Daisy's look both acknowledges and arouses. The soft focus also indicates, conventionally, that she is melting with passion as well, that she wishes him to look at her with desire. At another level, the soft focus obscures the boundary between fantasy and reality, suggesting that what is viewed within this frame is an apparition. Daisy frankly meets the lodger's gaze as if he were dreaming (although we do not know the whole of the dream—or nightmare—in which she appears). In his dream, she dreams of him too and meets his desiring gaze as if she herself were dreaming. In the picture Daisy presents to the lodger, then, his dream and her dream come together. But the status of this picture is ambiguous. We do not know the reality that the soft focus veils. We do not know whether Daisy really presents herself in this way or whether the lodger's picture is only a projection of his imagination; and if Daisy's inviting look is real, we do not know whether it reveals her true feelings or whether she is only acting, as if this were one of her fashion shows.

The asymmetry of the camera's relationships to these two figures is manifest in the next cut, which does not present the lodger as he appears to Daisy, but repeats the profile shot. Within this frame, the lodger grins, indeed all but leers. We do not know whether this grin is directed to Daisy or is viewed only by the camera, nor whether it is the grin of a murderer contemplating his next victim, a seducer, or an innocent man apologizing for a fright inadvertently caused.

Hitchcock now draws away from the ambiguous intimacy of this scene. When Daisy goes downstairs, we know from her expression that she is in a state of excitement. But when the lodger coolly takes out his newspaper and stirs his tea, we do not know his feelings or intentions. His coldness at this moment is the film's first direct indication that he may be manipulating Daisy in accordance with some design.

We are put further on the alert by a title reading "One evening, a few days later, the lodger made himself agreeable." The scene fades in on the lodger and Daisy playing chess beside a fire. He says, "Be careful, I'll get you yet," a remark that sustains our suspicions. He apparently means that he'll mate her, perhaps not only in chess; but perhaps he also intends to murder her. An air of suppressed violence as well as erotic tension hovers over this scene.

Hitchcock next cuts to a very different setup, in which Daisy's

1.29

1.30

1.31

1.32

blond hair occupies a conspicuous place (1.29). She accidentally knocks a chess piece off the table. As she bends down to pick it up, the lodger stares at her hair, once again in a kind of trance. In a closer shot, he too bends down, still staring (1.30), and his hand reaches for a poker. Then there is a cut to Daisy's hair, with the poker entering the frame, continuing its motion in the preceding shot (1.31). We imagine a frightful continuation.[9]

A bit maddeningly, Hitchcock cuts away to Joe entering the house. The mother is tightening the father's tie. As her husband turns to Joe, she tugs his head back, creating an image of hanging (1.32). This image bears ironically on the scene we have just left. It alludes to a murderer's fate, and it illustrates the mother's domination of the father in Daisy's family. When the next shot appears—a fire, stoked by a poker (1.33)— we do not at first recognize that we have returned to the lodger's room. This image is displaced; it is made intelligible only by the following shot of the lodger and Daisy bending toward the fireplace, which also explains his apparently menacing act of reaching for the poker. Once again, however, Hitchcock's presentation is disquieting. The blazing fire in the displaced image, projected larger than life on the movie screen, appears as a wild, frightful force. Like the wall lamp that signaled the lodger's arrival, this fire, I take it, alludes to villainy, as though the stoker of these flames were an agent of the devil. Perhaps the blazing fire is also a metaphor for Daisy's desire, which the lodger is coolly "stoking."[10] But perhaps he is not really in control. His impulse to reach for the poker coincides with his proximity to her hair, which appears to cast a spell over him. The fire stands in for that "other" scene in which he is once again absorbed. What corresponds, in that scene, to the stoking of the fire with the poker may well be something frightful. Then again, the displaced shot echoes the introduction of the lodger, when the hand entered the frame and grasped the knocker, setting the events of the narrative in motion. As at that moment, we can imagine the hand in the

1.33

frame as that of Hitchcock, metaphorically stoking the fires of his narration. After all, a melodramatic plot contrivance is about to be disclosed: Joe has been put on the Avenger case.

Daisy looks up. The lodger raises his eyes and she modestly lets hers drop. He looks down from her hair to the board. When he looks up again, she raises her eyes and their gazes finally meet. She then (shyly? properly? seductively?) lowers her eyes. He continues to stare, as if still entranced by her hair. Their eyes meet again, intensifying the erotic charge that, in movies, is conventionally released by a kiss. But the spell is abruptly broken by the mother, who announces Joe's arrival, and the scene of passion is deferred.

Downstairs, Joe is showing off a pair of handcuffs to the father ("A new pair of bracelets for the Avenger") as Daisy enters. Joe's next remark concerns her, but he directs it to her father. "When I've put a rope around the Avenger's neck" (he mimes a hanging) "I'll put a ring around Daisy's finger." In completing the pantomime, he uses the handcuffs, which served him as a noose, as a wedding ring.

Daisy's expression reveals that she is sickened by Joe's remark, which is less a proposal than a threat. That the camera captures such a revelation of Daisy's feelings marks a major development in the film. Full of himself, oblivious, Joe grins and slips the father a wink. All his arrogance comes to the surface in this gesture, which exploits a father's hold over his daughter and reveals the cynical camaraderie of men united in resentment of women.

Affecting coyness, Daisy breaks away. Joe catches her on the stairs and handcuffs her as if in jest. She looks at the camera—another significant development—and then at her manacled wrists. A quick cut to the handcuffs expresses her panic at this frightening glimpse of the bondage threatened by marriage to Joe. Upstairs, her mother and the lodger hear Daisy scream. Hitchcock cuts to a shadowy, menacing shot of the hallway, reminiscent of German films of the period (1.34), then to a low angle shot of the stairs. The lodger looks down from this height, the camera angle intensifying our

1.34

sense of his power (1.35); we next view Daisy, struggling to free herself from Joe, from the lodger's vantage on high; then we return to him, his face showing no expression as he surveys the scene from his perch.

Daisy goes into the inner room. Under her mother's eye, she appears to forgive Joe. To his surprise, she allows him to kiss her. But when Daisy looks at the camera, the gap is apparent to us between her feelings and his. He hugs her, overcome with joy, but she runs off, leaving him perplexed. From her look to the camera, we know that Daisy has made up her mind about Joe. For her, the kiss has settled all debts. For the first time, the mother looks at Joe with concern. Deflated but thoughtful, he asks, "Does this lodger of yours mean any harm to Daisy?" The question initiates the line of thought that will lead him to

1.35

conclude that the lodger is really the Avenger. He gives voice to the mother's suspicions and ours as well.

The scene shifts. A woman leaves a theater by the stage entrance and kisses a man waiting for her on the street. Hitchcock cuts directly to Big Ben, whose face presides over the London night

1.36

(1.36), then to a row of marching policemen's boots. We are back in the realm of the Avenger.

Hitchcock cuts to the lodger, creeping down the shadowy hall, then to the mother, awake. The intercutting between them suggests that she follows his every move in her imagination; it links our views of him to what she imagines. (The most memorable of these views is an overhead shot of the bannister, with the lodger's hand circling the concentric ovals [1.37].) The mother looks knowing, and we know exactly what she is imagining. The remainder of the sequence conjoins objective reality and the mother's nightmarish fantasy: our views are real and at the same time projections of her imagination.

This duality is crystallized by Hitchcock's presentation of what she sees when she looks out the window. Seen from her point of view, (1.38) repeats the shot of the newsboy hawking the *Evening Standard*. But the newsboy has now been displaced by the lodger, and the whole frame is composed to suggest an eye.

The woman and her escort squabble, and she leaves him. The next shot is of a courtyard dominated by a lamp and the pool of light it casts (1.39). Our view, framed by an arch, invokes the perspective of a theater audience. This is a symbolically charged setting viewed from across a proscenium: a dream stage. The woman enters, bending down in the pool of light to adjust her stocking. Presumably she takes herself to be unseen and hers is an innocent gesture, but it could also be a prostitute's come-on. Suddenly the shadow of a man spreads over her (1.40), reminding us of the lodger's introduction and the film's nightmarish opening. Like the woman in the opening shot of the film, she screams in the face of the being who has just stepped forward. The camera once again assumes the murderer's place.

A quick montage follows, in which beggars awaken, cats jump out of barrels, and birds fly off in alarm. The body is discovered, and the calling card the Avenger leaves on each victim's body is found. Then we return to Daisy's mother. Her expression suggests that her fantasy has just come to a grisly conclusion. She goes downstairs, providing occasion for an overhead shot (1.41) that echoes the overhead shot of the lodger on the stairs (1.37). In the earlier shot, the lodger appeared as if a projection of the mother's imagination. In the present

1.37

1.38

1.39

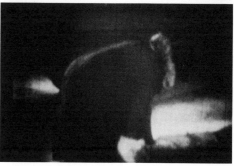

1.40

1.41

1.42

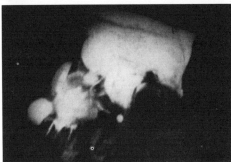

1.43

1.44

shot, the mother's corporeality is underscored. She drags her aging body down these stairs, wearied by the burden of her "knowledge."

A view of Daisy and her parents fades in. Daisy loads a tray and goes upstairs. The father reads that there has been a killing just around the corner. Joe arrives, looking grave. "The way that fiend did her in—" As Joe tells the father the details, the mother looks into the camera, anguished, absolutely transparent to us (1.42). Hitchcock then cuts to a view that is not immediately legible. In a moment, we identify it as Daisy's tray falling, the contents spilling over (1.43). Even before we understand what we are viewing, however, the shot's impact is visceral; it is a nauseating image, suggestive of garbage and vomiting. At one level, I take it, this image expresses the mother's nausea as she listens to Joe's account of the murder and imagines Daisy in the Avenger's hands. The succeeding shots as well can be viewed as projections of her fear: against a black background, Daisy screams, then a painting of a golden-haired girl falls through the frame.

Joe runs upstairs and the parents follow. At the lodger's door, Joe stops short. What he sees is briefly withheld, adding to our suspense. Then Hitchcock gives us Joe's view: the lodger and Daisy in an embrace. Joe lowers his hands to his sides and walks forward in the classic "monster" walk of the German cinema.[11] Joe has become an automaton, momentarily stripped of his will. When we return to his point of view, the camera tracks forward, advancing on the couple. In this frame, the lodger looks apprehensively right at the camera (1.44). This motion doubles the film's first camera movement, in which the lodger's presence was initially invoked, and also echoes the Avenger's advance on his victim. In the "dough heart" sequence, Hitchcock declared the camera's ability to penetrate Joe's theatricality, to expose his underlying capacity for violence. Now Hitchcock conveys that capacity for violence by having the camera assume Joe's place, as it had assumed the Avenger's and the lodger's. Hitchcock's gesture explicitly links Joe with the Avenger, and once more links the Avenger with the camera. Again, the possibility is raised that the camera represents something monstrous.

The lodger and Joe face off, as if about to come to blows (1.45; from this frame enlargement, we might imagine that the lodger is demanding that Joe take back some remark he made about his sweater). The lodger demands that the intruder leave. Theatrically asserting his prerogative, Joe pushes Daisy to the door. Her hair haloed with light, she looks back to the lodger—lovingly, invitingly, secretly declaring her freedom while not openly breaking with the role of Joe's girl (1.46).

1.45

In the parlor downstairs, Joe takes Daisy's shoulder, and she looks as if she might relent. The mother listens at the door. The encounter between her daughter and Joe is silent, and a look of satisfaction is on her face. Hitchcock then cuts to the other side of the door, where Joe and Daisy embrace, although she does not allow him actually to kiss her. The camera returns to the mother,

1.46

who looks serious, as though she suspects some such hitch. The father enters and she tells him that she heard the lodger go out late the night before. He invests a moment's thought in his wife's remark, but then sits down to enjoy the paper. When she says, "You don't think he—" the father chews gravely on his pipe, then takes it out of his mouth so as not to encumber his thinking. They agree that Daisy is not to be left alone with the lodger. The final image is of their shared view of the ceiling lamp, emblem of the lodger's secret.

The next sequence begins by fading in on the lodger, who looks right at the camera, a smile on his lips (1.47). This shot compels us to recognize that we do not really know who this man is or what he

1.47

1.48

wants. For all we know, the mother's suspicions are accurate and he is a murderer. The shot culminates the film's intimations, to this point, that the lodger is the Avenger, and that he has a bond with the camera. With a knowing look he meets the camera's gaze, as if he penetrated our act of viewing him and were acknowledging complicity with the author of the film. It is as if Hitchcock himself, wearing the mask of Ivor Novello, were meeting our gaze and smiling as recognition dawns on us.[12] Yet it is only the following shot (1.48) that allows us to recognize the setting: this is Daisy's salon, and the lodger is at a fashion show, sitting in the audience. This deferred disclosure takes up the implications of (1.22), the schematic framing of the lodger, the black bag, and the bed. It reaffirms his possession of a secret shared by Hitchcock and withheld from Daisy and from us. But it makes another suggestion as well. In the introduction of Daisy, the same setup represented an ambiguous perspective, invoking the viewpoint of the audience in the salon and also that of the Avenger. Now this ambiguous place is appropriated by the lodger, who bridges Daisy's two worlds. The effect is chilling.

Why is the lodger here? Perhaps he is the Avenger, with murder on his mind. Perhaps he is here to proposition Daisy: this is a market in which every article of clothing is for sale, and his look may reveal a belief that she too has a price. Perhaps he is intent on seducing Daisy. Perhaps he is courting her. A typical ironic touch plays on this last suggestion: a woman steps into view modeling a

1.49

white wedding gown; a title reads "Daisy," and precisely as the "bride" exits, Daisy makes her entrance (1.49). Then Hitchcock repeats the shot that opened the sequence. But we now read the lodger's smile as directed to Daisy, who is shown in the next shot (1.50). In this view, her face once again wears an inviting look, as it did in the soft-focus closeup in which she presented a picture to the lodger. This is an important

moment. The lodger's smile declares
that he only has eyes for Daisy, and her
look acknowledges his gaze and appears
to confirm that it is to him alone that she
presents herself. And this look is not
veiled by soft-focus; there is no ambiguity as to whether it is real. Yet we still do
not know the lodger's desire (does he
wish only to view her? to make love to
her? to kill her?) or whether his smile is
to be trusted. Nor do we know what

1.50

Daisy's look invites (does it invite him, as someone who sits in her
audience, to look but not touch? to step forward to seduce or proposition or court her?) or whether it is meant sincerely or is only part
of her act as a model. Our uncertainty cannot be resolved until they
again meet in private.

At this point, when an intimate, passionate scene appears imminent, the conclusion of the Avenger story also draws near. The
scene shifts to the police station, where Joe is meeting with his fellow detectives and their superiors. "If one makes a plan of the
Avenger murders, Chief, one can see that they have been moving
steadily in a certain direction." Joe takes out a map, and all agree
that the place to catch the Avenger is "near this small mark." There
is a dissolve to another map from the perspective of someone we
cannot see. A man—his face is obscured—leans into the frame
(1.51). The natural assumption is that he
is the Avenger. Yet we can just as well
imagine this figure, plotting the events
to come, as Hitchcock, poring over the
last pages of his script.

There is a gift for Daisy. Her parents
believe it to be a present from Joe, but
when Daisy opens it they discover that
it is the dress she modeled at the fashion
show, a gift from the lodger. Daisy looks
dreamy, but her mother is angry and
upset, and the father, for the first and

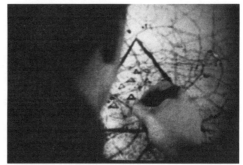

1.51

only time in the film, is roused to action. The improper gift must be
returned. He goes up to the lodger's room—to be sure, with some
hesitation—and puts the box on the table. "I can't have my daughter receiving presents from strangers."

A title reads, "The same evening." Daisy is in the bedroom.
Steam obscures her from our view as she undresses for her bath, but
we are aware of her nakedness (1.52). From this provocative view
Hitchcock cuts to the lodger, sitting with papers spread out before

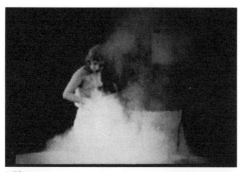

1.52

1.53

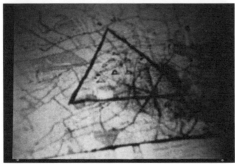

1.54

1.55

him (1.53). He looks up at the camera and then down again, as if authorizing, or at least cueing, the following framing, which shows us what is on the lodger's desk: the map that we took to be the Avenger's (1.54). This disclosure seems finally to confirm that the lodger is the Avenger. It sets the stage for a disturbing scene.

The lodger goes to the window. It is raining and the glare sends flickering lights and shadows across his face. He turns and advances toward the camera, a menacing figure. There is a cut to Daisy in her bath, the door to the hallway in the background of the frame (1.55). We do not need to have seen *Psycho* to sense that someone could enter this door, to be aware of Daisy's vulnerability. The next setup invokes both the lodger's introduction and the Avenger's. A hand, doubled by its shadow, enters the frame and grasps the doorknob. Then we cut to Daisy's legs viewed through rippling water (1.56), an intimate, erotic image. From the lodger at the door, the camera returns to Daisy, extravagantly beautiful against a black background (1.57); she is singing. The lodger hears her and smiles. He begins to leave but changes his mind and, with some timidity, knocks on the door. Daisy closes her eyes, as though in ecstasy. When the lodger announces himself, she gets out of the tub and wraps a towel around her body, and they speak through the door. She laughs when he tells her that her father thinks she shouldn't go out with him. The title "But Daisy didn't worry" drives home the obvious, that Daisy ought to be worried.

As the mother straightens up his room, the lodger prepares to go out. Framed in an expressionistic composi-

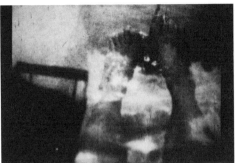

1.56

1.57

1.58

1.59

tion, he creeps into the hall (1.58). The view is through the bars of the bannister, and the frame is dominated by the bars in the foreground. I call this pattern of parallel vertical lines Hitchcock's / / / / sign. It recurs at significant junctures in every one of his films. At one level, the / / / / serves as a Hitchcock signature: it is his mark on the frame, akin to his ritual cameo appearances. At another level, it signifies the confinement of the camera's subject within the frame and within the world of the film. Like the profile shot, it announces that we have arrived at a limit of our access to the camera's subject; we might say that it stands for the barrier of the screen itself. It is also associated with sexual fear and the specific threat of loss of control or breakdown.

We return to the mother, who appears stricken. She looks down at something below the border of the frame (1.59). When Daisy goes toward the front door (1.60), the match between shots suggests that the latter is from the mother's point of view. Daisy and her mother are not within sight of each other, so once again the suggestion is that the mother somehow imagines what we view. When Daisy looks up and we cut to the lodger looking down (1.61), the setup reprises our view of the lodger overseeing the struggle between Daisy and Joe

1.60

1.61

1.62

1.63

1.64

(1.35); our view of Daisy is identified retroactively as also his. Hitchcock cuts again to Daisy, who turns to the camera. A shadow suddenly enters the frame and grows until it eclipses her from our view. Then the shadow turns into the figure of the lodger, who joins Daisy at the foot of the stairs (1.62, 1.63). The effect is of the passing of a dark cloud or the raising of a curtain. (Both this "curtain raising" and this "eclipsing" are to become staples of Hitchcock's technique.) When the camera returns to the mother, who bends over the bannister as the front door closes, we are reminded that her nightmare goes on. The father joins her. She says, "God forgive me! I let her go out with the lodger. And it's Tuesday!" While this melodramatic title draws a laugh, we appreciate the gravity of her plight. The scene fades out on the father, who stares into space.

The silhouettes of the lodger and Daisy fade in, framing the lamppost we recognize from the scene of the murder (1.64). They walk into the depths of this frame and sit under the lamp. There is a cut to a closer shot of the two figures, with the lamppost conspicuously placed to the left of the lodger (1.65).

Placing symbolically charged objects in the frame is a means of expression first systematically exploited, in film, by Griffith. Griffith's trees, flowers, garden paths, fences, and rivers are symbols with conventional connotations. Yet as they appear in film after film, they pick up connotations that make them private symbols as well, intimately embedded within the entirety of Griffith's work. In Hitchcock's films, lamps have their conventional association with enlightenment, with literal and metaphorical vision: it is in the light cast by this lamp, after all, that the truth about the lodger will be revealed. But lamps become

such a familiar feature of the Hitchcock
world and the Hitchcock frame that they
too become private symbols, yet another
signature of Hitchcock's authorship.
They are associated with illumination,
but also with a mysterious, private
realm that the light of reason cannot
penetrate. This is the realm of Hitchcock's acts of creation and our acts of
viewing; it is also the realm of sexuality.
Hitchcock follows G. W. Pabst, whose

1.65

Secrets of a Soul, a fictionalized psychoanalytic case study, was released in 1925, in using sexual imagery knowingly. (Griffith's
films, by contrast, are filled with images that he clearly had no idea
could be read in sexual terms.) In (1.65), the lamppost's phallic
shape appears deliberately emphasized by the precise placement of
the top frame line. In part, its presence in the frame is meant, I take
it, to offer mute testimony to the powerful, irrational force of male
sexuality that is unleashed in this dreamlike setting, this place
where murders are committed, where men wage battles for possession of women, where vengeance is conceived, where stories are
told.[13]

The lodger touches Daisy's hand. At this critical moment, there
is a cut to Joe, who is wandering the streets. When we return to the
two under the lamp, the lodger seems about to kiss Daisy. She looks

into the camera, and again Hitchcock
cuts to Joe, who suddenly sees something
that shocks him. Then we are presented
with his view: Daisy and the lodger
looking into each other's eyes. Just as
their lips are about to meet, Joe enters
the frame (1.66) and violently pulls the
lodger's hand away from Daisy. She
steps between them, tells Joe that she
never wants to see him again, and asks
the lodger to take her home. Joe looks as
though he might intervene forcefully,
but when his rival takes Daisy's arm and
they depart, he stands frozen on the spot.

1.66

Joe sits, frustrated, and buries his
head in his hands, his face blocked from
view (1.67). Hitchcock then cuts to
what Joe sees: a footprint in the mud
(1.68). Alert, he looks up at the camera
(1.69) and then his gaze again descends
to the mud. The footprint now be-

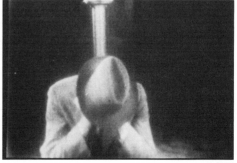

1.67

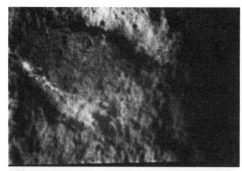

1.68

1.69

1.70

comes a kind of screen on which his thoughts are projected. First, we see a hand turning a painting toward the wall; then the lodger's bag crosses the frame-within-a-frame of the footprint. Joe hesitates but then excitedly wills the spectacle to go on. On this private screen, the lodger and Daisy appear locked in a passionate kiss, a scene that exists only in his imagination. Finally the ceiling lamp, emblematic of the lodger's mystery, is shown (1.70). Then there is a cut to a much longer shot. Joe looks up and rises, slowly and resolutely. We know that the idea has come to him that the lodger is the Avenger. It represents a solution to his investigation as a detective and to his personal frustration. He has found a way to put a rope around his rival's neck and a ring on Daisy's finger, as he had vowed.

At the house, the lodger and Daisy walk upstairs. He puts his hand on her shoulder and she looks upward. Walking stiffly, he follows her to the door of his room. At last, we gather, an erotic scene is about to take place between them. In the room, they are solemn, a mood that shows they both understand what her presence in his room authorizes. He grips her shoulder mechanically. She starts and looks up at him. His eyes are cast down. He turns her around to face him, raises her head with his hands, and only then looks up. But when he frames her face with his hands, he still averts his gaze.

That the lodger moves like an automaton and looks away from Daisy suggests that the act he is performing fills him with shame. He is unwilling to acknowledge the scene taking place or his own role within it. And we do not know what he takes this scene to be. In a close two shot, he takes off her hat and bends toward her. His lips part. She holds back, lowering her gaze. His eyes open wide and we see—with a frisson—that he is staring at her hair (1.71). He is again in a trance. His entrancement connects this scene with the one that earlier absorbed him, in which he was enthralled by a woman's presence. Under the spell cast on him by Daisy, the pres-

1.71

1.72

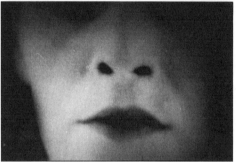

1.73

1.74

1.75

ent fuses, in his imagination, with that other scene to which we still have no access.

At this tense moment, Hitchcock cuts away to Daisy's anxious parents, who believe they have left their daughter in the hands of a murderer. When he cuts back, it is not to an intimate closeup but to a more formal long shot. Then we are shown the lodger's view of Daisy (1.72). Once more, she presents a perfect, erotically charged picture to his gaze. But when she now directs an inviting look to him, we know this is no act, no piece of theater. Her look is an unambiguous invitation to make love to her now. For the first time, the lodger's view of Daisy is followed by her view of him. In this frame, the lodger's face reveals longing and hunger. It moves closer to the camera until it is in extreme closeup, its lower half filling the whole screen (1.73). This amazing shot conveys Daisy's rapture even as it invokes the figure of the Avenger (what now fills the frame is the part of his face that the Avenger always covers); moreover, it is an image of the lodger as a seductive but frightening vampire.

Framed in closeup, the two kiss (1.74). From this erotic image Hitchcock cuts to another very close shot. Daisy looks up (1.75) and then closes her eyes in ecstasy. But the shadow formed by the lodger's silhouette sounds a disquieting note. It suggests that, even as he is kissing Daisy, he is thinking of that other scene. That his presence in the frame takes the form of a region of blackness intensifies the aura of impending violence and the sense that he is not completely present.

In a long shot, Daisy gently and tenderly puts a stop to the kiss. The two rise, turn away from the camera, and walk arm in arm to a couch. Under the "eyes" of a turned-away painting, they embrace

1.76

1.77

(1.76). She interrupts the embrace, momentarily holding him off as if he were going too far. There is no special mystery to this gesture: Daisy is not a child, but we take it that she has never before offered herself sexually; the well-behaved daughter within her momentarily rebels, although desire wins out. Yet when Daisy attempts to resume her part in this scene of passion, the lodger pushes her violently away. She all but throws herself on him, as he stands frozen on the spot, a grueling image of impotence (1.77). Finally, his paralysis is broken. He seizes her, and his kiss announces his intention to play this scene through to the end.

Though Daisy's hesitation is easily explained, the lodger's behavior is more mysterious. His resistance to her passion may reflect either innocence or inhumanity. Many different explanations are possible. He could be enraged, taking her to be a cruel exploiter of men's desires. He could be remembering his gentleman's duty to respect her honor. He could be revolted by her sexuality and unable to go through with the act of making love to her. He could be afraid that she would cease to desire him if he revealed his true nature. He could be afraid that he is monstrous, fated to destroy what he loves, and be struggling with himself to spare Daisy from falling victim to his curse. The violence with which he pushes her away could express a wish to do violence to her or a wish to spare her from the violence in his own nature; or it could be an expression of the violence of a struggle within himself. When he passionately kisses her, we have no way of knowing whether his action means that he has finally broken the grip of the other scene, or that he has submitted to it, allowing its spell to possess him completely.[14]

At this explosive moment, Hitchcock leaves us momentarily in suspense by cutting away to the mother and father at the front door. Joe has arrived with some other policemen to have a word with the lodger. When he enters the room, the lovers break off their embrace. Daisy speaks to him angrily, but he looks past her and announces that he has a warrant to search the room. The lodger withdraws into his private world; his back to the camera, he looks into the depths of the frame as though he were once again held spellbound by a painting (1.78). But he is brought back to reality when one of the detectives tries to open the cabinet in which the mysterious black bag is hidden. Joe makes a big production out of opening the bag. He finds in it a gun and then the apparently incriminating map. "A plan of the murders!" he announces. With disdain, the lodger replies, "Exactly." After this exchange, Daisy looks heavenward, her faith still intact. Joe seems to sense that she is slipping away from him. But when he pulls some newspaper clippings out of the bag, there is a shot of him—more specifically, his hat —which echoes our view when he looked down at the mud and the wished-for pictures materialized in his imagination (1.79). He looks up at the camera and pulls out the photograph of a blond girl. This is too much for the lodger, who breaks down weeping. Daisy offers comfort, as Joe looks on.

1.78

1.79

When Joe confronts the lodger with the photograph ("Your first victim, eh?"), he receives the reply, "My murdered sister." The lodger's answer does not by itself enable us to construct an innocent account of his behavior throughout the film, but it is the first clear indication in the narrative that such an account will be forthcoming. And Daisy responds to these words with a look that both pronounces judgment on Joe and expresses unshakeable faith in the lodger. Surely Hitchcock could still reveal that the lodger is the Avenger. But even if the lodger confessed to the murders, and indeed even if he confessed the intention of taking Daisy's life as well, her faith in his underlying innocence, I believe, would remain intact; even then, he would not be a murderer in her eyes. Her faith does not rest on tangible evidence or reason but rather on her love, which gives her, she believes, true knowledge about him.

Daisy's faith raises two related questions. First, in the world of Hitchcock's films, is love blind? Second, can innocence be recognized? If so, by whom and under what circumstances, and how are we to account for the fact that the guilty routinely pass for innocent and the innocent for guilty in Hitchcock's world as in our own? In *Stage Fright* Eve believes that her love for Jonathan gives her knowledge of his innocence, and yet it turns out that he has deceived her. Her discovery of his guilt coincides with her realization that she was never really in love with him but only playing the role of a woman in love. In Hitchcock's world, it is possible to believe mistakenly that one is in love, but love, if genuine, is not blind. If true love gives one knowledge, however, the question is only pushed back: how can one know whether one's love is real? (When a boy becomes a man or a girl becomes a woman in a Hitchcock film, that passage completes an education in recognizing feelings. However, help may well be needed if this treacherous passage is to be negotiated safely. For example, Eve needs directing or tutoring or both by her father, who suspects all along that she is not really in love, and by Hitchcock, who presides over *Stage Fright*'s world with Eve's sentimental education in mind.)

At times, Hitchcock treats the idea that innocence can simply be recognized as a joke. For example, in *The Saboteur*, the heroine's blind uncle—clearly a parody of the blind woodsman in *The Bride of Frankenstein* who intuits the monster's innocence—articulates the principle, with the support and encouragement of soulful violins, that the pure of heart can always recognize divine innocence. Yet Hitchcock is no skeptic on such matters, as many viewers assume. François Truffaut, for one, clearly wishes to think that Hitchcock recognizes no real distinction between guilt and innocence and believes that no one's nature can ever really be known. But Truffaut has no meaningful answer to Hitchcock's insistence that his protagonists are, typically, wrongly accused innocents. Hitchcock does not create guilty doubles for his innocent protagonists in order to deny that there is any real difference between them (that is, in order to deny that there is any such thing as guilt or innocence), but to assert a paradox at the heart of innocence. He designs events that compel his innocents to acknowledge their capacity for violence, or even, in order to protect their innocence, to perform acts of killing that, from the outside, look like murder. Similarly, the point of Hitchcock's insistence on the pervasiveness of theater is not to deny that there is any such thing as sincerity, or to assert that we can never tell the difference between sincerity and acting. It is Hitchcock's point, instead, that we must not take for granted our ability to see through insincerity, whether in ourselves or others. The human condition would not be what it is if we automatically knew ourselves or others, if we were incapable of knowing them, or if there were some outside authority we could rely on in making such judgments: this is Hitchcock's understanding, I believe.

As viewers, our task in assessing the lodger's guilt or innocence differs fundamentally from Daisy's. Daisy must come to terms with no one's testimony except Joe's, and she knows not to take his word. We, however, must come to terms with the author's ambiguous and contradictory suggestions. Hitchcock does not allow us to take his testimony for granted; we must judge for ourselves how to take his suggestions. We come to know him only by reading his films.

In a closeup against a black background, Joe registers the lodger's words (1.80). This shot again echoes the moment when Joe willed the images to appear in the mud. Daisy smiles, hoping he will still consider the possibility that the lodger may be innocent (1.81), but Joe hardens. Hitchcock cuts to a longer shot that reflects the formality of the moment as Joe says, "Tell that to the judge;" then there is a cut to a still longer, more impersonal framing. Joe points at the lodger and says, "I arrest you on a charge of murder."

1.80

I take it that Joe knows that, with this gesture, he is condemning himself in Daisy's eyes. He acts as though duty calls for him to sacrifice his own happiness, as though he were a victim, but I imagine him as secretly recognizing the spirit of revenge in which he acts. Joe, unlike the Claude Rains character in *Notorious* or any number of Griffith heroes, is not willing to let his rival prevail. His desire for vengeance against the man who won Daisy from him takes precedence over his wish for her love, for

1.81

happiness, or for justice. Joe wants the lodger to be the Avenger because he wants him to hang for stealing Daisy. It is not that he believes in his guilt the way she believes in his innocence. Her love fills her with a faith that vanquishes all doubts, but his vengeful act is performed in the face of doubts it refuses to acknowledge. And society, which has designated him as an agent of the law, has granted him powers apparently sufficient to satisfy his desire for vengeance. Daisy cries, "He's innocent!" Joe pulls her away, and handcuffs are placed on the lodger's wrists. At the door, Joe looks back one last time at the woman he loves. He turns his eyes away, looks up at the camera, and resignedly abandons the frame.

An emotionally charged encounter follows between the lodger and Daisy's parents. From a very long shot of the stairs, with him at the top and the parents at the bottom, there is a cut to the lodger looking down, then to the mother and father viewed from his point of view. In another long shot, he shakes his head sadly. Then the camera returns to the parents, who back away from him—that is,

1.82

from the camera—as he advances (1.82). They respond with terror and awe to his presence and are unable to meet his gaze. At this moment they appear overwhelmed by the enormity of the evil that has menaced their daughter. But perhaps the possibility dawns on them, or at least on the mother, that a terrible mistake has been made.

As Daisy and the lodger pass each other, she looks up at him and he says, "Meet me by the lamp." The lodger's all but magical powers, and their conjunction with the mother's unwitting agency, are nowhere more apparent than when he makes this apparently impossible appointment. Somehow he knows he will be able to keep this rendezvous, and, indeed, the mother allows it to take place by fainting, perhaps at the thought of the fate Daisy has been spared or her own implication in the condemnation of an innocent man. In the commotion that ensues, the lodger escapes. Hitchcock cuts back and forth to the lodger disappearing

1.83

into the darkness, Daisy waiting to break away to join him, and the police searching the streets.

The lodger sits under the lamppost, a pathetic spectacle. Daisy enters the frame and walks toward him. When he finds her beside him, he begins to tell his story, his face half in darkness (1.83). "That *was* my sister's portrait. We were dancing together at her coming-out ball." There is a dissolve from the lodger's face to the photograph of his sister, then to a view of dancing couples, including the lodger and his sister with their backs to the camera (1.84). Thus begins the film's flashback, which has two parts.

The camera begins to pull back from this scene of dancing, mov-

1.84

1.85

1.86

1.87

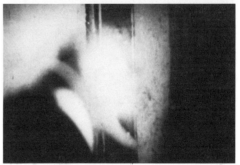

1.88

ing through the frame of a doorway and past elaborate grillwork (1.85). This is only the third camera movement in the entire film, its movement out reversing the earlier movements in. The shot ends with the dancers framed in a harmoniously composed frame-within-a-frame. The grillwork distances our view of the dancers; we have passed silently from within the space of the dancing couples to a position outside that space and screened from it. The next shot suspends this distanced perspective (1.86). But at the precise moment the lodger and his sister dance out of the frame, there is a cut to an extreme long shot in which the whole party appears perfectly framed, backlit, in the far background (1.87). Then there is an "unplaced" view of three switches on a wall. A hand sweeps through this frame, flipping the switches, and the screen goes dark (1.88).

The camera returns to the preceding setup. Within the frame-within-a-frame, the lights go out and the dancing stops. In a beautifully backlit closeup, the lodger's sister screams (1.89); this shot of course echoes a series of shots, the first of which is the opening of the film. Many hands grope at the switches and the lights go back on. Through the grillwork we see everyone running to one spot. There is a cut to a body lying on

1.90

1.91

1.92

the floor. A man stoops down and, in an insert, we view the Avenger's calling card. As the mother faints, the image fades out, bringing the first part of the flashback to an end.

The lodger in the present fades in. His account of the murder is completed, but his story is unfinished. "My mother never recovered from the shock. Before she died . . ." There is a dissolve to the lodger standing at the foot of his mother's deathbed, a cut to the mother viewed across the lodger's back, then a cut to a schematic half-white and half-black frame in which the lodger is visible only as a silhouette in the left foreground (1.90).

The mother sits up and speaks. In the title her words are italicized to indicate their status as an oath: *"Swear to me, my son, you will not rest until the Avenger has been brought to justice."* We return to the half-white, half-black frame, and the image dissolves to the face of the lodger in the present, its dark and light regions congruent to the dark and light regions of the frame in which we viewed his mother's deathbed (1.91). "Since then I have been tracking him down. Every week he moved nearer to your street." There is a cut to Daisy and the lodger; then the camera returns to his divided face (1.92).

In the conventional flashback, views of the past "objectively" present what has happened within the world of the film. Only a conventional sign separates off these events and declares their pastness. The camera claims precisely the same access to the past of the world of the film as to its present. Often, such a flashback is signaled when a character begins to tell the story of some past event at which he was present. The character may be in the midst of telling his or her story to someone else when the screen goes wavy and the flashback starts; may be recollecting events in solitude, speaking a kind of soliloquy; or may be telling us the story, as in many *films noirs*. But the character telling the story ordinarily has no privileged status in the frame, no special relationship to the camera, no control over the views that constitute the flashback. In the framing of these views, the camera does not acknowledge the storyteller as "I."

But what is the status of views within *The Lodger*'s flashback? One possibility can be ruled out quickly. The flashback cannot simply represent the lodger's memory, for nothing he could remember corresponds, say, to the view of the dancers framed by the grillwork or to the camera's passage from within the space of the dancers to a position outside, and screened from, that space.

Two possibilities remain. In the story the lodger tells Daisy, he plays a double role: he is a character and he is also the narrator. Perhaps within the flashback he plays a comparable double role. That is, perhaps Hitchcock authorizes the lodger to assume his own place behind the camera, lending his authority as author not to the truth of the flashback's presentation, but to its veracity as a transcription of the lodger's story. The other possibility is that the flashback, like the rest of the film, is simply Hitchcock's own narration. What complicates this issue is the fact that what the camera represents—the identity and nature of the camera's "I"—has been under investigation throughout the film.

As the flashback opens, the lodger, framed with the dancers, is one of the camera's subjects. But when the camera moves out to assume a vantage point outside that space, it invokes the presence of an unviewed viewer, as on several occasions throughout the film. At one level, the mysterious being invoked is the lodger in the present, telling his story to Daisy. He is barred from this scene that haunts him because the scene is past, and he must stand apart even from his own self within it. But this framing also invokes the *real* presence of an unviewed figure separate from the lodger, who views these dancers and is barred from the dance. After all, the hand that enters the frame, signaling the murder, cannot literally be the lodger's (although its entrance into the frame precisely echoes his first introduction, when his hand entered the frame and seized the knocker). The natural suggestion is that this is the Avenger.

Indeed, in the second part of the flashback, the unviewed viewer whose presence is invoked by the camera and the lodger as the camera's subject are telescoped into a single ambiguous, double figure. The lodger has assumed a position in the frame that declares his status as a mysterious incarnation of the author's agency and our viewing presence. Staring into the frame, possessing it with his gaze, he is the camera's double as well as its subject; and this schematic frame, half-light and half-dark, fuses with our view of the lodger in the present, his face similarly divided.

The ambiguity of the presence represented by the camera in the flashback is related to a significant fact. We possess no views of the figure whose hand enters the frame, nor of the scene of murder cued by that gesture. We cannot really say we know that this is the Avenger's hand. Indeed, nothing in the flashback decisively settles the issue of whether the lodger is the Avenger. The views that constitute the flashback do not rule out the possibility that the lodger has a monstrous other self, the Avenger, of which his innocent self remains unconscious, that this figure is an aspect of his divided personality, that he murdered his own sister in a kind of trance. The lodger could still be the Avenger, then, without the story's being a conscious lie. And he could also be lying, like Jonathan in *Stage Fright*. But assuming that the lodger's story is not literally false, I will sketch the rereading that the flashback mandates.

When the lodger first arrives at the door of Daisy's home, he has vowed not to rest until the Avenger is "brought to justice." Whatever his mother meant by justice, his plan is to track down the Avenger, then to confront and kill him. In effect, he is engaged in mounting his own piece of theater whose climax is to be the Avenger's death. The lodger is author, director, star, and audience for this production, which I will call his *project*.

This project can be viewed as reflecting the lodger's wish to fulfill the vow his mother exacted. Viewed this way, it appears not so much his own as hers. He is locked in a struggle with the Avenger, but it is his mother who binds him; he is driven by her will and she stands witness over him; through his project, she maintains her hold. Only by killing the Avenger will he be able to lay his mother properly to rest and be released from her domination. But the project can be viewed in a very different way as well. Perhaps his plan to kill the Avenger owes nothing to his mother, from whom he may even have withheld his murderous intention when he swore not to rest until justice was done (after all, he was already in shadow, had already assumed the relationship to the camera that binds him to the Avenger, when he spoke his vow). But why would he embark on such a project on his own? Although the idyllic image of the lodger and his sister dancing together, happy and laughing, establishes their love, it is striking that the flashback does not detail his reaction to her death. This omission invites the speculation that he believes himself somehow responsible for the murder, as if his sister were killed to punish him for his love for her or as if he had secretly wished her to die so he could be freed from his love for a woman he could never possess (she is killed at her coming-out ball; as of this night, she is eligible to be courted by any bachelor in society).

The lodger feels he must confront and kill the Avenger because he views the Avenger as his double—a reflection of what he imagines or fears himself to be. He strives to deny or undo or atone for his guilt. In advancing his project he operates coolly, like the chess player he is, and takes aesthetic pleasure in playing out his part. But the film also insists on his private anguish. He dwells within the past, haunting it with a ghost's presence.

The lodger is a divided figure. He is the Avenger's innocent, righteous enemy, but he is also the Avenger's vengeful double. He acts autonomously, but also under his mother's command. Yet the "mother" who dominates him is his projection and creation, to be kept alive within himself. He is her creature, but she is also his. His project makes him a composite figure, mother and son together; perhaps this above all makes him the ancestor of Norman Bates in *Psycho*. Then, too, the lodger's anguish reflects his knowledge that, if he completes his project, he will be a murderer. He is in a private trap from which he feels powerless to escape. Divided between a past that haunts him and a future that holds hope only for the closing out of that past, he has no life in the present. It is Daisy who brings his chronic condition to a point of crisis.

In the lodger's private production, the Avenger must play himself. But when the lodger first hears Daisy's laugh, I take it, he recognizes that she was born to play the role of the Avenger's victim. We can account for this recognition in two ways. Looking for a woman to use as bait, he coolly puts himself in the Avenger's place. From within the role of the Avenger, he hears Daisy's laugh as mocking the powers of men. As if with the Avenger's murderous gaze, he first views Daisy in her golden-haired splendor and recognizes her by her knowing look, first in his room and then in her salon. But perhaps Daisy's laugh also transports the lodger to the scene of his sister's death and reminds him of the woman who created the role.

Daisy's presence rededicates the lodger to his project, and he creates a part for her in his private play. Yet her presence also threatens that project because he is attracted to her. The conventions of movie romance entitle us to say that the lodger falls in love with her at the moment he hears her laugh. His desire reawakens him to the present and inspires a new undertaking, the courtship of Daisy, whose demands conflict with those of his project. For one thing, the lodger's plan calls for her to be exposed to grave danger without her knowledge or acquiescence. If his plan is successful, he will have turned himself into a murderer. A murderer who has exploited Daisy for his own ends can hardly court her honorably.

Also, the lodger's anguished impotence in Daisy's presence reveals his obsession with the Avenger. He must choose between his courtship and the violent piece of theater by which he plans to consummate his relationship with his murderous double. In a sense, the whole film turns on the conflict between the lodger's secret obsession with the Avenger and his desire for Daisy. The story of *The Lodger* is the story of a struggle with an obsession.

The lodger is afraid to reveal himself to Daisy. Throughout the film, he fears that, should she come to know him as he really is, she must reject him; and he fears that it may be his nature to kill rather than lose her. He harbors the suspicion that it may be his impotence that attracts her to him, and he suspects that she is drawn to him because he bears the Avenger's mark. I think that these fears erupt when he violently pushes her away and then passionately kisses her. The flashback's revelations do not resolve the ambiguities of this moment, but they do crystallize them. This kiss may declare the lodger's love and a renunciation of his project, or it may be a leap into madness, signifying that he has become completely possessed by the past scene that haunts him, that he has crossed a barrier into a world in which his sister and Daisy, himself and the Avenger, life and death, love and murder cannot be separated.

When Joe accuses the lodger of the Avenger's crimes and Daisy declares—so compellingly that even Joe pauses—her faith in his innocence, the lodger is inspired by her faith but feels unworthy of it. Filled with a sense of guilt, uncertain of his own nature, he arranges to meet her under the lamppost and there tells his story.

When the lodger finishes telling his story, the camera holds on his face, half in light and half in darkness. As much to himself as to Daisy he says, "But now—I shall miss him." Framed in a beautiful

closeup, her face overflows with tenderness (1.93). She kisses his hands and looks up at him. How will he now react? It is crucial that, at this moment, we remain in suspense. The lodger's secret, which is also the author's secret, is now told, but we still do not know how the scene will end. Even if he is not the Avenger, and even if he is by nature innocent, he could now turn violent. The flashback has not made nonsense out of our fears. The lodger could meet Daisy's

1.93

gaze, speak his love, and ask for her hand; but conceivably he also could say, "And it's your fault," and give himself over to a blind rage. If the lodger turned into the Avenger before our eyes, the film could end with a view of Daisy screaming, coming full circle. Or the film could take a specifically melodramatic turn, the Avenger now appearing on the scene, the lodger playing out his role and then disappearing into the night, a soul condemned. Or Joe could providentially arrive to apprehend the Avenger and then bless the union of Daisy and the lodger, redeeming himself and allowing the film a comedy ending.

None of these dramatic continuations is realized. The lodger simply looks up at Daisy and buries his head in her shoulder. Reality's intervention has been too strenuous. He has broken down, and even love cannot save him. They rise, Daisy draping her cloak over his shoulders. At this moment, there is a cut to a policeman walking in the London night, reminding us of the couple's jeopardy. Daisy says, "You're shivering. Keep your handcuffs hidden and we'll get some brandy."

The lodger and Daisy enter a pub. The travails of the handcuffed fugitive are a well-known Hitchcock specialty. Here the specific problem is how to drink a glass of brandy without exposing the "bracelets." (We might well marvel at Hitchcock's boldness, this early in his career, in inserting a brief scene played for laughs so close to the film's emotional climax.)

The couple disappears back into the night. Then Joe arrives and makes a phone call. Overhearing the words "He can't go far—he's handcuffed," the barmaid puts two and two together, and the patrons move out to take vengeance, as a mob, on the man they think is the Avenger. Thus they miss the news that catches Joe and us by surprise: the Avenger has just been caught red-handed. Joe rushes out to save the lodger from the mob.

There is no other suspense sequence in all of Hitchcock's work as harrowing as the Griffith-like rescue that ensues. Presented with absolutely no traces of the irony that become hallmarks of Hitchcock suspense, it builds to an agonizing tension. Pursued by the mob, the lodger comes to a spiked fence.[15] As the lodger attempts to climb over this fence, his handcuffs catch on a spike (1.94). This is companion to (1.77) as an image of anguished impotence. Graphic in its sexual symbolism, it also represents a notable occurrence of the / / / / motif. Unable to move, the lodger hangs suspended, hands tearing at him from all sides, tormented by the mob within which Hitchcock personally assumes a place in his second cameo appearance of the film (1.95).

Daisy arrives, pushes her way to the

1.94

1.95

1.96

1.97

1.98

1.99

front, and takes the lodger's hand. Viewed in closeup from her point of view, his eyes are closed and blood trickles from the corner of his mouth. His face is free from anguish, but there is no sign of life in it. Even when he opens his eyes, his face is blank (1.96). Finally Joe arrives at Daisy's side and tries desperately to save the lodger. It is only when a newsboy appears on the scene, hawking the news of the Avenger's capture, however, that the mob releases its deadly grip and the battered body is laid to the ground, the composition clearly invoking the *Pietà* (1.97). Joe cries, "Thank God I was in time!" He remains the old self-important Joe, giving himself sole credit for the rescue and not acknowledging the role played by the providential appearance of the *Evening Standard*. Joe's cry signals a cut to a low-angle portrait of the mob, seen as monstrous and inhuman, with Hitchcock himself now on the front line (1.98). Then in an intimate frame—this is a view the mob does not possess—Daisy kisses the lodger and the image fades out (1.99). Even Daisy's kiss does not have the power to make the lodger come to life. He has withdrawn into a private world to which we have no access. He has died to the world we can view.

The scourging mob, at one level, is a

projection of the lodger's anguished sense of guilt. It is as if he wills the mob's onslaught, takes upon himself a punishment fit for the Avenger. Yet if the mob seems to come in answer to his secret, silent call, it is not merely a phantom of his imagination; it is also real. But why does Hitchcock author a world in which reality and the lodger's nightmare coincide? We have seen the mob before: they are the newspaper readers, the radio listeners, the ordinary Londoners of the prologue. They hang on every detail of the Avenger story out of their fearfulness, their wish for vengeance, and their insatiable appetite for erotic violence. The mob is, at one level, the film's representation of its audience. It is made up of *viewers*.

Hitchcock's gesture here has the force of an indictment. In its desire for violence, its hunger for blood, the ugly mob is indifferent to the possibility that its victim may be innocent. So, too, we may say that the film's viewers have failed to have faith in the lodger's innocence and taken pleasure in, even willed, his torment. But more needs to be said. If the mob is guilty, it also suffers. It is frustrated, no more able to satisfy itself than the lodger is able to escape from its clutches. The lodger and the mob are equally trapped in this moment of impotence. They wish for opposing resolutions of the tension, of course, but Hitchcock fuses their frustrations in a single set of indelible images. The mob's desire for violence reveals its condition: it is not so much guilty as condemned.

If the film's audience stands indicted, justice would seem to demand that Hitchcock himself be included in the indictment. If the viewer is like the newspaper reader, *The Lodger* is like the *Evening Standard* itself, playing on the public's fears and unholy desires, selling violence for profit. Hitchcock enters the film in person as a member of the mob, thereby giving this sequence an aspect of confession. Hitchcock places himself with the viewers in the dock. If the mob represents the film's audience, it also represents the film's author. Hitchcock's cameos become a ritual, but *The Lodger*'s original audience could neither look for Hitchcock's appearance nor recognize it when it occurred. In this film alone—the film by which Hitchcock establishes his identity as an artist—his appearance is a private gesture, a secret.

In the face of the lodger and in his view of the mob, author and viewers come together. But Hitchcock also asserts his separateness from the lodger. The author releases the lodger to marry Daisy, bringing the film to a close, and the camera relinquishes its hold. The lodger's privileged position cannot be the author's, whose place is behind the camera. Hitchcock must abandon his dream of dwelling within the world of his creation. He too is not so much guilty as condemned. To the suggestion that the mob is Hitchcock's representation of his audience, I want to add that *we* have done nothing to justify such an indictment. *The Lodger* does not really assume that its audience is a mob. The film calls for and authorizes an attentive reading that acknowledges its authorship. Hitchcock does not avenge himself on viewers who acknowledge him; he exempts them from his indictment. *The Lodger* declares that it is not the *Evening Standard*.

In this light, Hitchcock's framing of Daisy's sad kiss, according us this intimate view, appears as an acknowledgment that his film is addressed to viewers who cannot justly be located within this mob. Indeed, the mob's scourging of the lodger feels like an assault on us as well. This sequence would not be so painful to view if we did not imagine ourselves in the lodger's place, suffering his torment. But why would Hitchcock place himself within a mob that attacks us with fury? The ambiguity in the mob's attack on the lodger—does it assail him, certain that he is the Avenger, or does it suspect that he is innocent?—extends as well to this attack on us. Perhaps there is justice in the attack because in our viewing we are somehow guilty. Perhaps we are to the film's author what the Avenger is to the lodger. Or does Hitchcock take us to be innocent? Then again we must ask ourselves how Hitchcock could regard himself as our victim, for we can also imagine the film's author represented by the lodger and the viewer by the mob.

Hitchcock's bond with the lodger and the Avenger has been apparent throughout the film. From the outset, the camera's intimacy with these figures has been declared. The lodger and the Avenger are surrogates for the author. The harrowing image of the lodger and the mob is a paradigm, if an enigmatic and paradoxical one, of the relationship between the lodger and the Avenger and the relationship between Hitchcock and us. The relationship of author and viewers, it declares, is at one level a struggle for control. We must suppose that, in making *The Lodger*, Hitchcock again and again imagined himself in our place. His intention is always "to get there first," anticipating and confounding our expectations of each moment so that emotions we cannot control are awakened within us. Hitchcock works to trap the viewer into becoming emotional the way the lodger works to trap the Avenger. But, in our reading, we have turned the tables by imagining ourselves in Hitchcock's place. In the creation of *The Lodger*, then, we may well wonder who is active and who is passive. Who brings the lodger to this moment of harrowing suspense?

The profundity of this image rests in part on its reversibility. We identify with the lodger and strain with him to keep those terrible hands from reaching his body; and we identify with the mob—*our* hands strain to rend his flesh. The fury and desire and terror of the two sides are fused in this image which, as it were, compels us to push the two sides together and pull them apart. The film that inaugurates Hitchcock's oeuvre declares murder to be a metaphor for his relationship to the viewer. Yet we cannot take for granted that Hitchcock judges his filmmaking and our viewing to be murderous. There remains the possibility that, despite everything, Hitchcock's motivations, and our own, are innocent. Perhaps Hitchcock's authorship is not like the lodger's secret project but like his courtship of Daisy. If we have faith in Hitchcock, we may assume that our violent struggle with him will be transmuted into a kind of marriage. *The Lodger* in fact establishes marriage as Hitchcock's other key metaphor for the relationship of author and viewers. The connection between murder and marriage is one of Hitchcock's great subjects. How concern for this subject could drive a good man to make such films as *The Lodger*, it might further be noted, is a principal subject of this book. But, then, what if Hitchcock is not a good man, but a monster?[16]

When Joe says, "Thank God I was in time!" we realize two things. First, as I have said, Joe is his usual righteous self despite his "redemption." He might also have thanked God that the newspaper story of the Avenger's capture appeared just in time. If the *Evening Standard* is implicated in the lodger's ordeal, it also plays an ironic role in bringing that ordeal to an end. Second, the "God" there is for Joe to thank can only be Hitchcock, who also acts within the context of his relationship with us. As Hitchcock arranges it, the lodger's salvation is conditioned on the Avenger's apprehension. This brings us to a fundamental Hitchcock paradigm: the innocent figure is freed for romantic union by the damnation of a guilty double who can never marry. The Wrong One—I adopt this chilling term from a number of Hitchcock films, most notably *The Wrong Man* and *Psycho* ("Did she look like a wrong one to you?") —is condemned from childhood to a life of isolation. He sacrifices himself, or is sacrificed, so that his innocent double can marry. If the lodger's violent ordeal is therapeutic (through repetition of the initial trauma, he is "cured"), there is a figure, the Avenger, who is beyond the efficacy of such a cure. Surely, Hitchcock's identification is divided between these two figures, one saved and one damned. Perhaps Hitchcock too is a Wrong One, and perhaps he calls upon us to acknowledge that we are Wrong Ones as well.

When the lodger is let down from the spiked fence, he is imaged as though dead. This is the first of the film's endings: death freeing the lodger from his curse as Daisy, faithful to the end, witnesses his passing with sorrow. But this ending is disavowed by an epilogue which informs us that the lodger completely recovers and becomes free to marry Daisy. Yet nothing can erase our haunting vision of the lodger's "death."

The immediate sequel—the first part of the film's epilogue—presents an equally indelible image of the lodger in a state of death-in-life, withdrawn into a private world we cannot view. The scene fades in on a very long shot of Daisy and a doctor standing over the lodger, lying motionless in bed. We might say that this is the film's second ending. But it too is disavowed. The doctor pronounces his diagnosis: "He has suffered a nervous strain." He touches his forehead to clarify his meaning. "But his youth and vigor will pull him through." (Those who know *Psycho* will recognize the mode of irony with which Hitchcock presents the testimony of this "authority.") What the doctor prophesies will become *The Lodger*'s third ending.

The lodger, in bed, opens his eyes, but barely. In a longer shot, the doctor leaves the frame, and the lodger slowly turns his head to Daisy. He does his best to reach out to her. She takes his hand when it flops weakly on the path to hers. As they look at each other, the image fades out.

In the second part of the epilogue, Hitchcock prefaces a tranquil coda with the title "All Stories Have an End": the storyteller steps forward to remind us that this is just a story. What we are about to view is not reality but only exemplifies the fact that stories have endings. The title is Hitchcock's reminder that he is free to choose the ending he wishes. Hitchcock presides over the lodger's miraculous resurrection and could as easily have withheld this miracle.[17]

The great hall of the lodger's mansion fades in. Daisy's mother and father are in the foreground of the frame. Daisy looks up as the lodger appears at the top of the stairs. He descends and walks over to Daisy. They embrace. He smiles with a Chaplin-like shyness as the parents enter the frame. A look of horror suddenly passes over the father's face. An insert reveals the cause: he trips on the unaccustomedly thick rug and almost falls. (This piece of business reinforces our sense that this scene repeats, but with a difference, the

lodger's entrance into Daisy's life.) The lodger and the parents shake hands: he has at last won their acceptance.

The father realizes that the young people should be left alone and pokes his wife. (The relationship between the mother and father has, as it were, been straightened out: the father now wears the pants in the family.) In front of tall windows, the lodger removes Daisy's hat. As they are about to kiss, a "TO-

1.100

NIGHT GOLDEN CURLS" sign flashes outside the window in the dark London
night. The camera starts to move in, specifically reversing the movement that
initiated the film's flashback. Daisy
lowers her gaze and the lodger kisses
her forehead. The camera continues to
move in as they kiss. Again, the "TO-
NIGHT GOLDEN CURLS" sign flashes. Finally, the camera's movement excludes
the sign from the frame, and we see
Daisy's ecstatic face and the lower half
of the lodger's face (1.100, 1.101, 1.102).
This last image echoes and reverses
(1.75), the kiss interrupted by Joe's intervention. It fades out, and "THE END" appears over an image of blowing leaves.

1.101

The epilogue, which on the surface
exorcises the specter of the Avenger and
asserts that the lodger's ghosts have
been laid to rest, is dense with invocations of earlier moments in the film.

1.102

This allusive quality is so marked, and the allusions so condensed,
that it might well be argued that Hitchcock composes the epilogue
to call attention to its own artifice and thereby undermine the authority of its disavowals. When the "TO-NIGHT GOLDEN CURLS" sign
reappears, it is stripped of its former ominous significance: it is
only an advertising sign. But in this setting it takes on a new meaning. As the camera moves in, both reversing its movement in the
flashback and echoing the introduction of the lodger and the
Avenger, the sign flashes. It is as if Hitchcock is declaring that
everything we have viewed is not real but a piece of theater or a
dream. The film begins by linking the camera with the mystery of
the act of murder and ends by linking it with the mystery of the
sexual act. Tonight, when our view fades out, when the lodger and
Daisy are at last alone, with no audience and out of the camera's
view, they will perform such an act for the first time. Do we really
know that this ending is a happy one?

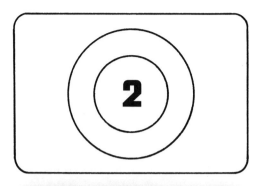

2

Murder!

After *The Lodger*, Hitchcock made six silent films: *Downhill* (1927), *Easy Virtue* (1927), *The Ring* (1927), *The Farmer's Wife* (1928), *Champagne* (1928), and *The Manxman* (1928). If we think of what is Hitchcockian only in terms of the development of a certain kind of suspense thriller, these films might be briefly passed over.[1] But these works, made at the height of the silent cinema's golden age, are substantial individual accomplishments—major additions, unjustly neglected, to the corpus of significant silent films. They can also be studied as a coherent body of work, complete unto itself. *The Farmer's Wife* and *The Manxman* are made with the clear knowledge that the silent cinema, already being supplanted by the talkie, is living on borrowed time. Whatever else they may be, they are summations of Hitchcock's understanding of the conditions of this doomed art. *The Manxman* in particular self-consciously declares the sizeable body of Hitchcock's silent films to be complete.

When production began on Hitchcock's next film, the studio planned to release it as a "part-talkie," but the triumph of talking pictures proved so complete that it was decided to add sound to all of it. Hitchcock had anticipated—and clearly wished for—this decision. *Blackmail* (1929) is Hitchcock's first sound film, and one of his most important and darkest. I have always thought of it as forming a kind of trilogy with *The Lodger* and *Murder!*

Blackmail is in the line of Hitchcock films that centers on a "girl on the threshold of womanhood" who wishes for a way out of the trap of marriage to the ordinary unromantic man her parents favor. But it gives the story of *The Lodger* a cruel twist. Its world is one in which there is no man for Alice who is her equal, no dream lover who is also innocent. Frank, Joe's descendant, wins this descendant of Daisy, and his is a victory of blackmail, not love.

In place of the lodger, and joining the lodger's role with that of the Avenger (although the blackmailer complicates this equation), is the figure of the artist, Hitchcock's surrogate within the world of the film. The artist's seductiveness, his capacity for violence, his necessary death, and the power of his art to haunt and mock those who behold it all testify to *Blackmail*'s status as, at one level, Hitchcock's reflection on his own art. A focus of this reflection is the act of killing performed behind a dark curtain, Hitchcock's declaration of his own theatricality and his own mystery.

Formally *Blackmail* is notable for its unusually resonant system of echoes and anticipations, which creates a texture in which every detail is significant and in which sounds, words, objects, gestures, and visual compositions are equally in play. It also elaborates on *The Lodger*'s ambiguous conjunctions of the subjective and the objective. This can be observed in the famous passage in which Alice is asked to pass a bread knife and we hear the word "knife" as it is colored by her imagination, and also in the inscriptions of sexual signifiers into the frame. But the passage in which the barrier between the real and the imaginary is most emphatically crossed—or perhaps denied—is the film's finale, the chase through the British Museum (a space dominated by ////s). In part, Hitchcock models this passage on the sequence in *The Lodger* in which the mother appears to imagine what we are privileged to view (the montage that invokes—but does not actually show—a scene of murder); and it becomes a fundamental Hitchcock paradigm. He films this chase by cutting back and forth between Alice, in the throes of an interior struggle, and the blackmailer, hounded by the police for the killing that Alice actually performed. The presentation suggests that Alice is imagining the chase we are viewing. (In one celebrated shot, a giant head dwarfs the puny figure of the blackmailer, its statue's face impassive and expressionless before the spectacle of this man's merely human desperation. This mask stands in for Alice and links our view with the private fantasy that absorbs her.) When she reaches her decision to confess at the instant the blackmailer falls to his death, it is as though our vision of this man's fate corresponds to her envisioning the consequences of her continued silence. It is a dark irony, characteristic of the bleakness of *Blackmail*, that the imaginary scene that edifies her is also real, and that the moment she arrives at her understanding is the moment at which it is, irrevocably, too late.

After two relatively unfulfilling assignments—in 1930 he was called upon to direct parts of *Elstree Calling*, the first British musical, and directed *Juno and the Paycock*, an admirable adaptation of the O'Casey play that allowed him, however, little scope for following up the ideas in *The Lodger* and *Blackmail*—Hitchcock turned to a project that came to occupy an important place in his work.

Murder! (1930) is the masterpiece of Hitchcock's early films. The philosophical dimension implicit in *The Lodger* and *Blackmail* becomes explicit in the arguments between the protagonist and the cunning and articulate murderer against whom he is pitted. (By contrast, the sophisticated lodger has no opportunity to argue his position, and *Blackmail*'s artist is killed early in the film.) We cannot follow the thinking in *Murder!* apart from a reading that comprehends the subtleties and ironies of Hitchcock's presentation of those arguments. Briefly, however, the philosophical concerns of *Murder!* are those of all of Hitchcock's films and include the problems of human identity; the relationships among love, desire, murder, dreams, madness, and theater; and the nature of viewing. And underlying the film's arguments are its reflections on its own nature as a film. The arguments about the conditions of art and the

film's testing of those arguments are placed within a series of invocations of theater: *Murder!*'s world mirrors and mimics theater, incorporating prosceniums, curtains, costumes, role playing, and
theatrical gestures; and the film's central strategy is to relate its protagonist's new play to *Murder!* itself. But the invocations of theater
are performed within the context of the film's declaration of its own
decisive separation from theater, its declaration of itself as a film.
The film declares the camera's powers and the limits of those
powers, and reflects on the camera's perplexing relationships to its
subjects within the world of the film, to Hitchcock, and to us.

In *Murder!* the camera's subjects at times appear to know they are
being filmed. They seem to possess the power to confront—hence
also to avoid—the camera's gaze, as well as the power to perform
for the camera, to command its attention. At times, the camera appears to penetrate its subjects' innermost wishes and fears, allowing them no privacy or secrets. What we view sometimes seems
projected within the imaginations of the camera's subjects. And
sometimes these subjects seem to have access to the views that
make up the film itself, as if they shared Hitchcock's position as author or our position as viewers. Beings who dwell within the world
of a film cannot literally view that film, of course; their relationship
with the camera grants them powers and subjects them to forces
that are, within the world of the film, magical. And that relationship also allows us to view them not as "characters" but as signifiers of Hitchcock's authorship and our own acts of viewing.

The film opens with a "hallucinatory" presentation of a scene of
murder, akin to the opening of *The Lodger*. Edna Druce, an actress,
is found murdered, a poker on the floor beside the body and an
empty brandy glass on the table beside her. All the evidence suggests that the murderer is Diana Baring, a rival actress in Edna's
company. The murder takes place in Diana's apartment; they had
been arguing and were known to dislike each other; and Diana is
found, in a trancelike state, at the scene of the crime.

A trial sequence follows. (No one's trial sequences rival Hitchcock's in drama, attention to the logic of the proceedings, and precise delineation of the discrete points of view of accused, judge,
jury, witnesses, opposed attorneys, and general audience. Consider, for example, the elaborate trial sequences in *The Paradine
Case* and in the silent *Easy Virtue*.) Diana does not confess to the
crime, but neither does she deny that she is guilty. She offers no
defense other than that, after a certain point in an altercation with
Edna, she remembers nothing.

The scene shifts to the jury room. The jurors who vote "not
guilty" on the first ballot are persuaded, one by one, to change their

votes. Throughout the lengthy deliberation, there is one juror, glimpsed during the trial, who is absent from the frame and not referred to. Today we may well notice this juror because he is played by Herbert Marshall, a familiar face to us. To *Murder!*'s original audience, however, he would only have been one of twelve anonymous figures; this was his first film, and all but the most attentive viewer would have been caught by surprise when, just as a consensus appears to have been achieved, the foreman says, "There's just Sir John," and Hitchcock cuts to the first shot in the sequence in which the film's protagonist appears (2.1). All faces turn, and he is isolated in a frontal framing (2.2).

2.1

Sir John has a bond with the camera. Retroactively our views of the other jurors are linked with his gaze: they suffer his scrutiny as they suffer the camera's. But Sir John also appears as if he were Hitchcock's agent and surrogate. When he begins to speak within this frame, it is as if the film's author were directly addressing the jurors, who indeed have momentarily become *our* representatives. The offscreen words of the foreman that cue his speech ("We mustn't be long. Time's money, you know") and the words of the address itself sustain this suggestion, whose irony will not fully emerge until the end of the film.

2.2

Sir John is a celebrated playwright and actor. He points out that he is not a man of business but a man of the theater who has trained himself "to apply the techniques of life to the problems of my art. But today, ladies and gentlemen, that process is reversed. I find myself applying the techniques of my art to a problem of real life. And my art is not satisfied." In the dock, Diana testified that she had no recollection of the murder. Is it possible that she committed the crime without remembering it? Does she possess a monstrous other self that her innocent self does not recognize? Sir John's statement amounts to this, that his views of Diana in the dock have given him knowledge of her innocence and sincerity. He asserts that his artist's gaze enables him to penetrate theatricality, to recognize acting when he sees it. But can one know another's nature with certainty merely by viewing? In *Murder!*'s reflections on the powers and limits of the camera, in which "the dock" is one stand-in for the film frame, deep questions about our knowledge of others, and the conditions of self-knowledge, are addressed.[2] The dock is dialectically opposed to the stage: on stage, Diana presents herself to be possessed in a desiring gaze; in the dock, she is subjected to stern eyes that judge her. But Sir John cannot make the other jurors see Diana as he does. He submits to them, acquiescing in their verdict. Diana is sentenced to hang.

At home in his bathroom, doubled in the frame-within-a-frame of a mirror, Sir John shaves and muses in stream-of-consciousness voiceover. His speech—in effect, a dramatic monologue—is accompanied by the passionate strains of the prelude to *Tristan und Isolde*, which comes in over the radio. He berates himself for failing to convince the jurors of Diana's innocence. Why couldn't the others have viewed her with his eyes?

2.3

Meditating on this question—our specific impression is that he is at this moment savoring his views of Diana in the dock—he stares into the mirror, lost in thought (2.3). To the other jurors, he had insisted that the impression Diana made on him had nothing to do with her "qualities" as they appealed to one of the jurors, a lewd, piglike man. But now, alone before the reflection of himself in his shaving mirror, he secretly admits to finding her attractive. When he thinks "I wonder what her feelings are now," we take it that he is possessed by a wish to view her at this moment. He looks down and reaches for the glass of red wine in front of him. His gesture is signaled by the camera's movement to the left, so that when he sips the wine, he is framed in profile, no longer face to face with his reflected image (2.4).

2.4

Sir John's gesture suggests that he is completely absorbed in a view he imagines or recollects, like the lodger spellbound before the paintings of golden-haired women. Sipping wine, perhaps he imagines himself possessing the object of his desire. On the other hand, his gesture, enacted in front of a mirror, seems so theatrical—the camera's reframing perfectly highlights his pose—that we might take him to be absorbed not by his desire, but by the *role* of a man possessed by desire. As the camera pans back, Sir John puts the glass down. He looks at himself intently. His offscreen voice urgently speaks the words, "Who drank the brandy?'' The staccato delivery of this line echoes the theme from Beethoven's Fifth Symphony which accompanied the title credits. That rhythm has already been taken up by the sound of knocking in the murder scene that follows the opening titles. And the knocking will again be invoked on several occasions in the course of the film. For example, a knock on the bathroom door will soon bring Sir John's meditation to an end.[3]

Whoever drank the brandy killed Edna. In this dark moment, framed by the camera's matched pans, the drinker of the wine conjures in his imagination the drinker of the brandy, his double. Yet this figure will turn out to be a real inhabitant of the world of the film. The camera bears witness to Sir John's imagining of the murderer, and appears to call forth this apparition. The camera reflects the power of the author when it frames Sir John's gesture. But does Sir John knowingly make a compact with Hitchcock, sealing this covenant with the wine, or is he Hitchcock's fool, blind to the agency that presides over this world?

At this critical moment, Sir John's valet knocks on the door, breaking the spell. Bennett, the secretary, has arrived, and is waiting in the sitting room. In the ensuing dialogue, we learn that Diana had once come to Sir John seeking a place in his roster of actresses, but he had sent her away "to gain experience." (This revelation is startling. We assumed that Sir John's interior monologue was giving us access to his private thoughts, but now it appears to have made no reference to what is really on his mind.) When Bennett points out the irony that Diana has now become a kind of star after all, Sir John announces that he himself plans to track down the drinker of the brandy. This is what I shall call Sir John's project. We discover a characteristic Hitchcock network of ambiguity—comparable to what envelopes the lodger's project—when we ask ourselves what Sir John's project really is and why he undertakes it.

Sir John failed to convince the other jurors of his view of Diana. But also, had he not once sent her away, she would never have had to join Edna's company and would now be free. His is a double failure: he failed to empower the other jurors to see her with his eyes, and in the past he himself failed to recognize what he now sees in her. He wishes to save Diana and redeem himself as a man (if Diana is not saved, her blood will be on his hands) and as an artist (his artist's powers have failed him; he must use theater to save Diana). But if Sir John embarks on his project out of a feeling of responsibility, he is also motivated by desire for Diana. At one level, his project is a courtship. To win Diana, she must be freed and he must redeem himself in order to be fit to declare his love. Also, he must satisfy his doubts about her. An S.O.S. report on the radio triggers his meditation in front of the shaving mirror. This suggests that he

viewed Diana in the dock as secretly entering a passionate plea for
help. Was it to his gaze alone that she really presented herself to be
viewed? Sir John's project is also an investigation into Diana's nature. She may be the murderer's double, and equally murderous.
The drinker of the brandy may be her lover. Sir John's investigation
is motivated, in part, by the question "Does Diana love me?"

Sir John's project is closely related to Joe's investigation in *The
Lodger*, and his relationship to the drinker of the brandy mirrors the
lodger's relationship to the Avenger. His project, we shall see, is
also a passionate struggle with his dark double, the drinker of the
brandy. He takes satisfaction at the thought of tracking this figure,
is obsessed with the wish to expose and confront him. But then
again, viewing Diana Baring with the eyes of a master of theater, Sir
John desires her for his company. He wants her to star with him in
his next production as his lover and bride: then others might see
her with his eyes. We have come to a crux of the film. Sir John is
swept up in a chain of events that would make a perfect play,
which might be called "The Inner History of the Baring Case". Sir
John plays a role in these events, but he also undertakes to assume,
as it were, their authorship. The outcome of his project will deter-
mine, for example, how the events will end. This in turn will deter-
mine what kind of play they would be if staged (among the possibilities alluded to in the film are "highbrow shocker," "blood and
thunder" melodrama, Shakespearean tragedy). He has a closing
curtain already in mind: Diana and himself locked in a lovers' embrace. However, he does not have a clear idea of the scenes leading
up to the ending, and the critical scene of the murder needs to be
filled in. Then, too, he does not yet know the identity of his villain.

Within the world of *Murder!* "The Inner History of the Baring
Case" is not a merely imaginary play. As the film unfolds, it gradually becomes clear that Sir John may well actually be immersed in
writing a play that follows the events of the murder point by point.
When the film ends with a view of the curtain falling on a performance of his new play, we take it to be "The Inner History of the Bar-

ing Case." This revelation, like *The
Lodger*'s flashback, transforms our understanding of everything that has come
before. In retrospect, we understand that
Sir John's project has all along been the
authorship of this singular piece of theater.

When Bennett finally leaves, Sir John
turns his profile to the camera (2.5) and
speaks: "Diana Baring—why did I send
her away? I told her it would be good for

2.5

her to gain experience in the provinces. Good for her! And now she's come back." We may accept these words as an authentic expression of love for Diana. But our impression of Sir John's theatricality is never stronger than in this speech, which he delivers as though it were a soliloquy. Even alone in his sitting room, he acts, performing for an imaginary audience. That he plays *himself* sustains the suggestion that the events in which he is swept up are the stuff of theater. Diana is a character to him; her suffering is not fully real. Insofar as we take him to be in the dark about his own theatricality, we might view him as speaking these words to convince himself that he really is in love. But we can also view him as consciously performing, impressing himself with his mastery as an actor, not with the sincerity of his character. Perhaps he is rehearsing lines he intends to put into "The Inner History of the Baring Case" and one day to speak on stage. It is clear from such considerations that his "self" cannot simply be identified with the role he is writing for himself in his new play. Sir John the character in "The Inner History of the Baring Case" must be distinguished from Sir John the actor/author within *Murder!* if his relationship to the camera is to be comprehended. In delivering this speech, for example, the character is anguished but the actor/author is coolly preparing his script. Viewed in this light, Sir John in *Murder!* (but not in "The Inner History of the Baring Case") is revealed as one of Hitchcock's gamesmen or aesthetes who try to author themselves and their world.[4]

Our sense of Sir John's theatricality is partly engendered by the way the camera frames him at this moment. Reciting his soliloquy, he is framed in profile, to maximum dramatic effect.[5] In (2.5) we can view the camera as performing in concert with Sir John, or as undermining his speech and exposing it as theatrical. Then again, we cannot even say whether he is subjected to this framing or whether he commands it. The camera's assumption of the position of Sir John's imaginary audience is ambiguous, as was its framing of his gesture of drinking the wine. The camera precisely poses Sir John's theatricality as a problem and links it to the enigma of its own bond with him; his sitting room is a stage and we are Sir John's audience.

Murder! is a whodunit. Much of its running time (92 minutes) is taken up with Sir John's investigation. First he enlists the services of the stage manager of Diana's theater, Markham, and his wife Doucie, an aspiring actress. Markham takes him on a tour of the murder scene, the dressing rooms, and so on. Markham is Sir John's Watson, amusingly incompetent at the process detective literature insists on calling "deduction." As usual with foils, however, his presence turns out to be indispensable: it is he who discovers the cigarette case, the key to the mystery. He remains in the dark about Sir John's deductions, however, and we are more or less in Markham's boat, not privy to Sir John's thinking until Hitchcock is ready to enlighten us. As is also customary, clues are planted for us. But in *Murder!* the clues relate less to the identity of the murderer than to his nature—specifically, his sexuality.

Hitchcock has summed up his attitude toward the whodunit format in a remark to Truffaut. "I don't really approve of whodunits because they're rather like a jigsaw or a crossword puzzle. No emotion. You simply wait to find out who committed the murder."[6] Because I share Hitchcock's distaste, I shall not dwell on Sir John's deductions. Two moments in the course of the investigation, however, merit comment. The first is Sir John's discovery of a photograph of himself in Diana's apartment, which deepens his sense of responsibility and increases his desire. But does her possession of this photograph mean only that he is her idol as a man of the theater or also that she is secretly in love with him? The second is the discovery of the murderer's cigarette case, after which the investigation can go no further without Diana's collaboration. Sir John visits the prison to confront her with this evidence, hoping that it will break her silence.

The scene fades in on the prison entrance (2.6). A conspicuous frontal setup invokes an audience's view of a stage set, introducing

a note of unreality. At the same time, this view, which belongs to no one in the world of the film, declares the camera's autonomy. There is a dissolve to an official paper that authorizes Sir John's visit, and also serves notice to us that in what is to follow he is to be our eyes and ears.[7] (As the sequence proceeds, though, the camera's relationship to its surrogate is revealed to be paradoxical.) Then there is a dissolve to the conference room in which the meeting

2.6

is to take place (2.7). In the course of the sequence, Hitchcock repeatedly cuts back to this shot, which serves as a conventional "master shot" that re-establishes the space each time it appears. Its full function, however, is far from conventional. In its frontality, its composition matches that of (2.6). This setup also invokes the perspective of a theater audience, suggesting that what we are viewing is staged, not real. A door is in the background, in the exact center of the screen, and within its frame is a window. The symmetry of this setup accords the window special prominence. In my reading of this passage, the empty frame-within-a-frame serves, at one level, as a reflection of the film frame, the "window" through which we view this world. It refers to our exclusive view and hence to the camera that frames it. Just as the view framed by the camera declares its separation from reality by invoking theater, so too it declares its separation from theater by acknowledging the film frame and the camera. The frame-within-a-frame of the window in (2.7) echoes the frame-within-a-frame of the clock-face in (2.8), the view that opens the film. This allusion to the film's opening is sufficiently important to justify describing that crucial passage in detail.

2.7

Over the sound of chimes, Hitchcock dissolves from (2.8) to an extreme long shot of a street in darkness, with the tiny lighted disk of the clockface in the center of the frame (2.9). This clockface, like Big Ben in *The Lodger*'s murder sequence, is a stand-in for the eye of the camera. It seems to preside over the film's world, as if the views that follow, accompanied by frenzied knocking, present us with what this eye sees or conjures. These views invoke a scene of murder without showing it. First we see a window shrouded in darkness. As a bird flies off, we hear a scream and then the sound of loud knocking. There is a dissolve to a street (2.10), with the frame divided diagonally between light and dark areas. Then Hitchcock cuts to a completely dark frame. Suddenly the darkness is pierced by a window that enters the frame and moves to the center of the otherwise black screen (2.11). Momentarily, we realize that the camera is panning across the wall of a building,

2.8

2.9

2.10

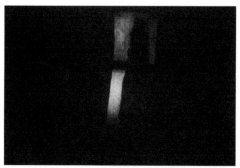

2.11

but the effect is extraordinary: it is as if a movie screen has been conjured out of the darkness.[8] As the camera continues panning, a series of windows pass through the frame. In the fifth window two people appear. They are the Markhams, who will figure prominently in the events about to unfold. Hitchcock cuts to the interior of their flat. They are talking as they dress to go out to see what is causing all the racket. It is by following Doucie Markham with the camera that Hitchcock effects a transition to the narrative proper.[9]

Within the prison visit sequence, the identification of the camera and film frame with the window in (2.7) comes into play at a number of crucial points. Hitchcock returns to this framing several times. Twice he isolates the window in a close shot. The first time it represents Diana's view; the second time it is not cued by anyone's gaze but is our view alone. Hitchcock frames this second shot, I believe, in part to declare his implication, and our own, in Diana's condition: her imprisonment is mirrored in her confinement by the camera's framings within the world of the film, a world presided over by an agency that bears an inhuman aspect. Finally, the sequence ends with the tableau of Sir John, back to the camera, staring at Diana's shadow framed within the emblematic frame-within-a-frame.

The significance of the window is complemented by that accorded a second frame-within-a-frame in the sequence, a barred

2.12

window through which light streams in (2.12). Both windows allude to the film frame and the camera, but the first is associated with Diana's imagination and the second with Sir John's gaze. It is when Sir John enters the room and looks offscreen to the right that the second window first appears in the frame. This shot begins as if it were from his point of view. But rather than cut back to his reaction, as we might expect, the camera pans to Sir John, indicating that this shot is *not* a point-of-view shot. The next shot represents the reverse of this presentation. Sir John looks screen left, and the camera pans to an empty chair. We take this to be an objective shot, but then there is a pan to the right until an empty chair at the other end of the table is framed. A cut to Sir John implies that the preceding shot was from his point of view after all.

In this pair of shots, Sir John's relationship to the camera is posited in contradictory terms, and this contradiction is linked to the frame-within-a-frame of the barred window, which represents the author's agency, the viewer's presence, and also Sir John's gaze and powers of imagining. In his mind, the scene about to take place stands in for all those wished-for future scenes in which he and Diana will sit across a much less austere table as husband and wife.[10] In addition, the table and chairs look like props: the stage is set, as it were, for the scene in "The Inner History of the Baring Case" whose counterpart in *Murder!* is the prison-visit sequence itself. And that scene in turn resonates with a real scene that has already taken place out of his—and our—view, one whose counterpart in the play remains to be written: the scene of Edna's murder, in which Diana and Edna sat facing each other across a table. Most significant of all, the panning repeats the camera's movement that was the keystone of Hitchcock's presentation of Diana's initial entrance into the film. Thus the present moment has an aspect of repetition for us that it cannot have for Sir John. To explain the significance of the repetition, it is necessary to pause again to turn to an earlier passage.

The passage echoed by this camera movement follows the cut to the Markhams that initiates the narrative. The camera tracks Doucie all the way from her front door to what turns out to be Diana's house, where a crowd has gathered. She pushes her way through the crowd and enters. The next shot neither follows her movement nor registers her point of view, but rather frames a formal tableau (2.13). The people we see stand frozen, staring at something below the frame line to the right. Diana sits in the middle of the room, in right profile. (In the course of this sequence, we will come to view her from many angles: right profile, full face, left profile, rear. We see her from all sides and yet she remains a mystery to us.) The

2.13

tableau once more invokes theater. But it declares the film frame by placing the object of everyone's gaze just beyond the screen's borders. We may anticipate that the next shot will show us what everyone is looking at. Instead Hitchcock cuts to a detail of the tableau, a policeman staring down at something offscreen (2.14). Instead of following his gaze, the camera tilts down until it frames a lantern

2.14

2.15

2.16

2.17

on his belt (2.15), then pulls back and pans left in the direction the lantern points until it frames Diana in profile (2.16). She appears to be in a trance. Not following her all-but-sightless gaze, the camera tilts down once more. Her hand, pointing limply to the right, passes through the frame, followed by her other hand, which hangs down lifelessly, and then by a poker lying on the blood-stained rug (2.17). The camera now changes direction, panning along the length of the poker until it frames the head and shoulders of the murdered Edna (2.18).

If we compare this elaborate panning movement with the zigzag pan back and forth across the table in the prison-visit sequence, we make a striking discovery. The pivotal role played by the lantern in the early passage is, as it were, displaced and split in the later one. The frame-within-a-frame of the barred window (rays of light streaming through it in precisely the direction the lantern points) and Sir John's gaze (his look points the camera on its trajectory) both link up with the lantern, which I view as a stand-in for Hitchcock's camera. Again, Sir John's relationship to the camera is presented as a problem. Does his gaze command the camera, or is he the camera's subject, oblivious of its power over him? To bring this issue into focus, I want to draw out the third of the allusions of this sequence to earlier passages. The frame-within-a-frame of the barred window invokes an earlier view that framed Diana against a wall crisscrossed by shadows cast by such a window.

The passage in question is prefaced by a view of the clockface from the film's opening shot. Then there is a fade-in on the entrance to Diana's the-

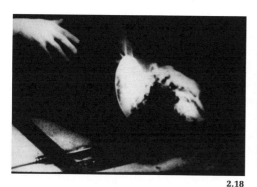

ater (2.19). In a shot reminiscent of the camera movements in *The Lodger*, the camera tracks in on the cashier's cage until the frame is completely filled with a posted notice: "Owing to indisposition, the parts played by Miss Diana Baring and Miss Edna Druce will be filled by understudies." (I read this as Hitchcock's jokingly direct apology to us for Nora Baring's abysmal performance in the role of Diana.) Then we are presented with a black frame and a white frame in succession. A "curtain" rises as if on a stage, but what we see is Diana in her prison cell. She is looking toward the right foreground, as if absorbed in some event offscreen (2.20).

Diana looks up at the camera, seeming to confront what disturbs her absorption (2.21). There is violence in her eyes. At this moment the camera pulls back to frame a window, retroactively revealing that our view has been through its frame and the curtain that opened onto Diana is the cover of the peephole on her cell door. As the camera continues pulling back to frame our view of Diana in this frame-within-a-frame, a hand is revealed (2.22). Within the world of the film, this unviewed viewer with whom our own view is linked is, presumably, a prison guard who lifts the curtain to view Diana. Like the track-in toward the door at the lodger's first entrance, this

movement is a declaration of the camera. And it goes beyond the camera's gesture in *The Lodger* by specifically alluding to the view through a camera's viewfinder. Although it is the hand and view of Diana's guard, this view also stands in for the camera's view and this hand for the author's hand. (Does Sir John's bond with the camera also make this *his* hand? Is this also *his* view?) The passage raises the issue, addressed by the prison-visit sequence, of what it is to be the camera's subject. It suggests that to be framed by the camera is to be imprisoned, confined.

Diana knows that she is being viewed. Her look at the camera expresses a wish to do violence to those who, unbidden, violate her

2.23

2.24

privacy. As if in response to this look, Hitchcock makes a remarkable move. Our framed view of Diana dissolves, with exquisite slowness, to the same view enlarged to fill the screen (2.23, 2.24). Throughout this passage into her private space, Diana continues to stare at the camera. Offscreen a voice calls, "Third Act beginners please!" As if awakened by this call, Diana shifts her eyes away from the camera, dismissing it. She resumes her absorption in a spectacle we cannot view. We do not know whether the voice is only part of Diana's fantasy, or whether there is a performance actually going on in her theater. What is clear is that the next words we hear must be a projection of her imagination, as the offscreen voice cries out, "Your call, Miss Baring!" Yet even now we do not know whether Hitchcock simply presents what Diana imagines, subjecting us to a voice projected from within her, or whether he presides over her fantasy, subjecting her to the voice and then projecting her fantasy so as to subject us to it as well.

As laughter sounds offscreen, Diana looks up proudly, and the implication is that she is making a stage entrance in a comedy. The laughter turns to thunderous applause and she humbly lowers her eyes, looks back off right, then again lowers and raises her eyes (this last time she seems to acknowledge her audience modestly as her merely human self). But when another offscreen voice says, "That's Miss Baring's understudy," she shuts her eyes, the fantasy spoiled. She is unwillingly brought back to the reality of her imprisonment, in which she is condemned to be viewed against her will by a cruel, judging gaze. The camera dissolves to Markham and others watching the stage from the wings, effecting a transition to the next sequence of the film.

We are not yet prepared to appreciate the full significance of this transition, which turns on the fact that Diana's understudy is the real murderer. Diana is to hang in place of the very person who has assumed her place on stage, a person who appears to fill her with revulsion. The seamless transition Hitchcock weaves between Diana's fantasy and the film's reality suggests that Diana somehow possesses the real scene that she cannot literally view. It is as if the spectacle in which she is absorbed, and from which she is momentarily distracted by the camera's intrusion, is nothing but the succession of views constituting the film itself. If these views are projections of Diana's imagination, however, how do we read her dismissal of the camera? In the face of the camera, she wills her reabsorption in a private world in which she is free to present herself to applause. Perhaps this show of distain is only an act performed for her real audience, the camera.

When Sir John visits Diana in prison, and she makes her entrance under his gaze, the issues attending our earlier view through the cell-door window are taken up and developed. From the point-of-view shot that ends as an objective shot and the objective shot that ends as a point-of-view shot—this pair of shots posing the problem of the camera's relationship to Sir John—we cut to a shot unambiguously from his point of view: the door with the empty frame-within-a-frame of the window (2.25). A guard appears within this frame, and Diana is admitted. The prisoner enters, followed by a second guard, who stations herself in the room. Diana smiles (2.26) and bows.

2.25

In Sir John's view, Diana appears and acts as though she were a creature of his imagination, acknowledging him as her true audience. Her smile shows that she identifies him not with the cruel guards from whom she had disdainfully turned away but with the longed-for audience within her fantasy. We may expect the next shot to detail Sir John's reaction to this apparition, but Hitchcock instead

2.26

cuts back to reprise (2.7), the master shot. Within this emblematic framing, Sir John and Diana sit in perfect synchronization, like mirror reflections; and as they do, a guard passes through the frame-

within-a-frame of the window (2.27). We have viewed Diana through Sir John's eyes, but not him through hers. We know how he imagines their encounter, but we do not know how she envisions the scene that has begun. For all we know, Diana is, at this moment, only acting.

With this cut to the master shot, Hitchcock sums up Sir John's fantasy. But it also breaks with Sir John's perspective on the encounter he has arranged, and asserts the camera's autonomy. It reminds us of the reality of Diana's situation, declaring the camera's presence to be an integral part of that reality. The camera's powers are manifest, for example, in the synchronization between the movements of the guard in the frame-within-a-frame and the "dance" Sir John and Diana perform. The master shot is followed by a cut to Diana which is similarly not cued by Sir

2.27

2.28

John's gaze (2.28). This view declares that she is a human being with private feelings, and is followed by a shot from her point of view. However, we pass to Diana's perspective only by way of the detour to the master shot: the transition from subjectivity to subjectivity is effected through the agency of the camera. Hitchcock asserts himself precisely to declare that Diana in her separateness is not encompassed by Sir John's perspective and to indict Sir John for his failures of acknowledgment. He fails to acknowledge the

grim reality represented by the guard framed in the window; to acknowledge Diana as a suffering human being; to acknowledge the camera and what it represents.

What Sir John does not acknowledge in Diana, the camera does. Hitchcock cuts to a chilling, low-angle shot from Diana's point of view: the guard stationed in the room, sternly watching (2.29); back to Diana; then to her terrify-

2.29

ing view of the other guard crossing the frame-within-a-frame (2.30). Uncannily, it is as if the camera's assertion of autonomy makes Diana mindful of the reality of her condition, a reality of which the camera is an integral part. Sir John's obliviousness of Diana's views, of her subjectivity, is also his unawareness of her attunement to the camera—an attunement that he lacks (despite Hitchcock's gesture of allowing him to appear to appropriate the direction of the camera).

2.30

When the camera now frames Diana in a setup that repeats (2.28) and then reverses field to Sir John (2.31), our excursion into her subjectivity is suspended. The body of the prison-visit scene, which takes the form of a shot/reverse-shot dialogue sequence, begins, as Hitchcock cuts back and forth between (2.28) and (2.31) until he is ready to break the pattern of repetition. What I am calling a "shot/reverse-shot" sequence is a dialogue filmed as a series of alternations between a pair of setups, each showing one of the participants. Conventionally, filming a long dialogue

2.31

as a shot/reverse-shot alternation rather than simply holding both speakers in a sustained two-shot serves primarily to add variety to a passage that would otherwise be oppressively dominated by immobile "talking heads." But in Hitchcock's work, shot/reverse-shot becomes a fundamental medium of expression. Complex and elaborate shot/reverse-shot dialogue sequences, whose formal compositions are intimately bound to the structure and meaning of the particular dialogues they set, become hallmarks of Hitchcock's authorship.[11]

The passage in *Murder!* is Hitchcock's first important shot/reverse-shot sequence, but all the basic principles and implications of the form as Hitchcock conceives it are in evidence. For example, Hitchcock already avails himself of the possibility of formally contrasting, as well as the possibility of formally linking, the alternated setups. Frames (2.28) and (2.31) are contrasted by their backgrounds: the crisscross graphic pattern that plays an important role in the film as a whole marks Diana's frame and is absent from Sir John's. And in both setups, the table juts into the bottom of the frame, giving the human figures a strangely incorporeal look, as if they were floating unrooted in the frame, and covering them from the waist down, as if to mask their sexual difference.

In this passage, as in all his shot/reverse-shot sequences, Hitchcock varies the pace and rhythm of the alternation of the two setups; his cutting is attentive to the dialectic of activity and passivity as people speak back and forth. And when a major shift in degree of intimacy occurs, Hitchcock characteristically effects a transition to a new pair of setups, which he then alternates, initiating a new phase of the sequence. In the later films, these principles allow the development of compound sequences of enormous complexity. In the relatively simple example here, the principle is already established that the new phase brings the camera closer to its subject, except in special circumstances. As the dialogue becomes increasingly intimate, the participants are locked more and more tightly into their separate frames. The tension thus created may or may not be resolved. The most satisfying possible resolution is the merging of the two isolated spaces into a single charged space within which a passionate kiss may take place. In the *Murder!* passage, however, this development is thwarted. It is typical of Hitchcock's shot/reverse-shot sequences that they present dialogues rooted in desire. Every significant remark in most of these dialogues tacitly (at times openly) expresses the wish that dialogue itself be transcended by union, that silence be attained. Usually they take the form of arguments whose implicit (at times explicit) subject is the unsatisfactory state of the relationship that the dialogue manifests, sustains, and throws into crisis. For these dialogues themselves are symptomatic of the very condition of tense separation that both parties long to overcome, whether they acknowledge it or not. Like the exchange between Sir John and Diana in the prison-visit scene, however, these passionate dialogues often break down, frustrating the participants and the viewer.

Within the compass of the alternation of (2.28) and (2.31), Diana thanks Sir John for coming. He begins to explain the purpose of his visit, but Diana keeps changing the subject. This creates suspense:

2.32

Is he prepared to declare himself, and will she allow him to do so? When she tells him how good his leading actress is, she looks right at the camera. Her remark and her look declare her wish to be free and in that woman's place. This is the signal for Hitchcock to break with the pattern of alternating the two shots. He cuts to a closer shot of Sir John (2.32), which he then matches with an equally close reverse shot of Diana

(2.33); then this pair of setups is alternated.

Sir John asks Diana whether she remembers their earlier meeting. She answers, "Of course. Very well." His pleasure in this answer is clear to us (if not to Diana). So when he goes on to say that he is here because he feels responsible, we know he is disavowing his true feelings. He does not acknowledge that he has also come because he desires her. He does not declare his secret project. Tilting her head slightly, Diana again looks into the camera. Her look suggests that she has recognized his withholding and silently rebukes him. This does not signal a cut to Sir John or a new shot/reverse-shot phase, but a break with the shot/reverse-shot mode altogether. Over Hitchcock's reprise of the master shot (2.34), Diana speaks. Her speech begins as a kind of soliloquy, not openly addressed to Sir John; the intimacy is broken. In this cut, the camera reasserts its autonomy, specifically its ability to penetrate Diana's feelings. It inaugurates a presentation in which Hitchcock undertakes to illustrate Diana's monologue and to articulate the conditions of her imprisonment.

As the guard once more crosses the frame-within-a-frame, Diana gives voice to her despair. "I knew that would happen. I knew someone would try and get me off and think they were doing me a kindness." Over her words, "Imprisonment for life," Hitchcock cuts, this cut not cued by Diana's gaze, from (2.34) to (2.35), an objective view of the nightmare of Diana's imprisonment. Then Hitchcock presents a new, oblique view of Diana (2.36). It is not Sir John's view, nor does it manifest the frontality by which, up to this point in the sequence, the camera's autonomy has been de-

2.33

2.34

2.35

2.36

clared. The framing suggests the gaze of the stern, watchful guard, and yet it is not literally the guard's point of view. The camera's perspective, indeed, *reverses* the guard's angle of vision. Does the camera then represent the guard's mirror image, her double, or is the guard the camera's "opposite number," dedicated to an opposing principle? This shot raises precisely the question of the relationship between our view and the guard's, but does not commit itself to an unambiguous answer.

Diana leans forward and speaks directly to Sir John. She would rather die than live a prisoner's life, she says. She has overcome her

2.37

fear of death, "Except at night." On this last word, Hitchcock cuts to the other guard, her lifeless face, still turned away, now closely framed in the window (2.37). This cut is also not cued by anyone's gaze within the world of the film. It is Hitchcock's illustration of Diana's darkest nightmare, the vision she cannot bear. This is the sequence's deepest penetration into Diana, and the camera's most profound declaration of itself. Imprisonment for Diana means

being subjected to a cold gaze that denies her sexuality and freedom, and being condemned to view a face inhumanly turned away. Who is the woman framed in the window? That this view invokes our first view of Diana (2.13) suggests that this isolated figure, cut off from all human warmth, is Diana's nightmare vision of herself.

To Diana, imprisonment means being always subject to this cruel gaze and always haunted by this face of stone. These are views of reality, but they are also projections of Diana's imagination, features of her inner landscape. In prison there is no escape from such visions. She cannot escape them by withdrawing into the private world of her imagination, locking reality out, for then she would only be locking the haunting visions in. She cannot escape into madness because the real conditions of her existence in prison are what it is ordinarily madness to take reality to be.[12] It is of great significance that Diana's vision of damnation is framed in the window that stands in for the camera and the film frame. Her horror at the death-in-life of imprisonment coincides with Hitchcock's declaration of the camera. Diana's imprisonment is a reflection of the condition of being framed by the camera within the world of a film. All of the subjects of Hitchcock's camera are condemned to its gaze. Diana is mindful that her existence is damnation, but beings in a film do not ordinarily view their world as a prison.[13]

Now Hitchcock cuts to a new shot of Diana, which returns to Sir John's point of view (2.38). This is a privileged frame, our closest approach to Diana; its intimate scale is never reclaimed or matched by any such view of Sir John. Within this frontal framing, addressing her question directly to the camera, Diana simply asks, "What is there I can tell you?" The counter shot of Sir John is not frontal but oblique (2.39), and does not represent Diana's point of view. The asymmetry between their situations, implicit throughout the sequence, is here declared, as befitting this moment at which he responds to her sincere appeal with a proposition. He says he will see to it that she is freed on the condition that she name the man she and Edna were arguing about on the night of the murder. When Diana refuses, Sir John levels a charge. "You

2.38

2.39

realize what you're admitting by your silence? You're shielding this man because you know you're in love with him!" If she remained silent or confirmed this hypothesis, would he go through with his project?[14] *Murder!* spares Sir John this test of character. When Diana insists that what he is suggesting is impossible, he replies, "I see no *reason* why it should be impossible!"

Part of Hitchcock's indictment of Sir John's character is that his imagination and his faith in Diana are too limited. In his obtuseness, he sees no reason where a reason exists. But in the dock of the film frame, he also stands charged for the vengefulness of his accusation. Diana disputes his reading of the murder scene; in effect, she criticizes the way he has written the corresponding scene of "The Inner History of the Baring Case." Her criticism is well-founded, yet rather than acknowledge that he needs her help to finish his play, he defends his reading as if she represented a threat to his authorship. His demand that she supply evidence of her love takes precedence over his human concern or even his desire. With a look of revulsion, Diana blurts out, "Why the man's a half-caste!" There is a swooshing, clicking sound and the camera pans right so quickly that all we see is a vertiginous blur until Sir John is finally centered in the frame. "What's that? What did you say? *Black blood*?!" He utters this last exclamation more to himself than to

Diana. It registers his private realization that the solution to the mystery has just been handed to him and that all the pieces are about to fall into place.

Hitchcock cuts one last time to the master shot. The guard again appears framed in the window. Now Sir John is ready to produce the cigarette case. "Will this help you to remember the name of the man you were quarreling about?" He slides it across the table to Diana, the camera panning quickly on the movement. As the guard confiscates the case and announces that the time is up, Diana identifies its owner. "It's Handell Fane's!"

The name finally spoken, the sequence draws to a close. Hitch-

2.40

2.41

cock cuts to Diana, reframing as she rises. The shadow of the guard, then the guard herself, passes through the frame-within-a-frame, while Sir John stands motionless, his shadow interposed between himself and Diana (2.40). He tells her about discovering his photograph in her apartment. She explains that she has been "keen on the stage" since she was a little girl and that "one has one's heroes." She urges him to say more, and he begins, "Diana, I . . . ," but the guard cuts him short. His back to the camera, Sir John watches Diana being led away. He stands before her shadow, perfectly framed in the doorway, like the lodger held spellbound by the paintings of golden-haired women (2.41). He is as cut off from Diana as we are. Her imprisonment is also his: he too is the camera's subject, confined to a world presided over by Hitchcock. Yet when he shouts "I'm going to find Fane," he persists in his hubris. He still claims for himself the authorship of Diana's, and his own, destiny.

As befits the murderer in a whodunit, Handell Fane plays a relatively small role in the film until he is identified as the drinker of the brandy. Up to this point, he has appeared on screen only once. This occurs at the conclusion of the passage in which we view Diana through the window of her cell door. As reality intrudes into her fantasy and she imagines her understudy's assumption of her place on stage, she shuts her eyes, and Hitchcock dissolves to the backstage of her theater. Stewart, a member of the company, is ex-

plaining to detectives that he and Handell Fane, another actor, saw
Edna and Diana leave the theater together the night of the murder.
"Is it very unusual?" asks a detective. "Unusual? I should say so!
It's an absolute miracle!" Presumably, he means by this "it" the
sight of Diana and Edna together: they hated each other and were
bitter rivals. But the line also embeds a barbed irony. The absolute
miracle, the "it," can also be Handell Fane, who cannot simply be
identified as a "he" or a "she." Fane is so adept at impersonating
women that he plays both male and female roles for the company.

Indeed, he is the understudy who takes
Diana's place, filling her with revulsion.
At precisely this moment, Fane exits the
stage and enters our view. Dressed as a
woman, framed frontally, he walks forward (2.42). Grim-faced, looking right
into the camera, he looms as a threatening figure.

2.42

This first view of Fane presents his
nature as a mystery. In retrospect, we
recognize it as a clue to his role in the
film. Although Hitchcock's treatment of
Fane in the remainder of this sequence is equally charged, I will not
analyze it in detail. A careful reading would call for explication of
the systematic juxtaposition of the farce enacted onstage and the
lines spoken, gestures performed, and roles played by the real characters offstage and on. Two brief points. First, when Fane returns to
the stage through an open door on the set, he has changed his costume and makes his entrance as a villain. At the same time,
Stewart, visible onstage through the frame-within-a-frame of this
door, engages in a comical series of exaggerated contortions.
Bound hand and foot, he attempts to free himself, his struggle a
metaphor for poor Fane's desperate efforts in reality to mask his nature from the world. Second, at the moment Fane speaks his first
words in the film ("I assure you, inspector, I'm not the other woman
in the case"), Markham finds himself unable to make his stage mus-
tache stick. Yet it is Fane who is this troupe's real villain.

Hitchcock certainly did not believe that it is impossible for a
good white woman to love a man she knows to have "black blood."
Nor did he believe it is impossible for a good woman to love, or
even to be, a killer, as is clear from *Blackmail*, *The Paradine Case*,
Dial "M" for Murder, *North by Northwest*, and *Marnie*. How then
are we to take Diana's assertion that it is impossible for her to love
Handell Fane? I am tempted to speak of the hapless love of half-
caste and miscast, considering the actress who plays Diana in the
film, or at least to note the parodistic aspect of the scene; it is as if

Sir John hits on the solution of turning "The Inner History of the Baring Case" into a mock melodrama. But although we are not yet fully prepared to comprehend Diana's relationship with Fane, her revulsion needs to be taken seriously.

In Clemence Dane's *Enter Sir John*, the novel from which the script of *Murder!* was adapted, the murderer's secret is that he is a homosexual. Truffaut says that *Murder!* is "a thinly disguised story about homosexuality." He argues that the murderer kills Edna as "she was about to tell his fiancée all about him, about his special mores," presumably thereby spoiling a marriage of convenience.[15] This is somewhat fanciful. Diana is not Handell Fane's fiancée, and there is no indication in the film that his are the "special mores" of the homosexual. On the contrary, *Murder!* makes little sense if we rule out the possibility that Fane desires Diana in the way, for example, the Claude Rains figure in *Notorious* is inflamed by the woman played by Ingrid Bergman. Fane does not want a marriage of convenience, and there is certainly no evidence that, say, he eyes Sir John with desire rather than Diana. (In the interview, Hitchcock does not directly contradict Truffaut's suggestion that Fane is "really" homosexual, but he does contest the claim that the film is about homosexuality. Truffaut appears oblivious, however, of the significance of the criticism implied in Hitchcock's insistence that what *Murder!* is all about is theater.)

The subject of homosexuality in Hitchcock's work is complex. Briefly, I believe that there is no major figure in a Hitchcock film who takes himself to be a homosexual. There *are* men bound together in mutual denial of the love of women. But if their relationship has a sexual dimension (and surely it does, in Hitchcock's understanding), these men are not cognizant of their desire. They view themselves not as desiring one another, but as joined in denying all love. That there is no redemptive homosexual love in Hitchcock's films surely reflects a form of censorship, but not one that can be undone by such naive expedients as reading "homosexual" for "half-caste." Handell Fane is a being for whom sexuality is a mystery, who does not know his own sexual identity and whose form of life is solitary. He is one of Hitchcock's Wrong Ones. It trivializes Hitchcock's conception to view the Wrong One as a closet homosexual whose condition could be cured by declaring love for his male double, or to view the violence in Hitchcock's world only as the inevitable consequence of repression. For this fails to consider the Wrong One's relationship to the camera, to Hitchcock and to us. The world of the film is the Wrong One's closet; there is no cure for his condition. Yet it remains a mystery what Handell Fane's condition really is, what Hitchcock thinks it is that marks some men as unfit for love, that makes them know they cannot reveal themselves to those they desire, that makes women unable to desire them.

Following the prison-visit scene, the next major set piece in the film is what might be called the play scene. In Hitchcock's words: "We had a play within a play. The presumptive murderer was asked to read the manuscript of the play, and since the script described the killing, this was a way of tricking him. They watched the man while he was reading out loud to see whether he would show some sign of guilt, just like the king in *Hamlet*. The whole film was about the theater."[16] The play scene is preceded by two brief transitional passages. The first is so remarkable in conception that it deserves to be set out in full.

It begins with a fade-in on a weather vane spinning in the wind (2.43). An offscreen voice asks, "Handell Fane? Handell Fane? What's become of Handell Fane?" Then the second shot of the sequence fades in: Diana pacing in her cell, viewed from overhead (2.44). We hear Sir John ask, "Any news of Fane yet?" and Markham reply, "Not yet, Sir John." In the third shot, the shadow of a gallows rises slowly into the frame (2.45), as we hear Doucie say, "Haven't you found Fane yet? I can't stand the suspense." The overall scheme of the sequence is simple. These three setups are repeated, in order, six more times. Each time, the duration of the shots is shorter, creating an increasing urgency. In the third shot of each successive cycle, the shadow of the gallows looms larger.

Over the weather vane we hear, "Oh for God's sake!" Over Diana pacing, "Hallo, hallo! Is that the Gramercy Agents?" Over the gallows, now higher in the frame, "You find Fane yet?" The cycle begins again: "Wanted for the most important job, you know. Yes, at once!" Then: "What's that?" / "Gone back to his old job?" In this last shot, the camera has moved in to frame the shadow of the gallows more closely. The next cycle: "What?" / "Trapeze artist?" / "Under what name?" In the im-

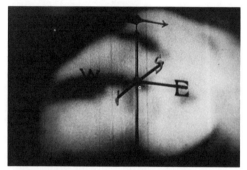

2.43

2.44

2.45

mediately following cycle, the shot of the weather vane passes by in silence. Over the shot of Diana, we hear only the word "Where?" And in the third shot, the camera has moved in so close that the

shadow of the noose is alone in the frame. The penultimate cycle passes by with great speed: "No, can't" / "Stop now." / Silence. The shadow of the noose is framed even more tightly (2.46). The final cycle is rapid and silent. In it, the place of the shadow of the gallows is taken by a totally black frame. A number of observations:

—The shadow of the gallows rises like a curtain. Diana's hanging is antici-

2.46   pated as a piece of theater.

—The noose is another of *Murder!*'s frames-within-a-frame. In the shadow of the noose, it might be said, the camera frames its own image. At the risk of being chastized for overinterpretation, I wish to claim that the gallows is one of Hitchcock's sexual symbols. The rising structure is imaged as phallic, yet the circle formed by the noose is a conventional female symbol. Handell Fane's sexual ambiguity is invoked, but so is the ambiguity of the camera, with its active and passive aspects.

—The noose is also a ring. It anticipates the circus ring, the setting for Fane's suicide, but it also alludes to the idea of marriage. Marriage is not an option for Fane, whose only fulfillment is in death.

—The spinning weather vane can be taken as Handell Fane's totem (Fane-vane; but also *feign*), emblematic of his ambiguity (he is black and white, male and female). It also links Fane with Diana, who was viewed from every direction when she was first introduced to us.

The second transitional passage begins by fading in on Sir John

and Markham at the circus. They are watching Handell Fane (a trapeze artist before he was an actor) perform. Sir John informs Markham of his scheme. For the first time, he explicitly refers to the new play he is writing; this is a turning point in the film. The passage ends with an echo of one of *The Lodger*'s barbed jokes. From the point of view of Sir John and Markham, we view Fane on his trapeze (2.47). Spotlights cast

2.47

twin pools of light on the tent canvas, in each of which Fane is projected as a tiny shadow, creating an image of a pair of watching eyes.

The play scene itself begins with another ironic touch. A date-book fades in. A hand enters the frame and flips the pages. Monday's page lists a 1:30 appointment with Handell Fane (the murder, we already know, also took place at 1:30). Tuesday's page lists no appointments. The only entry for Wednesday reads "Diana?" There is a cut to a watch from the point of view of the wearer. It is 1:30. Then a cut to Sir John, sitting at his desk. Cued by Sir John's gaze, the camera pans to the door as Handell Fane enters the study, and follows Fane until Sir John is incorporated in the frame with him. A cut to isolate Fane initiates the body of the sequence. Where the prison-visit sequence had a shot/reverse-shot alternation at its core, the play scene has one extremely long take. In the course of this extended shot, Hitchcock moves the camera a number of times, rather than cuts, to accommodate the characters' movements and to effect transitions from one temporarily stable framing to another.[17]

Fane looks right into the camera (2.48). This is Hitchcock's announcement that, in this long take, the camera frames a space in which Fane's private reactions—not accessible to Sir John's view—are intimately revealed only to

2.48

the camera. The viewer is privileged to see Fane's reactions as he comes to recognize the trap into which he has stepped.

Fane asks about Sir John's new play, for which he has come to audition, and receives the answer, "Well, you may question my taste, but as an artist you'll understand my temptation. My subject, Mr. Fane, is the inner history of the Baring case." On these words, the camera pans from Sir John to Fane, whose hand enters the frame and places an ashtray on the table, then pans to center on this object. On Sir John's offscreen words, "Really your indifference astonishes me," the cigarette drops out of this hand, and the fingers rub together. As Sir John goes on to ask whether he knew both women involved in the murder, the camera pans to isolate Fane's reaction. He looks down and then screen right. The camera now repeats the movement with which it opened the sequence, panning to the door by which Bennett and a detective are standing watching silently. This movement is now cued not by Sir John's gaze, but by Fane's. And when the camera pans back to Fane, it is apparent that he has figured out what is going on. Sir John, however, remains oblivious of this dawning of awareness. His offscreen "Now let's begin" signals the end of the long take, the main work of which is to effect a shift in the camera's identification from Sir John to Handell Fane.

Sir John sets the scene for the reading, which is to begin just before the murderer's entrance. As Sir John tells him that he is to make his entrance on the words, "Friends? I can tell you things about your friends that you don't know," Fane turns to the camera.

2.49

A look of resignation is on his face. The camera moves with him as he walks slowly to the window, and stops when he freezes as Sir John asks him how he knew to enter this way (2.49). Our view of Fane at the window, back to the camera, echoes our view of Sir John looking at Diana's shadow at the end of the prison-visit sequence (2.41). An enigmatic bond between Sir John and Fane is suggested.

Sir John's taunting, "And look, Mr. Fane, you've forgotten your script," is to be echoed forty years later in Frenzy's curtain line, "Mr. Rusk, you've forgotten your tie." But when Fane now turns to face Sir John, he is smiling. He has made one of those recoveries that reveal Hitchcock figures to possess resources beyond what we may expect. Hitchcock cuts on Fane's gaze—this insertion of Fane's literal point of view is another turning point in the film—to the two men at the door. Fane, now fully aware that he has an audience, is quietly sizing up his possible routes of escape. When Hitchcock now cuts back to Fane in a medium shot and Sir John momentarily enters the frame, the camera steps out of the role of Fane's intimate. The film frame now bounds a theatrical space within which Fane performs for an audience. At the beginning of this sequence, he was unknowingly subject to Sir John's direction. Now he has become cognizant of Sir John's attempt to author the scene and hopes to impose his own script.

Fane says, "Wouldn't it be better if I were to pick up the poker from the back fireplace *before* I made the entrance into the room?" Sir John looks at him, jots down his suggestion, and turns his gaze to the men at the door to be sure that these witnesses did not miss the self-incriminating remark. When Fane asks him for the poker, however, Sir John pauses. It is at this moment that it dawns on him that Fane has caught on. He asks for the poker, I think, not because he is too literal-minded to play the murder scene without a prop but because, armed with it, he might make his escape. With the reply, "Would a pencil do?" Sir John regains the upper hand. Fane resigns himself to going through with the reading.

Sir John walks past his desk, stopping some distance from Fane. In effect, he assumes a place in Fane's audience. When Hitchcock now cuts to Fane, that audience's perspective is also ours. As Sir John describes the action of the scene, Fane mimes it. With the approach of the climax, we begin to sense that Fane, reenacting a part he once actually played, is on the verge of losing control. He looks terrified as if a traumatic memory were about to surface. On the words, "Now you raise the poker that is in your hand, as the other woman says, 'You fool! Don't you know that he's a half—'" Fane opens his mouth in a silent cry (2.50). Hitchcock's cut to an overhead tableau (2.51) at this point is one of the most stunning effects in all of his work. In this frame, Fane and Sir John stand frozen in silence, scripts in hand; the floor and rug divide the frame schematically into black and white areas, creating an emblem of doubleness and linking this moment to the film's opening and to *The Lodger*'s flashback. Almost instantly there is a cut to a page of a script. (Though most of the page is illegible in available 16mm prints, it can be made out that this is not the script of "The Inner History of the Baring Case," but the shooting script of a film. The film is not *Murder!* itself, however, but an ironic stand-in: the scene described on this page has a magician pulling a rabbit out of a hat.) A hand turns the page—whose hand?—but the next is blank, causing a blinding flash of white. Hitchcock cuts immediately to Fane, viewed from a high angle (2.52). He does not meet the gaze of the camera. Then there is a cut to Sir John, waiting expectantly for a breakdown that never comes; to one, then the other, of the men

2.50

2.51

2.52

at the door; then to a two-shot of Fane and Sir John. The intended climax of Sir John's scene is aborted: Fane does not lose control. He pulls himself together and breaks the tense silence. "What a pity,

Sir John, the scene isn't finished. I was getting quite worked up to it." Sir John says that he had hoped for collaboration. But Fane puts the script down and prepares to leave, saying, "I am so sorry, Sir John. I am afraid that I understand so little about . . . play-writing. Perhaps later on, when the script is finished, you'll allow me to give you another reading." Sir John and Fane are locked in a struggle: at one level, a struggle for authorship of "The Inner History of the Baring Case"; at another, a struggle for ascendancy as artists.

The scene now shifts to the circus, where Fane's performance grants Sir John the collaboration he needs and allows *Murder!* its climax. As Sir John and Markham enter his dressing room, Fane finishes a letter he is writing, seals it, and rises in welcome. Sir John spots a bottle of brandy on the table and says, with an accusing undertone, "I suppose you find brandy steadying for the nerves." But he cannot comprehend, nor can we, the veiled meaning in Fane's reply, "Mine's very nervy work, you see, Sir John. You never know what may happen."

2.53

In the first part of his performance. Fane is once more a spectacle of sexual ambiguity. In a series of theatrical entrances, he moves into the camera's field of vision; into Sir John's view; and into the "stage" of the circus ring. A large black area momentarily eclipses almost all else in the frame (2.53). Immediately, this "shadow" is revealed to be a figure in a huge feather headdress. As this figure—apparently a woman—walks into the depths of the frame, blackness consumes less and less of the screen, creating one of Hitchcock's curtain-raising effects (2.54). Finally, "she" turns and we recognize Handell Fane (2.55). The second entrance follows momentarily. An elephant parades from background to foreground, screen left to screen right, blocking Fane from our view. As Sir John steps into the frame, the elephant moves by, repeating the curtain-raising

2.54

2.55

effect (2.56). Fane now turns and presents himself to Sir John (2.57), as the band starts up. Sir John takes a step toward Fane, who turns away disdainfully and steps forward into the circus ring, presenting himself to the audience at large. This, his third entrance, sets up the climax of the first part of Fane's performance: he opens his cloak and displays himself as a man-woman (and, in his feathered costume, also a man-bird) to the gazes that press in on him from all sides (2.58). Fane's form of theater is solitary. It does not consist in enacting roles but in self-exhibition. He is a creature condemned to live and die outside the human community. Fane's act stands opposed to the performances of which Diana dreams. Rather, it is like the death-in-life of Diana's imprisonment. Fane condemns himself to the cruel, inhuman gaze of his audience.[18]

2.56

2.57

In the second part of Fane's performance, his aerial act, Hitchcock intercuts shots of Sir John and Markham; Sir John and Markham placed within the general audience; and the audience's views of Fane (the last represent both the general audience's views and Sir John's private views from his place within that audience). The key to this sequence, which establishes a Hitchcock paradigm, is

2.58

that it images Fane's act in sexual terms. The passage details Fane's passion and ecstasy as, absorbed in his act, he appears on the threshold, then in the grips, of orgasm. This quasi-sexual performance culminates in the self-exhibition of the first part of his act. His "nervy work" requires him to get "all worked up" before a heartless audience.

First, he climbs the high pole. This accomplished, he looks down. The camera cuts to the circus ring from his point of view, then to Sir John and Markham attentively watching. Fane drops his feather headdress, dries his hands, grasps the bar, and begins swinging. Twin spotlights once again cast pools of light, with Fane appearing as a shadow in each, again imaging a pair of watching

2.59

2.60

2.61

2.62

eyes. This part of the sequence ends with Fane soaring through the air, to ringing applause. On this sound, Hitchcock cuts to Fane. He is swinging but remains stationary in the frame as his surroundings, an out-of-focus backdrop, pass first downward then upward before our eyes. This vertiginous effect conveys the loosening of the world's hold on him. In his ecstasy, he looks triumphantly into the camera (2.59).

From Sir John and Markham looking on without comprehension, Hitchcock cuts to a closer view of Fane, the background again vertiginous. His face now registers extreme anguish: his ecstasy is also pain. The camera turns again to Sir John and Markham, still oblivious of Fane's condition, then back. Fane's face, in dark shadow, becomes lit by harsh glare (2.60). At this decisive moment, Hitchcock penetrates Fane's being and gives us a series of three visions.

In the first, we see Sir John, in closeup, looking slightly off to the left, superimposed on Fane's surroundings passing through the frame (2.61). At one point, a string of lights momentarily crosses this face, creating an image of a death's-head grin (2.62). Should we take it that, in his anguish and ecstasy, Fane literally sees Sir John's face? We may be tempted to say that this is a superimposition of what he hallucinates (the face) and what he literally sees (reality passing before his eyes). The hallucinatory aspect of this image is what leads me to call it a *vision* rather than a *view*. But perhaps Fane has no hallucination at all; perhaps this face is nothing he sees or imagines; perhaps the superimposition simply serves Hitchcock as a conventional way of indicating that, at this moment of inwardness, Fane is haunted by Sir John, transfixed by him. Then again this shot may represent a real view of Sir John at this moment —a view that corresponds to the perspective of no one within the world of the film—superimposed on Fane's real view. Then this shot would represent no "private" experience of Fane's, but only serve as Hitchcock's reminder to us that, while Fane has turned inward, Sir John is still watching.

Thus the status of this image, Fane's relation to it, is perfectly ambiguous. Is this an "inner vision" projected from within Fane's imagination, or is the frame itself projected onto his imagination? Is he subjected to this image, as we are? We can't say whether, in effect, Fane's imagination subjects us to the image or is subjected to it. But, then again, we don't really know who Handell Fane is, or what he represents. What *is* his relationship to the camera (to the film's author and viewer)? Who is subjected to whom in this frame? And in a frame that constitutes a vision, what does the camera represent? One point at least is unambiguous. Whatever Sir John is looking at within this vision, he is not looking at the camera. In Fane's vision, Sir John lacks the power to confront his gaze, the power to penetrate or possess him with his gaze. Fane sees Sir John's powers as inferior to his own.

From this first vision, we cut back to Fane, wide-eyed, his face half in light and half in shadow, like the lodger telling his story to Daisy (2.63). Then Hitchcock presents Fane's second vision: a

2.63

closeup of Diana looking into the camera, likewise superimposed on the world passing through the frame (2.64). She comes to Fane as a goddess who compels men's gaze. In Fane's first vision, Sir John was looking off, his eyes turned from the camera. In retrospect, we can take it that Sir John, as envisioned by Fane, is held spellbound, like Fane himself, by a vision of Diana. But also Diana looks right into the camera. Within Fane's vision, she penetrates his gaze as if she possessed the inner world of his imagination. This apparition is projected from within his imagination, but he is also subjected to it. It is possible that Diana's powers are really magical, as Fane imagines. After all, when *we* viewed her through the cell window, she appeared to possess the power to imagine, to penetrate, perhaps even to conjure, our views. The interesting

2.64

2.65

2.66

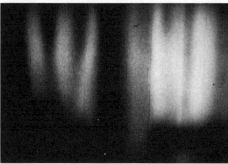

2.67

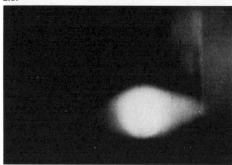

2.68

question is what powers are "natural" for a being framed by the camera who is attuned to, and may be in league with, the agency that presides over that framing. Is such a being human?

In the next shot of Fane, his eyes are almost completely shut (2.65), as if he were entranced by a siren's voice. If he now abandons himself completely to his vision, of course, he would fall to his death. But he does not black out. He opens his eyes and again looks up at the camera (2.66). But we can't know whether this gesture breaks the spell cast by Diana's gaze as Fane envisions it, or whether he bids his visions to continue, as Joe does in *The Lodger*. Does he look into the camera in defiance of Diana or at her bidding?

In the following frame, nothing is superimposed on Fane's vertiginous view of the world. I like to think of this frame as representing a vision of nothingness. It is not simply devoid of a superimposed human countenance; the blurred images that pass before Fane's eyes are charged symbolically, like dreams, and admit of a reading. The shadowy pole (2.67); the curious bell-like hanging lights, suggestive both of death bells and wedding bells, and also of sightless eyes (2.68); the death's-head grin (2.69); finally the blurred image of a couple (2.70): this vision is charged with images of death and with signifiers of the realm of human sexuality from which Fane is irrevocably estranged.[19] The vision of nothingness sums up Fane's nature in his own and—as he imagines—in Diana's eyes. It is also Fane's vision of his own death. Death is Fane's mark. In the world, he represents death, and only his own death can release him from his curse.

The series of Fane's visions now complete, Hitchcock cuts to an "objective" view. Fane lands on the high platform, relinquishes his grip on the bar, passes a rope through his hands, and turns to acknowledge his audience. The second part of his performance is successfully completed. But his strength is spent. His hands hang limp. He seems to be suffering an overpowering vertigo (2.71). If Diana should die in Fane's place, he would be responsible. His vision of Diana is a guilty one. Since it is, in effect, as a ghost that she appears to him, her death would not free him from her gaze, but condemn him to being forever haunted by it. His vision of Diana reminds him that his desires can never be satisfied. It is as if her envisioned gaze wreaks her own revenge on him. It corresponds precisely to her nightmare visions of her guards. Diana's imprisonment is the death-in-life of madness, but Fane, condemned by his visions, is also imprisoned, also mad and already dead. But his vision of Diana also arises out of his desire—he does not wish to be freed from it. I imagine him unwilling, for example, to confess and put himself at the mercy of a court, for then he would have to witness Diana's union with Sir John. Only through death can he keep faith with Diana without denying his desire.

2.69

2.70

2.71

As with all suicides, Fane's suicide is a private act, admitting no audience. We might think of Diana as Fane's real audience. But the "Diana" Fane envisions as bearing witness to his act and the "Fane" who is possessed by this vision of Diana are not separate beings who could stand in the relationship of audience and performer in a theater. For this Diana is also within Fane. Her possession of his act, which her gaze also commands, does not make it a piece of theater, does not mitigate its essential privacy. This Diana can no more sit in Fane's audience than we can. On the other hand, Fane does perform his suicide in the most theatrical way possible in a public arena before an audience that is hushed, waiting for the death-defying climax of his act. Fane's private act of suicide is also a consummate piece of theater that brings down the house. True, we can imagine that he kills himself this way not because he strives for effect, but because he needs to confront his demons and experience his passion one last time before he can bring himself to finish his nervy work. We can imagine that Fane must work himself up to it, overcoming his fear of death as if

2.72

2.73

2.74

it were stage fright. Nonetheless, when Fane passes the rope slowly through his hands, hardly appearing to attend to it, giving no sign that he is aware of an audience (2.72), the theatrical effect is stunning. But insofar as Fane's private act is also theater, who is its intended audience? We comprehend what is about to happen only an instant before Sir John does. Precisely when it appears that Sir John has finally understood, Hitchcock cuts to Fane, who only now makes it clear that he is tying a noose. It is as if he has deliberately deferred this revelation until the magnitude of his own obliviousness first dawns on Sir John. When the camera now cuts to Sir John, it is apparent that Fane's masterful theatrical stroke has its intended effect (2.73). Sir John has taken his place as a spellbound member of Fane's audience. Fane has demonstrated the superiority of his theater. Fane's art is triumphant.

From Sir John, taut with anticipation, Hitchcock cuts back to Fane. He tightens the noose around his neck and jumps. This framing is held, so that the rope swings back and forth across an empty frame (2.74) while Fane dies off-screen. If Fane's suicide is addressed specifically to Sir John, it is also addressed to the whole circus audience, within which Sir John has assumed a place. It says: "All along, what you have really wished to view is my death. Your unholy desire for the sight of blood is what drew you to the spectacle of my degredation. Here is the authentic climax of my act." In a rapid montage, Hitchcock details the audience's reactions of shock and ecstasy. Fane's audience breaks down, running amok. No one present can claim to be his superior—his case is proved.

Fane's gesture is the dramatic climax of *Murder!* The suicide casts a pall over the film. Even if *Murder!* ended with an unambiguous image of Diana freed and united romantically with Sir John, it would not have the feeling of a conventional happy ending. The film does not end in this way, however. Rather, it presents Sir John and Diana embarked on living happily ever after, then decisively draws back from this image, framing it and disavowing its reality.

Fane's body is carried to the dressing room, with Sir John and Markham among those attending. A letter is discovered—the letter Fane was finishing when they first arrived. Sir John reads in silence, continually glancing at Fane's body, placed below the frame line to the right. Then he reads the letter out loud to Markham, commenting as he goes along in a single static two-shot (2.75). Shadowy figures flit across the background of this conspicuously stylized frame, adding to its effect of unreality. "Fane says he has decided to collaborate on my play after all. He says, 'The two women are standing facing each other in dead silence. They are so lost in the tension of the moment that they do not hear the murderer creep

2.75

through the double doors . . . There's the melodrama for you, Sir John . . .' Well, Markham, do you have it all?" Sir John's remarks may well disquiet us. He seems concerned only with technical matters, as if it were only on this level that Fane's gesture was addressed to him, as if it really meant nothing (this anticipates Truffaut by thirty-five years). Sir John appears insensitive, even inhuman, in his failure to be moved by the fact of Fane's death. At this moment, he appears completely unmindful of Diana as well. When he asks Markham whether he has it all, it is clear that he takes his own understanding of Fane's gesture, and the events of the Diana Baring case, to be complete. We can't say precisely what his picture encompasses and what it leaves out, but of course he cannot know these events as we do; he has not had access to the totality of Hitchcock's presentation out of which our understanding emerges.[20]

When Hitchcock now dissolves to the prison gate (2.76), the air of unreality is sustained. This is in part due to the shot's invocation of a stage set viewed

2.76

2.77

2.78

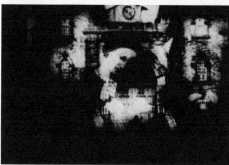

2.79

2.80

across the barrier of the proscenium. It is also due to this shot's clear echo of (2.6), the opening of the prison-visit sequence. The effect is uncanny when Sir John enters this frame from below (2.77) and walks into its depths, as if crossing the barrier separating the stage from the world. He passes from the region occupied by the camera, where his view and ours are one, and enters a region still haunted by his gaze. He is like a dreamer who awakens and passes, still awake, into the world of his dream. In the depths of this magical frame, Sir John and Diana join in an embrace (2.78).

There is a slow dissolve to a closer view of the couple locked in an embrace in the back seat of a limousine (2.79, 2.80). One effect of this dissolve can be summed up by saying that we do not know whether there are two embraces or one. The dissolve underscores the discontinuity between these scenes even as it smoothly bridges them and denies their real separation. The dissolve also calls attention to itself by its extreme slowness and by its echo of the passage in which we viewed Diana through the window of her cell door.

Diana is in tears. They are tears of thankfulness: she is sitting beside her hero, in freedom. But to whom does she give thanks? And does she also weep for Handell Fane, whose love was responsible for her ordeal but who finally sacrificed himself? In any case, we recognize this as the conventional moment for Sir John to declare his love and propose marriage. But what he says is, "Now my dear, you must save those tears. They'll be very useful—in my new play." By referring to it as *his*, Sir John claims sole authorship of this play. If it is indeed "The Inner History of the Baring Case," however, he claims responsibility not only for a work of theater, but for the conclusion of the real events surrounding the murder. Doing so, he still fails to acknowledge Handell Fane—fails to recognize the significance of Fane's final gesture and his need for Fane's collaboration. This failure surely confirms that he is not Fane's equal. Nor is he Diana's equal, in his continuing failure to acknowledge her. And if Sir John also means by his "new play" their marriage, then Diana will need all the tears she can muster. Like Alice at the end of *Blackmail*, Diana is condemned to a relationship that denies her equality. Alice bears the brunt of mocking laughter and knows that the joke is on her, but Diana is cut off at this moment from our privileged vantage point and does not yet know the bondage that awaits her. She weeps tears of joy at the prospect of her new relationship with this man who regards himself as her master, who confines her within the frame of his imagination, and who directs her to serve his art and his desire.

Sir John takes Diana's hand. As she gazes happily at him, he rests his face against her, pressing his lips to her hair. Looking right into the camera, he gives a half-smile (2.81), in a shot that precisely echoes the ending of *The Lodger*. His open eyes and smile reveal that he is not completely absorbed in the moment as Diana is. The smile expresses his self-satisfaction in completing his project and shows him looking ahead to enjoying the fruits of his success. This look could be viewed as addressed to the camera, an acknowledgment of it. I view him, however, as blind to the camera's presence, to the agency it represents and to us. I view him as so absorbed at this moment— with the scene he is imagining, not with Diana's real proximity—that he can look right into the camera without recognizing it. We are not, with Hitchcock, responsible for the scene about to be enacted. We bear witness, with Hitchcock, to Sir John's continuing hubris.

2.81

2.82

From this intimate view, there is a dissolve to an extreme long shot of Sir John (2.82, 2.83). As melodious music plays, Markham—dressed as a butler—opens the door to a drawing room. Diana makes her entrance, attended by Doucie in a domestic's uniform. Sir John holds out his hand and Diana steps toward him. They gaze at each

2.83

2.84

2.85

2.86

other, the Markhams looking on. The dissolve suggests that this is the scene Sir John imagines when he looks up and smiles at the camera. We take this to be an epilogue set in the future, with Sir John and Diana husband and wife and the Markhams impressed into nonthespian service more in line with their talents. As Sir John kisses Diana's hand, the camera begins to track out (2.84). At first, this movement strikes us as a gracious and tactful acknowledgment of the couple's right of privacy. The suggestion is that we are viewing the prelude to an act of lovemaking and that we have arrived at a conventional happy ending. Sir John and Diana appear poised for the kiss that signifies that they are destined to live happily ever after. The implication is that Sir John's half-smile was an anticipation of this scene about to take place out of the camera's purview.

However, as the camera continues moving out, it crosses the barrier of a proscenium and stops only when the proscenium frames the view that had filled the screen (2.85). Within this frame-within-a-frame, Sir John and Diana kiss, tiny figures in the distance. The curtain rings down to applause from an unviewed audience (2.86), the image fades out, and a title announces the end of the film. The scene that we took to be real was staged. Nor is this just *any* scene: it is, no doubt, the final curtain of "The Inner History of the Baring Case." So now the implication is that Sir John's half-smile was an anticipation of performing his new play. This play ends with the perfect fulfillment of Sir John's wishes, but we must ask what the ending of this play signifies in reality.

No kiss performed in private could

coincide with this kiss scripted by Sir John and performed under his direction in the public space of his theater. If the play's ending is modeled on a kiss that really took place, that kiss was at the service of the staged kiss, which presents itself to its audience as at the service of nothing outside itself. Within the play, the final kiss signifies the lovers' mutual acknowledgment of their love and their equality in marriage. But the real kiss serves an art in which Sir John acknowledges no partner. In finishing "The Inner History of the Baring Case," he completes his creation of Sir John as a character fated for the heaven-on-earth of marriage to Diana. But by doing so, he also effects his separation from that character. Sir John's play ends with the lovers joined in an embrace, but Hitchcock does not claim that the real events of his narrative end this way. *Murder!* disavows Sir John's ending as its own. Then does this camera movement declare that all our views of the world of the film have really been views of scenes staged by Sir John? At any moment, could the camera have pulled out to reveal a proscenium? Is *Murder!*—a combination of highbrow shocker, blood-and-thunder melodrama, aerial act, Shakespearean tragedy, romantic comedy—"The Inner History of the Baring Case" itself? Are Sir John's and Hitchcock's authorships one, and are we the phantom audience whose applause resounds as this curtain rings down?

We have already seen that Sir John's and Hitchcock's endings do not coincide. If there is a gesture within the world of the film that calls for comparison with the gestures that culminate in the camera's final pulling out to frame the stage, it is performed by Handell Fane, not Sir John. *Murder!* acknowledges Fane in its ending as "The Inner History of the Baring Case" does not, because nothing in Sir John's play corresponds to the camera. Sir John is not Hitchcock, and we are not the audience for "The Inner History." *Murder!*'s invocations of the stage are framed by and frame a succession of views that can be identified with no piece of theater, real or imagined. In the camera's gestures, Hitchcock's authorship is declared and our acts of viewing acknowledged. *Murder!* ends with its most decisive declaration that what Hitchcock has made is a film, not a piece of theater. My reading of *Murder!* returns to the point at which it began. What do the camera's gestures declare *Murder!* to be, when they declare it to be a film?

Hitchcock sets *Murder!* in a theatrical setting in part to dramatize the fact that, in the world of a film as in reality, acting is not confined to the stage. Traditionally the stage is the designated place, set off within the world, where acting is authorized, where performances take place before an audience, without real consequences. Roles may be played which fulfill wishes, as in a dream; staged, violence is only spectacle, sexuality saves and condemns no one, and death can be faced unafraid. (I am not suggesting that this description does justice to the most serious works of theater.)

The world of *Murder!*, however, is presided over by an author who sees to it that no one's fantasy lacks a real reflection. Within it there is no designated place where acting is exempt from real consequences. We might say that in a film's world there is no theater. But the other side of this is that to us the world of *Murder!* —the world of any film—is not fully real. The stage is banished from it, but all that world is a stage to us. We might also say that all that happens within the world of a film passes before us like a dream. Yet our viewing is an act with consequences. *Murder!*'s repeated invocations of the stage are, at one level, acknowledgments of the barrier separating us from the world in which Sir John writes "The Inner History of the Baring Case" and Handell Fane kills. Our views of that world, like the views that constitute a dream, might be called projections. (They are not, for example, representations.) But we cannot say whether Handell Fane's visions are projected from within his imagination or projected onto his imagination by the agency of the film's author. And we likewise cannot say whether the camera is subject to our wishes in its framings, or whether we are subject to views that emanate from outside ourselves. In the role of the camera, active and passive are fused, as are the subjective and the objective. We cannot say whether the views that constitute *Murder!* are ours, the author's, or those of beings who dwell within the world of the film. Insofar as the film's world is real, we are within it, and it is also within us. *Murder!* declares that film has no proscenium which can be crossed.

It is no accident that many of the greatest works of cinema center on gestures that, like the camera movement at the end of *Murder!*, are both invocations of the stage and declarations of the camera. In such films as Chaplin's *City Lights*, Renoir's *The Rules of the Game*, and Dreyer's *Gertrud*, to name just three, theater plays a central role. These masterpieces, which know and declare themselves as films, share *Murder!*'s understanding that something fundamental about film is expressed in the myth of film's drastic separation from theater. Hitchcock himself speaks to this point: "The idea of photographing actions and stories came about with the development of techniques proper to film. The most significant of these, you know, occurred when D. W. Griffith took the camera away from the proscenium arch, where his predecessors used to place it, and moved it as close as possible to the actors."[21] For Hitchcock, "pure cinema" was born when Griffith's camera crossed the barrier of the proscenium. This transgression freed film to discover a natural subject in theater. The interpenetration of theater and the world—reflected in the familiar ambiguity of the English word "acting"—is not material out of which theater is ordinarily made. The candid or unselfconscious can only be depicted, in theater, by performance on stage, and only the greatest theater acknowledges its theatrical condition. But when Griffith's camera broke the barrier of the proscenium, it assumed the capacity to depict theatricality as a matter of course. In movies, the camera regularly distinguishes between the candid and the staged, between gestures and expressions that are sincere and those that are theatrical.

The dialectical opposition between the theatrical and the nontheatrical is grounded in film's traditional way of presenting human beings in the world. In movies, typically, the camera alternately frames its human subject within public and private spaces. The frame of the "objective" shot is a stage on which a man performs, subject to view by others within his world. Within the frame of the reaction shot, he views the spectacle of the world, expresses a private reaction, and prepares his next thrust into the public world. Point-of-view and reaction shots together combine to effect the camera's penetration of his privacy. The human subject of the camera alternates tensely and hesitantly between acting and viewing as he prepares his entrances onto the world's stage, performs, and withdraws again into a privacy to which only the camera has access.

The opposition between the theatrical and the nontheatrical required the development of a mode of acting that owes little to the traditions of the stage. Before the camera, the film actor must appear unselfconscious; no way of acting in the theater corresponds to this look of unselfconsciousness, and no audience can stand in for a camera in registering it. Nor is the film actor's mode of presenting himself to the camera simply a direct application of still photography's experience in eliciting unselfconsciousness. The still camera's subject may be called upon to strike candid poses, but not in the same way to act.[22] The opposition between the theatrical and the nontheatrical is not simply a convention; it is essential to what makes movies what they are and not something else. Part of what *Murder!* declares is precisely that the role of the camera hinges on this opposition. This is why Hitchcock chooses to declare the presence and agency the camera represents by invoking a theatrical frame and asserting the film's separation from it.

Cinema's systematic exploitation of nineteenth-century theatrical forms must not blind us to its fundamental break with theater. Griffith's films are not melodramas; Griffith appropriates melodramatic conventions to make films that place the viewer in an intimate relationship, unavailable to a theater audience, with beings who find themselves both within and outside a world possessed of the spirit of melodrama. Griffith brings to the fore the encounters between the camera and the human subjects whose privacy it penetrates, encounters for which melodrama knows no equivalent.

I have argued that it is an expression and a measure of Hitchcock's self-consciousness that his films call for readings that interrogate each of the camera's gestures by which his authorship declares itself and our presence as viewers is acknowledged. In part, these gestures are declarations that the camera's "nature" or "identity" or "being" is bound up with the distinction between the theatrical and the nontheatrical. Our understanding that someone in a movie is at a particular moment acting, or that he is simply being spontaneous, always rests on what might be called the camera's testimony. *Murder!* declares that this testimony must never be taken for granted. The camera's framings may themselves, in effect, be theatrical: in suggesting that the camera has now penetrated its subject's theatricality, the film's author may even at this moment be taking us in. Hence at another level, *Murder!*'s assertions of the camera are declarations that the world of the film is not fully real. What is real, the ending of *Murder!* declares, is the film itself: these particular views with their active and passive aspects, the act of authorship and the acts of viewing that these views reflect.

Hitchcock makes the interpenetration of theater and world his subject in the same stroke by which he acknowledges his own theatricality as an issue and reflects on the enigmatic nature of the views that constitute a film. His work affirms what he called "the art of pure cinema." Yet he breaks with those films that do not declare themselves as films. But how can Hitchcock's films acknowledge their own capacity for theatricality while remaining faithful to film's break with theater? How can Hitchcock's camera declare itself with authority, when part of what it has to declare is its own capacity for deception?

Throughout my readings of *The Lodger* and *Murder!* a distinction between two aspects of the camera's agency has been implicit. *Within the real world,* the camera represents the author's act of directing its framings, choosing the views to be presented to us. The camera is the instrument of a real relationship between author and viewer. Following Griffith, movies are designed to arouse the viewer, to make the viewer emotional. The film's author subjects the viewer to his power. *Within the world of the film,* the camera has the power to penetrate its subjects' privacy, without their knowledge or authorization. Furthermore, it represents the author who creates and animates that world and presides over its "accidents," who wields a power of life and death over the camera's subjects. In part, Hitchcock designs the world of the film so that events mirror the secret fantasies of the beings who dwell within it. Events implicate the camera's subjects as though they were characters in a play or as though reality were only a dream. The camera's penetration of its subjects' privacy, combined with this control over accidents, gives the author what I have called godlike power.

But he is also impotent. Insofar as his place is behind the camera, he represents only a haunting, ghostly presence within the world it frames. He has no body: no one can meet his gaze, he cannot satisfy himself sexually, he cannot even kill with his own hands. If the beings within the world of the film do not possess the author's powers, they are also exempt from his impotence. Insofar as he is human, must he not harbor a wish to avenge himself on them for being spared his anguish? (I am not saying that the author does not love his creatures.) From the author's point of view, the conventional "happy ending" throws his own solitude into relief. The lovers' final embrace frees them from his dominion, although it comes about only because he has arranged this world's accidents with this end in view. A film that leaves its author unacknowledged, his feelings unexpressed, and his story untold also leaves his human desires unfulfilled and masks the inhuman, "monstrous" aspect of his role. Hitchcock, I have said, always makes films in which he declares himself. And his dedication to the art of pure cinema commits him to such declaration in principle. *The Lodger* and *Murder!* call upon us to acknowledge their author personally, but also to acknowledge his authorship and hence his art.

At one level, Hitchcock's films declare themselves by telling the author's story. Whatever else they may be, Hitchcock's films, like Renoir's and von Sternberg's and Ford's and Hawks's and Welles's, are also allegories of their own creation. One of the deepest functions of Hitchcock's Wrong One is to ground the film's allegory in a human figure. The Wrong One, like the author, is barred from fulfillment within the world of the film. He cannot enter into a true marriage, and he can save his soul only by accepting the necessity of his final withdrawal from the human circle. Handell Fane takes responsibility for his own death by performing a gesture that allows the romantic couple to marry. Fane "crosses over to the other side," with our blessing, and assumes a place beside the author, like Octave at the end of *The Rules of the Game*. But if the souls of some Wrong Ones are saved, others are not. Sir John never renounces the arrogant claim of authoring his own world. He is one of the figures who attempt to appropriate Hitchcock's power without abiding by the conditions of his authorship.[23]

As Hitchcock turns his camera on his surrogates and agents, filming their human stories, his films also declare themselves by acknowledging that, to the beings within the world of the film from whom his face is veiled, the author himself represents the threat of murderous violence. When the veil is lifted, an inhuman aspect is revealed. The Wrong One's fate reminds us that the author's assumption of his place behind the camera is a symbolic death. And the centrality of murder within Hitchcock's world reflects a wish for vengeance that is a natural expression of the author's role, a reflection of the fantasies that motivate the author's withdrawal. In part, it is by taking murder as a subject that Hitchcock's films acknowledge the conditions of their authorship and declare themselves as films.

Murder! does not call upon us to accept its world as real or as an alternative reality. Reality is reality. Hitchcock creates a film, not a world, when he authors *Murder!*. But what of films that do not declare themselves as films? Do they call upon their viewers to regard their worlds simply as real? I am inclined to say that, while viewing such films, the question of reality or nonreality does not arise, in the way that, while dreaming, the reality of the dream is not questioned (when that question does arise, the dreamer awakens). A dream is not a hallucinatory state which deceives one into believing that the unreal is real. A dream is not a delusion, and a film is not an illusion. Even a movie that does not declare itself does not usually delude its viewer, but attempts to avoid having the question of the reality of its world come up. Should that question nonetheless arise, rather than reflect on the real conditions of its making and viewing, such a film attempts to deny those conditions. An extreme form this denial may take is to maintain that the world of the film, the world filmed and projected, is simply reality. But then we are no longer speaking about ordinary movies, but that species of documentary commonly referred to as *cinéma vérité*, whose creed is that "truth" appears on screen only when the camera is brought out of the studio to confront reality spontaneously.

Yet cinéma vérité derives its entire picture of being-in-the-world from classical cinema. It is the old opposition between the theatrical and the nontheatrical. Those human subjects with whom we "identify" in a cinéma vérité film appear alienated from the displays of theatricality—the nonspontaneous, the manipulative, the noncandid—that surround them. This alienation makes them appear human even as it isolates them in the world; we recognize this humanity as the sign of the possibility of a human community that does not exist within the region of the world "documented" by the film.

Murder! declares that its camera represents a passive viewing presence and a godlike agency. A cinéma vérité film, on the contrary, denies that there is an invisible agency that directs the camera's subjects and scripts their words, or plots "accidents" in accordance with a secret design. It presents its views as neutrally and objectively captured. Of course, the cinéma vérité film inscribes a fiction: the camera's invisibility. In his dedication to minimizing this element of fiction, the cinéma vérité filmmaker withholds himself from the world in order to film it. Stepping behind the camera may appear an act of perfect innocence and purity. But it represses, it does not overcome, the fantasy of power and murderousness that *Murder!* declares to be an inalienable constituent of authoring a film. The cinéma vérité filmmaker's fantasy of virginity and impotence has as its secret other face the fantasy of being author to the world, commanding it to unmask itself. Claiming exemption from responsibility for forging community within the world he is filming, he trains the camera's eye on that world, wreaking vengeance on it. These twin fantasies of omnipotence and impotence come together in cinéma vérité's underlying vision of a world condemned to a lack of human community by virtue of the act of filming itself.

If a filmmaker intends to make a serious film about real human beings rather than "characters," he must give his film a form that acknowledges the camera's subjects as his equals, without denying the real privileges and liabilities of his chosen place behind the camera. Whether it declares or denies its author's implication in the condition of these subjects, it must acknowledge its authorship and take responsibility for its testimony. If the author takes his own testimony for granted, or assumes that reality itself gives authority to his film, he stands exposed under the harsh light of *Murder!*'s critique.[24] All films that tap the power first exploited by Griffith appear to us to be projected from within ourselves, even as we are subjected to these views from the outside. Their power cannot be accounted for without reflecting on the conditions of the act of making, and the act of viewing, a film.

Murder!, like every Hitchcock film, presents itself to us as a mystery, akin to the mystery of murder and the mystery of love. It declares itself to be no more mysterious, but also no less, than we are to ourselves. Its mystery is the mystery of our own being as creatures who are fated to be born, to love, to kill, to create, to destroy, and to die in a world in which we are at every moment alone even as we are joined in a human community that knows no tangible sign, a world we did not create and yet for which we are responsible. Or we might say that the mystery is that a film is made and viewed and a life is lived; yet both pass before us like dreams.

Hitchcock subjects us to his real power when he composes and realizes *Murder!* so as to elicit an emotional response. *Murder!* is the medium of the real relationship between Hitchcock and us, and the camera is the instrument of this relationship. For example, Hitchcock assumes the mantle of the storyteller, the gripping power of his narratives enhanced by film's power to weave a spell through visual rhythms and kinaesthesia. But *Murder!* is not simply a machine constructed to affect passive viewers. Its creation is also a human gesture, which may or may not be sincere and may or may not be seriously meant. The film is an expression of Hitchcock's individual, embodied human existence (it is, of course, also a product of an industrial system of production). *Murder!* is an utterance animated, as it were, by a human soul.

But how can a film communicate to its viewers that it is authored? After all, the camera has no voice (it frames its views in silence) and appears to have no body (it leaves no trace of itself within the frame). It might well seem that there is no natural human capacity corresponding to film's power of enabling the viewer to see with another's eyes. Even if the author succeeds in giving the camera his own personal style, how can a film, through the instrument of the camera, call upon the viewer to acknowledge its author's wish for acknowledgment? We might distinguish those films that call upon the viewer to recognize their authors from those that do not. We might make the further distinction between those films whose authors present themselves only through a style, as it were *theatrically,* and those whose authors call for their work, and their humanity, to be authentically acknowledged. These last —and it is my premise that Hitchcock's films are among them—are films that acknowledge their viewers' capacity for acknowledgment. In calling for acknowledgment of their authorship, they also acknowledge the viewer as their author's equal.[25]

What "fact" could I discover that would undermine my conviction that a human author stands behind *Murder!* and calls upon me to acknowledge him? I say I know Hitchcock through his films, with no fear of contradiction, although there are innumerable details of his biography I do not know, because it is his authorship that defines what I mean by "Hitchcock." I take his work to circumscribe and sum up a human existence, even while it circumscribes and sums up an entire art. Of course, what I mean by "Hitchcock" —the creator and creation of an authorship—cannot be separated from what Hitchcock's films mean to me from the history of my encounters with them.

It is not hard for me, sitting at my typewriter, or no doubt for you, dozing over your page, to conjure an image of the portly Hitchcock, alone in his study, composing *Murder!* shot by shot. We imagine him imagining our reactions when we view the completed film projected on the screen. But does Hitchcock imagine us to be mindful of *him,* mindful of his feelings as he steps behind the camera in his imagination and, addressing his fantasies and ours, creates *Murder!*? Or does he imagine his viewers as subject to his power at every moment, but unwilling or unable to recognize him? If Hitchcock wields power over us, he is also impotent in the face of the possibility that we will fail to acknowledge him. He cannot openly express the pleasures and terrors of his role, cannot compel our recognition. Insofar as he is human, he must wish—whether consciously or not—to avenge himself on those viewers who fail to acknowledge him. The fantasy of unleashing violence on the viewer who condemns him to his condition of impotence is built into the conditions of his role.

The violence inscribed in the author's role is not merely Hitchcock's alone. It is a condition of the art of film itself. On the other hand, Hitchcock has made this role his own, personally dedicating his life to his authorship. He is not willing to deny film's capacity for violence or to disavow his own implication in it.

As I read Hitchcock's films, they declare their intentions, which are honorable. His films invite us to enter into a relationship with him that is grounded in mutual acknowledgment, and in affirmation of the erotic bond that pure cinema has the power to forge. But on those viewers who do not acknowledge his art, Hitchcock avenges himself. Unread, its authorship unacknowledged, *Murder!* is seductive, treacherous. Those viewers who wish simply to avail themselves of its pleasures become the film's victims. And Hitchcock is so contemptuous of those viewers who are unwilling or unable to acknowledge him that he does not raise a hand to prevent them from remaining oblivious of, or even enjoying, his films' symbolic murder of them. Still he does not always allow viewers such liberties. In *Sabotage*, for example, the author's murderousness directs itself, shockingly, against an innocent boy and a little dog; in *Stage Fright*, Hitchcock's capacity for deception is declared so decisively that every viewer inclined to take the camera for granted must be distressed; and in *Psycho*, he compels even the blindest viewer to bow before the terrifying power his camera commands.

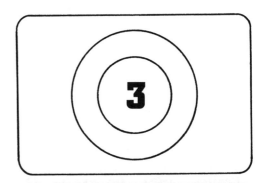

3

The Thirty-Nine Steps

The years between *Murder!* (1930) and *The Man Who Knew Too Much* (1934) were troubled ones for Hitchcock. During this time, he made *The Skin Game* (1931), *Rich and Strange* (1932), *Number Seventeen* (1932), and *Waltzes from Vienna* (1933). Of these films, none is of particular interest except *Rich and Strange*, a film close to Hitchcock's heart.

It is easy to like *Rich and Strange*, although, in my judgment, its execution does not equal its conception and the "writing" lacks the density characteristic of Hitchcock. The film appears sketchy and incomplete, the outline of a great work rather than a major one in and of itself. Yet it *is* a wonderful idea for a Hitchcock film. By a stroke of fortune, a couple whose marriage is reduced to the round of dreary routine is granted a voyage of adventure in which each rediscovers romance. Their relationship is threatened, but they fall in love with each other again and rededicate their marriage. At the conclusion of the film, they are back in the world of the ordinary, but that realm has been transfigured; and there is also the intimation that they are now prepared to embark together on another "voyage of adventure"; they await the arrival of a child.

Rich and Strange, with its redemption of an ordinary marriage, casts Hitchcock's other films, almost all of which concern protagonists who are single, in an unusual perspective. The film is an important precursor of *The Awful Truth*, *The Philadelphia Story*, *The Lady Eve*, *Adam's Rib*, and the other American comedies of the thirties and forties that comprise the genre Stanley Cavell terms "the comedy of remarriage."[1] And within the context of Hitchcock's work of this period, it bears a close and illuminating relationship to *The Man Who Knew Too Much*, which indeed can be viewed almost as its sequel. The later film opens on a couple bored with a marriage that appears held together only by the presence of a child. By a Hitchcockian "miracle," their secret wish is granted—if in a decidedly unwished-for way—when their daughter is kidnapped. Freed from this child, they are free to dissolve their marriage, but they choose instead to join forces. In their victorious struggle to track down the kidnappers and rescue their daughter, husband and wife reconfirm their commitment to each other. *The Man Who Knew Too Much* ends with a marriage restored, like *Rich and Strange*. The family anticipated at the conclusion of the earlier film is rededicated.

The Man Who Knew Too Much is generally regarded as the film that sets Hitchcock back "on track." I would not dispute this, although it is far from a uniformly successful film. Its strongest passages, I believe, are those that center on the wife, Jill (Edna Best). (*The Man Who Knew Too Much* is one of the films in which Hitchcock's sympathetic understanding of women is most strikingly manifest. He is commonly thought of as a misogynist, but this is a false indictment.)

The film's most celebrated passage is the Albert Hall sequence, one of the great set pieces in which Hitchcock places his art most theatrically on display. Jill arrives at the concert hall to try to forestall something frightful—she does not know what it is, but we know there is a plan to assassinate a foreign diplomat—from taking place. Hitchcock intercuts shots that detail her growing anxiety with a succession of views that together give us an overall picture of the public space of the hall, as the orchestra and chorus perform William Walton's "Storm Cloud Cantata." One effect of this cutting is to allow the rising excitement of the music to reinforce and to serve as a metaphor for this woman's private anguish. At the same time, the music serves as a metaphor for the power of the art of pure cinema on display in this passage. As Jill appears about to break down, the image goes out of focus to express her near loss of consciousness. When a focused image returns to the screen, we see a black curtain; then a pistol enters the frame and slowly turns toward the camera. Filmed this way, the gun appears conjured within, or projected onto, Jill's fevered imagination. It is as if, for this gun to kill, she must first be possessed by this vision and then *will* the bullet to hit its mark. And for the diplomat to be saved, she must find within herself the power to deflect the bullet's course, which she accomplishes by voicing a scream that distracts the assassin and stops the concert. (Within the film as a whole, this presentation is deeply resonant. It invokes the opening, the marksmanship contest Jill loses when her daughter distracts her with an untimely cry. At one level, what this woman acknowledges by conjuring her vision of the gun, what she exorcises when she screams, is her wish to avenge herself on the child she blames for binding her to her husband. What arises in place of this wish is a resolute determination to win her child back and to destroy her murderous antagonist.)

Jill's extraordinary power and burden testify to her intimate attunement to Hitchcock's camera and link her with Daisy and Daisy's mother, with Diana Baring, and with *Blackmail*'s Alice. (The Albert Hall sequence is, in part, modeled on *Blackmail*'s climactic chase.) The weaknesses of *The Man Who Knew Too Much* can be summed up by saying that it has no male figure who is Jill's equal and does not acknowledge the implications of this imbalance (the way *Blackmail*, for example, does). For one thing, the stature of Jill's marksman antagonist is diminished by Hitchcock's introduction of a second villain, a brilliant but perverted mastermind (Peter Lorre) who holds his hired gun in contempt. Lorre's disdain for the marksman blunts the effect of the film's most climactic moment, when Jill is once more pitted against her adversary and avenges her defeat. And Hitchcock seems confused by Fritz Lang's inspired use of Peter Lorre in *M*: Lorre looks like a refugee from a Lang film, rather than an authentic Hitchcock villain.

Then, too, Jill is married to a man (Leslie Banks) who is a caricature of a certain type of reserved Englishman. Despite the resources he discovers within himself in the course of the film, we do not believe that he will ever be capable of kindling his wife's imagination. In the fifties remake of *The Man Who Knew Too Much*, Hitchcock redresses the imbalance between husband and wife by casting James Stewart in the Leslie Banks role. Stewart is capable of representing as extreme a caricature of Americanness as Banks does of Englishness. But Stewart is also a great actor/personality, a deep and lasting subject for Hitchcock's—and not only Hitchcock's— camera. In this respect, what the 1934 *The Man Who Knew Too Much* lacks is a male protagonist in whom the audience may take a strong personal interest. It is above all this lack that Hitchcock addresses in his next film, of seminal importance to his work, *The Thirty-Nine Steps* (1935).

The early sound era was a period of confusion, compounded by international political unrest and economic dislocation. The year 1934 was a critical moment in the history of film. The institution of the Hays Office censors in Hollywood coincides with the onset of a new stability. By 1934, the landscape of the silent film was decisively altered, and a new complex of genres, which to this day dominates Hollywood production, was established. Perhaps the film that most clearly reveals the new landscape is Capra's *It Happened One Night,* the sensational hit that inaugurated the genre of the comedy of remarriage. Inseparable from the creation of such genres is the creation of a new type of star. A film like *It Happened One Night* is unimaginable without stars like Clark Gable and Claudette Colbert. The post-1934 stars call for new modes of relationship between the camera—hence the film's author and the film's viewers—and its human subjects.

In Hitchcock's American films, such stars as Cary Grant, James Stewart, Ingrid Bergman, and Grace Kelly become important subjects for his camera. These subjects provide him with the most pointed instances for raising and addressing the concerns that were always central to his work. The film in which he first discovers a deep subject in the new kind of star is *The Thirty-Nine Steps*. It is no accident that this is also the work by which he creates a new genre—the "Hitchcock thriller"—that is able to hold its own with the other genres that dominate post-1934 production, such as the comedy of remarriage.

The Thirty-Nine Steps is a major achievement. In the figure of Hannay/Donat, Hitchcock creates his first complete protagonist and figure of identification, the first of a long line of Hitchcock heroes. And it is the first Hitchcock film that "plays" as well as it "reads," working flawlessly as theater as well as taking theater as its subject. Every role in this film is cast with compelling sensitivity to the nuances of real human types. In this film, Hitchcock makes judgments of his human subjects and calls for agreement with these judgments. First and foremost, he calls upon us to accept his judgment that Hannay/Donat is a figure with whom we may identify. Those who accept this comprise Hitchcock's audience. The Thirty-Nine Steps is the first film in which Hitchcock calls forth an authentic audience—one in which we gladly assume our place. And it is the film that first grants the world its abiding sense of Hitchcock as the "master of suspense."

The Thirty-Nine Steps insists on a continuity between its protagonist and the figure of the lodger. Yet Hannay/Donat also represents a decisive break with the lodger in the fundamental respect that, from the outset, Hitchcock wants us to recognize him as innocent, possessed of no dark secret. However, while we know everything we need to know about this figure to know that he is no mystery to us, we know next to nothing about him as a character: our faith that we know him and the camera's respect for his privacy are intertwined. Hence The Thirty-Nine Steps is a bridge between The Lodger and the American films with stars like Grant and Stewart. Within that unknownness that is inseparable from our "knowledge" of a star, Hitchcock discovers a disturbing mystery. (It is only when he moves to America, and the idea of alienness takes on a poignant new aspect for him, that Hitchcock is prepared for this dialectical turn.)

The Thirty-Nine Steps opens with a panning movement along an electric sign. Against a black background, flashing letters spell out the words "MUSIC HALL," announcing a setting (one to which the film returns at its climax) and a metaphor (the mood and tone of the film, and its organization as a series of "numbers" designed to entertain, continually draw inspiration from the music hall).

The next few shots echo the introduction of the lodger. They follow a mysterious figure—we have no view of his face—into a theater and end with him ensconced in his seat, back to the camera, ready for the show to begin (3.1,

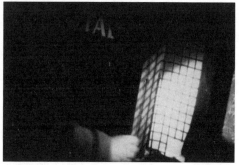

3.1

3.2

3.3

3.2). But when a few moments later the camera frames him frontally, we discover, not Ivor Novello's anguished mask but the intelligent, humane face of Robert Donat, with its characteristic look of dispassionate amusement (3.3). The break with *The Lodger* is declared. From this moment on, we accept *The Thirty-Nine Steps*'s protagonist, Richard Hannay, as exempt from the lodger's anguish. Hannay's assumption of his place at the center of the film's narrative, like his assumption of his place in this theater audience, is allowed for by the grace with which Donat takes to being filmed. In the series of shots that open the film, our identification with Hannay/Donat is secured.

When Hannay enters the theater, the music hall show commences, and Hitchcock's film likewise begins with the figure of Hannay and remains with him almost without a break. Hannay's centrality allows the film its dimension of fantasy, as we share his exhilarating adventures. The camera does not come between us; rather, Hannay's point of view is the regular medium of its "narration." However, there are critical moments when it breaks with his perspective. And even in its appropriation of Hannay's point of view the camera asserts a separation from him that is, paradoxically, a condition of his status as a figure of identification. We cannot understand the achievement of *The Thirty-Nine Steps* if we assume that identification with a figure on the screen is merely an effect. Our bond with Hannay/Donat is no illusion caused by the workings of a mechanism. To acknowledge this bond, we must be prepared to address such questions as who or what the camera reveals Donat to be, who or what Hannay is, what Hannay's world is, and who or what *we* are, that we heed the call to imagine Donat in Hannay's place. What imagining oneself in another's place comes to and what a figure of identification is are questions that underlie *The Thirty-Nine Steps* and all of Hitchcock's work. Two paradoxes might be singled out as at the heart of these matters. First, our identification is grounded in a distinct impression of Donat's individuality, of what separates him from all other stars and allows us our clear sense of Hannay's separateness from all other inhabitants of his world. How can recognition of this figure's separateness be a condition of our imagining ourselves in his place, of identifying with him? Second, this identification cannot be accounted for by reference to what we know about this figure, because we know nothing about him that is not already conditioned by our identification.

At the moment we first see Hannay's face, we discover that his place in this music hall audience is no mystery. Like us, he has paid his money and looks forward to enjoying a good show. Hannay's role in *The Thirty-Nine Steps* and his incarnation by Donat are linked to his role as music hall spectator. That role is like ours to the extent that the music hall corresponds to *The Thirty-Nine Steps* itself (of course, the film declares its separation from the music hall even as it invokes it). The possibility of our imagining ourselves in Hannay's place rests in part on this original link between his role and our own. Hannay is no ordinary spectator. Within the music hall audience, he stands out by his height, the ease and grace of his bearing, his well-tailored coat. Mr. Memory comes to refer to him as a "gentleman," and we might wish to say that Hannay stands higher in class than the rest of the audience. Yet Hannay is not upper-class like Sir John. The only moment when anyone looks to Hannay with deference occurs when he is taken for someone else at a political rally. His class comes down to his being Robert Donat, and what class is that? Hannay's identity as a Canadian—that he is a visitor to London from Canada and that he is single are about the only facts we ever glean from his biography—marks him as outside the rigid system of distinguishing Englishmen by class. At least this is part of the film's myth about Hannay: that he is outside and by nature superior to class, that he is neither a representative of one particular class of Englishmen nor is he no Englishman at all.

Hannay enters the theater just in time. As he finds his seat, the orchestra starts up and there is applause. It is as if his arrival is the signal for the show to begin. This coincidence reminds us that, while it is Hannay's entrance that allows Hitchcock's film to get down to business, a music hall show can go on even if Hannay's seat is not filled. No sooner does Hannay take his seat than there is a series of shots that steps back from his perspective to present a succession of vantages which together encompass a global view of the auditorium and allow us to be caught up with the show itself. Mr. Memory makes his entrance, following a respectful introduction ("Ladies and gentlemen, with your attention and permission it is my honor to introduce to you one of the most remarkable men in the world"). All present are entreated to test this man.

Mr. Memory's act calls for him to handle hecklers as well as to field serious questions. He comes alive in a witty give-and-take in which wisecracks are exchanged and set off by real questions and true answers. It is essential to this passage, as I understand it, that Mr. Memory win us over. We must be amused and take him to personify the spirit of the music hall. Mr. Memory's act is a winning piece of theater and a testament to an absurd but moving devotion. The poignancy of the film's ending, for example, requires that we be distracted from recollecting Mr. Memory until Hannay himself remembers him. Yet when, with Hannay, we do become mindful of this little man, we must be prepared to acknowledge both that we had stopped thinking about him and that he is truly memorable, that his spirit has been with us all along.

Hannay has a question. The global perspective is suspended as we are allowed our first view of his face. But another question is recognized first, and the camera reframes to include this questioner along with Hannay, who is amused by the whole scene. (Hannay sits in Mr. Memory's audience and in that audience's audience.)

3.4

When Mr. Memory finally recognizes Hannay, Hitchcock marks the occasion by a deep-focus shot that joins the two men—whose destinies, after all, are joined—in a single frame (3.4). Hannay's question is real ("How far is Winnipeg from Montreal?"), and Mr. Memory is more than equal to its challenge. Calling Hannay a gentleman, he welcomes him as a visitor, granting him a special place in his audience. He makes a little joke ("Miss Winnie who, sir?") and then gives the correct answer, ending with "Am I right, sir?" Hannay's "Quite right!" is an affirmation not only of Mr. Memory's "fact," but his whole performance and the form of theater he personifies. Amused and satisfied, Hannay claps his hands, calling upon others in the audience to applaud if they agree with his judgment. Hannay does not act with an aristocrat's prerogative to command applause. On the contrary, he gives expression to our own feeling, shared by those in this hall worthy of our community. Hannay's acknowledgment of the man's performance occasions an expression of approval that allows this audience momentarily to emerge *as* a community.

I take it that Hitchcock calls upon us to accept Hannay not only as a spectator, but as our full equal. It is not that, in the figure of Hannay, we believe we are viewing ourselves. Rather, we recognize in him a man whose testimony we would accept and whose company we would gladly share. Hannay's singleness within the world of the film—in this theater, he sits alone—binds him to our condition as viewers, whether or not we have entered the movie theater with a companion. Hannay's presence meaningfully marks our absence from the world of the film, and our condition as viewers, for we see eye to eye. Hannay's individuality and our sense of community with him are crystallized in his gesture of stepping forward within Mr. Memory's audience. *The Thirty-Nine Steps* is a fantasy or allegory about the condition of spectatorship.

This expression of community is short-lived. Heckling in the hall almost gets out of hand, and a fistfight breaks out. One of the most memorable images in the film is that of Mr. Memory in distress, unable to make his voice heard above the din while the man who introduced him—his respect for this "remarkable man" shows touchingly in the hurt expression on his face—speaks for him like a ventriloquist (3.5). (The disruption is germane to the politics of the film, since it clearly alludes to fascist hooliganism.) In an insert, a hand fires a gun as two shots ring out (3.6). The camera breaks with Hannay's perspective to frame the film's first declaration that there is a mystery in its world. The break is extended in a series of shots that gives us a global view of the resulting chaos. When the camera does return to Hannay, it frames the "accident" by which he finds himself entwined in an unknown woman's arms, an apparent consequence of their separate efforts to find an exit (3.7). Hannay leads her to the street, where she asks whether she can go home with him.

We later learn that it was this woman —Annabella Smith—who fired the shots in the theater to escape from two men who are on her trail. Had she already selected Hannay to play a role in her escape and arranged the accident of their meeting? Or does she only hit on a way to escape when she finds herself already in his arms? We cannot say whether their meeting is only Hitchcock's contrivance or this woman's as well. It is clear that Annabella's designation of Hannay represents a "magical" intervention in his affairs, whether we imagine her as a knowing or unknowing

3.5

3.6

3.7

agent of the author. This is not to say, of course, that she is not also a woman in desperate straits.

Hannay is designated by Annabella to play a role in some scenario. There is one and only one surface reading of her proposition. By inviting this stranger to take her home with him, she offers herself sexually. Hannay's reply ("well, it's your funeral") registers his wariness, but these ironically prophetic words also declare that he understands what, at face value, her offer comes to. Annabella casts Hannay as a bachelor at home in the world of casual sexuality, a man who would gladly make love to her. And how does she cast herself? She would like to go home with him, she says; she offers herself because she desires him.

Hannay's acquiescence declares no specific intention or desire. His "it's your funeral" frankly registers his sense that, in allowing this woman to go home with him, he is not so far making any personal commitment at all. He makes himself available and at the same time defers a decision, leaving his options open pending the revelation of her intentions. He neither reveals nor conceals a scenario of his own.[2] His reply raises specific questions about his life (for example, what is his history of sexual experience?) and his private feelings (for example, has this woman aroused his desire?). It is fundamental to our mode of identification with Hannay that we do not know, and never learn, the answers to such questions.

Hannay's sexuality and privacy locate the limits of his identity as a character. We might say that Hannay is not really a character to us at all (any more than we are primarily characters to ourselves). Otherwise this exchange with Annabella and the scene that follows would undermine our conviction that we know him. Hannay's withholding of himself, coupled with our ignorance of his biography and our inability to read his thoughts or feelings, would make us skeptical about his intentions. But this passage, on the contrary, assumes and reinforces our faith in Hannay. We know nothing and learn nothing to awaken us to skepticism about him. Almost all we know is that there is nothing essential that we do not know. Of course, this belief could be challenged. Indeed, if Annabella's scenario were played out, Hannay would stand before us revealed as a character. A moment would arise at which he would have to accept responsibility for his role or else refuse to continue to play it; he would have to declare his intentions, and we would discover his passion or have reason to condemn his impassivity. But the film systematically forestalls any development that would force Hannay to reveal his character or his sexuality. When they first arrive at his flat, he assumes the air of a man accustomed to entertaining women. But this reveals nothing. We never learn whether Annabella's scenario called for a scene of passion and, if so, whether

Hannay is prepared to play his part through to the end. He lights the stove to fry up a haddock fillet for his hungry guest. The sound of the gas catching fire startles her, and when the telephone rings, she reacts as though it spelled doom. Indeed, this ringing *is* a signal that renders her original scenario moot.

A condition of our identification with Hannay is that his situation is at every moment intelligible to us, while our understanding of that situation does not rely on knowledge of his character or on his own testimony (which could always be false). He declares no desire or intention *to Annabella* (a question the film pointedly raises but never answers is whether he possesses desires at all); nor does he declare himself *to himself* (this raises the question of whether he is capable of self-deception); nor does he declare himself *to the camera*. Hannay makes no declarations and has none to make: this is part of what I mean by saying that Hannay is not a character. But it also reveals something about what the film declares the camera's relationship to Hannay to be. We accept the "fact" that Hannay possesses no secrets. A condition of this is that he appears completely unselfconscious in the frame: he neither openly addresses the camera nor avoids such address. Hannay's innocence cannot be separated from his apparent obliviousness of the camera's framings, of his condition as the camera's subject. Unlike Sir John or the lodger, Hannay appears exempt from the need to choose between declaring and dissembling knowledge. The ease that is the most extraordinary feature of Robert Donat's presence on the screen—Charles Laughton called him the most graceful of all actors—reflects the naturalness with which he takes to being filmed and, in turn, the unselfconsciousness with which he accepts being within the world of the film. This figure is devoid of theatricality, in the specific sense that we do not admit the possibility that he is putting on an act for the camera or for himself. Hannay's exemption from theatricality is a condition of his stepping forward within Mr. Memory's audience. It allows for one of the basic strategies of *The Thirty-Nine Steps*. Hitchcock, the viewer, and Hannay himself are free to take pleasure when events conspire to frame Hannay, without his knowledge or responsibility, so that he is called upon to act. It is before our very eyes that this spectator discovers the exhilaration of acting: a mode of acting free from guilt, anguish, and theatricality.

Hannay's acting is a matter of reacting within a situation of which he is no more the author than we. Every situation in which he finds himself is a trap set for him. It poses a problem he must solve on the spot. In every case, his solution takes the form of discovering a role and performing it. Within the critical literature, there has been contention as to whether we should regard these roles as in or out of character for Hannay. But Hitchcock does not allow this issue to be settled. Hannay's acting is improvisation. His individuality manifests itself through his performances, but we discover in them no passion other than for performance itself. Nor is there anything we discover about *Hitchcock* from these performances other than his capacity to set Hannay up so that, after each improvisation, he emerges in a place already prepared. Hannay is, unbeknownst to himself, Hitchcock's straight man. Hitchcock's design for him coincides with his freedom to act.[3]

Hannay's exemption from theatricality is one of several aspects of the special relationship to the camera that specifically distinguishes him from the figure of the lodger. For example, he does not possess the lodger's capacity to look at the camera. It is without anguish that Hannay takes to being filmed, and in turn he does not threaten the camera with his gaze. This reflects the further fact that Hannay's gaze, within the world of the film, does not have the power of the lodger's. And there is no view that incarnates Hannay's desire. In turn, no one's gaze has the same hold on Hannay that Daisy's has on the lodger.

A cognate feature of Hannay's presence within the world of the film is what might be called his "invisibility." We can assume Hannay's point of view without pain, as we cannot assume the lodger's, because Hannay does not threaten the camera's invisibility, but rather participates in it. When Hannay must enact an ordinary anonymity on the train to avoid calling attention to himself—he is a

3.8

3.9

fugitive and his picture is in the newspaper—the camera is put in the literal position of his eyes, so that within the frame the act of looking at Hannay and the act of looking at the camera coincide (3.8). This is preceded by a view of Hannay warily stealing a half-glance at the camera. Surely, were our view of Hannay in (3.9) to fall into the hands of the other men in the compartment, all would be lost—Hannay would be recognized and caught. Yet the next shot of a man puffing a pipe, a trace of a smile on his lips (3.10), is from Hannay's point of view and forces us to recognize that our incriminating view of Hannay indeed *was* possessed by one of these men. The shock comes both from this shot's retroactive disclosure and its ambiguity: we cannot say whether or not this man's smile is one of recognition. It turns out that he has not recognized

Hannay. To such a gaze Hannay is, in effect, invisible. Hannay's invisibility is his capacity to recede, to blend into the background. Hannay draws on his protean quality, which allows him to avoid jarring others out of their distracted assumptions as to who he is, whenever he is called upon to perform an improvisation. It is illuminating to contrast Hannay, exempt from theatricality and capable of going unnoticed, with two

3.10

attractive, charming Hitchcock protagonists who follow in his line: Laurence Olivier in *Rebecca* and Cary Grant in *Suspicion*, *Notorious*, *To Catch a Thief*, and *North by Northwest*.

Olivier has a genius for cloaking himself in a character's singular style and manner. In his best film roles, he plays characters who partake of this genius, in whatever guise. The challenge for Olivier is in rendering the guise, whether he is playing a frankly theatrical figure known to the world as an actor (as in *The Entertainer*) or a man who deceives the world into mistaking his dissembling for sincerity (as in *Richard III*). In *Rebecca*, he plays a third type: a man who holds his extraordinary powers of acting in check. Olivier's particular genius makes him perfect for this romantic role. We can believe that his theatricality cuts so deep that he does not know where his role playing ends and his true self begins; at the cost of withholding himself from humanity, he bars himself from all intimacy for fear of being insincere. *Rebecca* calls upon Olivier to project an enigmatic, inhuman coldness that must strike us as no mere act, as though his gaze has the power to kill. Yet the film calls upon us, in the end, to accept him as an innocent who has fallen under a terrible curse.

If Hannay's exemption from theatricality distinguishes him from the Olivier figure in *Rebecca*, his invisibility separates him from that archetypal Hitchcock figure who nonetheless so clearly derives from him, Cary Grant. If there is a picture of Cary Grant in the newspaper, someone is sure to recognize him, as in *Suspicion* and *North by Northwest*. Grant is too striking to go unnoticed or to sit within Mr. Memory's audience. It is not that Grant plays actors the way Olivier does, however. In *North by Northwest*, the villainous Vandam calls him an actor ("You make this very room a theater"), but he does not know that Grant is who he claims to be.

In his discussion of *North by Northwest*, Robin Wood describes the introduction of the protagonist.

The film begins with shots of New York traffic and New York crowds . . . From this emerges Roger Thornhill, dictating to his secretary on his way home . . . In an exposition of masterly compression we learn all the essential things about him: he is brash, fast-talking, over-confident on the surface; entirely irresponsible and inconsiderate of others . . . a heavy drinker; a divorcé . . . surprisingly dominated by his mother . . . Indeed, he is a man who lives purely on the surface . . . A modern city Everyman.[4]

Wood's list of the essentials leaves out what *North by Northwest* insists is most essential about Thornhill: he is Cary Grant. By 1959, Cary Grant's face had long since become an icon; the film is filled with references to its familiarity. But a feature of Grant's face that had always been essential to its meaning on the screen is equally in evidence in *North by Northwest*: its great beauty. Grant's beauty is not an institution like John Barrymore's (Barrymore displays his beauty theatrically every time he turns his profile to the camera), nor is it to be relished in soft focus, like Gary Cooper's. It is as if Grant has made a pact with the camera: his face may be filmed as long as the camera does not stare long and hard at it or let its focus go soft. And this corresponds to a pact he appears to have made with the world: others may view him as long as they do not display their desire for him; in return, he will not display his feelings. Yet Grant finds himself continually gazed upon in ways that perplex and disturb him. He has a whole repertory of ways of addressing others' uncircumspect looks, and an equal repertory of ways of addressing the camera's gaze.

I have already cited the chilling moment in *Suspicion* when Grant looks right into the camera and we are compelled to admit that we do not know whether he is a murderer. We know that there is *something* on his mind, that he has some secret design we cannot fathom. All the pre-Hitchcock films that develop and explore Grant's screen persona, even remarriage comedies such as *The Awful Truth, Bringing Up Baby, His Girl Friday,* and *The Philadelphia Story,* play on our dark suspicion that Grant may be murderous by nature. And the much-maligned ending of *Suspicion,* as I read it, does not claim that Grant could not possibly kill, although it does not claim to unmask him as a murderer. The film declares that our suspicion about him can never be divorced from our understanding of who he is. And Hitchcock's subsequent films sustain this subtle position toward Grant. In *Notorious,* for example, Grant's silence reveals his love for Alicia, but it also has a murderous aspect: if she dies, he will be as responsible as Sebastian. And when, in *North by Northwest,* Thornhill deliberately makes Vandam suspicious of Eve, he takes pleasure in the knowledge that he may be costing this woman her life.

Grant's looks to the camera can also be comical. When Grant, unable to get a word in edgewise, tilts his head and looks right at the camera, he calls upon us to share his indignation until his presence is noted. This look bespeaks impotence, but it also suggests—is this suggestion only a bluff?—that he possesses a power he is holding in check. If those present are fools enough not to heed this look, Grant may have recourse to his famous whinny, which suggests that his is the power of a raging stallion. But this whinny, by which he blows off steam, gives only the barest suggestion of the explosion that would ensue should even this signal be ignored. His whinny unheeded, he may burst out in a display of anger that is at the same time an absurdly childish tantrum and a genuinely alarming signal that, should he be really aroused, *unimaginable* violence must be released.[5]

After the telephone rings, Annabella gives Hannay a tantalizing fragment of her story. She fired the shots in the music hall. She is a secret agent being trailed by two men directed by a sinister mastermind—he is missing the top joint of his little finger—in the employ of a foreign government, who plans to smuggle Air Ministry secrets out of England. At first, Hannay treats her as if she were joking or suffering from persecution mania. But when she wagers that the two men are on the street outside, he goes to look out the window in another room, and he carries a knife and hugs the shadowed walls. When he returns, he admits that she wins. Even now he may not believe her completely, but that she has a story he accepts as a fact.

The ringing telephone awakens Annabella to the reality of her situation. In her story, she preserves an air of mystery. But this is overshadowed by the mystery of her antagonist, whose brilliance blinds her, whose ruthlessness awes her, whose power to act with the speed of thought fills her with terror. The telephone is this figure's reminder to Annabella of his real power over her. It signals a halt to the unfolding of her scenario and announces that his script—which calls for her to die—has superseded hers. But if the ringing telephone is a signal to Annabella that her nightmare is real, it is also Hitchcock's signal to us that we are viewing a film, that these events have an author. The author's scenario supersedes even that of Annabella's antagonist. For a dying Annabella is soon to pass her struggle on to the unwitting Hannay, who is destined to defeat that monstrous figure.

Hannay asks Annabella what she wishes to do next. She replies that she wants first of all to get a good night's rest. With this remark, she voids her original invitation to Hannay to seduce her. He abides by this condition and settles down to a night's solitary "shakedown on the couch." In these changed circumstances, the issues about Hannay's sexuality and his character are not to be pressed. The image fades out. The scene next fades in on an open window, curtains flapping in the night breeze. Hannay awakens to this disquieting sight and sound. This is the first of a series of awakenings to reality that, at one level, comprises the remainder of the film. Hannay next "awakens," for example, to the sight of Annabella staggering in from the bedroom, a map clutched in her hand, the knife we last saw in Hannay's hand protruding from her back. She falls forward, saying only, "Clear out, Hannay, they'll get you next!"

Our impression that Hannay has awakened not *from* but *into* a dream is intensified when the camera zeroes in to frame the dead

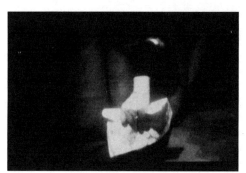

woman's arm (3.11).[6] But then Hannay "awakens" again, this time to the alarming ringing of the telephone. The repetition of the signal has an uncanny effect. When he looks out the window, he sees what he knows he must see: the two men are still there, and one is in the phone booth on the corner. This view alerts Hannay to the reality that this signal is meant for him. It announces that Annabella's nightmare is now his, that the dream into which he has awakened

3.11

is reality. These men really are out there; the man missing his little finger is real; Annabella is really dead.

If Hannay's sleep somehow allows Annabella's death, is this sleep guilty? Our initial impression is that Annabella's death is dreamed or imagined by Hannay. Then we realize that it is real. Has Hitchcock exercised his power to make reality coincide with the wish of a being who dwells within the world of the film? This is a Hitchcock film: that Annabella's murder is real counts neither for nor against the possibility that it is Hannay's projection or that it fulfills Hannay's wish. Have the Professor's agents, as it were, performed Hannay's murder for him, perhaps to demonstrate to him that he too is murderous by nature? To this must be added another possibility: that Hannay himself murders Annabella in his sleep. Perhaps Hannay possesses a murderous "inner self" of which he represses all consciousness, a self that is liberated by his sleep. (The open window does not prove that the murderer entered from "out there." And the presence of the two men on the street when Hannay looks out the window could be taken as evidence that, between the time Hannay first viewed these men and now, they have not moved.)

John Smith, in his reading of *The Thirty-Nine Steps*, sees Hannay's sleep as guilty. Annabella's death, he argues, is an expressionistic rendering of Hannay's "evil" impulses.[7] But I read this passage as reaffirming Hannay's innocence. Hannay is not the author of the reality to which he awakens, not implicated in the events that are unfolding. I take it that Hitchcock films the murder of Annabella without showing it and without giving Hannay an alibi in order that we may recognize that our belief in Hannay's innocence rests on faith and stands in need of no further evidence. Our faith in Hannay is also our faith in Hitchcock's narration, and both are vindicated by later events.

Hannay embarks on a project. It contrasts with those of the lodger and Sir John, however. For one thing, it amounts only to this, that he follow Annabella's itinerary to a town in Scotland and seek out the man she was to see. He has no further plans. He has come into possession of a fragment of a script he has not authored. The lodger's project is, at one level, the authorship of a script, one that defines a struggle against the Avenger and an internal struggle. But if the lodger's self—in the eyes of the world and in his own eyes— is at stake, Hannay's self is not at issue in his project. True, he sets out to clear himself in the eyes of the world. But he and Mr. Memory are the only witnesses we have encountered whose testimony matters, and they have already passed their judgment on Hannay, as we have. Hannay's trip to Scotland is not a spiritual journey or a rite of passage. Exempt from the struggle for selfhood, we might say that Hannay is exempt from having a self, as he is exempt from having the identity of a character. Or we might say that Hannay fulfills our dream of possessing a self that is completely secure. He has nothing to prove to himself, and he has no family, no past, no work that is real within the film, no entangling relationships, no commitments of any kind. He can face death without anguish, for he would depart from the world free of guilt, free of unfulfilled responsibilities.

Hannay owes nothing to Annabella: she died as she had lived. He would betray no one if he did not go to Scotland. Nor is his project a quest for vengeance since he has no special hatred of Annabella's killers. And he is not committed morally. Perhaps the lives of thousands depend on Hannay, but The Thirty-Nine Steps is unlike Sabotage, for instance, in that the consequences of the villain's plan are not detailed at all—the "Air Ministry secrets" are undisclosed. Also, Hannay does not come into a sense of responsibility as events unfold, as does, say, Roger Thornhill in North by Northwest or Robert Tisdall in Young and Innocent. This is not to say that Hannay remains unaffected by the events chronicled in the film. He does experience a series of awakenings. But these do not add up to a conversion: there is no article of faith he comes into or loses. He receives no edification, but then again he stands in need of none: Hannay is perfectly all right as he is.

Can we think of Hannay as undertaking to save England or the

English political system? Hannay goes on to make a speech at a political rally in which he describes the kind of world he would like to see: a world at peace, presided over by trust and human feelings. But this vision does not simply translate into support for England. After all, the English authorities also stand in Hannay's way. The film clearly sides with Hannay against his antagonist (although Hitchcock also identifies with that villainous figure). *The Thirty-Nine Steps* is silent on its alignment to the forces within the real political landscape of its time. In this respect it differs from *The Lady Vanishes*, made on the eve of the war, which through its irony calls upon England to act decisively against Germany; and from *The Saboteur*, made in America during the war, which commits itself to the struggle against Nazism.

In Hitchcock's films, Nazis are joined in a struggle to destroy all community. *The Thirty-Nine Steps* never says whether its villain is in league with others who share his vision or works in intellectual isolation (his two agents are not his equals). We might call him a "proto-Nazi," a lone prophet of the Nazi organizations of *The Saboteur*, *Lifeboat*, and *Notorious*. After the war, Hitchcock must abandon the useful figure of the Nazi. By the time of *Stage Fright* and *Strangers on a Train*, his villains have decisively fallen back on their original isolation. They know they must reconcile themselves to the death of the dream of Nazi conquest; they know their isolated murderous acts can no longer keep that dream alive.

The Thirty-Nine Steps also breaks with John Buchan's novel by not identifying the enemy as Germany. Buchan's picture of mankind allows for two races: the truly human, at best an Englishman, and the nonhuman alien, at worst a German. An extremely dedicated and crafty German might mask his alienness, given that Englishmen are prone to distraction and often take for granted that things are as they seem. But we—Buchan's novels, written in English, are by and for the truly human race—possess the power to recognize alienness if we concentrate. Once perceived as what it is, an alien trying to pass is a loathsome spectacle, and the killing of one is not murder. It must be emphasized that Hitchcock has no sympathy with this picture. (Buchan's picture of the German, of course, coincides with a certain German, and not only German, picture of the Jew; his novels are notorious for their antisemitism.) Indeed, Hitchcock's film mocks Buchan's book. Consider, for example, how he undermines Buchan's climactic unmasking scene. Hitchcock makes Hannay's antagonist a natural Englishman, not an alien (his Englishness stands out for his living among Scotsmen). Buchan's alien has eyes that hood like a hawk's. Hitchcock gives his villainous Cambridge professor a physical mark as well, but the missing little finger derides Buchan's belief that elements that defile society's purity can be recognized and destroyed. And, indeed, Hannay does not unmask the Professor; the Professor unmasks himself in a stunning theatrical gesture that catches Hannay and us by surprise. Hitchcock's Hannay, unaided, is no match for his antagonist.

Hannay is no patriot, but *The Thirty-Nine Steps* does not directly challenge the rhetoric of patriotism as do, say, *Notorious* and *Topaz*. Whether Hannay feels he owes allegiance to England is never allowed to come to an issue. The gesture by which he clears himself also saves England, and so patriots have no occasion to query his motives. Does *The Thirty-Nine Steps* at least affirm a democratic credo? To answer this question, it would be necessary to analyze in detail the speech Hannay gives at the political rally. I will confine myself here to a brief remark. The indifference of the crowd is overcome by Hannay's rousing oration, which even shakes Hannay out of his impassivity. But does this speech attain its effect by communicating an inspiring vision of community, or does his success simply testify to the power of theater, a power any demagogue could tap? Whether we take *The Thirty-Nine Steps* to endorse or mock the English political system, and whether we take it to affirm or deny the dream of community attained through reasoned conversation, depends in part on what we take Hannay's relationship to his audience to be when he delivers the speech. The performance that forges this gathering into a semblance of community at the same time isolates Hannay. As in the music hall, he is set apart from the citizens gathered. But at this moment he does not step forward from within an audience. Rather, Mr. Memory's place on stage is handed to him, and he has no choice but to appropriate it. The question of whether *The Thirty-Nine Steps* is a tribute to the myth of democracy or an affront to it, then, returns us to Mr. Memory's theater and to Hannay's calling.

There are many kinds of thriller. Some approach romantic comedy, as does *The Thirty-Nine Steps*. Others approach the horror film, as does *Psycho*. Some center on the adventures of a man seeking to complete an extraordinary project, and others on the nightmarish travails of a woman caught within a fiend's coils. Whether the thriller, in all of its forms, constitutes a true genre and whether the Hitchcock thriller is a genre unto itself are important critical issues. Perhaps at the most basic level we think of a thriller as beginning with a man suddenly and without warning plucked from an existence in which he is bound—but also protected—by all the rules and constraints of ordinary life, and thrust into a world of excitement, romance, and terror. This description holds for the Eric Ambler spy novel, but not for *The Thirty-Nine Steps*. Hannay is not plucked from the realm of the ordinary when Annabella singles him out. From the moment he enters the music hall—this is also the moment he is designated by Hitchcock's camera—he is already free from the ordinary. Hannay's original condition is freedom. In this he differs from the lodger, who is already burdened when we first encounter him with a project that makes him unfree. And even before the deaths of his sister and mother, he was bound to them. For the lodger, Hannay's condition of freedom could only be a fantasy, as it is only a fantasy to us. We acknowledge it as ours when we accept Hitchcock's invitation to identify with Hannay. The fantasy of *The Thirty-Nine Steps* begins with the fantasy that we are free like Hannay, which coincides with the fantasy that Robert Donat's grace is also our own. And it plays on the fantasy that, in a crowded theater, Annabella would single us out, asking to go home with us. But the film's fantasy is also our fantasy of possessing Hannay's calling, for which his freedom is a condition and to which he awakens as Hitchcock's design reveals itself to him. Originally, Hannay is oblivious of the reality that his world is authored and that the author has singled him out. He does not suspect that he leads a charmed life. He takes seriously every predicament in which he finds himself and performs every improvisation straight. Yet the value of his own life is not, to him, absolute. He is prepared to accept his death, should he recognize its imminence. At one level, our identification with Hannay is grounded in Hannay's awakening to his calling and his graceful acceptance of it.

Not every Hitchcock protagonist partakes of Hannay's grace. Consider, for example, Tisdall in *Young and Innocent*. Accused of a murder he did not commit, he assumes that the "someone up there" who likes him will see to it that he is vindicated. He has no compunctions about manipulating the girl of the film's title so that she falls in love with him and makes herself an accessory in his flight from the police. In the circumstances, his refusal to take his predicament seriously is self-serving and callous. We are gratified when he is chastened in the course of the film. Only when Tisdall acknowledges the arrogance of his cavalier attitude toward his own salvation does Hitchcock let him off the hook and arrange for the real murderer to be unmasked. But it is not Tisdall who effects this unmasking. In an extraordinary gesture, a masterstroke, the camera transports us "magically." We glide through the space of the Grand Hotel lobby, then through the space of the ballroom, until the camera frames a jazz band in blackface performing "No One Can Like the Drummer Man." Then the camera moves down and in until it isolates the drummer. It continues moving inexorably closer until it frames only his eye. The camera holds this framing until, unable to meet its unrelenting gaze, the eye flinches. The camera's gaze itself provokes the telltale twitch that allows us to recognize the murderer. In his despair, his drumbeat becomes so erratic that it disrupts the whole band. Finally he breaks down and laughs maniacally, giving himself away. That is, the camera provokes the murderer to unmask himself.

Hannay's next improvisation is called for right away. He is faced with the real problem of leaving the building without being spotted by the two men. Providentially, the milkman comes, cheerfully making his morning rounds. Hannay hits on the idea of borrowing his white coat as a disguise and explains his predicament. When his account meets with disbelief, Hannay is taken aback but then awakens to the need to make up a story. He asks the milkman whether he is married. "Don't rub it in" is the reply. Hannay then says that there is a married woman who lives upstairs. The intimation is that he has spent the night with her and has to escape without being observed by men planted by her suspicious husband. Saying "I was just wanting to be told," the milkman happily offers his coat and affirms their brotherhood ("You'd do the same for me some day").

Has Hannay's own disbelief simply come home to roost? But Hannay never failed to recognize the clear ring of truth: Annabella did not tell him the truth at the outset and, indeed, never told him the whole truth. The milkman's skepticism is not poetic justice. Yet there is a certain appropriateness to the story Hannay makes up. He casts himself in the same role in which Annabella cast him when she invited herself up to his flat. As I said, we do not know whether the role of "swinging bachelor" is or is not in character for Hannay. What Hannay has done is to size up the milkman. He shrewdly divines his subscription to a certain familiar myth about marriage: that marriage spells the end of freedom for a man, that it is an institution that denies men sexual gratification. No sane man from within however happy a marriage would freely choose, if he had the decision to make all over again, to exchange his freedom for the married state. Marriage makes all men brothers. They must join hands not to overthrow the institution of marriage (such a revolutionary step would be un-English) but to keep the torch of male sexual freedom burning.

From a strangely poignant shot of the milkman's pony, patiently waiting for its master, Hitchcock dissolves to the railroad station, a "TO SCOTLAND" sign prominent. Hannay is spotted at the last moment, but when the train pulls out he is safely on board, his pursuers stymied. Then the camera breaks with his perspective. A woman's head enters the foreground of the frame (3.12). A door opens in the background and she turns, opening her mouth to scream. But the sound we hear is a piercing whistle. With this,

3.12

3.13

3.14

Hitchcock cuts to a train passing out of a tunnel (3.13), then dissolves to Hannay, viewed in profile, lost in thought (3.14). The camera pulls out to place him in the company of two corset salesmen (a fourth man in the compartment, a minister, is disclosed in the next shot).

One effect of this surreal overlapping of sound and image—Hitchcock first uses this device in *Blackmail*—is to deny the reality of the separation between these places. The dissolve links the maid's discovery of Annabella's body to Hannay's imagination, as if he imagines or dreams what we have viewed; as if he is absorbed in the same scene that absorbs us, like Diana in her cell imagining her understudy's third-act entrance. Hannay's awakening to the reality of the present feels to us like our awakening as well: this transition creates the impression that whatever has happened is now behind us, as if it were a dream. Reality's momentary appearance of unreality makes all the more stunning its reassertion of itself. And Hannay's real situation is even more precarious than we might have thought. The police are convinced that he is the murderer, and his photograph is prominently displayed in the newspaper the minister is reading at this very moment.

After the clergyman leaves, the salesmen buy a paper to check on the racing results. Until they are distracted by an advertisement that announces a competitor's new line of brassieres, the only story in the paper that sustains their interest is the account of the murder. They subscribe to a mythology linked to, but distinct from, the milkman's. They take for granted the guilt of the man in whose apartment the body was found. Men desire women; certain women play to this desire, exploiting it; some men, aroused, are violent. The milkman idealizes free male sexuality, but these men view the human male as sexually depraved and the human female as predatory. And the minister's withdrawal, before his departure, into an opaque silence that reveals a personal and institutional embarrassment with the reality of human sexuality complements the salesmen's cynical hypocrisy.

Following this encounter, Hannay has his first—and decidedly unfelicitous— meeting with Pamela (Madeleine Carroll), the woman who is to become his "love interest." The train makes an unscheduled stop. Detectives come on board. Realizing that he must act quickly, Hannay looks through the window of the nearest compartment and sees a lone woman, reading (3.15). He bursts in, closes the door behind him, and says, "Darling, how lovely to see you!" There is a cut to the woman (3.16), who takes off her glasses and looks quizzical; then to a longer shot in which Hannay enters the frame, bends down, and appears to kiss her (their lips blocked from our view) (3.17); then to a closeup (3.18). Her eyes, at first wide open, almost completely close (3.19). In an insert, we see her eyeglasses slip out of her hands (3.20). A detective and then two uniformed policemen look in through the compartment window, and Hitchcock presents the clinch from their point of view (3.21). One says, "I wouldn't mind having a free meal in there," and they leave, fooled by another of Hannay's improvisations.

Hannay's intention is to present a view to the detectives whose privacy they will respect. Speaking in an urgent whisper, Hannay now throws himself on the woman's mercy. "I was desperate. I'm terribly sorry. I had to do it. Look here, my name is Hannay. They're after me. I swear I'm innocent. You've got to help me. I've got to keep free for the next few days." But hearing a click, he looks up to discover that a detective

3.15

3.16

3.17

3.18

3.19

3.20

3.21

has entered. The detective asks the woman whether she has seen a man go by in the past couple of minutes. This is a moment of suspense for Hannay and for us. The tension is broken when she says, in a hard cold voice, "I believe this is the man you are looking for."

When the stranger enters and forces himself on her, what do her widened eyes express? Does she think he is a rapist, a masher, a harmless clown? Is she spontaneously drawn to him, or is she terrified? Of course, even if she believes Hannay's story, she might feel obliged to hand him over to the authorities. Respect for the law could override sympathy for the plight of a desperate man perhaps wrongly accused. However, it is not regretfully that she turns him over to the police. Her pleasure is all too evident, and Hannay is surprised and angered by her apparent spitefulness. With a last protest of innocence, he breaks away. When the train stops on the Forth Bridge, he makes his escape.

But why is this woman so eager to turn Hannay in? The vehemence of her repudiation of him suggests that he has aroused her desire. The key to Hitchcock's presentation is the image of Pamela's face, her eyes shut as if in ecstasy, and the cut to her hands. When she relaxes her hold on her reading glasses, must we not imagine that she is transported by an erotic fantasy, that it is from a fantasy of making love that Hannay awakens her when he enters his plea? Then does she avenge herself on this man for daring to desire her or for denying desire for her? For awakening her desire or for refusing to fulfill it? In any case, her gesture is maddening. This woman stands in need of a comeuppance, a lesson in being human. If Hannay were not now desperate, he would be tempted to even the score by administering this lesson himself. One way of compelling her to acknowledge her willful inhumanity in denying his innocence would be by putting on his own piece of theater, in which he plays with a vengeance the role in which she has already cast him, in which he compels her to acknowledge her sexuality by giving her a real fright and making her fall in love with him.

Is Hannay simply innocent in this encounter? Perhaps his improvisation reveals a desire that he too fails to acknowledge. But as with all of Hannay's improvisations, there is no profit in pondering whether he chooses a role that is in or out of character. There is this asymmetry in the sequence: as Hitchcock films their kiss, he gives no sign that Hannay's desire is awakened, as he gives a sign that she has been aroused. What is unambiguous in Hannay's behavior, I have suggested, is his astonishment and outrage in the face of the woman's pleasure in turning him in. But didn't his encounter with the milkman teach him not to expect anyone to believe the truth about his plight? When the milkman failed to react in the expected way, Hannay caught on and drew on his intuitive grasp of the way men do things to come up with a happy solution. But with Pamela he is at a loss. In general, with all women Hannay runs up against the limits of his powers of improvisation.

This trying encounter is closely related to several scenes in comedies contemporaneous with *The Thirty-Nine Steps*. For example, Hannay's improvisation recalls Clark Gable's when faced with a similar problem in *It Happened One Night*, the seminal work made the year before Hitchcock's film. Under his direction, he and Claudette Colbert stage a marital row to deflect the suspicion of the detectives on her trail. This is a pivotal moment in the film: the couple's discovery of their mutual pleasure in collaborating on this piece of theater is what first transfigures their relationship. This reference precisely pinpoints the way the woman on the train fails Hannay. She refuses to allow herself to be animated by the spirit of the Gable/Colbert relationship (might we call this the spirit of comedy?). But perhaps the 1930s film with the encounter that corresponds most closely to Hannay's run-in with the woman on the train is the Astaire/Rogers *Swingtime*. Misreading an innocent gesture, Rogers publicly rebukes Astaire. The theatrical excess of her reaction gets his goat. Having no pressing piece of business to occupy him, he is free to make it his top priority to even the score, and he throws himself wholeheartedly into the task of compelling her to acknowledge both his innocence and her own desire.

When Colbert provokes Gable to teach her a lesson in humanity, it is apparent to us from the outset that it is only a matter of time before they realize that they are in love. And it is equally apparent that Astaire and Rogers will come to recognize the futility of denying that they are made for each other. But it is not in the same way apparent that, when the woman on the train spitefully turns Hannay in, they are fated for love. At this moment in the film's unfolding, we have no way of knowing what role romance and the spirit of comedy might play in this world. Pamela appears from out of the blue, like the milkman and the corset salesmen and the minister. This encounter seems to be just one of several that punctuate Hannay's journey; there is no sign that it is destined to have a sequel. When she reappears at the political rally much later in the film, also out of nowhere, it comes as a revelation that the film we are viewing might turn out to be a comedy.

A film like *It Happened One Night* opens with an announcement that it is a comedy, that love will not finally be denied (of course, we don't know what kind of comedy it is going to turn out to be; indeed, the world never before knew the genre of comedy that Capra's film inaugurates). But even when Hannay's love-interest-to-be makes her entrance, we are not apprised that romance and comedy have reared their heads. One key to the originality of *The Thirty-Nine Steps* is its juxtaposition of a romantic relationship with ties to 1930s comedies like *Bringing Up Baby*, *The Awful Truth*, and *The Philadelphia Story* with the world of a Hitchcock film, in which death, betrayal, mutilation, vengeance, madness, and terror are real threats. The crystallization of the Hitchcock thriller format in *The Thirty-Nine Steps*, the creation of a film in whose world the spirits of comedy and romance are so tardy in announcing themselves, and in which their power and efficacy are at issue, is an important development within the evolution of the genres of popular film.

And it is an equally important development within the evolution of popular literary genres such as the spy thriller. Hitchcock's film breaks with Buchan's novel, which has no romance and precious little wit. And it breaks with the Eric Ambler novel of the thirties, in which comedy is denied and romance plays a completely different role. In Ambler's *Journey into Fear*, for example, marriage belongs to the realm of the ordinary from which the protagonist is plucked. An essential element of the fantasy world into which he is thrust is its promise of an erotic fulfillment impossible within marriage. It is predictable that he meets a woman who almost succeeds in seducing him, and equally predictable that he sees through her deceitfulness just in time. When the events of the novel are over he returns, with mixed feelings, to his marriage and the only life that is real. The woman on the train awakens Hannay to a reality in which he is not the protagonist of an Ambler spy novel. Pamela is not Claudette Colbert, and she is not Annabella Smith.

The passage that follows the train escape is one of the most important in the film and among the most beautiful in all of Hitchcock's work. It begins with a series of shots of the treeless, rugged Scottish landscape, through which the solitary Hannay wends his way on foot. He comes to a crofter's hut, where he once more plays a role. Posing as a motor mechanic looking for a job, Hannay discovers that there is a newcomer to the neighborhood, a Cambridge professor. Clearly, this Englishman is the man Hannay has come to Scotland to see. But there is no way to get to the other side of the loch today. It is almost dark, and there are no boats or cars or buses. He offers to pay for a night's lodging, assuring the crofter that he can "eat the herring" and "sleep in the box bed." This promises to be a night's rest before Hannay completes his journey and meets the man who holds the key to the mystery. The crofter, John, is short of words, crafty, always thinking of ways of squeezing an extra penny's profit, puritanical, and suspicious, particularly of Englishmen. A stereotype of the Scotsman, he adds local color and his presence is somehow reassuring.

Hannay hardly endears himself to John when he mistakes his wife—at the end of the sequence we learn that her name is Margaret— for his daughter. Margaret's sweet innocence is as apparent as John's dour harshness. She contrasts equally with the cold woman on the train. As John orders her about, we have a clear and dismaying picture of their whole relationship. John leaves, and Margaret shows Hannay his bed and begins to prepare supper. When he tells her how tired he is, she asks him to sit down. It is clear that he takes comfort in her simplicity, openness, and kindness. But then a threat is revealed. There is a newspaper on the table, with some packages of food partly covering it. The reality of his situation returns to him: if there is an incriminating story in this paper too, he must keep it from being seen. Before he has a chance to see the headlines, however, Margaret moves the whole pile and begins to set the table. This means that everything Hannay now goes on to say and do has, as one of its aims, jockeying into position to get a good look at the paper.

Hannay asks Margaret whether she has been in these parts long. It comes out that she is from Glasgow and misses the cinema palaces, the women of fashion, and Saturday nights in the city. He assures her that at supper he will tell her all about the cities he has seen. But she informs him that her husband would not approve of that: John believes that it is best not to think of such places and the wicked things that go on there. Then why not talk about them now, Hannay asks. He intervenes in this couple's marriage, taking sides.

But why does Hannay's speak this way? As I read the passage, one aspect of Hannay's intention is to offer a piece of instruction. Margaret first asks whether it is true that women in the cities paint their toenails. We are overwhelmed—so is Hannay, we take it—by the poignance of this woman's innocent dreams. Hannay is amused and fascinated by Margaret, as well as grateful for her company.

And he believes that there is no evil in fashions or in movies or in a bit of flirtation, whatever John may believe. When Margaret's second question is whether London ladies look beautiful, his answer is, "They wouldn't if you were beside them." She replies, "You ought not to say that," at which point John enters. Were it not for this interruption, we could imagine Hannay going on to defend his remark. He wishes to instruct Margaret about her rights. She should not allow her husband to make her ashamed, or fearful, of her fantasies. She should not passively accept the conditions her husband has laid down. She should resent those terms and rebel.

If Hannay speaks from the heart, this is also another improvised performance. He plays the role of the sophisticated man of the world who knows the city and embodies the city's allure. He steps forward as the personification of Margaret's longing. Margaret is one of Hitchcock's girls on the threshold of womanhood. Hannay appears to her as the lodger to Daisy and Sir John to Diana. But she has already stepped into the trap of a marriage that denies her romantic dreams.

Hannay perceives that Margaret is not free. At this moment, he is—or so he believes—about to escape from his own private trap. After a good night's rest, he hopes to travel the last few miles to the Professor's house and there be delivered from his jeopardy. His teaching is, *You too can be free.* But Margaret's situation is not Hannay's. Freedom, for him, is the original condition he is about to reclaim; for her, freedom is only a dream. But does he understand this woman's situation, and does he know who he is in her eyes? Though Hannay is touched by Margaret, even as he speaks he is also intent on reaching the newspaper. Part of him stands off from her, remaining vigilant. If he is speaking from the heart, he is also distracting this woman with talk and winning her to his side so that, if it comes to it, she will not turn him in.

John enters the room on the words, "You ought not to say that," but does not immediately announce himself. We see the suspicion on his face before he asks what Hannay ought not to have said. Hannay replies evasively: "I was just telling your wife that I prefer living in town to the country." John's "God made the country" puts an end to this line of talk. Hannay asks John for his newspaper. Margaret turns on a lamp, and we see an article about the murder prominently displayed on the front page.

John asks Hannay his name—he identifies himself as "Mr. Hammond"—then asks him to put the paper down so he can speak the blessing over supper. Hitchcock cuts to John as he begins the prayer: "Sanctify these bounteous mercies to us miserable sinners." Then to Hannay, straining to read (3.22) as John's voice continues offscreen. "Oh Lord, make us truly thankful." To Margaret, who is

3.22

3.23

3.24

3.25

3.26

struck by the fixedness of Hannay's attention and looks down, following his gaze to its object (3.23). "For them and for all Thy manifold blessings." At this point Hitchcock cuts to Margaret's point of view: the newspaper (3.24). (Note the characteristic Hitchcockian joke, the "cold meat" on the top of the page.) "And continually turn our hearts." He cuts back to Margaret (3.25). "From wickedness." From her reaction, we realize that she intuits that Mr. Hammond is the fugitive accused of murder. There is a cut to Hannay (3.26), who sees that the truth has dawned on Margaret. He meets her gaze over John's words, "And from worldly things." Hannay silently mouths a plea for mercy and perhaps a protestation of innocence. An extraordinary shot of John—he faces the camera, and his eyes shift right and left (3.27)—makes it clear that he knows that a silent communication is taking place between his wife and the stranger. Hitchcock cuts back to a three-shot (3.28), as John views Hannay and Margaret surreptitiously. We know that John's thoughts at this moment hardly conform to the spirit of the prayer he speaks.

John is not wrong in thinking that an intimate communication, from which he is deliberately excluded, is taking place. And perhaps Margaret does desire Hannay. But John's suspicious na-

3.27

3.28

3.29

3.30

ture, his denial of his wife's feelings, his failure to acknowledge her innocence, and his confinement of her to keep her from temptation leave her open to Hannay's solicitation. John is a "miserable sinner" and well might he pray to be delivered from thoughts of "worldly things." Even now, he sins by regarding his wife as a possession over which he stands guard. Worldly things are not, for Hitchcock, evil. What is evil, and a source of evil, is avoidance and denial of reality. One cannot escape the condition of being human by withdrawing from the world.

Saying "Amen," John rises from the table, announcing that he forgot to lock the barn. (Again Hitchcock embeds a kind of joke in a moment of the utmost gravity. John's line invokes the countless "farmer's daughter" stories that turn on the folly of locking the barn only after the horse has been stolen.) The camera follows him outside. He hesitates, as if recognizing the portent of what he is about to do (3.29). Then he goes over to the window and spies on his wife, dreading and secretly wishing to see a clear sign of her unfaithfulness. The image of this man standing alone in the night, unable to keep himself from viewing, viewing in anguish, is one of Hitchcock's darkest and most frightful visions (3.30). To view like John, locked in the spirit of revenge, is to be damned. John's viewing contrasts absolutely with Hannay's gesture of stepping forward within Mr. Memory's audience, and with Margaret's frequenting of Glasgow's cinema palaces.

What of our own viewing? At this moment, the camera has broken away from its identification with Hannay. We share John's view of Hannay and Margaret, framed by the window (3.31). But while we comprehend John's nightmare, it is not ours. We know that Hannay is telling Margaret his story and imploring her not to betray him. The scene fades out on the image of John, his suspicious eye right on the camera (3.32), then fades in on Margaret lying in bed (3.33). She is wide awake, eyes open. Surely her thoughts are passionate ones aroused by Hannay. There is a cut to John, who is feigning sleep (3.34). The far-off sound of a car horn is heard, evocative and deeply resonant. This sound assumes a place within Margaret's romantic dream (it is the vehicle come to take them far away) and within her nightmare (it is the police, come to arrest the stranger). It is the nightmare that is real. Knowing what the sound threatens, she rises and goes to the other room to warn Hannay.

As Hannay is expressing his gratitude, John comes in on them, believing that he has caught them, as he puts it, "making love behind me back." Hannay protests Margaret's innocence of any such intention. He realizes that John does not believe him and that he has put Margaret in a difficult situation. She implores him to go. "And leave you like this? No fear!"

At this charged moment, Hitchcock performs an extraordinary gesture. He cuts to a shot with the three in the background, viewed through the bars of the back of a chair (3.35), the //// motif. With this signature shot, the author steps forward and declares the imprisonment of these people. John is imprisoned in his anguished, vengeful nature. Margaret is imprisoned in her marriage and can only dream of freedom (how can she leave her husband when his anguish is too terrible for him to bear alone and when she holds herself responsible

3.31

3.32

3.33

3.34

3.35

for him?). And Hannay is no more free to save Margaret than she is to release John from his curse.

Within this frame, Margaret says, "It's your chance of liberty." Hannay begins to argue with John. "Look here, you don't understand . . ." But he cannot finish his sentence. He had undertaken to instruct Margaret. Now he realizes that her understanding exceeds his own. What is there about freedom that this woman does not know? At this moment, it is Margaret who instructs Hannay. She helps him see that he must leave, even as she authorizes him to go. Hannay cannot free Margaret but, with her help, freedom can be within his grasp. Like Annabella Smith, she is an agent of the author, an instrument of Hitchcock's will.

The frame flickers with the glare of headlights. The car horn sounds, now loud and close: urgent, insistent, alarming. It arouses Hannay, triggering him to improvise. He hits on the idea of telling John the truth: the police are after him; Margaret knew, hence their secret communication. John believes this story, although he is not really convinced that the stranger had no intention of stealing his wife or that they were not making love behind his back. Hannay offers to buy John's silence, and John takes his money, apparently satisfied. The bargain struck, he goes out to meet the police, leaving Margaret and Hannay alone.

Margaret listens attentively to the muted voices coming from the other room. She reports that John is asking whether a reward is being offered, and predicts that he will turn Hannay in even though he accepted his money. She implores Hannay to leave at once, assuring him that John will "pray at" but not harm her. And she gives him an overcoat—John's "Sunday best"—so that he won't stand out too starkly against the landscape. Saying that he will always remember her, Hannay kisses her on the cheek and

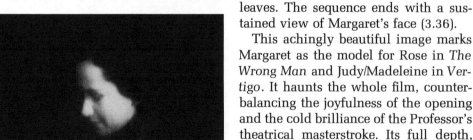

3.36

leaves. The sequence ends with a sustained view of Margaret's face (3.36).

This achingly beautiful image marks Margaret as the model for Rose in *The Wrong Man* and Judy/Madeleine in *Vertigo*. It haunts the whole film, counterbalancing the joyfulness of the opening and the cold brilliance of the Professor's theatrical masterstroke. Its full depth, however, is disclosed only retroactively. Hannay does not allow himself to question Margaret's assurance that John will do no more than pray at her. But later in the film, Hitchcock reveals the dark truth to us. Margaret tells John that she gave the overcoat to the stranger, and he savagely beats her. We do not take this revelation to mean that Margaret underestimated her husband's reaction. She knows full well that by helping Hannay she condemns herself not only to the death of her romantic dream but to violence at her husband's hand. She denies this knowledge to Hannay so that he will leave and secure his own freedom.

Thus the disquieting power of this image derives in part from Hannay's limitations. Hannay set out to instruct this woman about freedom, only to find her instructing him. We do not doubt his sincerity when he assures her that he will always remember her. But can Hannay, who lives a charmed life, really understand Margaret's gesture, which closes out her dream of freedom and accepts a hellish marriage as her fate? Can he acknowledge her passion in the way Hitchcock calls upon us to do when he gives us access to this view of Margaret and subsequently reveals its implications to us? Margaret accepts the limits of Hannay's capacity to acknowledge her when she authorizes him to take leave of her.

In the ensuing chase sequence, background music is used for the first time in the film. It combines with speeded-up motion and pratfalling policemen to parody the conventional movie chase, and shatters the gravity of the preceding passage. (The parodic chase music also reworks Mr. Memory's theme, invoking the mood of the film's opening and anticipating a later development, when Hannay will find himself unable to get the tune out of his head.)

When Hannay reaches the apparent safety of the Professor's warm and convivial home (this is daughter Hillary's birthday, and friends have dropped over after church), a second sudden shift adds to the sense of dissociation. The urbane Professor takes Hannay's abrupt arrival in stride. He assures him that they will talk as soon as he gets rid of the guests. In the meantime, "Mr. Hammond" is introduced to the party. Hannay believes that the Professor is Annabella's ally and that he will explain everything to him, perhaps recruiting him in the campaign against the ruthless agent who is missing the top joint of his little finger. This corresponds to our expectation as well. Their meeting comes exactly at the halfway point of the film. We expect the second half to be taken up with an organized search for the villain, to climax in his unmasking and apprehension. But the Professor is planning a coup: in a few moments he will reveal to Hannay that *he* is the monstrous figure who acts so quickly and stops at nothing.

The Professor is called to the door. When he returns, his hand

3.37

3.38

3.39

enters the frame and touches Hannay's shoulder (3.37). Then the camera pulls out to a two-shot. He explains in confidential tones that he has sent the police away. Switching to a public voice, he says to Hannay, "Come and look at the view from this window, Mr. Hammond. We're rather proud of it." So cued, Hitchcock gives us a view, framed by the window, of the fog-enshrouded, expressionistic landscape, the police and their dogs scurrying away (3.38). The Professor's jest in claiming authorship of this view is in anticipation of his coming coup, when it is his own hand he will hold up for Hannay to view, unmasking himself and asserting his secret identity as an author of views.

In the masterly long take that is the centerpiece of this sequence, Hannay and the Professor sit silently in the background, facing the camera, their backs to the window. In the foreground, we see the edge of Hillary's dress and part of her arm. We hear cynical banter off-screen about the thrill of having a murderer in the vicinity, punctuated by the expressive gestures of Hillary's hands, prominently displayed in the foreground of the frame (3.39). The fixed framing enforces our sense of the heartlessness of this chatter. Hitchcock does not show us any of the speakers' faces, freeing us to attend to the cutting edge of their words. And we are free to watch Hannay as he patiently endures the talk, and the Professor as he waits for an opportunity to declare the party over. It is clear that the Professor is amused by the irony of these words spoken in the presence of the ostensible murderer. The fact that the real murderer is also in the vicinity adds a level of irony we can recognize only in retrospect. Looking back, we realize that the Professor is amused that Hannay has walked into a trap and does not know it. But it is the camera's framing, the singling out of Hillary's hand, that is the cream of the jest. The Professor looks knowing, as if it were he who devised this brilliant framing and were "rather proud" of presenting it to us. Yet it is he who is the real butt of the joke. Hannay is oblivious of the Professor's design, but the Professor is no less oblivious than Hannay of Hitchcock's, which mandates Hannay's miraculous escape and the Professor's final defeat.

The Professor finally rises, saying, "There's no hurry. Still, if you *must* go . . ." The camera begins to pull out. As the Professor ushers his guests to the door, the camera continues its movement out. By the time all the guests have departed and the Professor himself disappears from our view behind the open door, the camera has traversed the whole room, whose broad expanse now separates it from Hannay, who has not moved (3.40, 3.41). Hannay has become a small figure engulfed by this space, dwarfed by the huge window and its view of the moor. "Louisa my dear, if you'll excuse us, Mr. Hammond and I would like to have a chat before lunch."

Hitchcock cuts to the door, which momentarily fills the whole frame. Closing the door, the Professor reveals himself to our view. His hand turns the key in the lock and surreptitiously palms it (3.42). We are put on the alert. Saying "Now Mr. Hannay—I suppose it's safe to call you by your real name now," the Professor walks toward Hannay. "What about our mutual friend Annabella?" The Professor's smile momentarily falters when Hannay replies, "She's been murdered." "Murdered? Oh, the Portland Mansions affair. What our friends outside are looking for you for." He turns away from Hannay and walks toward the foreground, the camera reframing with his movement. On the words, "But why come all this way to Scotland to tell *me* about it?" the Professor completely eclipses Hannay in the frame (3.43). We see, and see that Hannay does not see, the Professor give a

3.40

3.41

3.42

3.43

3.44

3.45

3.46

3.47

momentary start on the words, "I be-lieve she was coming to see you about some Air Ministry secrets. She was killed by a foreign agent who's interested too." Hannay sips his drink as the Professor turns to face him. "Did she tell you what the foreign agent looked like?" "Wasn't time. Oh, there was one thing. Part of his little finger was missing." "Which one?" "This one, I think," Hannay says, holding up his hand. "Sure it wasn't . . . this one?" On these words, the Professor holds up his hand (3.44). Then Hitchcock cuts to a close shot of the Pro-fessor's upraised hand, from Hannay's point of view (3.45). This hand, which fills the screen, is missing the top joint of its little finger.

This is *the* celebrated moment in the film. Everyone remembers it as a classic example of the Hitchcock "thrill." One need only think of the moment to recap-ture something of one's original terror and the impulse, equally strong, to laugh out loud. This time the Professor authors and presents to Hannay a view that shocks and rivets him. Showing his hand, he unmasks himself as the ruth-less and brilliant agent who will stop at nothing. When describing what hap-pens in a film, we frequently find our-selves identifying with the camera, say-ing, for example, "Now we see . . ." But the agency that presents us with *this* view cannot be thought of as "we." The view imposes itself on us, disrupting and compelling our attention. It is Hitchcock, as it were, showing his hand.

Hannay's smile freezes, his hand slowly dropping out of the frame. When he looks up to meet the Professor's gaze, he seems almost on the verge of smiling (3.46). The Professor looks expectant, a grin on his face (3.47). This grin is that of a hunter in the face of his prey. It expresses his delight at the turn of events. The Professor could not have designed a more perfect trap. He grins in appreciation of Fortune's blind genius. If the Professor's gesture unmasks him, it also claims to unmask the world. His grin declares that his hand, which bears the mark of his own nature, is also the perfect emblem for the divinity in whose place he has stepped forward. It celebrates his own brilliant gesture by which he appropriates Fortune's turns, takes them up boldly into his own design, and claims this world's authorship as his own.

The Professor's grin declares his gesture to be theater. In this sense it is reassuring, in that it disavows any wish to do Hannay harm and insists that what has happened is not real. It is an invitation for Hannay to acknowledge that his place is in the Professor's audience. The Professor holds out a hand of friendship if only Hannay will accept membership in his brotherhood, if he will affirm their natures as one and the spirit of the Professor's theater as also his own. But, of course, if this were really a world whose author is the Professor, there would be no escape for Hannay. The Professor's gesture really announces his intention to murder him, whether he returns the grin or not. The Professor's extended hand is a joke that *mocks* the helping hand of friendship. "You have come to the end of the road," it says. "You are face to face with your own murderer."

If Hannay thinks that the Professor means him no harm or offers a way out, he is the Professor's fool, a natural butt of the world's malignant joke: the Professor's grin is also a trap. For the spirit of the Professor's theater is murderous. His creed is that life has no meaning; there is no human community; nothing is of value except theatrical gestures that deny the world. The Professor's theater affirms the world's nothingness. Then does it matter at all whether Hannay grins back? Is the Professor's grin an authentic call for acknowledgment, or does it disdain such merely human needs? If Hannay returned the Professor's grin or refused to do so, and the Professor responded to that stand, both their "characters" would be revealed. But it is not in the cards that we should learn whether it is within Hannay's character to affirm the Professor's theater. As in Hannay's encounter with Annabella, a providential interruption deflects the course of events, and we never return to this moment of truth.

A thud is heard, clearly echoing the sound that startled Annabella when Hannay turned on the gas jet. In the present context, we can hear this as alluding to the sound of a gallows, hence as a reminder of the true import of the Professor's gesture (ironically, the death it really prophesies is the Professor's own, not Hannay's). It takes us a moment to recognize the sound as made by someone at the door trying to get in. The Professor's grin drops and he goes

3.48

3.49

3.50

3.51

over to unlock the door, casting Hannay —and the camera—a look of frustration indicating that he expects his impatience at the interruption to be shared (3.48).

The intrusion offends the Professor aesthetically, spoiling his exquisite performance, even as it gives the lie to the idea that he is too refined, too much the aesthete, to kill. The Professor knows that it is his wife, Louisa, who is responsible for this intrusion of vulgar literalness. His look expresses a distaste for this woman—perhaps it implies that women in general cannot rise to the demands of art—which he assumes must also be Hannay's own. Instead of opening the door, the Professor only unlocks it and then steps back to join Hannay in the region of the camera, out of the frame. By doing so, he appears to extend this stranger an extraordinary intimacy, presenting him with his secret view of his wife. She opens the door, says "Lunch is ready, dear" in an icy voice, nods, and leaves (3.49, 3.50). Yet this view is enough to "type" Louisa as a cold, overbearing woman, a nightmarish mother figure.[8]

The view the Professor shares with Hannay invites a specific interpretation of his villainy. The Professor's work is his one area of self-assertion within a sexless marriage. In the solitude of his study, he can escape from his wife and pursue his dream of possessing the world. The globe that figures prominently in several shots (3.51, for example) stands in for the Professor's wish to author the world, which is also a wish to deny it, to demonstrate its nothingness. But Louisa disdains her husband's project. When she reenters the room a few moments later, visibly impatient, the globe and the Professor's gun are

placed in contiguity in the frame, as
though they were one composite object
(3.52). Louisa glares at her husband
with contempt equal to what she feels
for "Mr. Hammond" (to whom she
clearly does not want to serve lunch).
The interpretation invited, then, is that
the Professor's traitorous schemes are
displacements of his real wish to murder his wife. But his secret wish to kill
Louisa is also a wish to do violence to

3.52

all women (hence the relentlessness of his designs on Annabella
Smith).

Viewed in this light, the Professor is a clear descendant of the
Avenger. Other interpretations of his villainy are possible, however. It must be kept in mind that we cannot simply assume that the
Professor has presented Hannay with a "true" vision of his wife.
Hannay would be a fool to assume that the Professor has really
granted him an intimacy, has exposed himself. If the Professor is
typical of Hitchcock's villains in his cool elegance, he is unique in
that his masterful manner never decisively breaks down. There is
no moment at which Hitchcock unambiguously discloses either
that the Professor is a monster with no soul or else that he is a tormented, impotent creature.

After Louisa's departure, the Professor's first words are, "Well,
Mr. Hannay, I'm afraid I've been guilty of leading you down the
garden path." Hannay replies, "It seems to be the wrong garden, all
right" (surely no Eden, although the Professor's name is Jordan and
no one wants to cross him). The Professor explains that his existence would be jeopardized "if it became known that I'm not—
what shall I say?—not what I seem." He gratuitously informs Hannay that he has already obtained the Air Ministry secrets and is
about to smuggle them out of the country. Then he makes an offer
that is no offer at all: "Supposing that I left you alone with this re-
volver?"

It is at this point that Louisa again enters. When she goes, leaving
the door ajar, the Professor asks, "Well, what do you think?" Hannay looks down and away, still not declaring himself. From his
point of view, we see the open door, which promises no exit (the
globe is again conspicuously placed in the frame). "Well, I'm afraid
you leave me no alternative." We cut to the Professor's gun, which
fires with a loud report and a burst of flame. In medium long shot,
Hannay starts, and his hand spontaneously goes to his heart. He
looks up at the camera and seems once more on the verge of breaking into a smile (3.53). Then his eyes close. The camera tilting

3.53

down with him, he falls to the floor with a thud. The screen fades to black.

This blackness signifies Hannay's death. Of course, after a moment, the narrative resumes. But when Hannay, alive, appears again on the screen, it is as if he has been reborn, his real death erased. The prayer book in the breast pocket of his overcoat—Margaret's gift to John, taken back from him, and given to Hannay—stops the bullet meant for his heart. (It is inscribed "To John from Margaret. The Lord bless thee and keep thee. Easter 1928.") Yet this gift is not a sufficient condition of Hannay's resurrection. When the gun goes off, his eyes open wide, as if in astonished recognition. But he must cap his string of improvisations by one last performance. He plays dead. What allows him to be convincing in this role, we later learn, is that at the decisive moment he blacks out.

For Hitchcock, "blacking out" requires relinquishing control, opening oneself to blackness, allowing it to flood in. And it requires that a "higher power" grant the gift of oblivion. When Hannay looks up at the camera, the blackness that engulfs the frame also represents his vision. Hitchcock blesses and keeps Hannay by granting him this "death," a glimpse of the author's power. But at this moment, when nothing appears on the screen, Hitchcock withholds his design from us. We are completely in the dark.

From blackness, the scene fades in on an empty coat hook (3.54). We hear John's offscreen voice saying "I canna find my

3.54

hymn book." Then the camera pulls back to frame John's face. We hear Margaret's voice: "Where did you leave it?" When John answers, "In the breast pocket of my overcoat," she replies gravely, "John, I'm afraid that I gave it to that gentleman who was staying here that night." John moves menacingly toward the camera, until he leaves the foreground of the frame. There is the sound of a violent blow and a cry of pain. Margaret's suffering is conveyed all the more powerfully for the fact that all views of her beating are withheld.

We pass directly to the sheriff's office, where Hannay is telling the story of his escape. Does this suggest the simultaneity of these two scenes? Does Margaret's ordeal rather take place while Hannay is, in effect, dead to the world? Margaret's exact words ("that night") rule out these possibilities and imply that it takes place some time in the future. Hitchcock breaks the continuity of his narrative to insert this reminder that the "miracle" that saves Hannay has a price. But perhaps Hannay only dreams this scene while blacked out. If the scene is dreamed, is it also real? (Again, in a Hitchcock film, it counts neither for nor against the reality of a scene that it is dreamed.) This brings us back to what Hannay sees when he looks up at the camera and blacks out. For Hitchcock calls upon us to acknowledge that John's violence and Margaret's suffering are inscribed in Hannay's glimpse of the author's power. Whether or not Hannay's vision encompasses this scene of violence, it reveals Hitchcock as surely as Hannay's miraculous rebirth does.

Then what is at stake in the second half of the film? The first half ends with the Professor's murderous act, Hannay's "death" and vision, and the author's denial of that death. This murder is only a rehearsal, but it is also a repetition; it doubles Hannay's encounter with Mr. Memory, the scene brought to a halt by Annabella's intervention. When blackness engulfs the screen, the film comes to a dead stop, and it also comes full circle. We see no way for it to go on. When Hannay survives the crisis, the world of the film is completely transfigured; the author's sovereignty and Hannay's state of grace have been unveiled. The second half of the film doubles back on the first until, at the conclusion, Hannay is back where he started. He does not continue his journey but rather retraces his steps. He does not discover and unmask the villain but finds him again and provokes him to unmask himself again. He again meets the woman he encountered on the train. And at the climax of the film, Hannay finds himself in a music hall, face to face with Mr. Memory. In his climactic replaying of this scene, which is also a replaying of his scene with the Professor, it no longer suffices to play dead. His calling originates in his spectatorship, but its fulfillment requires that he recognize the role he has been designated to play and accept that role, which in turn calls for Hannay to make the author's design his own. Hitchcock authorizes Hannay to act on his behalf, to perform the gesture that allows the film the ending he has designed for it.

The transition to the sheriff's office echoes the one from Annabella's murder to the train. It announces a new series of awakenings. Immediately following Margaret's cry of pain, Hitchcock cuts to the hymn book (3.55). The cut elides, or rather defers, an establishing shot. Hence when a man's cruel laughter resounds over our view of the book, the effect is uncanny. The laugh suggests that the

3.55

3.56

3.57

scene of Margaret's suffering has an audience that applauds John's violence, as if it were performed within the Professor's theater. When it is disclosed retroactively that this laugh is really the sheriff's—provoked by the implausibility of Hannay's story—one implication is that, whether or not he is actually in league with him, the sheriff is a natural member of the Professor's brotherhood. (The sheriff's affinity with the Professor is underscored by the presence of a globe within the frame (3.56).) It is in a world in which hatred between men and women is real, indeed ordinary, that Hannay leads his charmed life.

Hannay is irritated by the sheriff's bantering tone ("And this bullet stuck among the hymns, eh? Well, I'm not surprised. Some of those hymns are terrible hard to get through"). But only when two detectives arrive and he has Hannay handcuffed does he reveal that he has not believed a word of the story. Hitchcock cuts to the street as the Professor's two agents drive up. Suddenly Hannay leaps into view, crashing through the police station window, and another chase begins.

The camera cuts to a Salvation Army band. Hannay enters the frame from below, having fallen in with the marchers (3.57). He reassumes the place in the frame he occupied in the film's opening. "Providence" makes clear its special interest in Hannay's case. This is another celebrated moment, exemplifying Hitchcock's love of arranging coincidences as flamboyant as they are outrageously appropriate. Joining the Salvation Army parade, Hannay fittingly improvises the role of a sinner who has seen the light. Seeing a group of policemen, Hannay separates from the parade and enters a door that opens off an alley. He is met by a woman who leads him into a crowded political rally and offers him a seat on the platform. Meeting with heckling, the man at the podium steps down, and is succeeded by a meek man who swallows his words as he introduces the main speaker of the evening. At the completion of this introduction, Hannay is dismayed to find the others on the panel looking expectantly at him (3.58). He has no choice but to speak.

Hannay's speech is a parody—Hitchcock's as well as his own—of the clichés of ordinary political discourse, but its humor is enhanced by the fact that Hannay also means every word he speaks.

3.58

Ladies and gentlemen, I apologize in my hesitation in rising just now, but to tell you the simple truth, I entirely failed, while listening to the chairman's flattering description of the next speaker, to realize he was talking about me. May I say, from the bottom of my heart and with the utmost sincerity, how delighted and relieved I am to find myself . . .

Hannay's voice suddenly sinks. To this point, Hitchcock has cut back and forth between Hannay and the audience (3.59, 3.60). Now he cuts to a shot from Hannay's point of view. Pamela has entered the hall. On his words, "in your presence at this moment," she looks up and recognizes him (3.61).

3.59

Hannay is most decidedly *not* relieved to find himself in this woman's presence. Furthermore, he takes no pleasure in the thought that she could hear these words as addressed to her (they echo his first words to her on the train, "Darling, how happy I am to see you!"). As Hannay continues to speak, Hitchcock cuts back and forth between him and his view. With Hannay, we see Pamela talk to some people, disappear from view behind a curtain, and finally reappear, the Professor's men in tow.

3.60

Delighted, because of your friendly reception. And relieved, because as long as I stand on this platform, I'm delivered from the moment [the natural continuation, of course, is "of truth"] from the cares and anxieties

3.61

which must always be the lot of a man in my position. When I journeyed up to Scotland a few days ago, traveling on the Highland Express, over that magnificent structure, the Forth Bridge, that monument to Scottish engineering and Scottish muscle, I had no idea that within a few days' time I would find myself addressing an important political meeting . . .

Someone shouts out, "You meant for the moors to shoot something!" Hannay wins a laugh with his answer, "Yes, or somebody —I'm a rotten shot." Then he resumes his speech.

In support of that brilliant young statesman, that rising . . . um . . . the gentleman on my right, already known among you as one destined to make no uncertain mark in politics. In other words, your future member of Parliament, your candidate, Mr. . . . uh . . .

Hannay looks down at the poster spread out before him, hoping to read off the candidate's name. Hitchcock can aid Hannay by conjuring a Salvation Army band, but he can also make the name that has to be read upside-down "McCorquodale." Hannay pronounces it "McCrocodile," rousing the hall to robust laughter. A man shouts, "He doesn't know the candidate's name!" But Hannay's recovery is superb: "I know your candidate will forgive me my referring to him by the friendly nickname by which he is already known." One joke in this is that "McCrocodile" could be anyone's friendly nickname. Another is that members of Parliament are crocodiles. When Pamela reappears with the two men, a third joke becomes clear: she is also a deceitful crocodile.

Hannay's reaction to his realization that the game is up is a turning point in the film. Hannay joyfully launches into the body of his speech. He becomes animated the way Cary Grant does in Notorious when, in extreme jeopardy in the wine cellar, he becomes for the first time the "real" Cary Grant.

It is the spirit of the music hall that possesses Hannay, enabling his speech to turn this indifferent crowd into a semblance of community. Hannay takes his cue from Mr. Memory (this is not to say that he does so consciously) when he announces, "Now we're going to discuss some topic. What shall it be?" There are cries of "The herring fisheries!" "Unemployment!" "The idle rich!" On this last interjection, Hitchcock cuts from Hannay's view to a new setup: a slightly high-angle shot which suggests the point of view of someone in the balcony (3.62).

The idle rich? That's kind of an old-fashioned topic these days, because I'm not rich and I've never been idle. I've been busy all my life and I expect to be much busier quite soon.

In another new setup, a top hat—presumably McCrocodile's—is conspicuous (3.63), ironically suggesting that the politician they

3.62

3.63

are being asked to support is a member of the idle rich. And it casts Hannay—or perhaps Hitchcock—as a magician.

And I know what it is to feel lonely and helpless and to have the whole world against me, and those are things that no man or woman ought to feel. And I ask your candidate and all those who love their fellow men to set themselves resolutely to make this world a happier place to live in, a world where no nation plots against nation . . .

The audience has come alive. At this point, Hitchcock cuts to a closer shot of Hannay, from a low angle (3.64), and alternates this with (3.65).

3.64

Where no neighbor plots against neighbor, where there is no persecution or hunting down, where everybody gets a square deal and a sporting chance, and where people try to help and not to hinder . . .

The audience is excited now, united in approval. Hitchcock cuts to a much closer and more frontal low-angle shot (3.66). In this frame, Hannay looms larger than life, a hero. But the camera here also stands coolly apart from the crowd's fervor and parodies it. If this crowd can be aroused by a speech intended to keep them going for as long as possible, can it not be aroused by any demagogue?

As Hannay's speech draws to an end, the audience begins to applaud. Finally, all rise to give him a standing ovation.

3.65

3.66

A world from which suspicion and cruelty and fear have been forever banished. That is the sort of world *I* want. Is that the sort of world *you* want? That's all I have to say. Goodnight.

As Hannay begins to leave the stage, there is a cut from (3.67) to (3.68). He backs toward the camera, pushed by the advancing crowd. A hand enters the foreground of the frame, and after a moment Hannay's arm falls into its grip (3.69).[9] The cut to (3.68) awakens us to the reality of Hannay's situation, but he remains, as it were, in a spell. Our feeling that Hannay is entranced is reinforced by the way he backs toward the camera into the hands of the Professor's agent. The camera anticipates the entrance of the agent's hand into the frame, which then waits with the camera as Hannay completes his slow trajectory. We sense that Hannay will not look around him, will not avoid the agent's hand but will inevitably fall into its grip. It is not because Hannay is unsuspecting that he does not look around—he backs toward the camera as if hypnotized by it. He cannot literally see this hand, but it is as if he knows it is there and fatalistically allows the scene of his apprehension to be played out. At this moment, the agent's hand, the camera's prescient framing, and Hannay's will are all as one.

3.67

3.68

3.69

But no spell can survive a face-to-face confrontation with Pamela. They take up where they left off in the train compartment. "Didn't you realize I was speaking the truth in that railway carriage? You must have seen I was genuine." Pamela did misread Hannay's entrance into her life, but he does not simply ask her to reconsider her judgment. He attacks her for being blind, willful, and stupid. These attacks are understandable enough, in the circumstances, but they provoke Pamela to defend herself. Hannay's persistence in this tack, as surely as Pamela's original misreading and refusal to recant, is responsible for their becoming stuck in a ritual of attack and counterattack. And we recognize the irony in Hannay's charging Pamela with blindness when he fails to see that these "detectives" are not genuine. When he says, "An enormously important secret is being taken out of this country by a foreign agent. I can't do anything myself because of this fool of a detective . . . Has that penetrated?" Pamela's reaction is characteristic: "Right to the funnybone." But she now knows too much, and she is asked to come along as a witness.

In *North by Northwest's* art-auction sequence, Cary Grant, taking himself to have been betrayed by Eve, deliberately compromises her in Vandam's eyes, avenging himself. Hence, when he later discovers that Eve is a double agent and had no choice but to send him to a likely death, he feels guilty. By contrast, Hannay's remarks place Pamela in jeopardy, but they are fundamentally innocent. If Pamela should die, Hannay would bear no responsibility. And at this point in the film, we do not believe that Hannay or Pamela is in real danger. Hitchcock's power is superior to the Professor's, and he has revealed his intention to "bless" and "keep" Hannay. Throughout the remainder of the film, the antagonistic relationship between Hannay and Pamela is treated comically. Even this sequence ends humorously. As the foursome exits, the audience, which had settled down to the unrewarding task of suffering through the remaining speeches, spots Hannay and gives him another ovation. He waves, acknowledging their applause. This is, in the circumstances, a decidedly high-spirited gesture, and Hannay sustains his good cheer almost without a break until the end of the film.

In the detectives' car, Pamela notices that they miss the turn to Inverary. This tips Hannay off to the truth. His eyes shift back and forth (3.70). For the first time in the film, Hannay is engaged in premeditation. He is formulating the script for a production he is about to direct, with Pamela as audience. Hannay asks to see the detectives' warrant. As he expects, they refuse. He begins to whistle the tune that will run through his head until the climactic moment when he recognizes it as Mr. Memory's theme. Hannay makes this whistling part of his charade, but it also is a spontaneous expression of the

3.70

pleasure he takes in acting and the spirit that animates him. As long as he is in this mood he feels that nothing can stop him. He says, "Would you like to have a small bet with me, Pamela?" His bet is that the detectives' boss is missing the top joint of his little finger. To her astonishment, he receives a hard slap in reply. Anna-bella Smith once made a wager with Hannay. His "I win" completes the invocation of that earlier scene (and reconfirms the extraordinary tightness of the film's script).

A flock of sheep ("Ah, a whole flock of detectives!") blocks the road, and the car is brought to a screeching halt. The detectives handcuff Hannay to Pamela, saying, "As long as you stay, he stays," then leave the car to clear the road. Adding, "And as long as I go, you go," Hannay pulls Pamela out of the car with him and makes a break for it. Hannay forces Pamela under a stone bridge

and restrains her, as the men search overhead and the bleating of sheep fills the air. Then the fugitives hide under a waterfall. Warning, "One move out of you and I'll shoot," he presses something hard hidden in his jacket pocket against her body (3.71). But neither Pamela nor we ever seriously fear for her safety in Hannay's company.

Hitchcock fades out and in on the couple on the road. Hannay begins to whistle again, aggravating Pamela.

3.71

When he insists that the men after them are not real detectives, she reproaches him for his "penny novelette spy story." Exasperated, he says, "There are twenty million women on this island and I've got to be chained to you!" Then he patronizes her. "Now look here, miss. Once more, I'm telling you the truth." She replies, "The gallant knight to the rescue." She skeptically interprets Hannay's story as self-glorifying. On the other hand, her tone hardly suggests that she believes that she is, as Hannay puts it, "alone on a desolate moor in the dark manacled to a murderer who would stop at nothing to get you off his hands" (the pun, presumably, intended by Hannay as well as Hitchcock). In the middle of her reply ("I'm not afraid of . . ."), she sneezes, and Hannay takes out a handkerchief for her. This is a solicitous gesture, but at the same time he begins to get into the spirit of his murderer act. He grabs her collar and acts tough, which provokes her to say "You big bully!" and all but concede his point that he is no killer, since it is apparent that she is becoming comfortable with him. He smiles and says, "I like your pluck," but then—as if their mutual antagonism had not been exposed as a charade—he once more begins to pull Pamela along by the handcuffs and resumes his whistling (because he is enjoying himself in her company or because he knows it annoys her?).

Next there is a dissolve to the front of the Argyle Arms (3.72). (Compare this framing with the way Hitchcock frames the arrival of

Daisy and the lodger at the fateful courtyard.) Hannay stops whistling and announces that they are going in. The innkeeper's wife tells them that they have
just one available room, with one bed.
"You're man and wife, I suppose?" Hannay assures her that they are and prods
Pamela into a "yes," although she is out-
raged. The innkeeper catches Hannay's
eye. Hannay smiles, as if acknowledging that he has read his mind, and the
man grins in recollection of how it is to
be young and in love (3.73).

Our first view of the room echoes
(3.72), and gives special prominence to
the offending double bed, framed between the two in the background (3.74).
The innkeeper's wife enters with a tray.
Pamela blurts out, "I say, please don't
go!" This signals another insert of Hannay pressing something in his pocket
against Pamela's body. But the gesture
has an intimacy and an ambiguity it
lacked before. Still ostensibly threatening, it is now also reassuring. Perhaps it
even gently calls upon Pamela to respect this woman's romantic picture of
couples "terrible in love." In any case,
its intimacy testifies to how far their relationship has come, despite the fact
that, when he "confesses" that they are a
runaway couple, he squeezes her throat
(3.75) and releases his grip only when
the woman is out of earshot.

When Hannay now says, "What's next
on the program?" he registers his sense
that his life has become a music hall
show. But this remark is also directed,
jokingly but provocatively, to Pamela. It
suggests that squeezing her throat was
only part of a show and invites her to
choose whether the next act will be one
of violence or of love. Pamela's answer
is that they next get the handcuffs off:
she only wants the program to be over.

3.72

3.73

3.74

3.75

He teases her, assuring her that he wouldn't mind if she took off her wet skirt. She refuses, with a show of indignation, but does decide to take off her wet shoes and stockings. The camera tilts down to

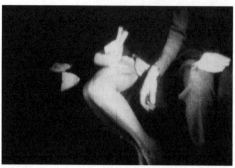

frame the memorable image of Pamela's hand slipping off her stockings, while Hannay's hand—manacled to hers— hangs limply (3.76). When the first stocking is off, his hand grabs her naked knee, and she thrusts a sandwich into it. When the second stocking is off, she takes the sandwich back, not missing a beat. Then she rises, pulling Hannay along with her, their roles momentarily reversed. When Hannay keeps his hand limp, he means to suggest that he is not

3.76

in the slightest aroused by Pamela's proximity. True, this limp hand comes to life when it touches her flesh. But its arousal does not constitute *Hannay's* making a pass. The joking implication is that Hannay is a gentleman, but his hand, aroused by the touch of a woman's flesh, acts on its own, independent of his will. When she holds out the sandwich, she joins in the charade, displaying her power to order the hand around, to keep it in its place. This hand is easily distracted and mastered.[10]

Hannay hangs the stockings by the fire, and Pamela—rather reluctantly but sincerely—thanks him. Yet Hannay cannot resist provoking her. He downs his whiskey in one gulp and pulls her to the bed: "Now, will you kindly place yourself on the operating table?" When she looks shocked, he insists that this is "Armistice Day." He reminds her that they are chained together. Her "Oh, don't gloat!"

echoes her earlier "You big bully!" but has a new gaiety. It leads to an almost openly playful exchange framed within an extended static setup (3.77). "Do you think I'm looking forward to waking up in the morning and seeing your face beside me, unwashed and shiny?" Pamela eats and Hannay again starts whistling. He wishes he could get this tune— where has he heard it?—out of his head. He yawns and Pamela remarks,

3.77

"You sound very sleepy." Hannay tells her that he last slept Saturday night, and then only for a couple of hours. "What made you wake so soon? Dreams? I've always been told murderers have terrible dreams." He mimes striking at her, and she pretends to recoil. She has begun to enjoy herself and wants him to continue. He does so, launching into a monologue: "I used to wake up in the middle of the night thinking the police were after me. Then one gets hardened. Killed my first man when I was nineteen."

He caps this story by predicting that one day Pamela will take her grandchildren to Mme. Tussaud's and say, "Chicks, if I were to tell you how matey I once was with that gentleman . . ." She suddenly turns away, and Hitchcock cuts to a new setup which sustains the ambiguity of her gesture (3.78). She complains that the handcuffs were pinching her wrists, but she may also have turned away from Hannay because she could no longer keep a straight face and did not want to give him the satisfaction of seeing her laugh. He concludes by telling of his Great Uncle Penruddy, "the Cornish

3.78

Bluebeard." Hitchcock cuts to isolate Hannay in a closeup, then slowly pulls the camera out until it frames Pamela as well. We see that she has lost a struggle to keep awake while Hannay, still absorbed in his performance, has not yet noticed that he has lost his audience. It is only when he yawns and says, "And that, lady, is the story of my life," that he sees, out of the corner of his eye, that she has fallen asleep. He smiles and the camera tilts down past their wrists to a burning candle, as the image fades out.

Freed from the ritual of attack and counterattack, Hannay can appreciate that Pamela too has been through a trying ordeal. He is satisfied that he has settled his account. His smile registers real affection. But it is also rueful: his performance put his audience to sleep before the issue of sex between them could even be broached. This beatific scene contrasts with the scene of passion the innkeepers imagine to be taking place at this moment, and the camera movement that ends this sequence parodies the conventional cutaway to signify an act of lovemaking. The candle functions like the control tower in *Casablanca*'s famous example of this convention, its phallic shape reinforcing its metaphoric status.

Hitchcock here asserts his narrator's prerogative and breaks with Hannay's perspective, interpolating a brief scene in which the Professor assures his wife, "As soon as I've picked up you-know-what I'll clear out of the country." When he kisses her, she turns her cheek to him. Her solicitude may or may not be real, but she will not allow him even the semblance of a lover's kiss. Then the scene fades out and the candle, now mostly burned down, fades in. Pamela awakens. With great effort, she succeeds in squeezing out of the handcuffs. Hannay rolls over in his sleep and places his arm across her legs. She daintily lifts the arm away, but like a cat moved in its sleep, it stubbornly returns to its chosen place. She ignores it and gathers her things to clear out, pausing only to satisfy her curiosity by reaching into Hannay's jacket pocket. She is not greatly surprised but nonetheless a little annoyed to discover that the gun

3.79

is only a tobacco pipe. Then she creeps into the shadowy hallway and looks down from the railing on the two agents immersed in a phone call (3.79). "Oh, he's gone to London already then, has he?" The innkeeper arrives with some whiskey and is sent away to get some water. Pamela opens her mouth as if to cry out but is stopped in her tracks by what she hears. "The girl handed him over to us thinking we were detectives." She listens intently to what the men say after they hang up. "He's warning the whole Thirty-Nine Steps. He's picking up our friend at the London Palladium on the way out."

The innkeeper returns, and the agents ask after a young couple. Just as it appears that he is going to give Hannay and Pamela away, his wife appears and sends the two men off. Then she kisses her "silly creature" of a husband. "You old fool, you wouldn't have given away a young couple, would you?" As they beam at each other, the camera tilts up to Pamela. She smiles upon this heart-warming scene, then makes her way back to the room where Hannay is still sleeping. She looks toward the bed. For only the second time in the film, background music starts up. Here romantic music conventionally expresses, but also gently parodies, Pamela's feelings. From her idealizing point of view, we see Hannay, sleeping like a child. She pulls the covers over him, then curls up on a divan by the foot of the bed, yawning and rubbing her arms from the cold. She sits up, looks over to the bed, looks away, visibly thinking. She comes to the conclusion that there is nothing wrong with what she is contemplating doing—she sees herself and Hannay as a couple, as if the question of sexuality between them had been resolved, as if they were husband and wife—and then pulls the lovingly tucked-in blanket from his body, wraps it around her own, and lies back down to sleep. We are still basking in the warm glow of the music as the image fades out.

When the scene fades back in, the camera pans to Hannay's face as he sits up and yawns. He gradually awakens to the fact that Pamela has slipped away as he slept. He looks up, and Hitchcock cuts to his point of view: the door to the hall, ajar. Then to Hannay's reaction, a warm smile (3.80). He smiles at Pamela's pluck in escaping from the handcuffs and at realizing that she has not, after all, turned him in. Now that he thinks she is gone from his life, Pamela is transfigured in his eyes. But his reverie of remembrance is rudely interrupted when her real voice, offscreen, says "Morning." Hitchcock cuts to Hannay's view, and we see Pamela beaming down on him (3.81). This shot retroactively discloses (3.80) to be inflected by Pamela's point of view, which means that Hannay has given his affection away to Pamela, to himself, and to the camera.

3.80

3.81

Pamela explains that she slipped out of the handcuffs during the night and was going to run away when she discovered that he had been telling the truth. This is an apology and an invitation to intimacy. He asks, in his old manner, "May I ask what earthquake caused your brain to work at last?" When she tells him about the telephone call, he becomes agitated. He starts pacing around the room, thinking out loud. When he notices that she is watching him, he returns her smile a little self-consciously. She says, "I feel such a fool, not having believed you." As Ingrid Bergman puts it in *Notorious*, she is "fishing for a little bird call" from her "dream man." He fingers the handcuffs distractedly. "Oh, that's all right." He again looks up and sees her watching him. Both are now self-conscious. She shyly looks away, as Hannay's bound hand drops out of the frame and his free hand fondles the bedpost. This is a moment of sexual tension. Pamela desires Hannay. But we cannot say whether he is straining to turn his thoughts from her to think about the Professor or straining to turn her thoughts from him to the urgent business at hand.

When she tells him that the two men left as soon as they got off the phone, the camera suddenly pulls out as Hannay steps back melodramatically. "You let them go after hearing what they said? You button-headed little idiot!" Hannay's reaction is too harsh. We sympathize with Pamela when she replies, "Don't talk to me like that!" And we remain sympathetic with her throughout the ensuing row, which ends when she angrily shouts that the current Palladium show—"Crazy Month"—should just about suit him.

Hannay acts as if Pamela means nothing to him. But perhaps the theatrical excess of his reaction expresses a feeling that it also disavows. Hannay's reaction corresponds precisely to Pamela's when she first turned Hannay in on the train. Their relationship has come full circle. It is as if this argument—so different in tone from their earlier comically antagonistic exchanges—confirms that they are now a couple, as Pamela believes. It is as if this is their first fight as a married couple, their first that could end in a reconciliation. Indeed, when they come together at the end of the film, the feeling is that of coming together *again*. But it is not as if the union marked by their taking each other's hand at the end of the film is simply a reunion. For they have not as yet even acknowledged their mutual desire.

The stage is now set for the film's great finale. But first there is a brief sequence in which Pamela talks to officials at Scotland Yard. They inform her that the Air Ministry does have a secret device England's enemies would love to get their hands on, but that they are absolutely certain that no papers are missing.[11] As Pamela leaves, she is reminded that she has not told them the whereabouts of Richard Hannay. "I haven't the faintest idea," she says, and stomps out. They have her followed.

The Thirty-Nine Steps establishes the paradigm of the grand Hitchcock finale. It improves on the ending of *The Man Who Knew Too Much*, which follows its magnificent Albert Hall sequence with an anticlimactic large-scale shootout that in turn frames the final dramatic confrontation between the heroine and her villainous enemy. *The Thirty-Nine Steps* in effect telescopes both sequences into one, pulls out all the stops, and at no point undercuts the sense of climax.[12]

As Pamela searches for Hannay, the auditorium rocks with laughter elicited by the comedy act on the boards. From the balcony, she spots him in the seats below and starts toward him, the police watching. There is a cut to Hannay, oblivious of her approach. He starts at something he sees, and we cut to his point of view: an extreme long shot of a box, empty except for a man in the corner whose hand rests on the rail. Hannay borrows a pair of opera glasses from the woman sitting next to him, and we are presented with his view, masked to register the limited field of vision of this instrument. The opera glasses—hence the camera—pan left until they frame a hand missing the top joint of its little finger (3.82). Hannay lowers the glasses and smiles.

The act of viewing defines a field of combat between the Professor and Hannay. In their first meeting, the Professor commanded Hannay's view. By framing the Professor with the opera glasses,

Hannay gains the upper hand on him. The aim of authoring the views he presents to the world is an aspect of the Professor's aim of authoring that world, which requires that he appropriate Hitchcock's power as his own. Hannay's view through the opera glasses undercuts the Professor's claim to power. When Hannay frames this view, Hitchcock allows that gesture also to effect the framing of our view. For the mo-

3.82

ment, Hitchcock allows these opera glasses to be the camera. By making this instrument available to Hannay, and by arranging for the accident that the Professor should unwittingly show his hand at the right moment, Hitchcock extends his own power to Hannay.

Yet we might well ask the Professor's old question: What does Hannay intend to do? For the second time, he finds himself in his antagonist's presence without a plan. And he is about to learn that the police still do not believe his story and are here in force, determined to apprehend him. Once again, it appears that all his efforts have landed him in a trap from which his powers of improvisation promise no escape.

Pamela makes her way to Hannay's side. He tells her that he found the Professor. When she breaks her bad news to him, Hitchcock cuts to isolate Hannay. The orchestra strikes up a new number. Hannay's smile fades. He looks down and then back up, as Pamela asks him what he is going to do. He seems to be struggling to formulate a recalcitrant thought. Suddenly the audience buzzes in anticipation, and Hannay finds himself whistling along with the music. He stiffens with excitement. "Do you hear that tune? It's that thing I couldn't get out of my head! Now I know where I heard it before. Of course! Music Hall! Annabella Sm . . ."

Hannay looks off to the left. As applause breaks out, there is a cut to his point of view, and we see the curtain rise on Mr. Memory. Our recollection floods back just when Hannay's does, as the introduction from the film's opening is repeated word for word: "Ladies and gentlemen, with your kind attention and permission, I have the honor to present to you one of the most remarkable men in the world." Hannay says, half to himself and half to Pamela, "It's the same little man!" As the intoning of the introduction goes on ("Every day, he commits to memory fifty new facts, and remembers every one of them"), Hannay looks through the opera glasses and, from his point of view, we see Mr. Memory glancing screen-right as if on signal (3.83): "Facts from history, world geography." Hitchcock cuts back to Hannay and Pamela. On the words "from newspa-

3.83

3.84

pers," he cuts yet again to Hannay's view. The Professor takes something shiny out of his vest pocket and catches the light with it (3.84): "From scientific facts. Millions and millions of them, down to the smallest details." The masked view moves left, past curtains and railings, so quickly that all we see is a vertiginous blur. Finally it rests on Mr. Memory, who nods significantly when the reflection crosses his face: "Test him, ladies and gentlemen." A cut back to Hannay as the introduction concludes with words that prefigure the solution about to dawn on him: "Ask him any question."

It is only when Pamela is told that no papers are missing that *The Thirty-Nine Steps* unveils its central enigma. How does the Professor plan to smuggle the secrets out of the country? Pamela imparts this riddle to Hannay, who must solve it. Hannay possesses all the facts he needs and must only connect the present moment with the scene that began the narrative. To make this connection, he must reclaim a memory. The opportune return of the figure of Mr. Memory enables Hannay to penetrate the Professor's scheme. At last enlightened, Hannay cries out, "I've got it! I've got it! All the information's inside Memory's head!"

But even solving the riddle does not release Hannay. As he explains the solution of the mystery to Pamela ("The details of the Air Ministry secrets were borrowed, memorized by this little man, and then replaced before anyone could find out. He's here tonight to take Memory out of the country after the show"), Hannay is informed that there are some gentlemen who want to speak to him. He rises and moves toward the detectives at the end of the aisle, as Mr. Memory asks for a question and the audience responds with the familiar mixture of real questions and heckling ("Where's the lavatory?" "When did Florence Nightingale die?" "What is the height of the Empire State Building?"). Hannay tries to tell the detectives that there is something they should know, but they will not listen ("Now look here, old man, you don't want to spoil people's entertainment"). Meanwhile, the questions go on ("What was the date of General Gordon's death?" "What is the capital of . . .?"). Suddenly Hannay breaks away, and Hitchcock cuts to an extreme long shot in which Mr. Memory's back is to the camera and Hannay is a tiny figure within the audience (3.85). This framing echoes the deep-focus frame in which Hannay originally posed a question and Mr. Memory answered it. Once again, Hannay has stepped forward to meet Mr. Memory face to face. He poses the question, "What are the Thirty-Nine Steps?" Mr. Memory momentarily looks dazed (3.86). But when Hannay's off-screen voice commands, "Come on, answer up! What are the Thirty-Nine Steps?" Mr. Memory answers the question, confirming Hannay's story in front of witnesses. "The Thirty-Nine Steps is an organization of spies, collecting information on behalf of the foreign office of . . ."

3.85

3.86

This is Hannay's greatest improvisation, by which he sees to it that a certain scene will take place. This scene is to be enacted within Mr. Memory's theater: to the people gathered in this hall, the question and answer are simply part of the show. Hannay has stepped forward to reclaim his special place within Mr. Memory's audience, and he is animated by Mr. Memory's spirit, which has possessed him throughout the second half of the film. Yet this is also a real scene of the revelation of truth, enacted before witnesses: the truth of Hannay's story, the truth about the Professor, and the truth about Mr. Memory (that he has allowed the Professor to appropriate his gift).

Our faith in Mr. Memory's innocence is not shaken by this revelation. *The Thirty-Nine Steps* no more elucidates how the bond between Mr. Memory and the Professor was forged than it explains how it came about that Margaret married John. We assume that Mr. Memory did not really know the Professor's nature, perhaps that his powers are wedded to a spirit of such purity that he is defenseless against all deceit (even Hannay, left to his own devices, is not equal to combat with the Professor), that, in his perfect purity, Mr. Memory does not really know what deceit, betrayal, or murder is. Without wishing to deny any of this, I find myself unwilling to say that Mr. Memory does not know he has been betrayed and party to betrayal. I see him as a soul in anguish, longing to be released from an oppressive burden. He knows, if only in his heart, who and what the Professor is and who Hannay is as well. His hesitation in answering this question shows that he recognizes it to be no ordinary one. I think he knows that Hannay is not an authorized agent but an enemy of the Professor; also that this is the "gentleman" he once welcomed into his audience and who once affirmed his theater. (Mr. Memory, like Margaret and the Professor, has the power to overcome Hannay's "invisibility." Could this be Mr. Memory if he were capable of forgetting Hannay?) That is, Mr. Memory chooses to answer Hannay's question, knowing it might cost him his life. Being who and what he is, he must answer truthfully, but this does not mean that he lacks flexibility. Rather, it manifests his commitment. (Would Hannay, the most flexible man in the world, do otherwise if he were in Mr. Memory's shoes?) Mr. Memory has no choice but to answer Hannay's question in the way that Montgomery Clift in *I Confess* has no choice but to refuse to answer the question posed by the prosecutor. For Clift to answer would be for him to violate his vows, to betray his calling as a priest. Mr. Memory's theater is also a kind of priesthood.

There is an act that the Professor, given his nature, likewise has no choice but to perform. Just before Mr. Memory can name the country served by the traitors, a shot rings out. He puts his hands to his heart and slumps to the floor, as the audience screams offscreen. Then we cut to the Professor in his box, a smoking pistol in his hand. The obvious suggestion is that Mr. Memory is shot to prevent him from speaking the name of the country the Professor serves. He has already said enough to validate Hannay's story, but not enough to uncover the whole of the traitorous operation. Yet it would be wrong to think of the Professor's act as the selfless one of sacrificing himself for the Thirty-Nine Steps (or the remaining thirty-seven or thirty-eight of them) or merely as an attempt to create a diversion. If he shoots Mr. Memory in his desperation to escape, the shooting is also a vengeful act. He wants Mr. Memory to feel his wrath. By answering Hannay's question, Mr. Memory declares that he places music hall, and the bond with Hannay that it grounds, above his bond with the Professor. He declares that there is a gulf between his nature and the Professor's. The Professor affirms this separation by his murderous act; he casts himself out of any community whose members, like Mr. Memory, are as they seem. In the spirit of music hall, Mr. Memory recognizes a higher power. Within the world of *The Thirty-Nine Steps*, this power is Hitchcock's. The author comes between Mr. Memory and the Professor when he invests his power in Hannay and calls upon him to step forward, animated by Mr. Memory's spirit. It is also Hannay, whose bond with Mr. Memory was forged at the opening of the film, who comes between Mr. Memory and the Professor. It is Hannay who provokes the Professor's vengeful act. The murder of Mr. Memory is real, but the Professor kills Mr. Memory in place of Hannay.

I have said that Hannay steps forward so that a real scene of revelation can take place. The truth about the Professor is revealed, and also a truth about the author's design, and about Hannay's calling. Hitchcock calls upon Hannay to perform the gesture that defeats the Professor. But Hannay's question, whether he knows it or not, cues the scene of Mr. Memory's death. In Hannay's gesture, Mr. Memory's theater and the Professor's theater come together. Then does Hannay betray Mr. Memory as the Professor does? Is Hannay also responsible for Mr. Memory's death?[13]

Hannay would be responsible for Mr. Memory's death if the Professor's act climaxed a scene of Hannay's own authorship. But does the Professor act out a role scripted by Hannay or supersede Hannay's script with his own? In addressing this question, we must note that the Professor's declaration of his own nature, addressed to Mr. Memory, is also addressed to Hannay. I take it that the Professor's gesture says to Hannay something like this: "I am monstrous. You are my double. Your will and mine are one. You too are author of this death." And if Hannay refuses to acknowledge the Professor's monstrousness as also his own, then the Professor means to say to him: "You claim to author my act? Here is *my* ending for this scene. To me, you and Mr. Memory are as one. I am your author, and Mr. Memory's death is also yours." (The Professor's murderous act is the perfect companion piece to Handell Fane's suicide.)

But the real author of this scene can only be Hitchcock. Mr. Memory and the Professor act as they must, given Hitchcock's design. Hannay also plays the role Hitchcock calls upon him to play. Hannay is, as always, free; his act is not dictated by his nature. One last time, he finds himself within a situation he did not create. I have been calling Hannay's acting "improvisation" to register that he acts freely and yet is at every moment framed. What is unprecedented is Hannay's unselfconscious acceptance of this condition, the other face of Robert Donat's graceful acceptance of being filmed. It is Hitchcock who frames Hannay's act and presides over the accidents in this world so as to sustain Hannay's original innocence. Although Hannay's improvisations lead inevitably to Margaret's suffering, the Professor's apprehension, and Mr. Memory's death, he remains exempt from the condition of authorship.

But if Hannay is not the real author of the scene of Mr. Memory's death, neither is the Professor. Does it follow that the Professor is innocent as well? Guilt, for a Hitchcock subject, cannot be separated from a failure to acknowledge the author's godlike power. The Professor is guilty for claiming to be above his world, for claiming exemption from the condition of being Hitchcock's subject. In the act of killing Mr. Memory, the Professor defiantly reasserts these claims. Of course, the Professor is no less subject to the author's power when he refuses to acknowledge that power. His hubris is integral to the author's design. When he kills Mr. Memory, The Professor kills a creature whose spirit is fundamentally opposed to his own. But knowingly or unknowingly—can we say he knows it in his heart without prejudicing the question of whether he has a heart?—he kills a being subject to conditions that are his as well. His act of murder also bears an aspect of suicide. The Professor kills Mr. Memory in place of himself.

At this climactic moment, the Professor is confronted with a vision of his own damnation. Hugging the wall of his box, he makes his way to the door. Suddenly the door opens, and he finds himself standing before the shadow of a policeman framed in the frame-within-a-frame of the doorway (3.87). This image, of course, is straight out of *Murder!*. It inscribes the Professor's nightmare vision of his fate and invokes the film frame and hence the author's agency. In this vision, Hitchcock reveals himself to the Professor, who knows he is damned.[14] The Professor jumps onto the stage. In a high-angle extreme long shot, policemen come toward him from all sides. The rear curtain opens to disclose yet more policemen (3.88). The circle swiftly closes and, with decisive finality, the curtains close off our view.

3.87

3.88

3.89

The floor manager, played by Miles Malleson, makes his way through the curtain and assures the public that there is no cause for alarm (3.89). Of all God's creatures, perhaps none comes so close as this familiar character actor—he is no less lovable for being almost chinless —to being Alfred Hitchcock's physical double. In *The Thirty-Nine Steps*, Hitchcock's ritual personal appearance —he passes by as the bus drives off bearing Hannay and Annabella to their fateful rendezvous—is particularly low-key and easy to miss. Perhaps Hitchcock is using Malleson as his stand-in.

Mr. Memory is helped backstage, and an order is put in for the "girls' introduction right away." As spirited music starts up, there is a cut to the final shot of the film: Hannay, Pamela, and a detective gather around Mr. Memory as the hast-ily assembled chorus line highsteps in the background (3.90). Hannay speaks in a respectful, affectionate voice. "Mr. Memory, what was the secret formula you were taking out of the country?" Mr. Memory looks up at his interlocu-tor. "Will it be all right me telling you, Sir?" He explains that he does not want to "throw it all away" because "it was a big job to learn it, the biggest job I ever tackled." Hannay gives his assurance

3.90

that it will be quite all right. As Mr. Memory begins his answer ("The biggest feature of the new engine is its . . ."), Hannay, the detective, and Pamela exchange glances. Mr. Memory's words vin-dicate Hannay completely and seal the Professor's fate. But they also bear the aspect of a confession. By asking Hannay for his assur-ance, Mr. Memory declares that he does not hold Hannay responsi-ble for his own imminent death. And he asks forgiveness for plac-ing Hannay's life in jeopardy. Hannay identifies himself as authorized to receive Mr. Memory's confession because he knows that it is he who must be forgiven, and whose forgiveness must be sought, if Mr. Memory is to die absolved.

The film's closing resonates with its opening. As Mr. Memory re-cites the secret formula, his powers fail. He slows down, omits words, and skips over whole sections. Yet he succeeds in reaching the end of his recitation ("This device renders the engine com-pletely silent"). Then he looks into Hannay's eyes and calls for judgment ("Am I right, Sir?"). Returning Mr. Memory's steady gaze, Hannay answers, "Quite right, old chap." The invocation of their initial encounter is complete. Indeed, Mr. Memory appears to be in a trance, appears to believe he is in his theater, concluding a triumphant performance. Hannay again affirms Mr. Memory's act, as if playing along with the illusion that nothing separates their origi-nal joyful encounter from the present grave one. But when Mr. Memory, still looking into Hannay's eyes, says, "Thank you, Sir, thank you," I take it that he suffers no illusion. He knows where he is and what has happened, and gives thanks to Hannay for releas-ing him to die in peace. On reflection, we realize that the unity of the two encounters is no illusion. For Mr. Memory's death warrant was already signed when the two first acknowledged each other. Hannay's presence in the audience shadowed Mr. Memory's theater, and it was already destined that Mr. Memory's death would finally lift this shadow. From the outset, Hannay possessed the power to grant Mr. Memory an audience. This moment brings to an end the series of Hannay's awakenings. By reaffirming their original bond and effecting Mr. Memory's redemption, Hannay awakens to his calling and fulfills it. Saying "I'm glad it's off my mind. Glad," Mr. Memory finds himself unable to go on. But he has said enough. His intimacy with Hannay is absolute. What remains to be said between them?

If Mr. Memory's death fulfills Hannay's calling, it fulfills Mr. Memory's as well. Through his death, Mr. Memory allows or authorizes Hannay's union with Pamela, as if it were his gesture of giving the bride away, bringing the film to a satisfying conclusion. As Mr. Memory slumps down, the camera pulls out and Hannay and Pamela step into the foreground of the frame, the synchronized movements serving also to block our view of the chorus line. The couple is joined in the sight of Mr. Memory's death, oblivious of the women who show their legs to an audience likewise excluded from the frame. Within this final framing, Hannay extends his hand, the

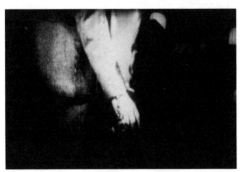

handcuffs still dangling. Pamela's gloved hand joins Hannay's just as the detective in the background rises to mark Mr. Memory's passing (3.91). Then the music cadences and the image fades out, ending the film.

In this final scene, the elements of the traditional ending of a comedy are all present, but rearranged to register a mood different from the festive one we usually associate with the union of comedy's lovers. A traditional comedy ends

3.91

with the lovers united. Society gathers to witness the public ceremony of their wedding, which culminates in a loving embrace that signifies an act of lovemaking to take place in private. Their embrace is also the signal for festivities in which all are celebrants except the melancholic ones untouched by the spirit of comedy, who have been cast out. These festivities celebrate the fertility of the lovers' union, the rebirth of society it promises, and the defeat of the spirit of melancholy.

But society does not witness or celebrate the joining of hands by Hannay and Pamela, which takes place in our view alone. Within the film's world, it is not witnessed but bears witness. The lovers have stepped back from the small circle attending Mr. Memory to join us "on the outside," witnesses to his death. Society is out of their sight as it is out of ours and attends neither to their embrace nor to the death of the little man who once won its applause. The spectacle that absorbs society—the chorus girls—is of no interest to Hannay and Pamela. The power to forge society into a community, we might say, dies with Mr. Memory. The spirit of his theater lives on only in the private union of Hannay and Pamela. The death of Mr. Memory and the union it allows close out our interest—and Hitchcock's—in this world. Our mood in taking leave of the world of *The Thirty-Nine Steps* is one with Hannay's and Pamela's as each takes the other's hand. If the casting out of the Professor is an occasion for celebration, the joy is tempered by the knowledge that he is not merely a "melancholic" but a murderer, and that it takes more than the spirit of comedy to defeat him. Mr. Memory has to die and the innocent Margaret suffer, and neither is privileged to witness the lovers' union. There is no abiding community in this world. In its absence, the lovers stand united but alone. In such a condition, the spirit of comedy and the spirit of melancholy are joined.[15]

Maurice Yacowar speaks of the union of Hannay and Pamela as tentative, insisting that they are still "disturbingly mismatched." But it is wrong to think of their union as in any way provisional. Their joining of hands is as decisive as the final embrace of any traditional comedy. It is joined as lovers that Hannay and Pamela take leave of the camera. (That their union is also a sexual one, soon to be consummated, is suggested in at least three ways. First, the slipping of hand into hand, as filmed, is erotic and also symbolizes sexual union in the manner of the wedding ceremony's thrusting of finger into ring. Second, the high-kicking chorus line declares the sexual source of society's interest in theater. And third, the final framing echoes (3.74), the view of Hannay and Pamela entering their room at the Argyle Arms, the double bed between them in the background.)

Nonetheless, Hannay and Pamela are not joined in marriage. There is no wedding—no public ceremony, witnessed and celebrated by society—to legitimize their bond. For in the world of *The Thirty-Nine Steps*, society has no authority to sanction their union. A silent joining of hands, which bears witness to Mr. Memory and to which we alone bear witness, authorizes this union in our eyes.[16]

The Thirty-Nine Steps, then, ends with Mr. Memory's death, the union of Hannay and Pamela, the Professor's damnation, and society's indifference as it turns its attention to the chorus line. But we can also say that *The Thirty-Nine Steps*, like *Murder!*, ends with a movement of the camera. In both films the camera pulls out to its final framing. When the camera moves out at the end of *Murder!*, it discloses that the lovers locked in an embrace are really on stage, acting. Their union takes place in the sight of society. But society is present not as witness and celebrant, only as audience. The camera movement at the end of *The Thirty-Nine Steps* reverses this. Hannay and Pamela are not revealed to be acting on stage in front of an audience, but are viewed by us alone. Our condition as viewers is joined with theirs as they step back to take in the moving spectacle of Mr. Memory's death. Their final embrace is no piece of theater. The camera's final gesture calls upon us to reaffirm our community with them. If we do so, we exempt ourselves from Hitchcock's indictment of the unviewed audience within the hall. We fulfill our calling as viewers.

We cannot be satisfied when Handell Fane dies unacknowledged and Sir John persists in his hubris. But though the ending of *The Thirty-Nine Steps* is not that of traditional comedy, its melancholy aspect in no way prevents it from giving us pleasure. There is justice in this world's fate. Hitchcock too must be satisfied with the fate of his subjects: the Professor's challenge to his authorship has been defeated and punished, and those who acknowledge his power have been saved. The camera's final movement in *Murder!* confronts us with our continuing failure to acknowledge the film's author. But the final gesture of the camera in *The Thirty-Nine Steps* grants us satisfaction. Why should Hitchcock not give his blessing to those who identify with Hannay, who join in affirming the author of this world?

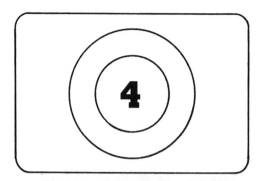

4

Shadow of a Doubt

The *Man Who Knew Too Much* and *The Thirty-Nine Steps* initiate a series of thrillers of which *The Lady Vanishes* (1938) is the most celebrated, but which also includes *The Secret Agent* (1936), *Sabotage* (1936), and *Young and Innocent* (1937).

These films are variations on the *Thirty-Nine Steps* formula. For example, *The Secret Agent* is a dark reversal in which the "innocent" protagonist is sent on a mission of killing (the plan he authors has the unfortunate consequence that an ordinary tourist dies, mistaken for the real enemy agent). *Young and Innocent* displaces our interest from its unsympathetic male lead to its female protagonist, who is played not by an adult actress, but by a real "girl on the threshold of womanhood," the sixteen-year-old Nova Pilbeam. It places this young and innocent girl within the setting of her bourgeois home, enabling Daisy's conflict between romance and family to resurface. (In this family, the father is a widower, and the daughter has younger siblings, so that she is the woman of the house.) Along with this shift, *Young and Innocent* reduces the role of the villain—he is not a theatrical genius like the Professor, but a decidedly ordinary man driven to distraction by his lover's betrayal—and makes the camera a prominent agency within the world of the film (I have already described the moment when the camera stares down the killer, provoking him to lose control and thereby to reveal his madness to the world). *The Lady Vanishes*, one of Hitchcock's most popular films, is the valedictory of the series. It is the film of the thirties that most fully acknowledges the Hitchcock thriller's roots in romance. (*The Lady Vanishes* opens with its girl/woman about to board the train that, barring a miracle, will take her to the man she plans to marry but does not really love: this is a situation that could be straight out of *It Happened One Night* or out of Shakespeare. And "Miss Froy" is a fairy-godmother who uses her magic to see to it that the true lovers are united.) At the same time, *The Lady Vanishes* takes on the aspect of a timely political allegory, unmistakable as a repudiation of England's stance of appeasement.

In this series of thrillers, *Sabotage* clearly stands apart for its emotional gravity. It traps its girl/woman within a marriage as frightful as Margaret's in *The Thirty-Nine Steps* and calls upon her to affirm her innocence by killing her husband—the film's villain—with her own hands. Hitchcock plays the violent, senseless death of her young brother—not to mention the puppy blown up with him in the bus—for suspense, forcing us to recognize that the author's capacity for cruelty equals that of his surrogate within the world of the film. It is also the thriller in the series that most emphatically declares that its real subject is film: the villain runs a movie theater, an "innocent" mask for his real calling, sabotage.

Yet *Sabotage* is not a major achievement. It does not successfully integrate its moments of horror with the theatricality demanded by the Hitchcock thriller format, which for the first time seems to constrict rather than liberate Hitchcock. This failure identifies the central problem that will come to absorb him: to discover how to give full expression to his theatricality while taking that theatricality absolutely seriously as a subject; to keep faith with *The Thirty-Nine Steps* while declaring continuing commitment to those aspects of *The Lodger* and *Murder!* that resist being encompassed by the *Thirty-Nine Steps* format; to hold his audience while acknowledging its capacity to acknowledge him.

Jamaica Inn (1939) reveals Hitchcock in a state of crisis. It is the only Hitchcock film I can hardly bear to watch. The film's violent shattering of the *Thirty-Nine Steps* mold makes clear his feeling of entrapment within the Hitchcock thriller genre. But *Jamaica Inn* makes it equally clear that he has no solution—or at least, this project offers no solution—to the problem of making a Hitchcock film that continues the *Thirty-Nine Steps* tradition while acknowledging its limitations. It was at this time that David O. Selznick invited him to America to direct a film about the sinking of the Titanic, and Hitchcock made the fateful decision to accept that offer. When the Titanic project foundered, Hitchcock began work—under Selznick's constant scrutiny—on an adaptation of Daphne du Maurier's *Rebecca*.

It is no simple matter to separate out the complex personal, professional, and artistic motives for Hitchcock's move to America or to assess what he thought it would mean to his life and work. The event raises important issues about Hitchcock's initiation into the American way of life, and the Hollywood system, represented by working for Selznick. Selznick's attention to detail was fully the equal of Hitchcock's, but their goals were completely opposite: Selznick aspired to productions so impressive, and so compellingly lifelike, that their audiences would be given no cause to meditate on the film's merely human author. Plausibility and production values were equally essential criteria in Selznick's efforts to achieve his goal, which required the effacement of all signs that would remind the audience it had access to the events of the film only through a mediator. *Rebecca* (1940), I believe, turned out to be a Selznick film that is also a Hitchcock film. But this means that Hitchcock succeeded in putting one over on the ever-vigilant Selznick, who was satisfied that what he had produced was his crowning accomplishment; and on the film industry as a whole, which awarded *Rebecca* the "best picture" Academy Award but did not recognize Hitchcock for his direction. Of course, Selznick was handicapped, in his efforts to supervise a production that would bear the imprimatur of the Selznick studio rather than the signature of Hitchcock, by the fact that he did not recognize Hitchcock's mark, did not know who the director he had hired really was. To those who know Hitchcock, his presence dominates *Rebecca* as surely as it does his British films, and as surely as the dead Rebecca dominates the world she haunts. (Indeed, *Rebecca* can be read as Hitchcock's ironic account of his experience in making the film. Like the first Mrs. de Winter, he suffers the intrusion of an interloper into his private domain. In contrast to the second Mrs. de Winter, who is acutely sensitive, despite her extreme naiveté, to every manifestation of the original lady of the manor, Selznick appears oblivious of Hitchcock's commanding presence.)

In *Rebecca* Hitchcock dons a new mask—and helps create a new myth about who he is—designed to deceive Selznick, Hollywood, and the public they pride themselves on representing. Hitchcock accepts the studio imprimatur, but ironically; and this reflects an ironic relationship to his new public and his new home. Yet it would be a serious error to suppose that it is only this new ironic distance, this alienation, that first manifests itself in *Rebecca*. For the film also clearly reveals Hitchcock's excitement at discovering the emotional weight, the sheer power, he can give to sounds and images by utilizing the sophisticated technology newly available to him. The Hollywood studio made it possible for Hitchcock to orchestrate the elements of cinematic expression to create incredibly rich and resonant emotional effects, although virtually every technique and formal device he comes to employ in his Hollywood films was already developed in his British films. Hitchcock's move to Hollywood is like Haydn's move to London: for the first time, he has a great orchestra at his disposal. It is in America that Hitchcock solves the problem of exploiting the resources of the Hitchcock thriller while addressing the meaning of its conditions. But if the original Hitchcock film is, in effect, born whole in *The Lodger*, the Hitchcock film that is also an American film does not spring into existence all at once.

Foreign Correspondent (1940) and, even more, *The Saboteur* (1942) reveal one approach that was to prove fruitful. This was to make a Hitchcock thriller that accepted America as a subject. In Joel McCrea and Robert Cummings, Hitchcock had access to two quintessentially American types (McCrea's Americanness is underscored by casting him opposite Herbert Marshall) and could experiment with the kinds of relationships his camera might develop with these American figures. The relatively bland and insubstantial

Cummings in particular—Hitchcock does not mistake him for a man cut to the measure of Robert Donat, John Gielgud, or Michael Redgrave—makes for a figure the American public can identify with or, more pointedly, Hitchcock can identify with the American public. Hitchcock takes pleasure in Cummings' obtuseness (an obtuseness that has more to do with his American propensity for the cliché than with the formal or metaphysical condition of dwelling within the world of a film).

The Saboteur is, in a sense, an Americanized remake of The Thirty-Nine Steps, and we may sense its author's amusement at the sea change. For example, Hitchcock's camera discovers the realm of the commercial everywhere in the American landscape: Cummings' love interest, played like a block of wood by Priscilla Lane, first appears to him as a picture emblazoned on an advertising billboard. And the camera repeatedly discovers that Americans have a penchant for action rather than words. The Saboteur assumes the form of a parody of The Thirty-Nine Steps, but what Hitchcock is really parodying is America and its culture, at least as it presents itself at first glance to this particular Englishman.

As in the case of Rebecca, however, the difference between The Saboteur and Foreign Correspondent and the British thrillers is not merely an increase in irony. For one thing, both American films allow their protagonists, and their viewers, to be touched more directly and more openly by the kind of horror that enters The Thirty-Nine Steps primarily through the marginal figure of Margaret. The vision of fiery death with which The Saboteur opens, for example, has no real precedent in the thirties thrillers, just as Hitchcock's British films do not quite prepare us for the moment in Foreign Correspondent in which the innocent diplomat is shot point-blank by a gun hidden in a camera.

Both Foreign Correspondent and The Saboteur amplify Hitchcock's discovery of the emotional effects that can be created with Hollywood technology. No one would seriously argue that they are major Hitchcock films, however. What they demonstrate is that, from the time of his arrival in America, Hitchcock was wrestling with the problem of making a Hitchcock film in Hollywood, the new form taken by his problem of continuing to make real Hitchcock films at all. In their own terms, Hitchcock's first American films are successful: they do satisfy an American public, and they are Hitchcock films. But they are at best stopgap solutions that leave unanswered the essential question: Can Hitchcock make a film in Hollywood that fulfills his ambitions?

Much the same can be said of Mr. and Mrs. Smith (1941) and Suspicion (1941), made between Foreign Correspondent and The Saboteur. Mr. and Mrs. Smith is usually dismissed as a misguided venture in a genre of comedy inimical to Hitchcock's work. But it is not really completely atypical. As I have argued, the Hitchcock thriller has always borne a close and complex relationship to the "comedy of remarriage" initiated by *It Happened One Night.* In *Mr. and Mrs. Smith,* Hitchcock applies his singular intelligence and sensibility to this distinctly American genre and creates a film that situates itself precisely in relationship to it, half inside and half outside its bounds, and illuminates the conditions of the remarriage genre even as it illuminates the conditions of Hitchcock's authorship. *Mr. and Mrs. Smith* breaks with, say, *The Awful Truth* by making the Robert Montgomery figure unattractive as well as immoral, and in any case decisively not Cary Grant. One consequence is that the Carole Lombard figure at times takes on the aspect of a Hitchcock girl/woman trapped in a marriage from which she wishes to escape. When the binding legal status of this marriage is "miraculously" dissolved, it is like a dream come true: the author has shown his hand in the characteristic Hitchcock manner. Furthermore, the repugnant tactics Montgomery employs to try to win her back—they culminate in his playing half-dead, raving like a madman to make her feel responsible for his suffering, although she really bears no guilt—clearly link him with the mysterious lodger figures who are obsessed with morally problematic "projects." Nonetheless, while *Mr. and Mrs. Smith* is a serious response to an American genre and is also a real Hitchcock film, it is no more a major Hitchcock work than it is a major Hollywood comedy.

Suspicion likewise is a fascinating film that keeps faith with Hitchcock's authorship without being a major achievement. Part of its significance resides in its initiation of the long-lasting and fruitful relationship between Cary Grant and Hitchcock's camera. It is also of interest for its strategy of forging, and then deliberately demolishing, a strong bond of sympathy between the Joan Fontaine figure and the viewer. But its solution to the problem of making a Hitchcock film in America—the denial of America—is again a stopgap. *Suspicion* sets its action within a conventional Hollywood-style England and fails to acknowledge the specific unrealities of that world. It fails to extend Hitchcock's satire on America to this "England" that is really an American fantasy, and it equally fails to discover the real England as a subject (as *Stage Fright* and *Frenzy* go on to do).

Shadow of a Doubt (1943) is Hitchcock's first American film that is the equal of his greatest and most ambitious British films. *Shadow of a Doubt* gives form to all he learned in Hollywood as it declares continuity with the whole body of his earlier work. It follows up on *Suspicion*'s investigation of the potentially tragic

consequences of skepticism, for example; it situates itself in relationship to American film genres, the way *Mr. and Mrs. Smith*
does; it extends the reflections on American types and American
culture begun in *Foreign Correspondent* and *The Saboteur*; and it
sustains *Rebecca*'s new mode of irony as well as its excitement in
exploring new emotional effects. In *Shadow of a Doubt*, we might
say that Hitchcock still wears his ironic mask, but he also unmasks
himself to declare that the Hitchcock film is still alive, that the man
who made *The Lodger*, *Murder!*, and the series of thrillers that
range from *Sabotage* to *The Lady Vanishes* is still dedicated to his
authorship. Rhetorically, *Shadow of a Doubt* takes the form of a
theatrical demonstration that is also a serious lesson. With this
film, Hitchcock accepts responsibility for educating a public from
whom he remains alienated. He creates a film that aspires to teach
its audience what a Hitchcock film really is.

   Shadow of a Doubt opens with an image that reappears on significant occasions throughout the film: waltzing couples, elegantly
dressed, dancing around a great ball-
room (4.1). It is over this image that the
film's title credits appear, accompanied
by strains of the Merry Widow Waltz.
This image is never placed. If the scene
of dancing is real, surely its world must
be long past, viewed through a screen of
nostalgia. If the scene is only a vision,
whose vision is it? The film's opening
raises the questions of who or what
commands the camera and what motivates the presentation of this view.

4.1

Shadow of a Doubt begins by declaring itself enigmatic, even before it announces that its projected world harbors a mystery within
it. Charles's mystery is from the outset linked to the author's gesture of opening his film as he does.

   In asserting the link between the mystery contained within the
world of the film and the mystery of the author's enigmatic presentation, *Shadow of a Doubt* returns to the strategy of *The Lodger* and
breaks with that of *The Thirty-Nine Steps*. (The dancing-couples
image specifically resonates with the picture of the lost idyll in *The
Lodger*'s flashback.) *Shadow of a Doubt* has no unproblematic, innocent figure of identification like Richard Hannay. The narration
continually raises disquieting questions about its protagonist and
about itself. But *Shadow of a Doubt* goes further than *The Lodger*
when it reveals that Uncle Charles is a killer like the Avenger, not
innocent of killing like the lodger. In turn, the female protagonist,

young Charlie (Teresa Wright), is an innocent like Daisy, but she is finally called upon to perform an act of killing with her own hands, like the girl/woman in *Sabotage*. *Shadow of a Doubt* is a complex and subtle film that bristles with paradoxes and ironies. Even more than *The Lodger* and *Murder!* and *The Thirty-Nine Steps*, perhaps, it reveals its secrets only to those who seriously interrogate it.

The titles completed, there is a dissolve to an urban panorama. The camera pans along a river and dissolves first to a closer view, panning across a junkyard; then to a city street, with boys playing ball; to a "bias shot" of a house with a "Rooms To Let" sign (the house is number 13, another link with *The Lodger*); to a window of that house. Then it dissolves "through" that window, and we discover a man lying on a bed (Joseph Cotten). He is lost in thought, and plays distractedly with his cigar, as the camera moves in (4.2, 4.3).

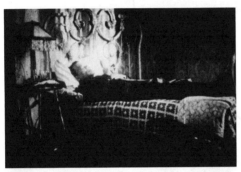

4.2

4.3

This series of dissolves establishes a milieu, urban America in decay—we later learn that this is Philadelphia, "the city of brotherly love"—that contrasts sharply with the film's Santa Rosa, California, a storybook American town. *Shadow of a Doubt* opens in the setting of the nexus of forties films that has come to be known as *film noir* (*Double Indemnity*, *Gilda*, *Out of the Past*, and so on). Part of *Shadow of a Doubt*'s originality resides in its deliberate juxtaposition of the dark world of film noir and the cheery world of sentimental Americana (Thornton Wilder is, after all, the credited screenwriter: Santa Rosa is Our Town). This juxtaposition is an extreme example of that characteristic of all of Hitchcock's films between the elements of "expressionistic" film genres (the murder mystery, the horror film, film noir) and the various forms of Hollywood romantic comedy. The film's double opening (Charles's introduction is to be repeated, almost shot by shot, in the introduction of Charlie) serves Hitchcock's insistence that a world that knows the posibility of fulfillment through romantic love and a world that knows the despair of love betrayed and love lost are subject to the same conditions and may be encompassed within a single frame. The reality of monstrousness and the possibility of redemption—even if, for some, redemption comes only through death—are equally allowed by these conditions.

This series of dissolves exemplifies Hitchcock's usual way of opening a film. The passage to the film's designated protagonist by way of a movement in, a narrowing of view, dramatizes the camera's choice of its subject. It suggests that this choice is at once arbitrary and inevitable, and provokes the question, What draws the camera—what leads the camera to draw us—to this figure? Hence it extends the declaration of the film's opening on the dancing-couples image and links the author to the mysterious figure of Charles. It is not that we can simply regard the Cotten figure as the protagonist of *Shadow of a Doubt*, since the film goes on to designate a second figure with precisely the same formality. And it is not that this first series of dissolves simply leads us to Charles. Having framed this figure lost in thought, the camera changes its direction, framing a nighttable on which rest a shot glass of whiskey, a water chaser, and a stack of money. Then the camera changes direction again, tilting down until it frames some bills that have spilled from the table to the rug.

This camera movement does not disclose the thoughts on which Cotten is dwelling. Why is this man, rolling in money, lying in bed in broad daylight in a seedy rooming house? Where has all the money come from, and why is he so indifferent to it? In introducing him in this manner—rather, in withholding a proper introduction, in presenting him to us as unknown—the camera's autonomy is asserted, its enigma declared. Charles's mystery, the mystery of the author's designation of him, and the mystery of the camera's gesture are linked.

If this were a film noir, Cotten would now begin to speak offscreen, telling the story of how he came to be reduced to despair. His narration would motivate a flashback that would occupy the film for most of its duration. But this is not how *Shadow of a Doubt* proceeds. We hear a knocking on the door that cues the film's first straight cut, and the effect is striking. The cut to (4.4) awakens us into the world of ordinary reality. It signals the beginning of a dialogue between Charles and his landlady, who has come to tell him that two men have been looking for him. She thought he did not want to be disturbed and told them he was not in. They are standing

4.4

outside now, waiting for him. Throughout this dialogue, the camera—which had so clearly asserted its autonomy by its movement to frame the money on the floor—allows its framing to appear subservient to the words and behavior of the subjects it frames, who in

turn become characters playing out a scene right from a form of "realistic" theater whose primary medium is dialogue.

Extended dialogue scenes played and filmed straight, all but unknown in Hitchcock's British films, become increasingly important
in his American work. By incorporating them into his films, Hitchcock elaborates modes of presentation that allow the camera at the
same time to mask and to declare itself (these modes include what I
have called shot/reverse-shot form and the reframing mode). The
dialectical relationship of film and theater is given a new twist.
And Charles also masks himself. In the presence of this woman, he
hides the alertness manifest in his solitary thinking. He acts like a
somnambulist, his somber voice betraying no animation. The framing of (4.4) befits a man lying in state, as if Charles were already
dead or waiting for death's release.

Charles passively suffers the woman's intrusion, but when she
notices the money lying on the floor and enters the room to pick it
up, he enacts a resigned indifference to the world ("It's funny. They
aren't exactly friends of mine. They've never seen me. Now that
they're here, I'll have to meet them. I may even go out to meet them.

But then again, I may not."). She pulls
the blinds so that he can continue with
his nap—blinds are always to be drawn
when there is a dead man in the room—
and glances back at him. As the shadow
of the lowering blind moves down Cotten's face (4.5), his eyes regain their
alertness, unobserved by the woman.
(We might compare the moment when
the lodger is "awakened" by the light
and then riveted by the sound of Daisy's
laugh.) Here the suggestion that Charles

4.5

is already dead or longs for death is refined: he awakens to darkness
like a vampire. (The idea that Charles is a kind of vampire runs
through the film. The issue of whether he can be photographed, for
example, relates to it. And when Charlie is told part of the truth
about her uncle by Saunders, Graham walks ahead with Ann, who
is told to occupy herself by telling the story of Dracula.)

On the sound of the closing door, Hitchcock cuts to a much
longer shot of the room. Alone again, Charles sits up, puts his cigar
down, and takes a drink. He looks toward the window as the music
swells. At the musical climax, he throws his glass violently against
the far wall. The violence of this gesture is stunning. It suggests
that Charles is, after all, very much alive. His display of world-
weary exhaustion and indifference was, it now appears, put on.
Equally stunning is the cool audacity with which Charles now acts.

He leaves and walks right by the two men waiting on the street corner, deliberately brushing by them, calling their bluff. Suddenly Hitchcock cuts to an extraordinary bird's eye view of a desolate expanse of city terrain. A tiny figure—Charles—turns and leaves the frame. The camera holds this framing until the two pursuers enter —the camera disdains to move, anticipating this entrance—and then go separate ways. There is a cut to another barren expanse (4.6). The two men—viewed from this height, they are tiny antlike figures—meet, evidently bewildered by their prey's disappearance. In a gesture whose audacity matches Charles's own, the camera twists elegantly to the left, spanning this cityscape and finally settling on Charles himself, in profile (4.7). Fully come to life, he surveys the scene with amusement and contempt as he puffs on his cigar. Again Hitchcock has declared a bond, itself enigmatic, between the camera and this figure, the bounds of whose power and theatricality we find ourselves unable to survey.

4.6

4.7

We dissolve to Charles on the telephone in a dingy poolhall. "I want to send a telegram to Mrs. Joseph Newton, Santa Rosa, California. 'Lonesome for you all. I'm coming out to stay with you awhile. Will wire exact time later. Love to you all, and a kiss for little Charlie from her Uncle Charlie.' That's right, that's the signature. 'Uncle Charlie.' That's right. Santa Rosa." We know that Charles goes to Santa Rosa to get away from the men who are pursuing him. But we do not know that he is not also lonesome for his family, that he is not also sincere in sending his love "and a kiss for little Charlie." We cannot plumb his real intentions or his real wishes.

Over Cotten's voice repeating "Santa Rosa, California," there is a dissolve to a panoramic view. It is as if the series of views of Santa Rosa that follows, accompanied by sunny music, illustrates Charles's private meditation on the town; or as he is presenting these pictures to us. Once more we sense an attunedness between Hitchcock and Charles.

This series of views, doubling the introduction of Charles, moves in on Charlie, lost in thought (4.8). But before we have an opportunity to wonder about her thoughts or Hitchcock's emphatic sugges-

4.8

tion of Charles's link with her, the ringing of a telephone signals a cut to the
downstairs of the house. Charlie's nine-
year-old sister, Ann, is lying on the
floor, eating an apple and reading *Ivan-
hoe*. The camera follows her as she
walks—with   comically   exaggerated
slowness, keeping her nose buried in
her book—to the phone, and pulls over
a stool so she can reach it. A telegram
has arrived.

One of the most striking features of *Shadow of a Doubt* is the
boldness with which it passes from tone to tone and mood to mood.
Such shifts are characteristic of Hitchcock, but this film exploits
them with uncommon abandon, as in this transition from a film
noir milieu to a household that could be straight out of Capra's *You
Can't Take It With You*. The Newton family is made up of lovable,
eccentric screwballs, such as precocious Ann, with her fervent dedication to literature ("I read two books a week. I took a sacred oath I
would") and belief in its literal truth ("I get everything from my
books. They're all true"). Each of the family members is, whatever
else he or she may be, a running joke. But unlike Capra Hitchcock
does not suggest that his "pixillated" family is blessed by true san-
ity that a topsy-turvy world mistakes for unreason. The Newton
family has not innocently escaped the traps set by the world, and it
does not provide safe harbor for true lovers. Charlie cannot escape
into her family or from it, just as Charles cannot. And when he
wishes, Hitchcock makes these screwballs ring true (we may sense
that he has modeled Ann on his own daughter, Pat, who appears in
several of his later films). But this does not prevent Hitchcock from
exploiting his characters as stereotypes in a satire on America: Joe
(Henry Travers) is the henpecked American father, for example.
Nor as caricatures, or emblems, of his own *coups de théâtre*: Joe's
dialogues with Herb, in which they "relax" by analyzing the latest
murder mysteries, are not designed to appear real. They are as stylized as vaudeville turns, and stop Hitchcock's show. But for Hitchcock to allow his show to be stopped by a framed piece of theater is
also for him to show his own hand. And these characters are stand-
ins for philosophical positions in a complex discourse that is, at
one level, a reflection on the film itself. Ann's faith in a literature
dedicated to romantic love is opposed by her father's understanding of literature and his practice of "literary criticism." If wed-
lock is holy in Ann's literature, in her father's it is a condition
that motivates murder. But are we to take *Shadow of a Doubt* for
Ann's kind of literature or Joe's, and what form of criticism might

be appropriate to it? Then, too, both Ann's and Joe's positions are opposed by little Roger's belief that science and logic have conquered all provinces of mystery ("Superstitions have been proven 100% wrong") and his obsessive practice of quantification ("Do you know how many steps I have to take to get from here to the drugstore? 649"). And all three positions are in turn opposed dialectically by the principles Graham articulates when he presents himself as a documentary photographer undertaking to capture the reality of the typical American family.

These characters' articulations of their contrasting world views contribute to the specific texture of the dialogue of *Shadow of a Doubt*. Debates run through the whole film that take up the issues central to the confrontations between Handell Fane and Sir John and between Hannay and the Professor. The arguments are framed within the complex discourse Hitchcock addresses to us. The words are often charged with ironic meanings of which only the viewer can be aware. The scenes involving the various family members provide counterpoint to the main lines of dramatic action. The ironies they embody are, at one level, dramatic. For example, the first words spoken by the mother, Emma (Patricia Collinge), "My those back stairs are steep," ironically anticipate the accident that is to take place, much later in the film, on those stairs. But then getting to know *Shadow of a Doubt* is partly a matter of coming to recognize how every line of dialogue is charged with multiple meanings and functions, how it participates in the film's philosophical discourse and in a system of anticipations that both serves and undermines the suspense.

I have argued that such a texture of significance is characteristic of Hitchcock's films in general. Beyond this, *Shadow of a Doubt*'s specific arguments, and its unifying system of signs and linkages, deeply embed it within Hitchcock's oeuvre. When Joe hears there is a telegram, he immediately assumes that his sister, a new driver, has caused an accident. Throughout the film, the word "accident" is highly charged: this film, as surely as *The Rules of the Game*, is about the nature of accidents (can a world authored by Hitchcock have any accidents?). The line will be echoed when Emma tells the chilling story of Charles's accident. But the resonance of the line, which is spoken with such comical casualness, goes beyond the bounds of this film: when Marnie's mother speaks of her "accident," and that word is taken up into *Marnie*'s discourse, it is a mark of the continuity of Hitchcock's work.

The character of *Shadow of a Doubt*'s dialogue, combined with the consistent brilliance of its parody of ordinary ways of using meaningful language thoughtlessly (in its rendering of the absurdities and meaningfulness of ordinary language, the Wilder/Hitchcock dialogue is worthy of Beckett), makes it eminently quotable. This film contains no line of dialogue that is merely conventional or "ordinary."

A brief exchange between Ann and her father follows. As in the exchange between Charles and the landlady, the camera masks itself, apparently depicting a scene straight out of "realistic" theater. What is realistic on stage emerges as conspicuously stagy within Hitchcock's frame, but the continual intrusion of staginess is not a

4.9

flaw. It is part of a strategy for making theater a subject of the film. Now Hitchcock cuts back to Charlie (4.9), a shot that is the mirror image of (4.4), our first close view of Charles. Like Charles, Charlie is interrupted in her solitary thinking by a knock on the door. Her father opens the door and stands in the doorway. She tells him of her despair about the state of the family ("I give up. We sort of go along and nothing happens. We're in a terrible rut"). When Joe reminds her that the bank gave him a raise last January, Charlie replies, "How can you talk about money when I'm talking about souls?" What disturbs Charlie particularly is her mother's unfulfillment ("Dinner, then dishes, then bed. I don't see how she stands it"). She proposes that they do something for her. But what? It will take a miracle. Suddenly, Emma's voice sounds offscreen, and she makes her entrance. Charlie takes out her irritability and frustration on her mother ("Oh, I've become a nagging old maid"). Then she has a brainstorm. She announces that she's going downtown to send a telegram to "a wonderful person who will come and shake us all up, who will save us." The one "right person" to effect their salvation is Uncle Charles. Emma resists this suggestion, but Charlie is insistent.

Charlie argues that, if they are to "do something for" Emma, if the family is to be "saved," what is needed is a "miracle." The coming of Charles, in answer to Charlie's call, is to provide that miracle. But what is the miracle that Charlie calls upon Charles to perform? It is all too plain that Joe has no authority or power within this household. He is sweet but ineffectual. Married to Joe, Emma can never feel fulfilled. The only "miracle" that could "save" Emma would be for a real man, one who possesses the potency Joe lacks, a man like Uncle Charles, to come to take Joe's place. And Emma's resistance to Charlie's idea suggests that she does indeed desire Charles, that he is the lover of her dreams.

But surely there is another "miracle" in Charlie's fantasy as well.

When she speaks of herself as "a nagging old maid," we are reminded that she is a young woman discovering her own sexuality, one of Hitchcock's girls on the threshold of womanhood. Will her own marriage, when it comes, be as unfulfilling as her mother's? Will the lover she longs for come, enabling her to escape the trap of a sexless marriage into which her mother stepped? When Charlie calls for Charles, she sees him as her own, as well as her mother's, longed-for lover.

At the telegraph office, Charlie learns of the arrival of Charles's wire, and marvels at the coincidence. Then Hitchcock cuts to Charlie on the street, walking toward the camera. Beaming, she says, "He heard me! He heard me!"—Does she believe that Charles has heard her call, confirming their "magical" bond? Or that God heard her prayer? To Charlie, Charles *is* divine. To us, Charles's "divinity" is his mysterious bond with Hitchcock, who arranges this miraculous coincidence in accordance with a secret design. In ironic counterpoint to Charlie's sublime assurance that the agency that engineered Charles's coming must be benign, Hitchcock dissolves from Teresa Wright's beaming countenance to a locomotive going full steam. The dissolve is sufficiently slow for us to note the momentary superimposition, which creates the impression that a monstrous engine is advancing menacingly on the unsuspecting Charlie (4.10). Then the camera reframes on the locomotive as it advances, finally holding on its grinding wheels.

4.10

There is a dissolve to the interior of this train. Then the camera moves in to frame a black curtain that shields a compartment from our view. Charles, masquerading as the sick "Mr. Otis," is behind this curtain, which serves as an emblem of his mystery and capacity for theater. (Compare the lodger, viewed through the transparent ceiling, framed with the curtain that is emblematic of his mystery.) In this brief interlude, Hitchcock makes his ritual personal appearance. Although we do not get to see his face, we have no trouble recognizing

4.11

him as one of a party playing bridge (4.11). In the midst of talk about the "poor soul" behind the curtain, a man turns to Hitchcock and says, "You don't look very well either!" Hitchcock then pre-

4.12

4.13

4.14

4.15

sents an insert, from "his own" point of view, of the bridge hand "he" holds: thirteen spades.

Hitchcock's affinity with Charles is reasserted. Both are "veiled," both appear unwell, but perhaps both really hold all the cards.

Over cheery music, there is a dissolve from the bridge hand to the Santa Rosa train station. The train arrives. As a porter helps the supposedly sick Charles dismount, Charlie runs toward him, but stops, uncertain. We cut to her point of view; then to a medium shot of Charles, who straightens up, smiles, and walks forward jauntily; then back to Charlie, who also smiles, and again runs forward reassured. A series of alternating shots ensues: Charles, smiling and walking forward, followed by Charlie, smiling and walking forward, and so on (4.12, 4.13). This alternation once more presents the two figures as matched or linked or bound to each other: each becomes the other's mirror reflection or double, as if they were but one being with two aspects.

These frontal shots with marked depth of perspective are followed by a frame devoid of foreground figures, shallow in focus, and conspicuously lacking in depth. The sudden transition to this flattened frame underscores the special significance of what is to happen within this frame.[1] Charles and Charlie simultaneously enter the frame from opposite sides. But first to enter the frame is Charles's cane—magician's wand and, like his ubiquitous cigar, emblem of his phallic power (4.14). Only then do the two human figures enter the frame and embrace (4.15).[2]

The camera moves out slightly as Joe, Roger, and Ann join Charles and Charlie in the frame. There are greetings all around and the whole group begins to walk toward the camera, which recedes before them but does not quite keep pace. One after another, the family members pass out of the frame, leaving Charlie and Charles, then only Charles. The frame to himself, he smiles with satisfaction. This virtuoso passage is followed by an equally important sequence, composed with equal care.

The car drives up to the Newton house. Emma, not yet seen by Charles, hurriedly takes off her apron and prepares herself to be viewed, the depth of her feeling apparent. Leaving the car, he looks toward the house. From his point of view, we see her wave her arms and come running down the stairs: he too has perceived her emotion. But the shot that follows, a low-angle medium shot of Charles, haloed by trees, does not in the same way reveal his feelings. On his line, "Emma, don't move," we might expect a continuity cut to a shot that again frames Charles at mid-range and has Emma join him in the frame; or a shot from Charles's point of view which frames Emma like a picture (as in the lodger's deferred view of Daisy). Instead, Hitchcock gives us another frontal shot, this one dominated by trees and devoid of human presence. Again, the human figures enter this "empty" frame simultaneously from opposite sides (4.16). But with the meeting of Charles and Charlie as precedent, we are surprised by the scale of this shot: Charles and Emma are viewed from a great distance, and when they pause they are

4.16

still very far apart. Only when Charles says, "You look like Emma Spencer Oakley of 46 Vernon Street, St. Paul, Minnesota, the prettiest girl on the block," do they run toward each other and embrace, upon which Hitchcock cuts to a closer shot, and Roger and Ann join them.[3] Ann and Roger start to walk toward the house, the camera reframing with them, and we discover Charlie, who has been standing silent all this time, slightly apart from the rest of the family, proud and happy witness to this scene that she takes herself to have authored.

But this part of the film ends on a disquieting note. Joe and Charles enter Charlie's room. Joe explains that it was Charlie's idea to have Charles stay there. Joe stops Charles as he is about to put his hat on the bed. "Superstitious, Joe?" "No, but I don't believe in inviting trouble." But when Joe leaves, Charles goes over to a photograph of Charlie on the wall. He looks at her bed, plucks a flower and sticks it in his lapel, and then tosses his hat on the bed after all.

On the movement of the hat, the camera pans left so rapidly that everything momentarily becomes a blur, until the hat on the bed is framed in a stable composition. On this framing, the image fades out to mark the end of the film's first "act." Structurally, it is like the fade in *The Lodger* on the ceiling lamp, emblem of the lodger's mystery. Tossing the hat on the bed, Charles affirms that he has lodged himself within the Newton home.

Charles's behavior has a sinister aspect. When he plucks the flower after viewing the photograph of Charlie, it is clear that he has designs on her. When he tosses the hat on the bed, violating Joe's injunction and challenging Joe's God, the clear suggestion is that Charles's designs on Charlie are sexual. But why exactly has he lodged himself in this household? What are his intentions?

It is significant that this camera movement doubles the movement from the perplexed would-be pursuers to Charles looking disdainfully down upon them. That earlier camera movement, I argued, suggested a bond between Charles and the camera. Its repetition makes a further suggestion. It is now Charles's own gesture that precipitates the camera's movement. It is as though Charles, claiming his place in this home, his domination of Joe, his willingness to take on the gods, and his possession of Charlie, also manifests a power to direct the camera. Has Hitchcock authorized Charles's appropriation of this power, or is Charles's gesture an act of hubris of an order that cannot go unpunished?

The scene fades in on the family at dinner. Charles is holding forth, ensconced at the head of the table and center-frame (4.17). "It

wasn't the biggest yacht in the world, but it had a nice little library and the bar was paneled in bleached mahogany. You pushed a button, and . . ." At this moment, Charles looks right into the camera. This reminds us that there is someone absent from the frame, sitting at the other end of the table, Charles's designated audience, in whose view he occupies center-stage. On the words, "What am I talking about? That's all over. Let's talk about you," there is a cut

4.17

to Emma, who smiles, speechless at the attention paid to her.

Emma envisions Charles as central, but his feelings toward her are unclear. At one level, he is toying with her: simply by meeting her gaze, he in effect "pushes a button, and . . ." Women are puppets who may be manipulated at will.

I hear the line "You pushed a button, and . . ." as, at one level,

Charles's reference—over Emma's head—to his own methods of operation with women. But the line has another level of reference as well and exemplifies a strategy basic to *Shadow of a Doubt*. It is also Hitchcock who refers, no doubt over the head of most viewers (which is precisely the point), to his own practices. Hitchcock pushes a button and brings the viewer, however oblivious, into focus.

Charles changes the subject. He has gifts to hand out: inappropriately, a toy pistol for Roger and a stuffed animal for Ann. A much more appreciated gift: Joe's first wristwatch. Then, for Emma: "I've two for you, Emmie. One old and one new." (There turns out to be "something borrowed" for Charlie.) The "new" is a fur stole. The "old" is a pair of photographs of their mother and father. How can we reconcile Charles's thinking about "all the old things," and his sentimental act of keeping these old photographs, with the disdainful gesture of plucking the flower and throwing the hat on the bed, and the condescending manipulation of Emma?

Charlie's "My, she was pretty!" sets the stage for the first unveiling of Charles's power to hold an audience in thrall by the sound of his voice. But as he spins out a vision of an idyllic vanished past, something else emerges as well: the ease with which his speech, steeped in poetic nostalgia, slips into a dark, brooding meditation on the fallen present. "Everybody was sweet and pretty then, Charlie. The whole world. Wonderful world . . . Not like the world today. Not like the world now. It was great to be young then. [He squeezes Charlie's shoulder.]" The truth is that the world today knows neither happiness nor beauty. The world is not what Charlie thinks it is, and she is wrong about him, wrong to imagine that his coming signifies the rule of a divinity that prizes human happiness.

Charlie takes issue with Charles, however tentatively. "We're all happy now, Uncle Charlie, look at us!" Rather than directly argue his point, Charles constructs a demonstration—or is this Hitchcock's demonstration, or one on which they collaborate?—which Charlie is incapable of grasping. He says, "Now for your present, Charlie," and we get the only shot in the sequence that isolates Charlie in the frame. As she gets up to go to the kitchen, the camera follows her. On Charlie's "I don't want another thing," a shadow passes over her (4.18). As the camera continues reframing with her movement, the shadow's source is disclosed. She passes behind Charles, whose back, startlingly close to the camera, fills the frame (4.19). The whiteness

4.18

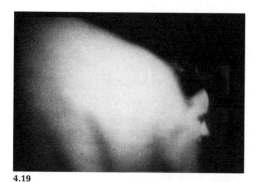

4.19

that engulfs Charlie at this moment is an image of Charlie's "present" in two senses: Charlie's present is shadowed, and she is screened from us, by Charles, and the emptiness that he stands for —he is not another "thing," he is nothingness—will be his present to her.

Charles's and Charlie's exchange in the kitchen is filmed in shot/reverse-shot mode.

I can't explain it. . . . I'm glad that mother named me after you and that she thinks we're both alike. I think we are too. I know it. It would spoil things if you should give me anything. We're not just an uncle and a niece. It's something else. I know you. I know that you don't tell people a lot of things. I don't either. I have the feeling that inside you somewhere there's something nobody knows about. . . . Something secret and wonderful and —I'll find out. We're sort of like twins, don't you see? We have to know.

It is because she takes them to be twins that Charlie wishes for no gift. She knows that there is something inside him that nobody knows about. It is her right as his twin, and indeed her duty, to come to know of this something. And of course she has this same something inside her that he has inside him. When she knows him completely, she) will at the same time know herself.

Does Charles share Charlie's belief that they are twins? If so, does he, without knowing it, really share her innocence, or does she too have darkness in her heart? Or is it that he believes that Charlie, in her innocence, represents a principle with which he is at war? We must not jump to conclusions about the bond between Charles and Charlie, or about who is destined to learn what, and with what consequences, as the narrative unfolds. One thing is clear about Charles's gift, however. With whatever irony, it invokes a specific conventional scene. Within the frame of a two-shot, Charles says, "Give me your hand, Charlie." The camera moves in as he sol-

4.20

emnly places a ring on her finger (4.20). Twins or enemies locked in struggle, they are now betrothed.

After Charlie's "Thank you," Charles points out that she did not even look at the ring. When she does so, Hitchcock cuts to an insert closeup from her point of view. We can almost immerse ourselves in the emerald's greenness, despite the fact that the film is in black and white.[4] Charlie discovers an inscription:

"TS FROM BM." Upset, Charles wants to take it back, but she won't let him ("Someone else was probably happy with this ring"). This ring becomes for us an emblem of Charles's mystery, as well as a clue. Who are TS and BM, and what was this couple's fate? How did Charles come into possession of this really good emerald, and what does giving it to Charlie mean to him?

Charlie steps out of the frame and Charles walks toward the camera. The dancing-couples image—for the half-minute or so leading up to this moment, the musical track has been invoking it—appears superimposed on his advancing figure (4.21), suggesting a link between this image and Charles's subjectivity. What Charles is really like "within" is his mystery.

4.21

The image fades out. From the dancing couples, Hitchcock cuts to the dinner table. Now Charles sits at one end of the frame and Emma at the other. Charlie is at the center, but she is small in the background and her back is to the camera (4.22). Charlie starts to hum the Merry Widow Waltz (it provokes Ann's characteristic line, "Sing at the table and you'll marry a crazy husband"). Then there is a reprise of (4.17), with Charles center-screen. The effect is to bracket everything that has occurred between—the giving of the gifts, the betrothal—and to reanchor the scene in Emma's view.

4.22

Charlie tells Joe that he wants to put $40,000 in his bank. Over the following shot of Charlie, who is still humming, Emma's voice offscreen says, "Goodness, the way men do things!" This framing, which takes in the whole scene and places Charles center-screen, gives her observation a comprehensiveness that is intrinsic to its obscurity. It sums up all she has seen and also has a curious aspect of prophecy, as if what is about to take place within her view will represent even more perspicuously "the way men do things" (I am not suggesting that Emma is consciously a prophet). But also, I hear in this line one of the author's self-references that run through the film. Emma speaks words Hitchcock gives her, and he speaks through her, referring to his own practice as this moment exemplifies it. Hitchcock's composition of this sequence is fully exemplary of that way men do things which so fills Emma with wonderment. At this level, the remark reflects what has already been screened, what is on screen now, and what is about to take place within the frame. A character's words are a medium through which Hitchcock can in effect say "Look at this!"—this means in part, "Look at me!"—without breaking his narrative discipline. With Emma's offscreen line, Hitchcock alerts us to the sequence's masterful example of his practice.[5]

Unlike Charles, Emma never claims the power to direct the camera. She remains consciously oblivious, but unconsciously attuned to the dark turns of the author's scenario, like Daisy's mother in *The Lodger*. (Perhaps this is Hitchcock's idea of the way *women* do things.) Despite her apparent absolute inability to put two and two together, her utterances repeatedly make her, in effect, the author's unconscious spokesman, and her actions the author's unconscious agent (for example, when she attempts to fix Charles up with the widowed Mrs. Potter, or when she sends Charlie out on the shopping trip that almost leads to her death). The writing of Emma's part and the magnificent performance by Patricia Collinge combine to create a figure of great originality and power.[6] Emma manifests the all but inhuman brilliance of Hitchcock's design, while giving the film emotional weight. She is both the author's creature and an individual character. As a character, she is both a precisely delineated individual and a representative of a certain type of American woman, whose belief in bourgeois American verities is absolutely sincere. Through the reality, but also the institution, of her psychological frailty, she dominates the life of the family. This oppressive domination is rendered the more maddening by her palpable innocence: she asks nothing for herself, wishes only happiness on the family. We can almost imagine that she is her brother's equal in malignancy and his superior in deceitfulness, except for the inescapability of our recognition of her innocence, an innocence that shadows the family in guilt.

The scene anticipated by Emma's remark begins with Charlie's "I can't get that tune out of my head." We know that Charles is lying when he identifies it as the Blue Danube Waltz. Hitchcock cuts from Charles to Charlie on her words, "No it isn't, Uncle Charlie. I know what it is . . ." Then there is a sudden cut to a closeup of a crystal wine glass. As Charlie's offscreen voice continues ("It's the . . ."), Charles's hand knocks the glass over. As it falls, the camera pans sharply to the left, echoing the earlier movements that suggested the camera's bond with Charles; then there is a cut to a long shot of the family in commotion. Why won't Charles allow the words "merry widow" to be spoken?

The scene that follows first broaches the subject of murder. Joe's friend Herb arrives. "You never were much on helping," Emma says to Charles as a pleasantry, adding "There now, lead a life of luxury" as she takes the newspaper out of Joe's hand and pulls away the cushion on which Herb was about to sit, giving both to Charles and at the same time driving the "literary critics" to the porch. Does Emma resent Charles for his privilege? She appears unconscious of the *possibility* of such resentment. In any case, the process, in part unconsciously directed by Emma, by which Charles appropriates the place of the head of this household is already well advanced.

The dialogue on the subject of the perfect murder is set off formally by its framing within a single static two-shot, which underscores its character as a vaudeville-like stylized set piece (4.23). Herb (Hume Cronyn) is the stereotype of the mama's boy: small, frail, slightly effeminate, lacking the capacity of effective self-assertion. We are expected, I take it, to regard Herb's obsession with murder as a displacement of a wish to commit a specific real murder he does not have the courage even to contemplate. His mother may be only "middling" but has enough life in her—or so he imagines—

4.23

to keep her son from living a life of his own. (Herb is a study for Norman Bates.)

Herb is acutely alert to the major and minor ways people put him down. His entrances are routinely treated as intrusions, and he feels slighted whenever any of his ideas is not appreciated. Since he advances them already smarting from prior slights, he feels slighted all the time. His assertions take on a hostile tone that only half conceals a desire for violence. It is perhaps above all in the original and singular inflection of Hume Cronyn's portrayal of ordinary vengefulness that his performance matches Patricia Collinge's in brilliance.

Herb's anger when Joe points out that he is confusing writing a murder mystery with performing a murder is characteristic. It also helps embed this dialogue within the film's discourse about the relationship of literature (and by extension film) and reality. On Herb's "If I was going to kill you, I'd murder you so it didn't look like murder," Hitchcock cuts abruptly to Charles, almost hidden by the newspaper he is reading. This cut suggests that something in the newspaper bears on murder. But to what murder-that-doesn't-look-like-murder does this cut refer? What murder has Charles performed or does he intend to perform? Or is this another of the author's self-references? Is it he who is planning a kind of murder, and who is to be his victim? Is it Charles, who is, after all, fated to die in what his world will remember as an accident? Are *we* Hitchcock's designated victims?

Charles plays a game with Joe's newspaper, ostensibly to entertain the children but really to give himself an opportunity to rip out a page. From Charles's hand pocketing the purloined page, Hitchcock dissolves to Charlie on the landing, standing outside the door

to her—for the time being, Charles's— room. The frame is dominated by the huge shadow she casts on the wall and the vertical shadows of the bannister (another occurrence of the //// motif) (4.24). Entering the room, Charlie tells Charles that she knows a secret. She goes to his jacket, pulls the page from the bulging pocket, and holds it up like a trophy.

4.24

Hitchcock allowed us, in the preceding sequence, to witness Charles's deception of the children. But now we, like Charles, are surprised by Charlie's revelation that she has seen through Charles's charade. Hitchcock gave us no sign that Charlie possesses such power to penetrate Charles's deceptions. Charlie's revelation triggers a violent response from Charles. As he suddenly rises, he looks right into the camera. With frightening swiftness, he walks forward ominously. Hitchcock cuts to Charles's hand violently seizing Charlie's wrist; to her anguished face; and only then to a medium two-shot that registers the passing of the moment of intense fear. Charles apologizes and says goodnight as Charlie leaves. Alone in the room, he picks up the newspaper page and folds it neatly, smiling to himself.

This is the first time that Charles directs a violent gesture at the camera. Firsthand, as it were, we feel its force. But then Hitchcock allows us this view, withheld from Charlie, which suggests the possibility that this is only an act performed by an actor who remains unmoved inside. Charles's violent gesture, perhaps only an act, becomes another clue to his mystery. This passage suggests that the locus of Charles's frightening power, hence his mystery, is his hand. Another implication may be approached through the observation that, whether or not Charles is bluffing when he frightens Charlie with this display of violence, the capacity for violence with which Hitchcock confronts us is real. (It is only in *Psycho* that Hitchcock allows this power free rein.)

A last statement of Charles's mystery concludes this part of the film. Hitchcock cuts to the exterior of the Newton house, then to Ann's bedroom (now shared by Charlie). After Ann says her prayers, the camera moves in on Charlie, the framing invoking her

mysterious bond with Charles. She
hums the Merry Widow Waltz and looks
dreamy. We take it that she is thinking
thoughts of Charles, and at this moment
Hitchcock cuts to Charles, sitting in his
easy chair smoking his cigar. As he
blows a perfect smoke ring, the image
fades out (4.25).

4.25

Charles has the same air of disdain he
had when he plucked the flower and
tossed his hat on the bed. Is Charlie, to
Charles, as insubstantial, as subject to
his will, as this smoke? Or is this smoke,
as it forms a ring, symbol of their betrothal, the medium through which
Charles's desire, not subject to the dic-
tates of his will, reveals itself? If desire
draws Charlie to Charles, does it also
draw Charles to Charlie?

4.26

The scene fades in on the exterior of
the Newton house, then dissolves to
Charles in bed (4.26). Emma comes into
the room with breakfast and a piece of
news: "You're not the only celebrity in
this town. The whole Newton family is
going to be in the limelight. A young
man called this morning. Said his name
was Graham."

Charles tears the piece of toast he
holds in his hands (4.27). Throughout
this sequence, Charles reveals himself
through his hands.

4.27

He's being sent around the country by some sort of institute or committee
or something and is supposed to pick representative American families and
ask them questions. It's kind of a poll. It's called the "National Public Survey." He said he wanted a typical American family. I told him we weren't a
typical American family. He's going to take our pictures too.

Charles's response renders Emma speechless. Wagging his knife
at her, he says, "Emmie, women are fools. They'd fall for anything.
Why expose the family to a couple of snoopers?" (It is obvious to us
that Charles takes Graham to be on his trail.) When Charlie arrives,
Charles tells her how Emma "made the Newton family into all-
American suckers." As Charles cuts his food in the foreground of

the frame and listens intently while Emma protests that "As Mr. Graham told it, it wasn't that way at all; it's our duty as citizens," Charlie intervenes on her mother's side. She points out how it would be a chance to have a free photograph made. When Charles insists that he's never been photographed in his life and doesn't want to be, Emma says, "I had a photograph of you. I gave it to Charlie. I guess you've forgotten."

Charles prides himself on being the man who has never been photographed and on being the man who remembers all the old things. This forgotten photograph chal-

4.28

lenges his understanding of who he is. To mark the occasion, Hitchcock reframes to a three-shot with Charles in profile and in shadow and the two women standing in the background behind him (4.28); then cuts to an insert of a photograph of Charles—that is, of Joseph Cotten—as a child (4.29); then cuts back.

Charles is placed in a passive position, stripped of his power, forced to endure Emma's story in silence. "It was taken the Christmas before you got your bicycle. Just before your accident." On the charged word "accident," Charles looks down, visibly uncomfortable. Charlie chimes in, "Uncle Charlie, you were beautiful!" "And such a quiet boy, always reading. I always said papa never should have bought you that bicycle. You didn't know how to handle it."

4.29

It is the father who is to blame: Emma no more respects her own father's authority than Charlie's father's. She now begins to speak of Charles in the third person, as though he were not in the room. Her speech rolls back the years: Charles becomes once more the "baby" dominated by the women in his life. As Emma's story unfolds, it becomes more and more painful for Charles to listen, while the palpable relish with which she throws herself into her narrative grows. Charles may possess the power to shatter Emma's composure with frightening ease, but she has her ways of digging beneath his skin. Her pleasure is innocent, yet it is also cruel, as she recollects Charles's bygone suffering and makes him relive it.

Charlie, he took it right out on the icy road and skidded into a streetcar. He fractured his skull. And he was laid up so long. And then—when he was

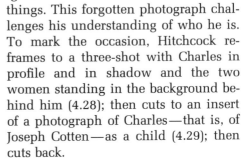
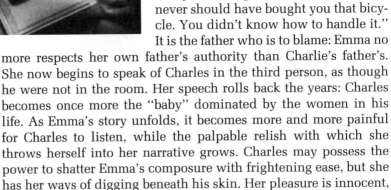

getting well, there was no holding him. It was just as though all the rest he had was, well, too much for him, and he had to get into mischief to blow off steam. He didn't do too much reading after that, let me tell you. It was taken the very day he had his accident. And then a few days later, when the pictures came home, how mama cried. She wondered if he'd ever look the same. She wondered if he'd ever *be* the same.

Finally, Charles speaks. "What's the use of looking backward? What's the use of looking ahead? Today's the thing." But Emma has the last word. "Then you'd better finish your breakfast and get down to the bank." As the two women leave, Hitchcock reframes to a frontal shot of Charles, who sips his coffee, expressionless, his mystery intact. (Does Hitchcock take Emma's story to be a serious account of what causes some people to become murderers? Emma's understanding of Charles's case and her way of telling his story are not Hitchcock's. Charles's condition cannot be reduced to complications of a skull fracture. What Hitchcock does take seriously in Emma's narration is the idea of the accident. In the world of *Shadow of a Doubt*, over which he presides, a man's nature cannot be separated from the accidents that befall him.)

Charles, sportily dressed in a smart suit with a flower in his lapel, a bold tie, and a Panama hat, walks down the street, arm in arm with Charlie. They pass two of her friends, who are obviously bursting with curiosity and envy, then enter the bank. In the lobby, Charles jokes out loud about embezzlement ("We all know what banks are"). People stare, and Joe cautions him not to joke about money in front of his boss, Mr. Green. Charles replies, "$40,000 is no joke, not to him, I bet. It's a joke to me. The whole world is a joke to me." They follow Joe into Mr. Green's office, where Charles says that he thought he would put some of his "loose cash away for safekeeping." When Mr. Green questions the wisdom of carrying so much cash around, Charles replies, "I guess heaven takes care of fools and scoundrels." Mr. Green nods slightly in agreement but he is distracted; he can't take his eyes away from all that money just beyond the corner of the frame, and he doesn't want to disagree with Charles. Of course, we take it that part of Charles's motivation in speaking this cynical homily is his assessment that Mr. Green is the embodiment of folly and a scoundrel to boot. In the manner of his acquiescence, Mr. Green unwittingly confirms that Charles has gauged Mr. Green's hypocrisy perfectly. His comtempt—it is, surely, also ours—for the spectacle of Mr. Green is absolute.

As Mr. Green hands Charles a deposit slip, Joe turns his gaze from his boss and looks right at the camera (4.30). Charles says, "Ah details—I'm glad to see that you're a man who understands details, Mr. Green. They're most important to me. Most important.

4.30

4.31

4.32

4.33

All the little details." Hitchcock then cuts to Charles, with Charlie looking on in the background (4.31). I take this view to be Joe's, with the implication that, when Joe looked at the camera in the preceding shot, he was looking at Charles. This in turn suggests that Joe has become attuned to Charles's contemptuous view of Mr. Green. Charles is, but Mr. Green really is not, a man who, in his concern for large matters, truly recognizes the importance of details. For Hitchcock too, "all the little details" are "most important." This cut is another example of Hitchcock's inscribing self-reference in a detail, and it signals that a consummate example of the author's mastery over detail is imminent. A woman's voice suddenly sounds offscreen. On the words, "Oh dear," Charlie turns screen-left. Almost immediately, Charles also turns. Spurred by his turning, the camera quickly pans to the left (this is the panning movement regularly associated with Charles's power) to place two middle-aged women with him in the frame (4.32). One looks past him, presumably to Mr. Green; the other looks right at Charles. The camera then pulls back to reincorporate Charlie into the frame (4.33). She makes the introductions. "Mrs. Green," Charles repeats, nodding to the first woman. Hitchcock then cuts to a new angle, which reverses the positions of Charles and Charlie, who is now framed between Charles and the second woman, Mrs. Potter, and is witness to their exchange (4.34).

Mrs. Potter's jeweled handbag glitters, and she has assumed a theatrical pose.[7] Charles nods. "Miss Potter." She corrects him. "Mrs. Potter." With charm, he replies, "Something about you made me think . . ." Eager to hear the flattering end of this sentence, she prods him. "Yes?" But Mr. Green's annoyed voice leaves that wish dangling. "What do you want, Margaret?" "We were shopping and I only had five dollars so I . . . ." Mrs. Potter cuts in to remark to Charles that an advantage of being a widow is that you don't have to ask your husband for money. (Mrs. Potter has no intention of allowing this eligible man to believe that she is unavailable or could not afford to keep him in style.)

4.34

At the door of Mr. Green's office, Charles speaks a mischievous exit line: "Oh Joe, keep your eyes open. You may have his job in a couple of years." Mr. Green and Joe stand frozen in the frame. But before Joe exits, he raises his eyebrows as though reflecting on Charles's words. For a moment, he even walks with his nose in the air. Then he makes up his mind to act as though Charles's words made no impression on him, although at least for this moment his eyes have been opened. The image fades out.

The scene fades in on two men in a car parked by the Newton house. One says, "Here he is," and Hitchcock cuts to their point of view, as Charles and Charlie approach the house, not seeing them. Within the frame of an objective shot, Charlie gives Charles her word that he won't have to see the questionnaire men. The camera follows her as she goes toward the house, leaving Charles out of the frame. Hence when there is a cut to Graham and Saunders at the door and they introduce themselves to Charlie, this shot, while perhaps not literally from Charles's point of view, nonetheless appears inflected by it (4.35). When Charles enters this frame, the effect is startling: he is, as it were, viewer/author of, and actor within, our view (4.36).[8]

4.35

Unwitnessed by Charlie, Charles's and Graham's gazes meet. Without saying a word, Charles opens the front door and goes inside. Charlie then invites the two men to enter. They go through the door and turn into the parlor, exiting the

4.36

4.37

4.38

4.39

4.40

frame one after another. By this time, the camera, in a virtuoso move, has passed through the doorway, crossing the threshold (4.37).[9] Finally, only Charles is left in the frame. He pauses and then goes up the stairs. There is a cut to Graham in the parlor. This is one of the cuts that Hitchcock treats as if it were a dissolve; its point can be appreciated if the two shots are superimposed (4.38). Graham assumes Charles's exact place in the frame, and both figures are linked with the charged image of the staircase, this conjunction announcing a series of developments of the greatest importance.

As Graham goes through the motions of conducting the interview, he tries to pump Emma about Charles, while Charlie attempts to protect her uncle. On the leading question, "There are six in your family?" Charlie breaks in with "Five. My uncle's just here on a little visit." Hitchcock cuts on this line to a slightly low-angle shot of Charlie, inflected by Graham's point of view (4.39), then reverses field to Graham. This cut suggests that Graham is acutely attentive to Charlie's reference to her uncle. But it makes another suggestion as well, if one that becomes intelligible to us only retroactively: this is the moment of the dawning of Graham's desire for Charlie, provoked by her combative intervention. "When someone asks for privacy, they should have it. Mr. Graham, perhaps you'd better choose another house." But Emma's will prevails. "Charlie, why don't you let the young men go ahead, so long as they're here?"

At this point there is a cut to a low-angle shot of Charles looking down from the top of the stairs (4.40). (Compare the lodger looking down on the struggle between Daisy and Joe.) We now realize that during the whole scene downstairs, Charles has been at this station. He has not literally had access to what we have viewed, but, in retrospect, we sense his gaze possessing all we have seen. It is as if he had magical access to Charlie's defense, Graham's ominous, ambiguous interest, and Charlie's acquiescence in this violation of his privacy.[10] At this mo-ment Charles leaves the frame, as if vol-untarily relinquishing his grip on the scene, and Hitchcock cuts back down-stairs (4.41), the ceiling lamp—the lodger's emblem—a secret stand-in for Charles's haunting presence.

4.41

Saunders wants to photograph Emma baking a cake. "If you'll start by break-ing an egg, Mrs. Newton . . ." "But you don't start a cake by breaking an egg. You have to put the butter and sugar in first." Saunders' tribulations are a joke on the process of filming. One clear target is a certain theory and practice of documentary. Saunders pretends to be engaged in a documentary project of which Emma has no comprehension, not understanding the docu-mentarist's belief in the ordinary and the candid, while Charlie touches on the serious issue of the responsibility of photographers to respect the privacy of their subjects. But the joke is also on the Hollywood method of filming, which *Shadow of a Doubt* itself ex-emplifies. Emma's maddening insistence on following the real order of steps in baking her cake links her with the actor who does not appreciate the need for scenes to be shot out of sequence and insists he can only play a scene straight through.[11] The joke is com-pounded by Hitchcock's identification with his well-known con-ceit—reference to it was *de rigueur* in Hitchcock interviews—that his films are slices of cake, not slices of life.

Emma's "My brother Charles loves maple cake" gives Graham an opening to return to the subject Charlie is trying to ward off (char-acteristically, Emma serves as the author's unwitting agent, ad-vancing the plot). But realizing that getting information out of Emma is a hopeless task, Graham asks Charlie to show them the upstairs. Charlie refuses to let Saunders photograph her room, ex-plaining that her uncle is using it now and doesn't want to be pho-tographed. She won't let Graham knock on the door to see if Charles is in; *she* knocks. Only when she sees that the room is empty does she allow Saunders to photograph it. Graham suggests that Saunders work with the door closed ("Might as well let him work in peace. Besides, I'd like to talk to you").

On Charlie's line, "You know, your picking us as an average fam-

4.42

4.43

4.44

4.45

ily kind of gave me a funny feeling," Hitchcock cuts to Charlie (4.42). On her "I guess I don't like to be an average girl in an average family," he cuts to Graham (4.43), who replies, "Average families are the best. Look at me. I'm from an average family. Besides, I don't think you're average." Then Hitchcock cuts back to Charlie and alternates (4.42) and (4.43) in shot/reverse-shot mode.[12] Charlie says, "That's because you see me now instead of a few days ago. I was in the dumps, and then Uncle Charlie came." There is a cut to Graham. The smile leaves his face and he says, "But your mother said that he only got here last night. Maybe you just think that." We cut back to Charlie, who replies forcefully, "I don't think, I *know*. It's funny, but when I try to think of how I feel, I . . . I always come back to . . ." As Charlie hesitates, Hitchcock cuts to Graham, who appears at a loss for words. She finishes her thought, ". . . Uncle Charlie," and we cut back to Charlie, who has picked up on Graham's silence. "Are you trying to tell me that I shouldn't think he's so wonderful?"

Suddenly, Charlie looks down. As music starts up, her left hand grabs her right wrist, as though responding to a pain or chill. On this motion, Hitchcock cuts to a shot of Charlie's arms, disrupting the shot/reverse-shot alternation (4.44). In this shot, viewed from neither Graham's nor Charlie's vantage point, Charlie's hands are framed as though they were alien to her, not subject to her will; as though, at this moment, their autonomy asserts itself, this assertion linked to this framing's assertion of the camera's autonomy. This cut forcibly brings us back to the ring giving and to Charles's violent seizing of Charlie's

wrist. Charlie too, we take it, is as-
saulted by this memory.

When the camera returns to Graham,
his face is turned sharply away and he
appears unable to speak (4.45). Not surprisingly, it is Emma's offscreen voice
that breaks the spell, allowing the narrative to proceed. "Mr. Saunders, I'm
ready for the eggs!" There is a cut to
Charlie, who is also turned away from
the camera in a Hitchcockian profile
shot (4.46). She gasps audibly but then
violently wrenches herself back into her
normal stance. Recovering, she turns
back to Graham. "I hope Mr. Saunders
doesn't move anything in there. My
uncle's awfully neat and fussy." Graham looks up, and Hitchcock cuts to a
highly charged, schematic shot from his
point of view (4.47). Charles, framed by
the curtain, is coming up the backstairs.
Graham shifts his eyes toward the
closed door of Charlie's room. When he
shifts his eyes back and speaks—
loudly, so that Saunders will be sure to
hear his cue—we know he is acting. "Is
this your uncle you were"—a cut to the
closed door (4.48)—"telling us about?"
The effect of this cut is to identify what
we see on the screen with the subject of
Graham's inquiry. As so often in
Shadow of a Doubt—and this becomes
a recurring strategy in all of Hitchcock's
later films—a line of dialogue and a
framing specifically comment on each
other, combining dramatic irony and
self-reference: Uncle Charles, like the
author who presents us with this view,
is a closed door and a blank screen. No
one is neater or fussier than Hitchcock.

The door opens and Saunders appears, looking right at the camera, his
camera poised ready to shoot (4.49). We
cut back to the highly charged setup of
(4.47). At the exact moment Charles

4.46

4.47

4.48

4.49

4.50

enters the door, the whole frame flashes white, nearly blinding us (4.50). Hitchcock's white flashes always have a "natural" explanation. Here, as in the climax of *Rear Window,* an exploding flashbulb causes the screen to flash white. But I have pointed out that the white flash is also a sign associated with the threat of subjective breakdown, and this is clearly true of this moment. Of course the moment also plays on the related idea, basic to Hitchcock's work, that the camera is a kind of gun. That this white flash blinds both the camera's subject and the film's viewer reflects the depth and ambiguity of the camera as symbol. There is no simple answer to the question of who or what the camera's real target is.

On the line, "My sister told me to remind you something about eggs," Charles looks right into the camera and advances menacingly. Hitchcock then cuts to a three-shot of Graham, Saunders, and Charlie, which suggests Charles's point of view. As once before, Charles enters a frame inflected by his perspective, and he and Graham face off at opposite ends of the frame. Charlie looking on spellbound, Charles holds out his hand and demands the roll

4.51

of film. Saunders bends down, presumably to remove the film from the camera. But the result is that he is blocked by Graham from our view (4.51). We later learn—or do we?—that Saunders switches films at this moment. Saunders' sleight-of-hand, if it really occurs, is matched by that of Hitchcock's framing. Charlie looks down, momentarily withdrawn. We cut to a closer shot, with Charlie in the background and Charles's extended hand in the foreground (4.52). Charlie finds her gaze compelled by this hand, which is for the first time to Charlie, and more clearly than ever to us, the emblem of Charles's mystery. Her gaze runs the length of Charles's arm as Saunders' hand enters the frame. When the exchange is made in the foreground of the frame, Charlie does not witness it: she is looking right at Charles's face, which lies beyond the

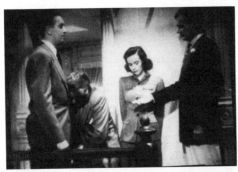

4.52

frame line, for the first time recognizing that she may not really know him (4.53). Then she looks back down, troubled. Charles walks into the frame, completely blocking Charlie from our view (4.54).

4.53

The appropriation of the roll of film reverses the bestowal of the ring. Charles's eclipse of Charlie doubles the eclipse that immediately preceded the gesture. Expressively, it obliterates her, as if in revenge for her failure to keep her promise, her failure to keep Graham from coming between them. (Of course, the full implications of Charlie's "failing" are not yet apparent, to Charles or Charlie or to us.) Emma's voice ("I'm going to fold in the eggs!") again breaks the tension, and there is a cut to downstairs. Graham asks Emma whether he can borrow Charlie for the evening to show him around Santa Rosa. Smiling,

4.54

Emma suggests that Ann would be a better guide, because she knows everything. But it is clear that Emma gives her blessing to Graham's request. Her feelings toward him are unmixed: from the first, I think, she spotted him as the kind of nice young man she would like her daughter to marry. Charlie, open-mouthed, says she doesn't mind. Graham then moves to the foreground of the frame and opens the door, the camera moving out through the doorway, reversing the movement that initiated this scene. A bracket is closed, and this important passage is enclosed between a pair of declarations of the camera's capacity to cross the threshold of this possibly representative, possibly not so representative American home.

The next sequence begins with Charlie and Graham, laughing, exiting from Gunner's Grill. We dissolve from their amusing encounter with Charlie's friend Katharine (who has an opportunity to envy Charlie another glamorous male companion) to a stunning shot of Charlie framed against a dark background (4.55). The camera pulls out and twists to frame her with Graham. She has had a sudden insight. "I know what you are really. You're a detective. You lied to us. You just wanted to get in . . ." At this moment, Hitchcock cuts to a shot of Graham viewed over Charlie's shoulder, as she rises, completing her line (". . . our house") (4.56). Much

4.55

4.56

later in the film, he tells her that it was during this encounter that he first knew he was in love. The framing, which conspicuously juxtaposes Charlie's hair and Graham's eye, embeds Hitchcock's veiled declaration of Graham's desire.[13]

Graham pleads with Charlie to listen to him. "Why should I, when you lied to me?" He sits her down, takes her hand, and proceeds to give her an account meant as an answer to that question.

I had to. When I came here to this town to find a man, I hadn't counted on you. I hadn't counted on your mother or your family. There's a man loose in this country. We're after him. We don't know much about him. We don't even know what he looks like. Your uncle may be that man. We followed him. We think he is. But in the east there's another man who's being hunted too. He may be the one.

Graham believes, but does not know, that Charles is guilty of some unnamed crime. Graham knows, but Charlie does not, what that crime is. On the other hand, neither Charlie nor Graham has had access to Hitchcock's intimations to us that Charles may be a murderer. But why should we trust these intimations when Hitchcock has, if not exactly lied, at least deliberately deceived and misled us?

Graham must now swear Charlie to secrecy. Taking a different tack, he represents himself as the exemplar of the ordinary citizen. He argues that he has to be more important to her than Charles could ever be because ordinary people matter most. Graham argues that he does not have to force her hand because it is not within her nature *not* to help him. He claims to know that her nature and his own are fundamentally the same. Graham's opposition to Charles corresponds to a clash between two different pictures of Charlie's nature. Is she ordinary like Graham or extraordinary like Charles? One irony is that, of the two men, it is Charles who seems to believe that she really is ordinary, while Graham has already told her that he doesn't find her "average" at all. Another irony is that Graham's argument coincides exactly with Charlie's earlier argument that she and Charles are like twins and thus have a deep bond. And the scene of Charles's and Charlie's "betrothal" is also invoked by the suggestion that Graham's presentation is only one step removed from a proposal (indeed, shortly he will declare love and all but propose), turning as it does on his testimony as to how much Charlie means to him ("If it weren't for you . . .").

Graham promises that, in any case, they won't arrest Charles in Santa Rosa. But the effect of this assurance, given the way Charlie's mind works (hesitantly, indirectly, by the articulation of a claim she knows on reflection to be false, and then by the grudging acknowledgment of the truth), is to plant in her imagination the terrifying picture of Charles's arrest in front of Emma, which is also a picture of Emma's breakdown, in effect her death. "Arrest him in town with mother?" "I tell you we won't." Her response is inarticulate, numbed. "Oh." Then she gives Graham her word that she won't say anything to Charles about their conversation.

Shortly after Graham's departure, Charlie runs into her father and Herb. She says goodnight, setting the stage for the second dialogue between the "literary critics." Herb informs Joe that he put a little soda in his coffee, "about the same amount I would have used if I wanted to use poison." When Joe points out that he hadn't tasted anything but might have if it had been poison, Herb reacts with characteristic petulance. "Notice the soda more than you would the poison. Ha, for all you knew you might just as well be dead now!"

The cut to the following shot is ironically charged (we can taste the poison in it): Charlie, on top of the landing, small and vulnerable in a frame with the silhouette of the stairpost in the center (4.57).

4.57

Charlie enters Charles's room and rummages in the waste basket, presumably looking for the missing newspaper page. She goes into her temporary bedroom and spreads out on her bed the papers she found, telling Ann that she's looking for a recipe. Ann points out that they have newspapers in the "liberry." A brief suspense sequence ensues, as Charlie rushes through town to try to get to the library before it closes at 9:00, only to make it just in time to see the lights go out. She goes to the door and knocks loudly, passersby frowning at this disturbance. The librarian lets her in and relishes the opportunity for a stern lecture.

Music swells and the camera follows Charlie as she looks for the day's newspaper. In a medium-close profile shot, she mutters, "It can't be anything really awful. *I'll prove to him it isn't.*" Then her attention is riveted, and Hitchcock cuts directly—the cut creating the effect of a white flash—to the headline "Where is the Merry Widow Murderer?" The camera tilts down as the story slowly passes through the frame, the Merry Widow Waltz theme sounding.

Nationwide search underway for strangler of three rich women. The whereabouts of so-called "Merry Widow Murderer," stronghanded strangler of three wealthy women, is a question which baffles detectives today who are conducting coast to coast search for the killer. . . . His latest victim . . . was Mrs. Bruce Matthewson, the former musical comedy star, known to audiences at the beginning of the century as "the beautiful Thelma Schenley."

There is a cut back to Charlie, and then to a closeup of her hands from her point of view. She removes the ring. In an extreme closeup, we reread the inscription: "TS FROM BM." In the most exceptional shot in the film, technically and expressively, the camera pulls out from Charlie's hands (4.58), passes over her shoulder as she rises (4.59) and continues rising as she crosses the room, until finally she is framed in the shadows from a great height (4.60).[14]

4.58

4.59

4.60

We are fully convinced that Charles is guilty. His crime is far more horrible than we had imagined, despite Hitchcock's warnings. It is repellent enough to shake whatever attachment we had formed, even the perverse attachment that would have thrived on a less loathesome revelation. It is a bold break with film convention that Hitchcock has accomplished here: his enigmatic protagonist disclosed, halfway through the film, to be guilty of a crime that effectively precludes continued identification with him.

Our knowledge and Charlie's for the first time coincide. This framing that isolates her human figure, looking down on it (but not condemning her, not scorning her), is expressive of her situation. She feels small because she knows she is trapped in a struggle against a monstrous adversary. But she also feels small because she knows she has a large responsibility. The knowledge she possesses gives her a terrifying power over Charles. The framing expresses both her real vulnerability and her recognition of her stature as a moral agent, an adult. It is as if she is reflected both in that small, trapped human figure and in the camera's powerful gesture of encompassing that figure in its frame. The great crane shot that culminates in this framing reminds us of Charles, even as it marks Charlie's frightening yet exhilarating acquisition of self-consciousness. But it also represents the film's most perfect manifestation of its author's power over Charles and Charlie, and over us. Hitchcock's formulation of Charlie's coming to self-consciousness declares the camera's autonomy as well. With this gesture, Hitchcock definitively shows his hand. Yet with this gesture, the author forswears his acts of withholding information from Charlie and from us. We do not have answers to all of our questions about Charles; we do not know what motivates his murderous acts, nor even their real nature; and we do not know the nature of Charles's and Charlie's bond. But these are not questions that Hitchcock can answer by revealing any further secrets. With this camera movement and framing, Hitchcock renounces, for the remainder of the film, the practice of cloaking his narration in mystery. From this point on, the status of the narrative and our relationship to it are transformed.

This transformation is completed by the superimposition of the dancing-couples image: its meaning has been told. Over these two images is superimposed yet another: Charles, reading a newspaper, his back to the camera, walking into the depths of the frame (4.61). It is this view that opens out onto a brief interlude in which Emma informs Charles that Charlie has been asleep all day and is still asleep.

4.61

There follows a dissolve to the exterior of the house as evening falls, then to Charles with a glass of milk—an echo of *Suspicion*—the bars of the bannister casting tall shadows in the background (another occurrence of the / / / / sign). Charles looks up as Emma, preceded by her shadow, descends the stairs (4.62). She explains that Charlie just now awakened ("Pehaps I shouldn't have let her sleep so long, but I think she needed it. She doesn't look quite herself"). When Emma leaves the frame, Charles continues staring. The effect of the ensuing quick cut to Charlie on the landing

4.62

4.63

upstairs is to make Emma turn into her in the frame, as though Charles looks right through Emma to Charlie (4.63). Faced with the prospect of making what amounts to a stage entrance, Charlie demurs and goes down the backstairs. She joins her mother in the kitchen and takes over the mashing of the potatoes.

We do not in fact know whether Charlie slept. Her nightmares, sleeping or waking, are closed to us, but not because Hitchcock wraps her in an enigma as he had cloaked Charles. If Charlie's newly acquired knowledge has indeed changed her, we will be witness to that change. Her first test is to face her mother's maddening banter. When Emma begins humming the Merry Widow Waltz, Charlie now attaches the same specific meaning to it that we do. Her mashing becomes an expression of the violent, conflicting emotions that pass through her, like Daisy's mother's obsessive scrubbing in *The Lodger*. Charlie's hands, like Charles's, have become signals and conduits of her feelings.

Driven to fury by the nerve-wracking humming, Charlie says, with startling force, "Whatever you do, please don't hum that tune any more!" Then her tone abruptly changes, as if to deny that anything unusual has taken place (we have seen Charles's manner shift like this): "You just sit there and be a real lady." Charlie will serve the dinner tonight.

Emma calls the family in. As Charlie watches, Ann asks her mother whether she can sit next to her, not next to Charles. Charlie supports this request, but Emma says, "Certainly not. Uncle Charlie might think . . ." Emma needs no external interruption to keep from finishing her sentences: "Certainly not." But of course she lets Ann have her way. The camera cuts to the dining room. Seeing the new seating arrangement, Charles asks, "Have I lost my little girl?" (In this line, Charles casts himself as Ann's father.) As Emma is on her way to the kitchen, she sees Joe with the newspaper. Charles has so much appropriated the place of head of the family that the newspaper that was once Joe's has now become his. Emma just has to say "Joe!" and her husband recognizes that he has stepped out of line and apologizes. "Had it in my hand, I guess. Nothing special in it." He passes the paper screen-right, the camera panning to follow this motion. The exchange occurs precisely as the camera centers on Charlie's empty chair.

Over Emma's offscreen words, "Roger, don't make so much noise with the soup!" we cut to Charlie in the kitchen, readying her entrance. The nausea of stage fright, and Charlie's nausea at the

thought of Charles, are expressed by charged snatches of dialogue
we hear offscreen: in this passage, the objective presentation and
the presentation of Charlie's subjectivity are intertwined. As Charlie starts to move toward the door to the dining room, we hear: "If
he keeps his lips close together, he can draw carefully, same as a
horse"; "Ann, don't be disgusting";
"Mom, may I dip my bread in it?"
Thankfully, this soup is not at this moment shown (not until *Frenzy* will that
outrage be perpetrated). Finally, Charlie
leaves the frame, walking screen-right.
The camera pans with her until the door
frame blocks her from our view. For a
moment, the screen is a blur. Finally,
the camera holds on the frame of the
door seen from the dining-room side. By
this vertiginous camera movement, the
shot transforms itself into one from
Charles's point of view. (4.64).

4.64

Charles says, offscreen, "You're right,
Joe." Charlie opens the door, making
her entrance into Charles's view and
ours (4.65): "Nothing special." Charles
means not just that there is nothing special in the newspaper, but that *Charlie* is
nothing special. He does not even suspect that she has made good on her
promise or threat to find out his secret.

4.65

The next shot retroactively places the last as from Charles's point of
view (he is looking right at the camera), and is itself read as from
Charlie's point of view. If he takes his view simply to expose her
(because she is not, he believes, special enough to acknowledge his
view or to deceive him), that view has been, unknown to him, authored by Charlie. By contrast, what Charlie views is an act she can
now see through. When on this cut Charles completes his sentence
("Nothing special tonight"), his words take on an unintended significance that reflects Charlie's perception and not his own. To
Charlie, Charles's act is nothing special tonight.

This passage is modeled, I think, on the moment of Saunders'
taking of Charles's photograph. But now Charlie has appropriated
the place of Saunders' camera. Her view possesses Charles as if in a
photograph. Registering what has occurred, the camera pulls out
until the whole dinner table is encompassed (4.66). But then the
mad mindlessness of the family's dinner chatter resurfaces, until
Charlie rises, ready to perform a daring act.

4.66

I slept all right, and I kept dreaming. Perfect nightmares. About you, Uncle Charlie. You were on a train, and I had a feeling you were running away from something. And I saw you on the train and I felt terribly happy.

In retrospect, we may recognize in this nightmare (it may be made up) a prophecy of the film's climax. The ironic congruence between Charlie's dream and the film's resolution is integral to Hitchcock's design. What Charlie does not and cannot know, of course, is what it will be like—how it will feel, what it will cost—for her to assume her place in her own vision. When Emma asks how Charlie could feel happy at the prospect of Charles's departure, she replies, "Well, he has to leave sometime. We have to face the facts." Hitchcock cuts to Charles, who eyes Charlie very closely. He says (and

4.67

here we assume he really means it), "I like people who face facts."

Charles sends Roger into the kitchen to get "the big red bottle." While Charles is gesturing with his hands, making what looks like a throttling gesture as he describes the bottle (4.67), Charlie turns at the door on her way to the kitchen and says sarcastically, "You can throw the paper away. We don't need to play any games with it tonight." When she goes out the door, not waiting

for a response, Charles looks downcast. Not only her words but her manner and above all her timing (with his hands in a strangling pose, he is caught as if in the act) are deliberately provocative. Her devastating exit line suggests that she has seen through him so totally that she disdains him even as an audience.

While we view Charles reflecting on Charlie's provocative line, Emma's voice sounds offscreen: "Ann, you can help Charlie carry in the vegetables." But we must not underestimate Charles's resources. He is not so easily to be outdone, to be reduced to a vegetable by these women. The bottle of wine will play a role in an improvised charade, performed for Charlie as audience, by which he will top Charlie's theatrical coup and regain the upper hand, reasserting his new place as head of this household.

Roger emerges from the kitchen, holding the wine bottle—it looks comically large in his small hands—and scrutinizing it as if not quite sure what it is (4.68). The camera reframes in such a way that at a certain point Charles must pass through the center of the

frame. As Roger is about to sit, the camera hurries its movement, as if to get
Charles past the center as quickly as
possible. In this sequence, Charles has
not yet been placed in the center. The
moment in this shot at which Charles
passes through the center of the frame is
the moment of his reference to Saint
Paul: "You know what Saint Paul said,
'Take a little wine for thy stomach's
sake.'"[15] Emma now speaks up: "Wine

4.68

for dinner. It sounds so gay. Charles, remember the time they had
the champagne, when the oldest Jones girl got married?" Emma's
remark is cued by Charles's reference to Paul and can only be
viewed as secretly provoked by Charles: he is once again "pushing
a button." In turn, Emma's remark cues the camera to reassume her
point of view (4.69). In this frame, Charles's centrality is decisively
reclaimed, just as Emma raised the subject of marriage in order to
reassert her special intimacy with him. In this scene Charles has
arranged, and arranged to be enacted while Charlie is out of the
room, Emma's desire, and hence Charles's power over her, is unambiguously revealed. This is how I understand Hitchcock's motiva-
tion in making this one of those frames
in which he inscribes a sexual signifier.
In (4.69), the bottle—Charles holds it in
his hands, which obsessively play with
its cork—is accorded a prominent place
in the frame, one that underscores its
clear schematic significance: it is the
stand-in for Charles's penis.

4.69

    Charles's initial response denies
Emma's intimacy and puts her down a
bit. "This is sparkling burgundy." But
Emma is not squelched. "Well, one sip
and *I'll* be calling it 'sparkling burgledy.'" The camera cuts now
from Emma to Joe, who is excluded from the memory his wife
shares with her brother. "Oh, imported," Joe says of the wine, as
Emma giggles disconcertingly offscreen at the thought of that bygone wedding. Emma continues. "Charles: 'Imported Frankie' and
his tweeds . . . And his loaded cane?" Over a shot of Joe's embarrassed face, Charles adds, shockingly, "His loaded everything!"
When Hitchcock cuts again to the closed kitchen door, it is clear
that, this charade under his belt, Charles is ready for Charlie's entrance. Ann comes through the door and then Charlie. Emma says,
"Charles, I promised Mrs. Green, the president of our club, that

4.70

4.71

4.72

4.73

you'd talk to the ladies." On Charlie's glance, there is a cut to Charles, who is almost finished peeling the foil from the bottle. "What sort of audience will it be?" Precisely on the sound of the popping cork, Hitchcock cuts to Emma, chewing. "Oh, women like myself." As Charles begins his great, spellbinding speech, Hitchcock returns to the framing to which the camera pulled out immediately after Charlie's coup.

Women keep busy in towns like this. In the cities its different. Cities are full of women, middle-aged widows, husbands dead, husbands who've spent their lives making fortunes, working and working. Then they die and leave their money to their wives.

At this point Hitchcock cuts to Charlie's view of Charles (4.70). He is looking off to the right, presumably at Emma. As he speaks, the camera moves in:

Their silly wives. And what do the wives do, these useless women? You see them in the hotels, the best hotels, every day by the thousands. Drinking the money, eating the money, losing the money at bridge, playing all day and all night. Smelling of money. Proud of their jewelry but of nothing else.

He shifts his gaze. The poetry in his voice disappears as his speech turns to an indrawn, private vision (4.71): "Horrible, faded, fat, greedy women." Then Charlie's voice sounds offscreen, undertaking to speak for the form of life that is "ordinary," speaking for us. "But they're alive, they're human beings!" At this moment, Charles turns his gaze directly to the camera (4.72). "Are they?" he asks coldly and dispassionately, not allowing her to appeal to outside authority in formulating her answer, forcing Charlie and us back on ourselves. In the following shot (4.73), Charlie has momentarily become, visually, like a small figure within Charles, his interlocutor. She does not meet his gaze.

Charles continues, now explicitly directing his remarks to Charlie, and the camera pulls out until finally the two are facing off at opposite ends of the frame: "Are they, Charlie? Or are they fat, wheezing animals? And what happens to animals when they get too fat and too old? But I seem to be making my speech right here." Charles pours the wine, and Hitchcock cuts to Emma. "Well! For heaven's sake, don't talk about women like that for my club. The idea! And that nice Mrs. Potter's going to be there too. The Greens are bringing her here to a little party I'm having after the lecture."

At this propitious moment, Herb arrives. In a deep-focus shot, he waddles in and waits to be invited to join them. In the scene with Joe that follows—framed as usual in a static two-shot—Charles is a spectator, even as he is also the dialogue's real if of course unintended subject. Herb suggests poison mushrooms as a murder weapon. Joe proposes a counter-suggestion. "A bathtub. Pull the legs out from under you. Hold you down. Been done, but . . ." Suddenly, Hitchcock cuts to a high-angle long shot of the room (4.74). Charlie has jumped to her feet. It is as though by her decisive gesture she commands this shot's break with the passive framing of the theatrical routine, its break with the point of view of Charles as spectator. Her father's blindness cannot at this moment be borne, and

4.74

Charlie's protest is angry and violent. She both exercises a real, hitherto dormant power and loses control, relinquishing the upper hand to Charles. "What's the matter with you two? Do you always have to talk about killing people?" "We're not talking about killing people. Herb's talking about killing me and I'm talking about killing him." Emma seconds Joe's claim that this dialogue is innocent: "It's your father's way of relaxing." Exasperated, Charlie rushes out, with Charles offering to "catch up with her."

Charles and Charlie meet outside the Til Two Lounge (4.75). (Note that the frame line cuts the neon sign in half, leaving only the word "cock" visible.[16]) Charles directs Charlie to go in with him. She says she has never been in a place like this, but acquiesces. Hitch-

4.75

cock cuts to the smoky, dark, noisy interior of the bar. Charles and Charlie sit across from each other. Their conversation must be delayed, however, as a waitress sidles up to their table to take the order. She is Louise Finch. She explains who she is with a deadpan explicitness that is comical, vulgar, touching.

I was in Charlie's class in school. I sure was surprised to see you come in. I never thought I'd see you in here. I've been here two weeks. Lost my job over at Kern's. I've been in half the restaurants in town. What'll you have, Charlie?

Charlie whispers "Nothing thank you," but Charles orders for both of them, deliberately treating Louise Finch as just a waitress. "Bring her some ginger ale. I'll have a double brandy." Taken aback, Louise says "Uh huh" and looks twice at Charles before leaving. Music starts up, suggesting that the scene is about to start in earnest.

Charles asks, "Well Charlie?" as if *she* had sought this encounter. But then he begins, Hitchcock filming their exchange in a simple shot/reverse-shot alternation. "Now look . . ." He folds his hands on the table in plain view. "Something's come between us." Knowing what he does not know she knows, Charlie can see through Charles's act. The more he speaks, the more he exposes himself. "We're like twins. You said so yourself." His hand enters her frame and takes Charlie's. Charles invokes the scene of the giving of the ring, recalling and now endorsing her argument that they are twins. She flinches from his touch and looks only at his hands, not his face. Under her gaze, his hands start folding a paper napkin.

4.76

"I'm not so old. I've been chasing around the globe since I was sixteen. Guess I've done some pretty foolish things." A cut to Charles's hands twisting the napkin, from Charlie's point of view (4.76). "Nothing serious. Foolish." Hitchcock then cuts to Charles, looking down, a little boy's sheepish grin on his face.

Charles is shyly talking around some subject. In part, he is still fishing to find out what Graham told Charlie. But I take it that Charles's circumlocution invokes a specific conventional context. Charles is speaking precisely as if he were about to make a proposal. Invoking the earlier scene of betrothal, he is repeating it, maybe hoping that what has come between them will go away. Suddenly, the grin leaves his face. Looking down, he has become aware of something and realizes that she is aware of it too. On a sickening sliding sound, we cut to Charles's hands. Very slowly, they withdraw from the table, until they are completely blocked from view. This is one of Hitchcock's most devastating images of impotence. When Charles next says, "Aw, Charlie, now don't start imagining things," he means, among other things, "Don't start imagining that I really did what Graham told you I did," and also, "Don't start imagining that I desire *you*."

For the first time now, Charlie speaks directly to Charles, although she refuses to look at him. "How could you do such things?" He answers, "Charlie, what do you know?" (not "what do you think you know?"). The gesture Charlie is about to perform calls for a framing that registers its formality. Hitchcock cuts to a longer shot as Charlie takes off her ring and places it on the table. This gesture constitutes a direct answer to Charles's question: she knows what this ring means. At this dramatic moment, Louise Finch returns. There could not be a more frustrating interruption, rendered comic by the perfect irony of its details (when she sees the ring, she says, "I'd just die for a ring like that"). Again Charles cuts her off. "Bring me another brandy." Charlie rises to leave, but he demands that she sit down. "You think you know something, don't you. There's so much you don't know. So much."

Charles is no longer denying the truth of what he thinks Graham has told her, but arguing that she does not really know him or the world. As if to demonstrate that Charlie knows nothing (the demonstration is over her head, but that is again part of its point), at this moment, with the swiftest gesture, Charles palms the ring (the ring has been lying in plain view on the table, but so spellbound are we by the force of Charles's speech that we are little more likely than Charlie to notice it). Charles no longer denies his guilt but declares it, and exhibits his inhumanity theatrically, in the most shocking of his great speeches.

What do you know really? You're just an ordinary little girl living in an ordinary little town. You wake up every morning of your life and you know perfectly well that there's nothing in the world to trouble you. You go through your ordinary little day and at night you sleep your untroubled, ordinary little sleep filled with peaceful, stupid dreams. And I brought you nightmares. You live in a dream. You're a sleepwalker, blind. How do you know what the world is like? Do you know the world is a foul sty? Do you know that if you rip the fronts off houses you'd find swine? The world's a hell. What does it matter what happens in it? Wake up Charlie. Use your wits. Learn something.

Charles has answered Charlie's question. His actions are grounded in his vision of the world as a hell (whether Charles really believes that people are beasts and their fate is of no importance is another question). Charlie heads for the exit, and Charles downs his drink and follows her. The level of the ambient noise suddenly rises, the sounds of the bar coalescing in laughter that takes on a cruel, hard edge. The laughter is mocking, and its mockery is cued by Charles and, as it were, in his voice. The Til Two Lounge—a conventional "fallen" setting, although Hitchcock, unlike Capra in *It's a Wonderful Life*, insists on its underlying tameness and innocence—has become a nightmare extension of Charles's performance. Hitchcock has doubled the cliché back on itself.[17]

Charlie goes out the door, with Charles close behind. (Note the device of having the clockface painted on the swinging door of the lounge take on the aspect of an eye (4.77), like the clockface in *Murder!* and Big Ben in *The Lodger*.) He catches up with her on the street in front of the house. Holding her arm, he appeals to her.

4.77

The same blood flows through our veins, Charlie. A week ago, I was at the end of my rope. There's an end to the running a man can do. You'll never know what it's like to be so tired. I was going to . . . Well, then I got the idea of coming out here. Charlie, give me this last chance.

His implication is clear: at the end of his rope, he was going to kill himself. Part of the power of this moment comes from the fact that we have seen Charles's weariness in the dreary rooming house. His suggestion that his homecoming was a last refuge from the vision of his death has the ring of truth about it, although we recognize that he is also being theatrical. But what is he asking of Charlie? He asks her not to tell Graham what she knows. But he is also asking her to let him stay. When Charlie replies, "Take your chance. Go," Charles answers, "I'll go, Charlie, I'll go. Just give me a few days." We sense, I take it, that he does not really intend to abide by Charlie's condition but is playing for time. He touches a vulnerable point. "It would kill your mother." She looks at him, accepting this. He presses. "You realize what it will mean if they get me? The

electric chair." He has gauged the line's effect correctly: Charlie almost breaks down. "Charlie, I count on you. You said yourself we're no ordinary uncle and niece."

Charles's plea has become a demand. She agrees to its terms. With Charlie in the foreground looking into the depth of the frame, he goes into the house (4.78); this composition echoes Hitchcock's framing of the lodger at the moment he

4.78

first hears Daisy's laugh. We hear the voices filtering from inside ("East west, home's best"; "Where's Charlie?"; "Oh, she said she was a little edgy; I persuaded her to go for a little walk"). Hitchcock reframes as Charlie turns until she leaves the frame, and the image takes on the reflection of her point of view, as cheerful goodnights are spoken and happiness reigns within the house (4.79). Then Charlie turns until she faces the camera, and weeps. We hear Charles and Emma laughing. Charlie's beautiful dream of Charles in her father's place has come true and turned into a nightmare.

4.79

The scene fades in on the exterior of a church. Services are ending, and people pour out. Graham tells Charlie that Saunders wants to speak with her, while Graham, Katharine, and Ann walk ahead (Ann is telling Katharine the story of Dracula). Saunders says to Charlie,

I want to tell you about the photograph we took. I gave him the wrong film. Yes, we got the picture all right. We've got witnesses in the east who can identify the man we want from that picture. The moment the witnesses see that picture we know whether or not Oakley is the man. It's ready for the wire now.

Why doesn't Graham speak for himself? Saunders can explain that he is doing the talking because of Graham's consideration for Charlie and her family; Graham could say these words himself only by declaring his feelings to Charlie, deepening the impression of impropriety in conjoining professional obligation and courtship. (Graham is, after all, a clear descendant of *The Lodger*'s Joe, although the film does not seriously press the issue of the possible impurity of his motives and impropriety of his methods.) Saunders can in character, as Graham cannot, back his request with a threat. And he also serves as go-between in Graham's courtship.[18]

Saunders gives Charlie two hours to get Charles to leave town. She reluctantly agrees to tell them when he goes. When Graham joins them, Charlie tells him that they've made a bargain. They say goodbye, and Charlie walks back toward the house with Ann and Katharine. Charlie suggests that Ann pick some flowers for the dinner table. Ann replies, "Simple flowers are the best," and Charlie, amused, says, "I didn't ask for orchids." On Charlie's line, Hitchcock cuts to a long shot of Charles on the porch, reading the newspaper and smoking a cigar. Charles is an "orchid" that Charlie *did* ask for. (This makes Graham—whose courtship of Charlie is encouraged by Ann—the "simple flower.")

When Katharine says goodbye, we get a medium frontal shot of Charlie walking forward, smiling. But then her face drains of expression as she is brought back to reality. Hitchcock cuts back and forth between Charlie, walking forward toward the house, and Charles, from her point of view, beginning to descend the stairs, the shots getting progressively closer.[19] When Charles asks, "How was church, Charlie? Count the house? Turn anybody away?" she reels

4.80

with the punch and rejoins, "There's room for everyone." We view Charles at this point from fairly close up and from a low angle. Puffing his cigar, he directs a knowing look right at the camera (4.80). "Show's been running such a long time I thought the attendance might be falling off."

Charles's look at Charlie, his blasphemy, his play with the cigar, and his subtle smile all challenge her to look at him and acknowledge that he is back to his old tricks. And he has reclaimed his special relationship with the film's author, who once again uses dialogue as a medium of self-reference. At one level, Hitchcock speaks through Charles, referring to his own "show." *Shadow of a Doubt* has been running so long that it may appear in danger of losing its audience, and perhaps it has become too much like a church service. But Hitchcock is about to perform a theatrical turn whereby he reasserts his presence and manifests his undiminished power, and brings his film fully back to life. Indeed, the twist Hitchcock here anticipates surprises even Charles with its perfect address of his desires.

As Charles is about to lower the cigar from his mouth, Joe's voice —conjured by Hitchcock as effortlessly as Charles conjures smoke rings—sounds offscreen. "Anything special on the news broadcast?" The tag phrase "anything special" links this moment to Charles's theatrical entrance into the dining room, and Charles's

4.81

trumping of Charlie. Something special *is* about to be unveiled: the shot in the film that is Hitchcock's second most extraordinary display of virtuosity. First he cuts to a shot dominated by hedges, from behind which Joe and Herb appear (4.81). "The fella said they caught that other fella, the one they call the Merry Widow Murderer." At this moment Hitchcock cuts to a beautifully composed image of rich texture, with

Charles and Charlie facing each other, gazes locked in intense confrontation (4.82). As the voices continue, they both look up, suspending their own intimate scene. "State of Maine. Portland."[20] Herb and Joe now walk into this frame, as Charles and Charlie follow them with their eyes. The camera begins a spiraling movement clockwise, first effecting an elegant transition from a long shot of Charles and Charlie to a medium shot of Herb and Joe (4.83). "They were just about to nab him at the airport, and he ran right into the propellor of an airplane. Cut him all to pieces." Just about now, Charlie reenters the frame, her back to the circling camera. "Had to identify him by his"—at this point Charlie is eclipsed by Joe—"clothes. His shirts were all initialed." Now Charles enters the frame, as Charlie, her eye perfectly framed between Herb and Joe, turns toward the camera. "Well, it makes a good ending." Charles, who had been eclipsed by Joe, passes into full view. "I guess that closes that case pretty final." "It sure does." Now Herb obliterates both Charles and Charlie from our view (Charles disappears completely just as Charlie is about to be uncovered). Hitchcock has planned a "good ending" for this incredibly choreographed shot, which anticipates the imminent announcement that the film itself is approaching its ending. On Joe's words, "Never cared much for that case," Herb finally leaves the frame, uncovering Charlie and then Charles (4.84, 4.85). The effect is precisely that of the lifting of a veil or the drawing of a curtain, as at the beginning of Handell Fane's climactic performance in *Murder!*. What is disclosed when the curtain is raised is that, in the course of this shot, Charles's and Charlie's positions

4.82

4.83

4.84

4.85

4.86

have become reversed. Charles is now at the left and Charlie at the right of the frame.

Charles smiles and says, "I think I'm going to get ready for dinner. I'm hungry. I can eat a good dinner today." The camera moves with him to the door, then through the door frame, crossing the threshold of the Newton home once more, as the music nears a climax. Charles climbs the stairs so that our view of him comes from an increasingly low angle. As the camera holds and the music pauses without resolving, he stops and very slowly turns to face the camera. Hitchcock cuts to his point of view: Charlie, doubled by her shadow, centered in a highly charged, symmetrical frame (4.86). He turns around again agonizingly slowly, as though all the weight of the world is now on his shoulders, and the screen fades to black.

When Charles hears the news, he momentarily feels free. But as he runs up the stairs, he suddenly senses Charlie's presence. His anticipation and dread coalesce in (4.86), the climax of this sequence. This view is objectively real, yet its composition marks it also as a projection of Charles's interiority, a vision. This vision crystallizes and reveals to Charles himself his ambiguous desire for Charlie—his desire to be joined with her in an authentic marriage grounded in mutual acknowledgment and his desire to possess her completely, like a thing. The vision also reveals that Charlie herself stands in his way. If Charles is to fulfill his desire or else free himself from the curse of unfulfilled desire, Charlie must be confronted, the source of her power acknowledged. If this vision is Charles's projection, the mark of Charlie's authorship is on it as well. Stepping into Charles's view, holding her ground and meeting his gaze, Charlie presents herself to him, confronts him with what is most disturbing: her reality and autonomy. Of course, it is only the unfolding of the remainder of the film that discloses in full, to Charlie and to us, the nature of the life-and-death struggle to which her gesture at this moment commits her.

Charlie's knowledge gives her gaze its power over Charles. What she knows is that he has killed. But she also knows the secret desire that animates his gaze *at this moment*. Her gaze, so to speak, beats his to the punch. Anticipating and meeting his look, she declares her knowledge that his murderousness and also his impotence are now exposed to her. As long as he remains in this home, her gaze must possess him, fixing him in an anguished impotence. As with Diana Baring's nightmare vision of her guards in *Murder!*, Charles's vision of Charlie, the conjunction of inside and outside, is a vision of madness. How can Charles free himself from possession by Charlie's gaze? His desire is too consuming for him to consent to banishment from her world. Part of the meaning of his vision, of course, is that it marks the onset of his obsession with killing Charlie. He realizes simultaneously that he desires her, that her gaze has the power to possess him, and that he must view her with a murderer's eyes. Charles's vision of Charlie is also his nightmare vision of himself as a Wrong One condemned to kill the thing he loves most in the world. Killing Charlie means not release from his curse but the sealing of his fate, the fulfillment of that curse. The blackness that engulfs the frame as the image fades out expresses his despair.

In this image, which bears the marks of Charles's projection and Charlie's act, Hitchcock shows his hand as well. This moment's perfect coincidence of frame and subject, nightmare and reality, act and vision displays the order of the world of Hitchcock's creation. The conjunction marks a fundamental turning in the film. We might say that this is the moment the film's ending comes into view.

To the accompaniment of agitated music, the scene fades in on Charles pacing in his room, cigar in hand. He goes to the window and looks out; Charlie is in front of the house. The camera tilts down as his hands rise into the frame.

4.87

As though involuntarily, they make a strangling gesture, and the cigar drops from their grasp (4.87). Charles is apprehensive and jealous. His hands reveal his anguish: the dropping of the cigar reflects his frustrated sense of impotence and also registers his fear of the murderous power his hands possess. From Charles's point of view, we see Graham drive up and begin to speak with Charlie. As they are about to pass out of Charles's sight, we cut to Charles at the window, straining to keep them in view. This image suggests that the scene that follows, while out of his literal view, will be imagined, magically possessed, even conjured by Charles, like the scene of the first encounter between Graham and Charlie.

Graham wants to tell Charlie the good news and has something else on his mind as well. They go into the garage to talk. From a very long two-shot, with Graham at one end of the frame, Charlie at the other, and a dark, impenetrable shadow between them in the center of the frame (Charles's stand-in?) (4.88), we proceed to a shot/reverse-shot alternation (they stand far apart so that there is,

4.88

4.89

4.90

4.91

in each frame, a striking disparity of scale between the two figures) (4.89, 4.90). Having told Charlie the news, Graham announces his aspirations as a suitor. "I wanted to wait and come back and then tell you. But I can't help it. I want to tell you now. I love you, Charlie. I love you terribly. I know it's no time to tell you now and I'm sorry." She would like them to be friends and promises to think about his words. When she invites him to come back, he steps forward, swelling with happiness and pride. At this moment, we might expect him to take her in his arms to kiss her, but he does not. He points to the wall, saying, "You know, this is a swell place. I'll put a bronze plaque right up there." Charlie laughs, and a shadow advances on the frame as the garage door slams shut with a frightening bang.

Charlie is waiting for them outside. The tense encounter that follows passes without incident. "When I was young, we sat in the parlor," Charles jokes, underscoring the age difference between them and also implying that Graham's courtship is really a seduction. Graham joins Charles in the frame, facing off against him, and Charlie takes her place at Graham's side. Graham tells Charles that he'll be back, only not on business. Charles replies, "I can understand your coming back." He frames Charlie's face with his hand, suggesting affection but also a strangling (4.91). "She's the thing I love most in the world." She turns away. Graham says goodbye, having given Charlie his addresses in case she needs him. As the car pulls away, she has second thoughts and cries out "Jack!" But it is too late. Accompanied by a sudden surge of dramatic music, the camera moves in on her hair. She turns slightly, then looks to Charles, and walks around to the back-stairs, avoiding him.

The scene fades in on Charlie, about to go down the backstairs on a shopping errand for her mother. Suddenly she falls down the flight, the camera quickly pulling back in a vertiginous movement. Charles stealthily enters the frame and looks intently at Charlie, then leaves. On Emma's "Oh darling, you might have been killed!" there is a cut to Charlie, then to her view of the broken stair, then back. Charlie looks up. The following shot of Charles, upstairs in the hallway, surrounded by dark shadows, is as if from Charlie's point of view, suggesting that Charlie suspects Charles and is at-tuned to him at this moment.

That night, Charlie sneaks out to see if Charles really did tamper with the stairs. As she climbs the stairway, she discovers him, and they face off against each other, their silhouettes outlined against the lights within the house. He tells her that he's not leaving.

I want to settle down. Be a part of this family. I know what you've been thinking. How do you think your mother would have felt? What would it do to her now? How about your father's job at the bank? What would be-come of you if everything came out? What would you tell? Who would be-lieve you?

As Charlie replies, "I don't want you here, Uncle Charlie. I don't want you to touch my mother," the camera moves in to frame their silhouettes—to all the world like lovers' silhouettes on a window shade—in me-dium shot (4.92). The image fades out on Charlie's threat, "Go away or I'll kill you myself."

Charles's sawing of the stair, I gather, is not a serious murder attempt. It is a message to Charlie, meaning, "Let me stay or I'll kill you," and further, "Ac-knowledge me or I'll kill you." The latter implies, "Don't tell Graham," and also, "Don't let Graham come between

4.92

us." When Charlie explains why she doesn't want Charles to stay ("I don't want you to touch my mother") she does not acknowledge the reality of Charles's desire. She does not say, for example, "I don't want you to touch *me*." Is it that Charlie does not yet fully know her own desire? She does not yet know, after all, whether she will accept Graham's proposal; she does not know which of her promises she will keep. If Charlie forced Charles to leave by con-vincing him of her resoluteness, would she inform on Charles and then marry Graham? Charlie has given back Charles's ring and Charles has broken his pact: she is now free to accept Graham's proposal. But is Charlie's bond with Charles so easily broken? Has her desire for Charles been overcome? The terms of the remainder of the narrative are definitively established and understood by both Charles and Charlie. Whether or not they desire each other, they are locked in a struggle to the death.

The second—and perhaps more serious—murder attempt follows immediately. The setting, appropriately enough, is the garage. A view of the garage door fades in. We recognize the shadowy figure of Charles. In an insert closeup, we see the exhaust pipe of

4.93

a car (4.93). This exhaust pipe, spewing forth poison, recalls Charles's ubiquitous cigar.

Then Hitchcock cuts to the family in the house. It is the night of Charles's lecture to Emma's club. The family is all spruced up. Emma squirts scent on Joe, visibly uncomfortable in a tuxedo. "No perfume!" he objects. "Just the nice, fresh, clean smell of lavender. You look very handsome, both of you. I must say I'm pretty proud of the two men in my family. Oh Joe, I *wish* you could drive a car." The camera moves in from a three-shot, isolating Charles. Synchronized with this movement, Charles looks off-screen to the right. There is a quick cut to Charlie's huge shadow, framed by the bannister, followed by Charlie, who enters the frame and walks down the stairs (4.94).

4.94

When she awoke from her long sleep, Charlie took the backstairs to avoid making this entrance into Charles's view. Charles is mesmerized by the vision of Charlie, who now makes her deferred, defiant entrance. Charlie wants to arrange things so she won't have to ride with Charles. Charles's line, "Charlie, I want you to hear my speech on the way. After all, you're my severest critic," is a private joke, no longer between Hitchcock and the knowing viewer, but between Charles and Charlie. Emma, offscreen, settles the controversy. "Well anyway, we need a taxi." Charles announces, "It's all arranged." He means by this that the seating arrangements are now final. And what we are about to witness, the second murder attempt, is also all arranged: he claims authorship of what is to follow. But Charlie whispers urgently, "Mother, please ride with me . . . *Please!*" When Charlie leaves to start the car, Emma is in a quandary.

In the garage, Charlie finds the car already running. In the darkness, she gropes for the key to turn the motor off, but it is missing. At this moment the garage door closes, engulfing the frame in darkness, and there is a cut to the interior of the house (our eyes accustomed to the darkness of the preceding shots, this cut has the effect of a white flash; we are momentarily blinded by it, as we were when Saunders took Charles's picture). Charles comes down the stairs. Then Joe goes up, leaving the frame to Emma and Charles. She touches his shoulder, casts him a loving smile, and then leaves the frame. The camera reframes with him as he goes to the window and closes it, then turns on the radio. "Might as well have a little music while we wait." But the waiting is cut short when Herb unexpectedly appears on the scene. Agitated, he announces that someone is trapped in the garage. All leave and run to the garage door, which has been wedged shut by a stone. Surreptitiously, Charles kicks it away, and Charlie falls through the door frame, unconscious.

Charles takes charge. He goes into the garage, inserts the key in the ignition, turns the motor off, and comes back out. He carries Charlie into the yard and lays her down on the grass, ordering Joe to get a bottle of whiskey, Emma to rub her feet, Roger to get something with which to fan her. Ann, breaking down, hugs Charlie emotionally, a deeply affecting gesture. Then, framed as though lovers, Charles leans over Charlie, his hands clasping hers. In a close shot from Charles's point of view, Charlie opens her eyes and says, "Go away." As we cut to a long shot with the whole family in the frame, Charles says, "Emmie, she wants you." Charlie slowly rises and begins to tell what happened. Herb, wanting a little recognition, tells his story ("Lucky thing I passed by. I was walking across the yard and I heard this beating on the door and I figured there must be a human being in there."). Paying no attention to Herb, Emma says to Charles, "She might have died. *You* saved her."

Joe's first thought is to cancel the lecture. But Charlie insists that they all go and she will stay home to prepare for the party. Emma, bewildered by what has happened, reluctantly agrees. As she gets into the cab, she mutters uncomprehendingly, "I don't understand. First the stairs, then . . ." But she cannot finish her thought, and the cab pulls away. When Charlie sees that she is alone, she runs back to the house. There is a dissolve to her on the phone, viewed from a slightly high angle (4.95). Upset, Charlie says, "He isn't there? And you don't expect him?" Then there is a dissolve to a longer, higher-angle shot with the bannister crowding Charlie in

4.95

4.96

4.97

4.98

the frame (4.96). "Can you tell me where . . ." Then to an extreme long shot in which Charlie is viewed through the //// bars of the bannister (4.97). Within this framing, she finishes yet another attempt to track down Graham. The camera twists left, holding on a view looking down the flight of stairs to the front door (4.98) that echoes Charles's view of Charlie framed in the doorway.

Has Graham let her down? In any case, the agency that arranged for Herb to arrive just in time appears determined to let the struggle between Charles and Charlie be played out as a private matter between them. That agency once more declares itself. As Charlie comes up the stairs, the camera twists again, its direction reversed this time, until it frames her, doubled by her own shadow (4.99). As the music builds in dramatic intensity, she opens the door and goes inside. Viewed through the frame-within-a-frame of the doorway, she turns on the light, goes to the dresser, and passes from our sight (4.100). Charlie's search for the ring is closed to us; Hitchcock's framing declares a limit to our access to her. As if reaffirming the significance of the camera's gesture here, Hitchcock cuts directly to another empty frame-within-a-frame (4.101). This setup is the precise double of that in which Charles viewed Charlie in the doorway and completes this sequence's invocation of that moment. Charlie is absent from this frame, which does not depict Charles's view. It frames no one and represents the view of no one within the world of the film.

For some seconds, the camera holds this framing, marked by the absence of human figures and invoking Charles's fateful vision. When people finally

throng through this door, buzzing with
sociability (4.102), it is as if the camera's
gaze itself has brought the frame to
life.[21]

Charlie emerges from the bedroom
and closes the door behind her, clasping
the ring in her hand, as sounds filter
from the party downstairs. Emma's
voice rises above the general hubbub
("Joe, will you take care of everyone?").
Charlie calls, "I'll be right down," and
looks one last time at the ring. The audience has arrived, and Charlie is preparing to step out on stage.

4.99

Downstairs, Charles is about to pour
champagne for the guests. There is general laughter as the minister says, "I
thought champagne was only for battle-
ships. None for me and none, I'm sure,
for my wife." Charles fills a glass and
gives it to the Widow Potter, with a
show of cordiality. Then he holds up his
own glass. "I'd like to propose a toast
too . . . Isn't Charlie coming down?"
"She'll be down in a moment," Emma
answers and proceeds to serve Mrs. Potter from a tray of sandwiches, her words
evoking a series of grisly images ("Oh
don't take that one. I don't know why I
make tomato. They always soak through
the bread when they've been standing.
Try one of these. Just whole wheat bread
and cream cheese. It's the paprika
makes it pink"). Mr. Green toasts "our
distinguished visitor, the man who
made the best speech heard in this town
for years." As Charles passes a glass to
Herb over Mrs. Potter, she and Charles
exchange glances. This brings us to one
of the most disturbing passages in the
film.

4.100

4.101

With the minister framed beside him,
Charles turns, looks up, and smiles
(4.103). (In the course of this shot and
its repetitions as the sequence proceeds,

4.102

4.104

4.105

4.106

the minister gradually edges to the left, until he is all but completely excluded from the frame.) There is a cut to Charles's view of Charlie, as she makes her entrance and begins to descend the stairs (4.104).

Up to this point, the filming is modeled on the moment when Charlie descended the stairs just before going to the garage. Charles's smile reveals his real happiness at seeing Charlie still alive. And she is radiant, a vision of beauty. She looks at the camera as she descends, as if reveling in Charles's—it is also our—gaze. Hitchcock cuts back to Charles. "Now for my toast." What might Charles's words be? Hitchcock's filming precisely invokes a toast Charles cannot make (and perhaps does not consciously realize he desires to make). The stage is set for Charles to toast Charlie as his intended bride.[22]

The smile freezes on Charles's face as he sees something that transforms his vision. Hitchcock cuts to a closer shot of Charlie from Charles's point of view (4.105). She is wearing the ring, and her look to the camera now signifies recognition of Charles's recognition of that fact.[23] The camera moves in, its movement sensuously meshing with the movement of her hand as it glides down the bannister, until that hand nearly fills the frame: a shot powerfully evocative of erotic fascination (4.106, 4.107).

By presenting herself in public wearing Charles's ring, Charlie shows him that she once again possesses the evidence to condemn him and that she knows exactly what that evidence is. Of course, no evidence poses any threat to Charles unless Charlie is willing to use it against him. Charlie's bold gesture is meant, at one level, as a declaration that she is prepared to expose Charles or kill him rather than let him remain in this home, even if it means Emma's breakdown. Charlie makes her entrance into Charles's view dressed as a promised bride. Further, she invokes that act about which bridegrooms fantasize. She presents herself to Charles's vision as if offering herself to him and claims the power to satisfy him (the locus of Charlie's erotic power, like Charles's, is the hand). She penetrates his fantasy and

4.107

possesses it. Her entrance, I think, inscribes a pledge as well as an ultimatum. If he leaves, she will not turn him in (in any case, she has given up trying to reach Graham; Charles will be able to leave town without being apprehended). She wears Charles's ring and vows her faithfulness to him, on the condition that he depart. She will not accept Graham's proposal: her hand is already given.

Charles's glass, still raised for a toast, appears in the exact place in the frame occupied by Charlie's ring (4.108). He lowers the glass below the frame line and fills it out of our view. When he lifts it back into the frame, he is again smiling. His words appear to concede Charlie's terms. "Charlie, you're just in time for a farewell toast. Hate to break the news to you like this, but tomorrow I

4.108

must leave Santa Rosa." At the foot of the stairs, Charlie removes her hand from the bannister as though it reminded her of Charles's touch and reflects on her victory. One disturbing implication reveals itself immediately. Mrs. Potter says that this is a real coincidence: "I was planning to go to San Francisco myself tomorrow morning." The widow will fall victim to Charles if he really does leave on the train and Graham is not notified. Charlie's agreement with Charles makes her party to the murder of all the future Mrs. Potters.

Then the devastating effect Charles's departure will have on Emma reveals itself. For Charlie, an elegiac note is struck. "Oh Emmie darling, I didn't mean to spoil your fun tonight. I got a letter today and I've got to catch the early morning train." He looks at Emma and smiles. As we reframe with him to a two-shot, he bends down to kiss her, then turns away, directing his speech not to Emma alone, but to the whole party. "But I want all of you to know that I'll always think of this lovely town as a place of hospitality and kindness. And homes." Emma is dazed. "But I can't bear it if you go, Charles." Then there is a cut to Charlie, deeply troubled. She moves into the parlor and takes a seat as Charles explains that he's arranged with Dr. Phillips for a memorial to the town's chil-

4.109

dren. Then Hitchcock frames Emma so as to underscore the match between her pose and Charlie's (4.109, 4.110). "It's just the idea that we were together again." Emma has lost sight of the fact that she is in public and sobs out loud. At this moment, Hitchcock cuts to the guests looking right into the camera, which he places in the literal position of Emma's eyes (this is a gesture also addressed to us). In the face of this public breakdown, no one knows what to do. The minister is conspicuously awkward and ineffectual. Everyone looks down or away, embarrassed, unwilling or unable to acknowledge Emma at this moment. Of all the guests, only Mrs. Potter continues meeting the camera's gaze (4.111).

4.110

Hitchcock may at times appear to endorse Charles's professed inhumanity or to treat despair cynically or frivolously. People who don't understand Hitchcock might think that he would be inclined simply to make a joke out of Mrs. Potter. But this detail, embedded so that one recognizes its significance only if one attends knowingly and sympathetically to Hitchcock's framing, can serve as a revelation of Hitchcock's humanity as well as a declaration of his method. For Hitchcock, the absence or loss of love makes the world a hell. The widowed Mrs. Potter has a knowledge of grief and

4.111

understands Emma's sorrow. Only she has the strength of character to stand by Emma at this moment.

If Mrs. Potter is the true type of Charles's victims, what does that suggest about Charles's acts of killing? In his conversation with Truffaut, Hitchcock speaks of Charles as a killer with a mission. One way of understanding that mission is to think of it as ridding the world of "fat, wheezing animals" that incarnate lost beauty and grace. But we can also understand Charles's mission as a commitment to listening for and responding to these lonely women's desperate, heartfelt calls (of course, Charles may be mad in believing he hears such calls). It is fundamental to *Shadow of a Doubt*, as I read it, that Charles's killing can be viewed as expressing either contempt for his victims or compassion, indeed love, for them. Failure to acknowledge this ambiguity, and to appreciate its implications, is a failure to comprehend the film.

And what does Charles envision Mrs. Potter to be calling upon him to do? To fulfill her as her husband never did, hence to betray her marriage? To take her dead husband's place, hence to bring that marriage back to life? To release her from the curse of dwelling in a world in which love has died? To allow her to keep faith with her marriage by joining her husband in death? Whether or not Mrs. Potter acknowledges it, the truth about "marriage" to Charles is that its consummation is death. (I am not suggesting that Charles's acts can only be understood as the selfless giving of the gift of death. Hitchcock also does not allow us to rule out the possibility that Charles's selflessness is a mask, that his really *is* the monstrous creed he professes, that he mocks all who put faith in love.)

As Emma goes on, speaking to no one in particular (although her words are weighed by Charlie, by Charles, by Mrs. Potter, and by us), Hitchcock cuts to Charlie. "We were so close growing up. Then Charles went away and I got married and . . ." The camera moves in as Emma's voice trails off. "Then you know how it is." Charlie begins to weep. "You sort of forget you're you. You're your husband's wife . . ." The image fades out.

Charlie weeps, I think, for her mother, for the likes of Mrs. Potter, for Charles, and for herself. She has forsaken her own romantic dreams as well as her hopes for an "ordinary" life by consenting to a marriage that makes her party to Charles's acts of killing, in which her being is submerged in Charles's. She has consigned herself to becoming her husband's wife, even to Mrs. Potter's condition of widowhood and consigned Charles to the death-in-life of banishment from his love. Dead to Charlie's world, he must haunt the earth, trapped in an endless cycle of killings. But Charles's true intentions have not yet been revealed. The stage is set for the film's climax and conclusion.

The scene fades in on the train station. The Greens, the minister and his wife, and the Newtons, along with Herb, are gathered for Charles's departure. Mr. Green says, "We'll be looking for you, Mr. Oakley. We believe you're one of us. Don't we, Margaret?" She concurs. He adds, "And bless you for your gift to our hospital. The children will bless you too in all the years to come." Charles's trib-

4.112

4.113

4.114

4.115

utes to this town are ironic—if no one but Charlie is capable of recognizing his irony—but we cannot assume that they are not also sincere. Emma and Charles take each other's hands, and there is a cut to Charlie, who is dressed in black: dressed, that is, as a widow. Absorbed, she has her back to the train as it pulls into the station (4.12; this image was anticipated early in the film by the dissolve to the train bringing Charles to Santa Rosa).

Roger, Ann, and Charlie board the train to see Charles off. Then, in a framing fit for the farewell of Richard III, Charles bids adieu to Santa Rosa and to Emma (4.113). He says his goodbye—this is his farewell to the world he dreamed of calling home—almost soundlessly, disdainfully blowing it out like a puff of smoke. He turns, a secret smile on his face, and absents himself from the frame, leaving it momentarily void of human figures.

The frame that follows is composed schematically, perfectly divided in two (4.114). The right half, in its surrealism, takes up the metaphysical mood of the previous shot. The corridor, centered in this half of the frame, tunnels into the depths of the illusionistic space and gives this region a graphic symmetry that recalls both Saunders' photograph and Charles's vision of Charlie from the top of the stairs.[24] Charles enters the corridor at the far end and quickly bridges the distance between background and foreground. Through this potent movement, the frame's opening into depth is closed. And when Charles walks forward, he looks right into the camera and waves (4.115). The strangeness of the gesture is magnified by our perception of Charlie's obliviousness of it. The left side of the frame is hers as the right side of the frame is his. Her region is as flat as his is deep. Her back is to the camera, so that she is imaged by her black hair and widow's dress, the object of Charles's desire and his potential victim. She stands motionless, lost in thought before one of those "private rooms" that so intrigue Roger. Behind her, we can make out just enough of the compartment to see Roger at the apogee of each of his bounces on the unseen bed. This girl on the threshold of womanhood is reflecting on what goes on in a private room, contemplating the empty double bed.

On Charles's wave, the camera reverses field to Charles's view of Mrs. Potter at the far end of the car; she waves back on her way to the adjoining car. Mrs. Potter's wordless invitation to Charles is unseen by Charlie, but we know that, if Charlie leaves this train now, Mrs. Potter's fate is sealed, and with it Charles's and also Charlie's own. As Charlie is about to follow Ann and Roger down the corridor, there is a continuity cut to a medium shot, which frames her like a picture within an empty rectangle on the wall behind her (4.116). Charles advances and takes her arm: "Charlie, I want you to know I think you were right to make me leave. It's best for your mother. Best for all of us. You saw what happened to her last night. She's not very strong, you know. I don't think she could stand the shock. I remember once when she was a little girl . . ." He never gets to complete this memory. A flicker in the corner of the frame indicates that the train has begun to roll. Charlie, panicked, tries to break away, but Charles advances relentlessly. "Listen, I want you to forget all about me." She looks down at his hands, then back up at him as he advances, then away. She stares down in horrified recognition. "Your hands!" At this point Hitchcock cuts to Charles, his face absolutely grave (4.117). For the first time, he allows himself to be viewed without his

4.116

4.117

mask; he appears as a monstrous figure, condemned to haunt the world and to represent death.

In the next shot, the landscape hurtling by is for the first time visible. Within this frame, Charlie struggles to free herself, but Charles holds her fast (4.118). As the music continues to build in intensity, there is a cut to a much closer shot, in which the moving landscape

4.118

4.119

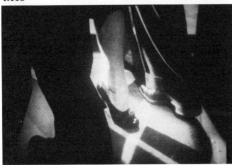

4.120

4.121

almost fills the frame (4.119). "I've got to do this, Charlie, so long as you know what you do about me." The "this" to which Charles refers, we take it (as does Charlie), is his act of killing her, already begun; and a key to this act is Hitchcock's imaging of it as sexual, like his imaging of Handell Fane's trapeze act. The landscape hurtling by, the roar of the train, and the swelling of the music combine with the rising curve of excitement of the action to give this climactic passage its passionate, erotic force. Charlie presented herself to Charles as his bride, imagining she would wear his ring and remain faithful to him if only he left Santa Rosa never to return. But Charles's look now denies that their relationship can remain chaste; it declares that this marriage must be consummated.

The camera tilts down to the couple's legs, intertwined and violently locked (4.120). When we cut back to a shot of them grappling, Charles blocks Charlie from our view, creating one conventional Hollywood image of a lovers' clinch (4.121). From their intertwined legs, Hitchcock cuts to a shot of her gloved hand grasping the door latch: she is struggling desperately to keep from being pushed to her death. Then he cuts to the two framed by the landscape hurtling by, to her hand losing its grip on the latch, and again to the two struggling. Charles has gained the upper hand and is waiting for the moment of climax. As he says, "Not yet, Charlie, let it get a little faster," there is a cut to a tight closeup of her, his hand at her mouth and throat (4.122). She looks down, her eyes wide, and Hitchcock cuts to a shot from her point of view, in which the tracks move by in a blur (4.123).

This is more than a conventional point-of-view shot. For one thing, what Charlie objectively sees at this moment is nothing determinate. Her "view" has broken down. It is not that she sees nothing, but that Charles has presented her with a vision of nothingness, akin to Handell Fane's third vision and to the vision the Professor presents to Hannay when he shows his hand. And this shot has a powerful, unsettling kinaesthetic impact: we do not so much see as feel it. It is a representation of Charlie's vision, but also a metaphor for it and an expression of the vertigo it engenders.[25]

4.122

Charles makes Charlie attend to this vision. She wants to turn away, but he forces her to keep looking. And he continues to address her about the act he is performing. His words ("Not yet, Charlie, let it get a little faster") establish that this act is not simply one of killing, but

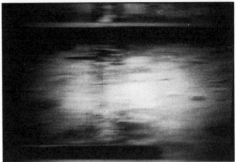

4.123

also one of instruction and initiation. He is preparing her for the part she will be called upon to play when the right moment comes —when "it" gets just fast enough. At one level, this "it" refers to what is contained within the frame of Charlie's vision. To know what she must do, and to do it, she must acknowledge the seductive, spellbinding power of the vision to which Charles directs her gaze. And by the cut to (4.123), Hitchcock compels us to attend to this vision too. When Charlie interrupted Charles's speech at the dinner table, she undertook to speak for the likes of us. Now Charles casts her in the role of viewer, and she assumes our place— as we assume hers—in silence. Hitchcock calls upon us to accept Charlie as "one of us," as he calls upon us to accept Charles as his own representative and to accept Charlie's vision (her vision of Charles, of her world, of her own fate) as also our own (our vision of the film's author, of the film itself, of our acts of viewing). There is a part Hitchcock will call upon us to play, and to play our part we too must attend to this vision.

In *Rebecca*, Mrs. Danvers, speaking in a soothing, hypnotic voice, lulls Joan Fontaine into an ever-deepening absorption in a vision of the seductive, beckoning sea; she encourages her to accept that vision's invitation to plunge to her death. Perhaps this is how it is most natural to understand Charles's words, at least at first: he compels Charlie to attend to her vision so that she may be transported into such a state that, at the climactic moment, she will submit passively, or even surrender gladly, to his murderous thrust. He presents her with this vision of her own nothingness and of the awesome power he represents: the power of the divinity that holds sway over this world. This is at the same time Charlie's vision of her own desire and a terrifying vision of unfreedom, of nothingness, of death, of all she dreads.

Yet Charles is not, I take it, simply seducing Charlie into submission. He is also performing a demonstration, for her as audience, within the context of their ongoing argument. Like the Professor when he shows his hand to Hannay, or Handell Fane when he demonstrates the superiority of his form of theater, Charles performs his demonstration in order to clinch his case. But Charles's gesture goes beyond the Professor's and Fane's by also being a serious act of instruction, one that is addressed to someone for whose education he takes a real responsibility. Charles presents Charlie with this vision in order to complete her initiation into the adult world in which real and symbolic acts of killing are commonplace, ordinary; in order to complete her education and thereby her transformation from a girl to a woman. Charles wants Charlie to *know*. He wants her to know that she has stepped into a trap, what that trap is, and who has set it. He wants her to know who he really is, what life has really been like for him, his monstrousness and his despair. He wants her to know how he envisions the world and what she harbors within herself. He wants her to know that he has allowed her, as it were, to see inside him and to know that what he has inside, she has too. He wants her to know that they are twins after all, but that what joins them is something frightful, not something wonderful. He wants her to know that he has come at her bidding, but that he is separate from her and cannot be willed away like a phantom in a dream. He wants her to know that this vision reveals her desire, but that it also announces the limits of her freedom, announces that she must do what she is about to be called upon to do regardless of her desires.

Hitchcock cuts once more to the nightmare vision of the rails, then to a two-shot. The tension raised to an excruciating pitch, Charles cries "Now!" Cued by this signal, Hitchcock cuts to Charlie's hand, which has regained its grip on the door. Then to Charles, who looks ready. Suddenly, he cuts to a much longer view. Looking away from the open door, Charlie pushes Charles to his death (4.124). To comprehend this moment, I believe, and to understand *Shadow of a Doubt* as a whole, we must acknowledge the haunting possibility that Charlie's act fulfills rather than frustrates Charles's real wish, that Charles—whether consciously or not—directs Charlie to push him off the train. This is, after all, the only possible resolution: Charles released by death from his curse, Charlie freed from her monstrous marriage by widowhood, the circle of killings broken. And it is a beautifully appropriate one: the man who believes he has the power to hear and answer the desperate calls of women who long for death calls upon his twin, who has vowed faithfulness to him and vowed to penetrate all his secrets, to perform the act that frees him

4.124

(as she once called upon him, the only person in the world capable of performing the requisite "miracle," to come and save her).

With this possibility in mind, Charles's presentation to Charlie of the vision of the tracks takes on a new meaning. In retrospect, we may take him to be acknowledging his own powerlessness to fulfill his desire or effect his salvation. That is, he concedes her victory and calls upon her to respect the responsibilities it imposes, which are also consequences of her acceptance of the role of his promised bride. He calls upon her to save him, to allow him to die redeemed, and also to free herself from his curse. But to do so, she must kill him herself, must take his death into her own hands. What completes Charlie's education, then, is her discovery of Charles's longing for death, of her desire for his death, and of her own capacity for killing. For Charlie to become a woman, her innocent self—and the world of her innocence—must die and be reborn. The innocent Charlie dies when Charles dies by her hand. If Charles is a murderer, Charlie is a murderer too. Yet there is an even deeper irony. If Charlie's act of killing is necessary and conceived in innocence, Charles's acts of killing also were not really murders, were necessary and conceived in love. Charlie now knows that evil is real and death is final, but she kills to affirm her innocence and to acknowledge Charles. She fulfills her calling when she hears and responds to Charles's desperate plea, and we affirm her act, as we affirm our community with Hannay and Pamela at the end of *The Thirty-Nine Steps*. Hitchcock calls upon us to acknowledge that, when Charlie pushes Charles to his death, she acts in our place and in completion of the author's design. In this gesture, Charlie's hand and our hand and Hitchcock's hand and Charles's hand are one.[26] We acknowledge our community with Charlie and join with her in acknowledgment of Charles. What she gains at this moment is also what she irrevocably loses within her world, a true community. If she discovers the power of evil and the finality of death, she also discovers the reality of love as a human bond. Within Charles and within herself she discovers "something wonderful" after all.

By insisting that Charles and Charlie can both be viewed as acting out of love and a shared condition of innocence, I do not mean to be denying the obvious. Of course, it is also possible to view Charles as murderous to the end, as acting out of a desire for violence rather than a longing for love; and it is possible to view Charlie as compromised, fully implicated in his immorality. It is possible to view Charles as like the Professor rather than like Mr. Memory. The truth is, I take it, that the ending of *Shadow of a Doubt*—and indeed the entirety of the film that turns on this ending—is designed to pose its ambiguities, not to resolve them. We cannot say whether, when she turns away and pushes Charles to his death, Charlie asserts her power over him or, acknowledging his power over her, fulfills his secret wish. We cannot say whether her turning away breaks decisively with the vision he presents to her, or whether it completes her possession by that vision. We cannot say whether she discovers within herself the power to overcome her vision, or whether what she finds within herself *is* the power revealed in that vision. We cannot say whether by her act she exorcises Charles or accepts him into her heart. It is not that Hitchcock avoids taking a stand on these matters. His articulated

4.125

ambiguity *is* his stand, his affirmation that love and murder (and the act of making a film and the act of viewing a film) are, as I put it at the conclusion of the reading of *Murder!*, mysteries. *Shadow of a Doubt*, like every Hitchcock film, does not claim to solve for us its deepest mysteries, but to acknowledge them.

Our vision of Charles's fall is particularly harrowing and haunting. As he falls from the train, another train rushes with terrifying force from the background to the foreground of the frame. (4.125). We do not actually witness the impact, but we imagine him as horribly crushed, mutilated, dismembered. As the music shifts to a ghostly reprise of the Merry Widow Waltz, there is a dissolve to the dancing-couples image. Dream and nightmare are momentarily superimposed, and the entire film is coalesced into a single image (4.126).

4.126

Then the mood lifts. There follows a cut to an extreme long shot of Santa Rosa, the streets lined for a funeral procession; then to the front of the church; and finally to Graham and Charlie. The camera moves in, then holds this framing (4.127). From this point on, the soundtrack develops in two separate lines. As Charlie and Graham talk, we hear the minister's eulogy (sometimes drowned out by the foreground voices).

4.127

Santa Rosa has gained and lost a son. A son that she can be proud of. Brave, generous, kind. With all the splendid dignity of . . .

Without looking at Graham, Charlie says, "I'm glad you were able to come, Jack. I couldn't have faced it without someone who knew. I did know more. I couldn't tell you." "I know."

He came into our community and our lives were finer and richer for it. For those who loved him most, those who knew him best, and for you, his beloved family . . .

Charlie continues, "He thought the world was a terrible place. He couldn't have been very happy ever. He didn't trust people, seemed to hate them. Hated the whole world."

Let this thought, in this sad hour of . . . No true love ever died . . .

Charlie completes her thought: "He said that people like us had no idea what the world was really like." Graham then sums up his understanding of the moral. "Things aren't as bad as that. But sometimes it needs a lot of watching. It seems to go crazy every now and then, like your Uncle Charlie." After looking at each other, they look away, as though lost in their own private worlds. Charlie sighs and says nothing further, as the minister completes his eulogy.

The beauty of their souls, the sweetness of their character, live on with us forever.

There is a dissolve to the front of the church. As the music, now dominated by the organ, resolves, the title "The End" appears. The circle of killing has been completed, the chain broken. The widows' money, the fruit of Charles's murders, has been left not to Charlie (Charles's "widow") but to all of Santa Rosa. It now may do, as it were, God's work. Charlie's original wish that she receive no gift from Charles is finally fulfilled. And Charlie is free to marry if she wishes. But the tone of this ending is ambiguous and disquieting.

The Lodger, Murder!, and The Thirty-Nine Steps all end with the union of lovers. The Lodger avoids Shadow of a Doubt's downbeat ending in part by having its Charles-like figure be innocent, or in effect reborn as innocent, while the shift of Daisy's affection from Joe to the lodger is complete. *Murder!*'s ending is ironic and bitter because its world, which knows no justice, is unworthy of Handell Fane's final gesture. *The Thirty-Nine Steps'* ending is rendered bittersweet by the death of Mr. Memory, but it lacks the specifically unsettling quality of the ending of *Shadow of a Doubt.* (The lovers' innocence is uncompromised, the Professor can be destroyed with no regrets, and the dying Mr. Memory forgives and is forgiven by Hannay.) To this group, we might add *Stage Fright,* whose Charles figure turns out to be a murderer and, like Charles, suffers a horrible death at the film's climax. But by the time of Jonathan's death, Eve has fallen out of love with him and fallen head over heels in love with "Ordinary Smith," the Graham figure.[27]

Shadow of a Doubt's ending refuses to maintain that Charlie is in love with Graham, but also refuses to rule out the possibility that, after the final fade-out, she will marry him. But that is hardly her dream come true. When Charlie says, "I couldn't have faced it without someone who knew" (words that Charles might have spoken to Charlie with real authority), we are not satisfied with Graham's assurance that he knows. Graham does *not* know. Not having access to Hitchcock's presentation to us, he does not know what we know. He does not speak for Hitchcock, nor does he speak for us, when he gives his summation that the world is basically all right as it is but only needs a little watching. Not only the world needs to be watched, and the world needs more than watching. Nor do we believe that Charlie feels for Graham what she felt, and still feels, for Charles. We sense that Charles's death leaves Charlie isolated, weary, depressed. The possibility of marriage to Graham holds no promise of fulfillment. Graham knows only that realm of the ordinary within which, but also apart from which, Charlie is fated to stand. A part of Charlie that Graham does not know, but which Hitchcock has allowed us to share, dies with Charles; and a part of Charles lives on within Charlie, and within us.

5

Psycho

Shadow of a Doubt is separated by as many years from Psycho as it is from The Lodger. This period may naturally be divided into two parts, with Stage Fright (1950) and Strangers on a Train (1951) the boundary. The remainder of the 1940s was, manifestly, a time of searching for Hitchcock, while the decade of the fifties represents the full flowering of his mature art.

Shadow of a Doubt establishes that Hitchcock can make a film in Hollywood that is the equal of his greatest British work. But it is, along with its underrated companion piece Lifeboat (1943), in many respects an isolated accomplishment. Shadow of a Doubt in no way represents a general solution to the problem of the form an American Hitchcock film might take, in the way that The Thirty-Nine Steps represents a model for the remainder of his films in the thirties. After a gap of two years, when he made only two short films for the British Ministry of Information, his next feature, Spellbound (1945), was released, a film strikingly different from Shadow of a Doubt.

Spellbound, like The Paradine Case (1947), was made under the aegis of David O. Selznick. These films are far from the equal of Shadow of a Doubt or even Lifeboat, in my judgment, although there is of course much of interest in them. After Rebecca, Hitchcock had no need to prove that he could make a Selznick film that is also a Hitchcock film. Between these two projects, however, Hitchcock made Notorious (1946), which he produced as well as directed. Notorious is, with Shadow of a Doubt, the greatest achievement of Hitchcock's first decade of work in America. I have no inclination to disagree with Truffaut when he singled out Notorious, among all Hitchcock's films, as the one that gives the most perspicuous picture of Hitchcock's art.[1] Notorious transforms the Hitchcock thriller of the thirties into a fully American film, as Foreign Correspondent and The Saboteur do not; it creates a Hitchcock paradigm, with Hitchcock's subsequent Cary Grant vehicles—To Catch a Thief and North by Northwest—among those cast in its mold. Notorious is the first Hitchcock film in which every shot is not only meaningful but beautiful, as beautiful as are Ingrid Bergman and Cary Grant photographed by Ted Tetzlaff under Hitchcock's direction. For the first time in Hitchcock's work, two great romantic stars are matched against each other, and their romance is wedded to a richly expressive, romantic visual style. In Notorious, Hitchcock's camera expresses the full-bodied passion that vibrates in his greatest later films, such as Vertigo. In Notorious, the camera's lush romanticism, for the first time, is equal and constant partner to its wit, elegance, and theatricality.

After The Paradine Case Hitchcock made, in the unsettled atmosphere of Hollywood at the end of the forties—a Hollywood threatened with economic dislocation and political division and repression—two strange and disquieting films, his first in color, *Rope* (1948) and *Under Capricorn* (1949).

Rope is the film in which Hitchcock employs the famous ten-minute take, with no cutting. Over 150 discrete camera movements effect transitions from setup to setup, simulating every kind of classical cut. Yet André Bazin was wrong when he wrote that "*Rope* could just as well have been cut in the classical way."[2] For the deliberateness of every move that the camera makes creates a state of perpetual tension. At every moment, our sense that the camera is poised to move enhances our sense that it represents a palpable presence within the world of the film. What *The Lodger* declares at certain crucial junctures, *Rope* embodies throughout.

At the center of *Rope* is a secret—there will be no cuts, only camera movements—that is no secret at all. This separates the film completely from the stage play from which it was adapted, defines the film's conception, determines the details of its planning, and makes its execution a virtuoso performance. *Rope* presents what is ordinarily taken for granted in a film, continuity, as its signal achievement. Hitchcock's desire for his achievement to be acknowledged is as manifest as its central character's desire for the conception, planning, and execution of his perfect murder to be acknowledged. Indeed, the crux of *Rope*'s secret is that it allows the film to be a perfect counterpart to the murder at the heart of its narrative. Like *Shadow of a Doubt* and *Murder!* before it, and *The Wrong Man* after it, *Rope* is one of Hitchcock's studies for *Psycho*.

Next to *Jamaica Inn* and *Torn Curtain*, *Under Capricorn* is, despite its exhilarating camera movements and its legion of admirers in France, the Hitchcock film that gives me least pleasure. *Stage Fright* (1950), on the other hand, is a Hitchcock film that is greatly underrated. With *Murder!* it is one of the works in which theater, always a preoccupation, becomes an explicit subject. Yet *Stage Fright* presents its central philosophical arguments about film and theater with subtlety and complex irony, as it presents its characters and the events of its narrative. Few Hitchcock films are studded with as many traps for the unwary viewer or critic who thinks it is child's play to penetrate the author's thinking. It is a film that can give the impression of having been put together casually, but is one of Hitchcock's most carefully composed and crafted works.

Rope and *Stage Fright* are remarkable films. But they are alike in expressing themselves with extreme, almost obsessive, indirectness. Both films reveal an author whose thoughts are veiled from his public. (I say this despite *Stage Fright*'s lightness of tone and its declared allegiance to romantic comedy.) It is only with *Strangers* on a Train (1951) that Hitchcock once again unveiled his mastery of theatricality and commanded the attention of his audience.

Strangers on a Train is noteworthy for the brilliance of its conception and the masterful execution of its details; and for Robert Walker's riveting presence and performance. And it was Hitchcock's first collaboration with the cinematographer Robert Burks, who photographed all the remaining Hitchcock films of the fifties, endowing them with a look that has become indelibly impressed on our understanding of what a Hitchcock film is.

Of these films, I Confess (1952) stands out for the austerity of its black and white photography, and for a stark, tormented mood that is accentuated by the poetic quality of its language and the subdued, repressed tone in which Hitchcock's actors were directed to speak. I have always associated this film's bleakness with the dark moment in the history of Hollywood at which it was made: its story about the courage and despair of a man scorned for his refusal to testify under interrogation is a thinly veiled allegory of McCarthyism and the blacklist.

Dial 'M' for Murder (1954) is a highly accomplished Hitchcock film that looks much more like a major one when it is viewed in the 3-D format in which it was made. But it is with Rear Window, from the same year, that Hitchcock's mature period really begins. Rear Window is generally recognized as one of Hitchcock's greatest films: funny, touching, almost inhumanly brilliant, profound, completely worked out formally, dramatically, and philosophically, worthy of the most attentive scrutiny. To Catch a Thief (1955) is its considerable inferior, while The Trouble with Harry (1956), a personal favorite of Hitchcock's, is an endlessly fascinating, if highly idiosyncratic work (it is also his first film with music by Bernard Herrmann). The remake of The Man Who Knew Too Much (1956) is a rich and rewarding film, which demands to be placed alongside the 1934 version: few experiences in film study are more eye-opening than thinking through the relationship between these two films, shot by shot.

The Wrong Man (1957), Vertigo (1958), and North by Northwest (1959) are, like Rear Window, among Hitchcock's most accomplished films. They are profound studies of the conditions of human identity, knowledge, and love, and sustained reflections, at the highest level of seriousness, on the conditions of the art of film.

Psycho (1960) is the masterpiece that culminated the period in which Hitchcock and his public were in closest touch, and announced, I shall argue, its necessary ending. Its astounding success capped the decade in which "Hitchcock" was a household name. After this triumph and the publicity campaign that preceded the release of his next film, *The Birds* (1963) disappointed Hitchcock's public. Who at the time was prepared for the loving concern accorded the relationship of Melanie and Mitch, the tragic death of Annie, or the haunting figure of Mitch's mother? Dissatisfaction centered on Tippi Hedren. To an audience longing for another Grace Kelly, she was awkward and ill at ease on camera, often painfully and embarrassingly so. Yet Hitchcock used her again in *Marnie*. Indeed, he insisted in placing her at the center of that film. She came between Hitchcock and his audience as no star had ever done.

Hitchcock's camera discovers in Tippi Hedren an exemplar of the difficulty and pain of expressing love. She is quite pretty, but we do not take easy pleasure in viewing her. She does not repel us and we are not unsympathetic to her, but something calls upon us to keep our distance. Indeed, the camera moves us too close and confronts us with our wish to avoid intimacy with her. Hitchcock calls upon us to acknowledge film's ordinary avoidance of intimacy, and our own in our ordinary lives. Is it that we are fearful that our appetite for love is so voracious that we do not dare give in to it at all?

The Birds and *Marnie*, his two last masterpieces, are infused with a deep sense of loss, an urgency, and an emotional directness that set them apart from all other Hitchcock films. They declare something about the human need for love that was always implicit in his work. Hitchcock's subsequent films—*Torn Curtain* (1966), *Topaz* (1968), *Frenzy* (1972), and *Family Plot* (1976)—make no further declarations of such an order.

Torn Curtain, made after the death of cinematographer Robert Burks and without the collaboration of Bernard Herrmann and editor George Tomasini, is an ambitious but aborted work. *Topaz* is a melancholy film about loss, betrayal, death; about the failure of the old to pass on hard-won knowledge; about the end of romance. It contains passages as beautiful as anything in Hitchcock, yet is, manifestly, another failure. *Frenzy*, a self-conscious return to Hitchcock's origins, and specifically to *The Lodger*, is more successful, if apparently more modest. In *The Lodger*, murder is invoked but not shown; in *Blackmail*, it takes place behind a curtain; in *Murder!*, *The Thirty-Nine Steps*, and *Stage Fright*, it is still not shown; in *Psycho*, the murder in the shower is presented in a montage that withholds all views of the knife penetrating flesh; in *Torn Curtain*, with the killing of Gromek, *Blackmail*'s curtain is opened, but murder is still a theatrical scene; in *Topaz*, it is treated poetically (a dying woman's dress, viewed from overhead, billows out like petals as she falls). Only in *Frenzy* is there a full revelation. We

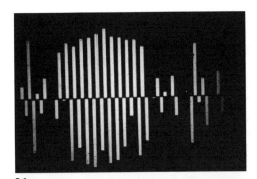

5.1

5.2

5.3

5.4

see the murder of Mrs. Blaney, in all its horror, from beginning to end, its presentation stripped of theater and poetry, and it is perhaps the most heartbreaking passage in Hitchcock's work.

The author's cameo appearance in *Family Plot*—the familiar silhouette is seen through a translucent window, the word "DEATHS" superimposed—posits the film as coming to us from beyond the grave. I think of *Family Plot* as a curtain call: light, assured, intended for pleasure, it is an acknowledgment that the body of the concert is over. What could be a more satisfying farewell than the wink to the camera that closes Hitchcock's last film, a medium's intimate salute to a medium? In this knowing yet joyful wink, *Psycho*'s darkness is acknowledged and a lifetime's dedication to the art of film is affirmed.

Psycho's title credits are dominated by graphics that play tensely on the Hitchcockian //// (5.1). They give way to an aerial view of a large city (5.2), and the words "PHOENIX, ARIZONA" appear. The camera begins to move right, hesitates, then resumes its movement. There is a dissolve to a less lofty perspective, the movement continuing as "FRIDAY DECEMBER THE ELEVENTH" appears; to a yet less elevated shot, the camera zooming in and panning right; to the wall of a building, over the words "TWO FORTY-THREE P.M.," the camera moving in toward a bank of windows. There is a barely perceptible cut to one window, its blinds almost completely closed. The camera moves in toward this window (5.3) until the darkness under the blinds fills the frame. Then, from within the dingy hotel room, it moves in to frame a double bed and a half-dressed couple (5.4).

This opening transforms that of *Shadow of a Doubt* in ways that begin to suggest *Psycho*'s singular import. For example, the documentary aspect of the opening of *Shadow of a Doubt* is taken up and extended. Indeed, *Psycho*'s opening approaches *The Wrong Man*'s assertion of the reality of its world. In *The Wrong Man*, Hitchcock personally appears, framed in one of his patented tunnel images, to tell us that the events we are about to witness really happened. As *Psycho* opens, we see the real city of Phoenix spread out below the camera and, for all we know, it really was Friday, December 11, 2:43 P.M. when these shots were taken. The precise specification of date and time reinforces the suggestion that what we are about to view is no ordinary fiction. *Psycho*'s fiction is that its world is real.

And in the opening of *Psycho*, as in that of *Shadow of a Doubt*, the camera also declares itself, dramatizing its choice of subject. But *Psycho*'s rhetorical claim for the reality of its world is also a claim for the reality of the camera's gesture of singling out this room and entering into it. In order to enter the room, the camera must descend from the great height at which it soars freely like a bird—*Psycho*'s myth is that the phoenix is the kind of bird the camera is—and plunge through this narrow opening, where it is immersed in blackness. The camera's descent and penetration suggest that it possesses a corporeal presence in the world of *Psycho*, a body; thus that it represents a being that could be viewed—a creature whose powers, however extraordinary, are only natural. A precedent is the camera's plunge through the narrow opening of the cell-door window in *The Wrong Man*. In *Shadow of a Doubt*, by contrast, the camera appears incorporeal, a spirit possessed of magical powers that enable it to breach the barrier of Joseph Cotten's window with an effortless dissolve.

The lodger enters Daisy's world possessed of the camera's powers and animated by its spirit. The camera magically possesses him, cloaks itself in his human form. In *Psycho*, however, the camera itself is called upon to suffer incarnation. Passing through this narrow opening, the camera is engulfed in blackness, suffers a symbolic death, before it emerges "on the other side," born into *Psycho*'s world. But this is at the same time the birth of that world to us. By imaging the creation of its world as a birth, *Psycho*'s opening revises and outdoes that of *North by Northwest*, the Hitchcock film immediately preceding it, which begins by imaging a magical conjuring of its world out of nothingness. Mythically giving birth to the world of *Psycho*, the camera is its mother, its gaze a mother's gaze. But the passage of the camera through the window is also its penetration of a world that, as the titles announce, already exists. This penetration reveals the masculine aspect of the camera's mythic identity; if the camera gives birth to Marion Crane's private world, it is born into it as a son. Hence the phoenix as the camera's totem: rising from its own ashes, alive and dead, mother to itself and its own son. Hence too the camera's role as harbinger of the being known to this world as "Norman Bates," who is at the same time living and dead, son and mother.

In *Shadow of a Doubt*, the camera's opening gesture is posited as enigmatic. There is a mystery in this world, that film's opening declares, incarnated in the figure of Charles, whose enigma and the camera's are one. The corollary is that the author of *Shadow of a Doubt*, represented by the camera, possesses knowledge, withheld from us, that cuts through the mystery. At one level, the film is the deferred revelation of this secret knowledge, this secret design inscribed in Charles's every knowing look and the camera's every knowing gesture. But the opening of *Psycho* is not in the same way enigmatic, does not declare that the author has a secret design. It may well be obscure to us what impels the camera to suspend its majestic soaring to descend to earth to undergo death and rebirth, penetrating and giving birth to Marion Crane's world. But it is not that Hitchcock could mitigate this obscurity by disclosing to us something he knows (about Marion, about himself, about us, about the camera).

That the camera descends to earth at all, that it singles out this woman, violating her privacy, is not posited as an enigma but as a spontaneous act that manifests the camera's nature, specifically its appetite. ("Appetite" is a concept given great prominence in *Psycho*. The next shot in the film shows Marion's uneaten lunch. Almost the first thing we learn about her is that she has lost her appetite.) At one level, *Psycho* is an allegory about the camera's natural appetite. But it is not a secret knowledge about that appetite, possessed by him alone, that impels Hitchcock to make *Psycho*. What lies at the heart of *Psycho*, what the film unleashes, is something that Hitchcock's work has already made known to us.

When the camera singles out Joseph Cotten in *Shadow of a Doubt*, it does not hesitate, as it does before committing itself to the course that leads it to Marion. Are we to read this hesitation as *in-difference*, as if it were on a mere vagary of its appetite that the camera singles out a human subject at all, and this human subject rather than another? The camera enters this window and follows Marion to her tragic fate; would a different whim have led it to a different window, a different subject, a different fate? Or is Marion, to the camera, a perfectly representative human subject? Hitchcock speaks of Marion as "an ordinary bourgeoise," yet the fate she suffers is hardly representative. It distinguishes her from others in her world, who all come to recognize that she is in some terrible way marked. Then does the author single Marion out knowing her fate? But, surely, no more than Norman Bates can Hitchcock be said to know or to fail to know Marion's fate. For the camera also *seals* Marion's fate when it singles her out. Its entrance into Marion's life is fateful; the mark she bears is also the camera's mark. If she is representative, it is only because every human subject in her world could have been fated by the camera.

As the film opens, the camera appears spontaneous, unselfconscious, free. Then it hesitates. This hesitation might be read as indifference, but its deep resonance within Hitchcock's work as a whole attunes us to its ambiguity. It recalls, for example, Joe's hesitation before he looks back down into the mud, Handell Fane's before he confronts his third vision, the crofter's before he claims his view of his wife's unfaithfulness, and Charles's before he turns on the stairs to frame Charlie with his gaze. Within *Psycho*, it is to be echoed by Norman's hesitation before he hands Marion the key to cabin 1, condemning her, and by Marion herself, when she turns to the old house from which voices are emanating. The camera's hesitation suggests a momentary doubt, a revulsion at what its gesture really calls for. Yet its nature makes it inevitable that it will overcome its hesitation, that it will plunge into blackness to be born into, and to give birth to, Marion's world.

I argued that the lodger can be seen as entering Daisy's world in answer to her call. Then does Marion also solicit the camera's coming (whether or not she is conscious of making such a call)? To be sure, Daisy knows her own romantic dream and recognizes the lodger the moment he reveals himself to her. By contrast, the camera slips secretly into Marion's world, without awakening her to its coming, and never reveals itself unambiguously to her. But if we nonetheless take the camera to be responding to Marion's call, what might we imagine Marion's real wish to be? What appetite does she possess? Does her violent death, when it occurs, satisfy her desire or deny it?

Daisy is a being all men desire to view. *The Lodger* assumes our appetite—the appetite of the man in every viewer, we might say—for Daisy. But if the camera views Marion Crane as an object of desire, to what does it wish to subject this "object"? *Psycho* does not take for granted that we will fall in love with Marion. Janet Leigh is not Ingrid Bergman, say. Not that she is unattractive or unsympathetic. If *Psycho* did not acknowledge Marion's humanity, her killing could not serve, as it must, as a paradigm of murder. Yet, with her flat affect and stiffness, she lacks a certain spark we once took for granted in a Hitchcock heroine. Would Cary Grant look twice at her?

It is crucial to *Psycho*, I take it, that we feel abandoned in its world, a world in which romance, indeed even the dream of romantic fulfillment, has all but died. And a basis of our alienation is the camera's commitment of its attention to this "ordinary bourgeoise" who is, as Uncle Charles would put it, "nothing special." Even if we possessed magical powers, we could find no fulfillment, no community, no real home, in *Psycho*'s world. It is often said that Marion's death less than halfway through the film deprives *Psycho* of its anchor. We would feel cast adrift if Richard Hannay failed to come back to life after his "death" halfway through *The Thirty-Nine Steps*. But when Marion's life is unexpectedly cut short, we have long since felt anchorless in *Psycho*'s world. We wish neither to be nor to marry Marion Crane.

The closeness of *Psycho*'s world to our own, and our alienation from that world as from our own, marks *Psycho*'s affinity with the Hitchcock-directed teleplays of the *Alfred Hitchcock Presents* television series, such as "Breakdown" and "Bang! You're Dead." Characteristically, the camera commits itself only ironically to the nominal protagonists of the teleplays. This allows free rein to the series' hilarious but disquieting satire on America in the 1950s, particularly on American television and that aspect of the series itself that Hitchcock identifies as its "sponsors." The show's sponsorship is also a censorship: "they" allow Hitchcock's teleplays to affirm, but only within limits to exemplify, "the art of pure cinema." Hitchcock composes his teleplays seriously as movies-in-miniature. But if they were unframed by Hitchcock's personal appearances, they would be devoid of a human center. We are the only human subjects whose capacity for vision the show takes seriously, and the only vision we are allowed that bears comparison with, say, Diana's or Fane's visions in *Murder!* is the vision of Hitchcock inscribed in the show's ritual opening. In this familiar opening, the camera frames the author's "signature," the line-drawing silhouette that both represents Hitchcock and manifests his hand. Hitchcock enters the frame, but only in shadow. Hitchcock's shadow steps toward Hitchcock's silhouette until it fills its outline. Then a metamorphosis is effected, as if by the agency of the camera's gaze. The shadow becomes transfigured, and Hitchcock stands before the camera in the flesh. When he is brought magically to life each week by the camera, he is not born into the teleplay's world. He addresses his remarks about "them"—flippant yet literally meant— directly to the camera. He situates himself and us and also them— the dreaded sponsors—outside the world of the teleplay.

Psycho's world is close kin to the world of the typical Hitchcock teleplay. Marion Crane might have stepped right out of such a world. But Hitchcock does not give *Psycho* a teleplay's frame. The camera does not remain outside *Psycho*'s world but is born into it, as I have said. Part of *Psycho*'s myth is that there *is* no world outside its own, that we are fated to be born, live our alienated lives, and die in the very world in which Norman Bates also dwells. In Norman Bates, the world of *Psycho* possesses a denizen who could not be enclosed within the world of a Hitchcock teleplay. Hitchcock and we do not stand safely apart from Norman's world. But a corollary of this is that *Psycho*'s world is not ruled by "them." *Psycho* has no sponsors.

The question of whether the author knows Marion's fate from the outset encompasses the question of the camera's self-knowledge: its knowledge of its own impulses, nature, appetite. *Psycho*'s opening suggests that the camera is neither like Uncle Charles, who knows his own role and fate, nor like Richard Hannay, who enters his calling blindly. And this question of what might be called the camera's self-possession in turn encompasses the question of the camera's freedom and what circumscribes it, and the question of its innocence or guilt. *Psycho*'s opening announces its deep concern with these questions about the camera. Of course, part of the significance of this announcement emerges only retroactively, when we reflect on the camera's bond with Norman Bates. In its appropriation of Marion Crane's subjectivity, the camera reveals its appetite; but in Norman Bates, the camera discovers a singular subject fit to stand in perfectly for itself. The camera's relationship to Norman puts its relationship to Marion, and indeed all its subjects, in a new light. In Marion's ultimatum to Sam, in the theft of the money, in the journey to Fairvale cut short by the stop at the Bates Motel, in the dialogue with Norman in the parlor, in Marion's violent death, and in the aftermath of Marion's murder (in particular, Norman's irreversible metamorphosis), Hitchcock formulates perhaps his profoundest reflection on the nature of the camera and the conditions of his own authorship.

If *Psycho* is an allegory about the camera's natural appetite, then, it is also about the making and viewing of films. Marion Crane's dead eye and Norman/mother's final grin prophesy the end of the era of film whose achievement *Psycho* also sums up, and the death of the Hitchcock film. In *Psycho*, Hitchcock's camera singles out a human subject *as if for the last time*, then presides over her murder. Marion Crane's death in the shower, mythically, is also our death—the death of the movie viewer—and Hitchcock's death. Yet *Psycho* is made out of a continuing commitment to the art of film to which Hitchcock had dedicated his life. Perhaps this art may yet be reborn out of its own ashes.

Over a man's voice saying "Never did eat your lunch, did you?" Hitchcock cuts to Marion's uneaten meal, then to Sam (John Gavin).

Marion and Sam, unmarried, have just made love, meeting in secret in this cheap hotel room. He has come to Phoenix pretending to be on a business trip, and this is her lunch hour. But Marion announces, "This is the last time for meeting like this." She will no longer allow Sam to make love to her in secret. From now on, they can see each other, but respectably ("In my house, with mother's picture on the mantel"). But when Marion exclaims, "Oh Sam, let's get married!" he reminds her that he is still paying off his dead father's debts and paying alimony to his ex-wife. When Marion insists that she would be willing to share a life of hardship with him, he responds, "Marion, do you want to cut this off? Find yourself somebody available?" Looking him in the eye, she answers that she is thinking of it.

This is a sad moment for Marion. She will probably have to write off her relationship with Sam. (The poignancy is expressed not by her face—she remains wide-eyed and expressionless—but by Bernard Herrmann's music.) On the other hand, nothing rules out the possibility that he will yet come around. The scene leaves him with a decision to make. (Psycho's great irony has Sam finally penning a letter to Marion in which he admits she was right, as her dead body, crammed in the trunk of her car, lies at the bottom of the swamp.) Yet even should he decide to propose, he knows that, by letting this moment slip by, he leaves himself with no claim on her. Marion has a decision to make as well.

Sam's desire for Marion is clear, but she remains inscrutable (her opacity is declared most emphatically when the camera frames her in a profile shot, then moves in to underscore this framing). The passion that animates Hitchcock's girls on the threshold of womanhood appears to be all but extinguished in Marion. Would Daisy long for the likes of Sam? We are not attracted to this wooden figure. Marion appears more than willing to settle for a kind of marriage—if she can even attain it—that earlier Hitchcock heroines rejected. To be sure, we cannot simply rule out the possibility that Marion really desires, even loves, this man and that they could win through to a union that represented the fulfillment of romance. But Sam would have to conquer his ghosts and worries about money and declare himself like a man. And Marion would have to discover and declare love for Sam, overcoming her fixation on marriage as such.

What urgency possesses her at this moment, then, provoking her to plunge her relationship with Sam into a state of crisis? Time is running out. She has long since given her virginity away, and not for much longer will her sexuality be a marketable asset. Life is slipping through her fingers, and she has nothing to show for it. Daisy is unwilling to settle for what everyone has but wants what no one else possesses; Marion, however, is convinced that she alone possesses nothing and longs to be like everyone else. Marriage devoid of passion is at least something.

Marion feels that death is at hand, that she amounts to nothing, that her mother's gaze (the picture on the mantel) is passing judgment on her. In the aftermath of the sexual act just completed, she feels empty. The recollection of that act and the prospect of its repetition fill her with a revulsion that erupts when she suddenly rises, moves away from Sam, and decisively rejects his suggestion that she call her office so they can spend the rest of the afternoon making love. Her rising signals the camera's first appropriation of Marion's literal view of Sam. And her sudden motion is in turn registered by the camera, which tilts, pulls out, and twists in a vertiginous movement, closely related to the rapturous, circling camera movements with which Hitchcock characteristically renders ecstatic passion.

This camera movement serves as an expressive representation of Marion's revulsion, but it is also as if it were the camera's dizzying movement that subjects her to nausea, as it subjects us to vertigo.[3] Marion's revulsion is for the world and for herself. At this decisive moment, her whole life turns on a wish. But we cannot say what that wish is. We cannot say whether Marion wishes for full awakening and fulfillment or for release from desire in a passionless marriage or in death itself.

Psycho's central strategy is to conjoin the onset of Marion's crisis with the camera's entrance into her world, and in turn to conjoin that with the coming of Norman Bates. Marion's crisis and Hitchcock's innermost concerns bear intimately on each other, in ways I have begun to describe. And Norman Bates—he is Marion's, but also the camera's, projection, yet within the world of the film he is real as well—perfectly mirrors the camera itself. Marion's revulsion, the resolution it provokes, and Norman's nature and fate also bear on each other point by point. The camera anticipates the coming of Norman Bates when it enters Marion's world in conjunction with her intimation of her own nothingness and mortality; her feeling that her mother's gaze presses upon her; her thoughts of finding "somebody available" who might take Sam's place. For Norman Bates is the being destined to be Marion's murderer, the incarnation of nothingness (we don't even know whether "Norman Bates" is really alive or dead), the bearer of "mother's" gaze, the "somebody available" who is prime candidate for the role of Marion's dream lover.

There is a dissolve to a real-estate office. Hitchcock, wearing a ten-gallon hat, stands on the street by the door, framed by the window. Marion passes him to enter the office, and he casts her a side-long glance. Marion has a brief conversation with Caroline (Pat Hitchcock), another secretary in the office, before the arrival of Mr. Lowery, their boss, who is late from his lunch with Mr. Cassidy, "the man who's buying the Harris Street property." Perceiving that something is bothering Marion, Caroline asks whether she has a headache and offers some pills. "Mother's doctor gave them to me the day of my wedding. Teddy was furious when he found out I'd taken tranquilizers." (Presumably it was not the prospect of the ceremony that filled Caroline with apprehension. That her mother's doctor prescribed the tranquilizers suggests that it was a tradition of the women in her family to face sex only in a tranquilized state. What is astounding is the nutty, offhand ease with which she makes public her fear of sex. And by casting his own daughter Pat in this role, Hitchcock makes a joking suggestion that the sexless marriage alluded to is his own.)

The men's arrival is signaled by Mr. Cassidy's "Wow! Hot as fresh milk!" The continuation ("You girls ought to get your boss to air condition you up") establishes that Cassidy is talking about the weather.[4] But Cassidy also is, or could be, talking about Marion, who attracts him. As Mr. Lowery impatiently tries to get him to concentrate on business, Cassidy speaks directly to her: "Ah, tomorrow's the day, my sweet little girl. Oh, oh, not you. My daughter. My baby. And tomorrow she stands her sweet self up there and gets married away from me. I want you to take a look at my baby. Eighteen years old, and she never had an unhappy day in any one of those years. You know what I do with unhappiness? I buy it off. Are you unhappy?" To Marion's guarded "No, not inordinately," Cassidy replies, "I'm buying this house for my baby's wedding present. $40,000 cash. Now that's not buying happiness, that's buying off unhappiness." He pulls out a big wad of bills, causing a sensation.[5] "I never carry more than I can afford to lose," Cassidy adds. We cut from a strongly disapproving Lowery to an astonished Caroline, who exclaims "I declare!" "I don't," Cassidy says, proffering another confidence. "That's how I get to keep it." When Lowery remarks on the irregularity of such a large cash transaction, Cassidy expresses his disdain for such conventions: "It's my private money; now it's yours." Then he reminds Lowery about the bottle in his inner office, and the two men go inside, Lowery first whispering to Marion that she should put the money in the safe deposit box over the weekend.

Marion takes the money from Caroline and knocks on the inner office door. She tells Lowery that she has a slight headache and would like to go right home after the bank. Cassidy tells her she should take the rest of the afternoon off. Lowery does not object, and she closes the door and prepares to leave. Caroline remarks to Marion, expressing astonishment, that Cassidy was flirting ("I guess he must have noticed my wedding ring," she adds). This makes explicit what has been clear to us. Brandishing his wad of bills, Cassidy is showing off to Marion. Money spells manhood to Cassidy. His remarks indeed announce that he has the wherewithal to buy Marion's favors. But on the eve of his "baby's" wedding, he offers these confidences instead of propositioning her. Surely, he knows that Marion is not in a position to buy off her unhappiness and must bitterly compare her own fate to his daughter's. Intentionally or not, his remarks also suggest a remedy for her condition. They are a direct challenge to Marion; Cassidy could just as well have said, "Take this money, if you dare!" (If she took the $40,000, she would be following Cassidy's own maxim. Besides, he bragged that this is money he can afford to lose and that it is not rightfully his anyway.)

When Marion tells Caroline, "You can't buy off unhappiness with pills," she acknowledges that she is suffering from no mere headache. It is clear that she applies Cassidy's remarks to her own case. But does she accept or reject his creed that unhappiness can be bought off with money? This question is directly pertinent to our understanding of her act of taking the $40,000. Two distinct pictures of this act suggest themselves. Perhaps Marion accepts Cassidy's thesis and takes the money to give to Sam in the hope of buying off her unhappiness. But perhaps Marion takes the money to avenge herself on the likes of Cassidy. Then are Cassidy and Sam as one to Marion? Does she also wish to avenge herself on Sam?

We have no way of knowing, even in retrospect, when Marion first thinks of taking the money and when she decides to give in to this temptation. When she announces her intention to go to the bank and then home to sleep, has she already formulated the very different scenario she actually follows? As she goes to put the money in a large envelope, her entrance into the frame is preceded by that of her shadow (5.5), and her figure is momentarily doubled. Is this only an accident of filming, or is it a secret sign?

5.5

The scene dissolves to Marion's room, her bed in the foreground. Half-dressed, she enters the frame, once again preceded by her shadow, and goes to her closet. Everything suggests that she is following through with her announced plan. But then the camera tilts down and moves in on

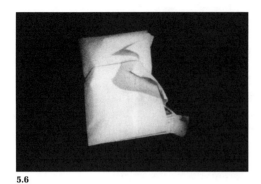

5.6

the envelope filled with money, lying on the bed, as pensive music starts up. The camera now pans diagonally up and to the left to a packed suitcase lying open on the bed. She is going to leave town with the money.

On Marion's glance, we cut to the envelope (5.6), initiating a passage in which shots from her point of view are alternated with extended objective views of her preparations to leave. This passage is acute psychologically. We recognize in her behavior— she acts as if this were an ordinary occasion—a charade of indifference designed to avoid reminding herself that she has made a decision. For example, by leaving the money in plain view on the bed, she all but convinces herself that she is not avoiding it. It is as if in a trance that this woman goes through the motions of packing, almost lulling a region of herself to sleep, acting so as not to awaken it.

Throughout this passage, the camera stands outside Marion and scrutinizes her like an entomologist studying an insect. Even when the camera appropriates her perspective, it stands neutrally apart, taking note of the gravitational pull exerted on her gaze by the money-filled envelope. Yet we are also attuned to her behavior as if from within. We too know this frame of mind pitched between decision and indecision, this mode of avoidance, this dissociation, this charade performed for the self as audience. Hitchcock has gotten the subtleties of this presentation exactly right. In standing outside Marion, even in appropriating her gaze, the camera manifests its separateness from her but at the same time reveals close familiarity with her mind. The camera's separateness from her corresponds to her alienation from herself, her dissociation. She stands apart from her own gaze, her own hands, even her own reflection in the mirror. The camera is alert to the subterfuges through which

her entrancement is woven, as if, in its wakefulness, it were one with what slumbers within her. Or is the camera something truly alien that takes possession of Marion in her trance? Who or what really authors the scenario that has already begun to be enacted?

We next see Marion behind the wheel of a car (5.7). Then we hear Sam's voice: "Marion, what in the world . . . What

5.7

are you doing up here? *What is it, Marion?"* Marion is imagining her arrival at Sam's, and we have access to her stream of consciousness.[6] Sitting silently, starting forward, expressionless, she is imaged as though she were viewing a film. The scene she is imagining is a "private film" projected onto the inner screen of her imagination (whether from within or by an outside agency).

5.8

Completely unexpectedly, Mr. Lowery appears in the crosswalk, framed by the windshield, and smiles in recognition. This apparition arises uncannily from the texture of Marion's imaginings, even as it presents itself to her as real, an "accident" out of her control. On Lowery's smile, the camera returns to Marion, who smiles back mechanically (5.8), then once more to her point of view. Lowery turns back to the camera, his smile replaced by a troubled look (5.9). When it cuts again to Marion, the camera frames her tightly (5.10). The smile has frozen on her face, too. The red light changes to green, and she begins to drive away, as Herrmann's music takes on a tense urgency. There is a dissolve to a landscape at dusk, the car hurtling into the gathering darkness; then to Marion's anxious face, harshly illuminated by glare from the oncoming headlights (5.11).

5.9

5.10

In the novel by Robert Bloch from which *Psycho*'s screenplay was adapted, Marion—she is Mary in the book—rehearses the story she intends to tell her lover when she arrives with the money. She has a realistic plan, one that perfectly well could succeed. But Hitchcock's Marion has no worked-out plan of action. So is it not folly for her to go on now that she has been spotted by Lowery? It is painful for Marion to look into the approaching headlights, but she

5.11

cannot turn her eyes away from them. If her private film has started up again, we have no access to it, or it unreels in silence; yet the blinding light suggests that it has become a nightmare. Is Marion's nightmare that her fate is in her hands, that she is madly condemning herself, destroying any chance for happiness? Or that her fate is

in the hands of a monstrous agency indifferent to human suffering? When Hitchcock reverses to Marion's view, glare blinds us as it blinds her (5.12). If this blinding light stands in for what is conjured within her imagination, we are also subjected to it in her place. This light joins Marion's private film with the film that holds us spellbound: *Psycho* too has taken a nightmarish turn. Hence we are relieved when there is a cut to Marion. She looks down and the image fades to black, the anxious music subsiding.

5.12

5.13

A road in broad daylight fades in. Marion's car is parked on the shoulder. A state police car pulls up. The policeman gets out and knocks on the window of the parked car. Marion, stretched out across the front seat, awakens with a start and impulsively starts the engine. He tells her to turn it off, and Hitchcock

gives us Marion's view of the trooper staring from behind opaque sunglasses (5.13), a memorable realization of everyone's paranoid fantasy of being scrutinized by the cold eyes of the Law. Marion explains that she almost had an accident on the road and had pulled over, not intending to sleep all night. "Is there anything wrong?" "Am I acting as if there's something wrong? There's

nothing wrong, except that I'm in a hurry and you're taking up my time." She starts the motor again, but he demands that she shut if off and asks to see her license. He studies it interminably before finally allowing her to drive off. From her point of view, we see his car behind hers, framed in her rear view mirror. Her relief is also ours when the police car turns off at the "RIGHT LANE FOR GORMAN" sign (5.14).[7]

5.14

Marion drives on to California Charlie's used-car lot. She wants to trade in her car, with its Arizona license plate. It does not ease her mind when she sees the state trooper pull over across the road, get out and lean against his car, watching her. But California Charlie's affability is hardly dented by Marion's nervous impatience. However, it does violate his sense of propriety when she picks out a car and insists she does not want to take a spin around the block or to take the usual day and a half to think it over. Saying, "Why, this is the first time the customer ever high-pressured the salesman," he makes her an offer—her own car plus $700—which she accepts, making him uneasy and suspicious. When she comes back from the restroom with seven hundred-dollar bills along with the necessary papers, he makes one last effort to get her to act like a normal customer. As the transaction is completed, the trooper gets in his car and drives across the street to the lot. The policeman, California Charlie, and another salesman all watch incredulously as Marion drives off in her new car.

5.15

We again see Marion at the wheel (5.15). Offscreen voices are heard. First the salesman's voice: "Heck officer, this is the first time I've ever seen the customer high-pressure the salesman." Then the policeman's: "I better have a look at those papers, Charlie. She look like a wrong one to you?" (A Wrong One, indeed.) Then these voices segue into a series of fragmentary scenes, set on Monday morning and conjured within Marion's imagination. But from these scenes, unlike that of her arrival at Sam's, she is absent: they do not center on a view of Marion, invoked but withheld.

There is a dissolve to Marion's view through the windshield—the dissolve indicates a passage of time—then Hitchcock cuts back and forth repeatedly between Marion and her view. We hear the voices of Caroline and Mr. Lowery, concerned that Marion has not shown up for work; Lowery on the phone with Marion's sister; a telephone conversation between Lowery and Cassidy; then an exchange with Cassidy in Lowery's office. In the shots through the windshield from Marion's point of view, afternoon gives way to evening and evening to night. Cars turn on their headlights, so that she must again drive into blinding glare (5.16). As the world before her darkens, there is a darkening of the mood of the scenes invoked by the voices, culminating in Cassidy's rage and threat of vengeance. And as outer and inner worlds darken, Marion's face reveals a deepening anguish, conjoined with a strange exhilaration

5.16

5.17

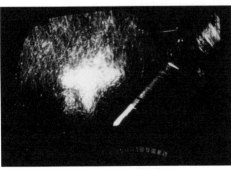

5.18

(at the moment Cassidy's voice is conjured, her face is frozen in a grin that anticipates the film's penultimate image (5.17)). And as Marion's suffering intensifies, the camera subjects her to progressively tighter framings.

Cassidy's words, scripted by Marion's imagination, are charged with double entendre. They sustain the suggestion that the loss of his wad of bills feels to him like the theft of his manhood ("She sat there while I dumped it out!"). Marion's grin reveals the pleasure she takes in contemplating the aftermath of her act of taking the $40,000, which exposes that act's violent aspect. (Again, we must recognize the possibility that her real target is Sam.) Marion's grin also reveals that she imagines Cassidy's rage, and in particular his threat ("I won't kiss off $40,000. I'll get it back, and if any of it's missing I'll replace it with her fine soft flesh"), as impotent. If Cassidy tried to make good on his threat, he would fail. Then he would really feel her power. That is, underlying the scenes conjured in Marion's imagination is a fantasy of vengeance against the likes of Cassidy, men who regard her as a piece of flesh to be bought and consumed. But Marion's fantasy also has a masochistic aspect. Cassidy lacks the power to make good on his threat to make Marion pay with her "fine soft flesh." But nonetheless the fantasy of being subject to murderous violence (a fantasy destined to be fulfilled) also underlies the scenes Marion imagines.

When the erotic tension of these imagined scenes finally erupts in Cassidy's impotent rage, Marion's inner voices become silent, as her private film approaches its climax. It starts to rain, and the windshield wiper begins rhythmically cutting a swath across her field of vision (5.18). This slashing blade implies that the climax of her private film is a silent scene of erotic violence. We do not know whether, in this scene conjured in Marion's imagination, she is agent or victim of this murderous violence. Of course in retrospect we may recognize the rain, and the vision of blade slashing through water, as prophetic of her fate. Linked to the privileged status of this vision is the fact that the blade slashing the frame-within-a-frame of the windshield forms a perfect ////.

The reverse shot is the tightest framing of Marion in the sequence. The screen flashes with blinding glare as she opens her eyes wide, closes them as if in pain, and again opens them wide as the music's crescendo reaches its peak (5.19, 5.20). But although the tension begins to subside after this moment of climax, signaled by a cut to a slightly longer shot of Marion, neither she nor we have been offered any real satisfaction or release. We are left in an uneasy calm. With no traffic behind her, for the first time she is framed against a plain black background (5.21). Suddenly, something offscreen strikes her attention, and we cut to her view, again slashed through by the wiper blade. A neon sign ("BATES MOTEL VACANCY") emerges out of the rain and darkness, as if, like Marion's inner voices, this apparition were conjured within her imagination. In this sign, Marion's private film and *Psycho* converge.

The motel comes into view (5.22). Marion drives up, and we cut to an objective shot of the car stopped in front of the office (5.23).

The silence broken only by the rain, Marion runs into the office. Finding no one inside, she comes out and the camera cuts to her view of the old house adjacent to the motel, a light in one window; back to Marion; and then to a somewhat closer view of the house, the window occupying a more prominent position in the frame. (I take this window to be a descendant of the frame-

5.19

5.20

5.21

5.22

within-a-frame of *Murder!*'s prison-visit sequence.) What appears to be the silhouette of a woman passes back and forth across the window (5.24). Marion honks the car horn, and a man—this is Norman Bates, played by Anthony Perkins—runs down the stairs from the house into the foreground. In an objective shot, he opens an umbrella and leads Marion into the office, saying, "Gee, I'm sorry I didn't hear you in all this rain."

Psycho's shower-murder scene has passed into the consciousness of the world. An uninitiated viewer—one who does not already know Norman's story or Marion's fate—can scarcely be found. It is difficult for us to remember or even to imagine how Norman Bates must have originally appeared to *Psycho*'s audience. One of the functions of the encounters with the trooper and the used-car salesman is to invite the expectation that this motel keeper will be only a minor character, one more shrewdly drawn American type encountered by Marion, punctuating her journey only to pass out of the film, like the milkman and the corset salesmen in *The Thirty-Nine Steps.* But the groundwork has also carefully been laid for another expectation. Perhaps Norman Bates will instead play a role like that played by Pamela, the woman on the train in *The Thirty-Nine Steps,* or the role played by Margaret. (Marion's stop at the Bates Motel and Hannay's stop at the crofter's cottage are, in important ways, analogous.) Marion told Sam that she is on the lookout for "somebody available." Perhaps Bates will be the man destined to provide her with an edifying perspective on Sam. California Charlie—his sales pitches are all matchmaker's talk in any case—recognized her as a woman "in the mood for a change." Perhaps Bates will turn out to become her love interest in the film. Perhaps she will decide that she prefers him to Sam (*Stage Fright* establishes a precedent for such a change of heart). Or perhaps Norman will reawaken her love for Sam (unintentionally, by becoming a cautionary example in her eyes, or intentionally, by undertaking to instruct her about her feelings).

What is clear is that the uninitiated viewer is unlikely to suspect the role Norman Bates will actually play. How could it be known that his mystery is to dominate the film? Yet when he makes his entrance, there are some signs of his mystery. Consider, for example, the passage that depicts the entrance of Norman and Marion into the motel office. Viewed attentively, it reveals a precision of significant detail that more than matches the first meeting of Charles and Charlie in *Shadow of A Doubt*.

The passage begins with a shot of the office interior. A mirror placed in the empty frame (5.25) links this setup with the master shot of *Murder!*'s prison-visit sequence. The mirror occupies the place of the window in the shot from *Murder!*, which invokes the film frame and hence the camera's presence and agency. By making its frame-within-a-frame a mirror rather than a window, *Psycho* deepens this invocation. For who could view this shot without

5.25

wondering where the camera was placed so that its reflection is not visible in the mirror? The mirror calls attention to the camera's general exclusion from the frame. If a mirror may stand in for the frame—viewing a film is like looking through a window, but it is also like looking into a mirror—then why has the camera—why have we, why has Hitchcock—no visible reflection in this mirror or the larger frame that contains it? But then again, are we sure we would recognize our own reflections within the frame of a film?

Psycho's transformation of *Murder!*'s frame-within-a-frame is characteristic of its self-consciousness. And within this setup, both inside and outside the frame-within-a-frame, a symbolically charged presentation is about to be inscribed. First, Marion, carrying her handbag, appears reflected in the mirror (5.26). Momentarily, she enters the frame in the flesh and turns to face the mirror, her turning precisely synchronized with the appearance of Norman's reflection (5.27). At this moment, Marion (in full face) and Norman (in profile) are contiguous, as if the mirror framed not two people but a single composite being (a creature with a male and a female face, a creature turned toward and away from the camera at the same

5.26

5.27

5.28

5.29

5.30

time). Then his reflection separates off from hers, at the very moment that Norman in the flesh enters the frame (5.28). He passes so close to the camera that he momentarily eclipses both the mirror, with her reflection within it, and Marion herself, (5.29). Finally, he assumes a place across the desk from Marion, who has turned from the camera to face him (5.30). As he breaks the silence, saying simply "Dirty night," Norman occupies the right side of the frame, while Marion—doubled by her reflection, framed like a picture in the frame-within-a-frame of the mirror—occupies the left.

When Diana makes her entrance into Sir John's view, she appears as if she were a projection of his imagination; they seat themselves in synchronization, like mirror images. In this passage from *Psycho*, Sir John's role is, in effect, played by Marion and Diana's by Norman. Within the frame of the mirror, Norman and Marion appear as aspects of a single self, even when his reflection separates off from hers. Marion faces the mirror when Norman's reflection splits off from her own. Our vision of Norman emerging as if from within Marion's self is available to her, but she takes no note of it. The presentation framed within the mirror appears to sustain the suggestion that their encounter is conjured within Marion's imagination, a continuation of her private film. Yet Norman's eclipsing of the figure of Marion, like Charles's eclipsing of Charlie before his gift of the ring, strikes an ominous note. It suggests that Norman possesses a mysterious power over Marion. And it is not simply because she is oblivious that she does not possess this ominous vision as we do. How could she have access to our vision of Norman stepping between the camera and herself? Rather than being framed in the mirror, hence available to her—if she awakened to it—the obliteration of the figure of Marion, which is also the obliteration of the mirror itself, is framed only for us. In retrospect, we may recognize this moment's aspect of prophecy, its anticipation of Marion's death at Norman's hands.

This symbolic presentation is a piece of theater for which we are the only possible audience. Yet even we are likely to be too oblivious, too entranced, to acknowledge the performance that has just been executed before our eyes. Certainly, the sequence testifies to the camera's virtuosity. It also raises a specific question about Norman. Does he act in complicity with the camera when he steps between the camera and Marion? This question is closely linked to a number of others that bear on our assessment of Norman's knowingness. Does he know that he keeps his mother alive within himself? Does he know that his hands—whether animated by his mother's will or his own—have committed murder? Does he know that he is face to face with a woman fated to die by his hands? When he speaks the words "Dirty night," is the irony only Hitchcock's, or does Norman already know what dirtiness lies ahead this night?

We pass into a brief shot/reverse-shot alternation between (5.31) and (5.32). In the framing that initiates this sequence, the camera assumes a distance greater than we might expect. We do not simply view Norman over Marion's shoulder. Instead, both figures are given equal weight in the frame; Norman, viewed frontally is matched by Marion in silhouette, back to the camera. This framing underscores our sense that Marion is a viewer and that she is entranced: she faces into the depths of this frame as if she were turned inward, as if Norman were a creature of her imagination or her mirror reflection. We have encountered similar framings in each of the films we have examined: the lodger riveted by the sound of Daisy's laugh, Hannay face to face with Mr. Memory, and so on. This framing invokes another

5.31

5.32

Hitchcock paradigm as well: a man's desire for a woman crystallized in his view of her hair. Marion is an object of desire. (A further resonance of this shot is revealed only at the climax of the film, when this framing is reprised, the mother's corpse in Marion's place.)

Norman explains that "They moved away the highway." Only

those who turn off the main road ever stop there any more. But "There's no sense dwelling on our losses. We just keep on lighting the lights and following the formalities." Norman's words are ripe with irony, as are most of his lines throughout the film. They have a secret self-referential level: like Sir John's words to the other jurors in *Murder!*, Norman's words can be heard also as Hitchcock's, spoken directly to us. Heard this way, they register the observation that Hitchcock's art has been passed by: we would not now be in this place unless we too had wandered off the main road, but nonetheless, *Psycho* finds Hitchcock still "lighting the lights and following the formalities," despite the fact that "they" have moved away the highway. This present shot/reverse-shot passage, and the extraordinary setup that is its keystone, exemplify this "formality," at the same time occasioning the remark and serving as its veiled subject.

Hearing Norman's words as Hitchcock's reveals the close link between this passage and a number of passages in *Shadow of a Doubt*. But the flamboyant theatricality of the "Goodness, how men do things!" passage, for example, has given way to a gesture whose rhetoric is that of an expression of resignation by a performer whose audience has been lost. This expression resonates with Marion's announcement to Sam that "This is the last time" for "meeting in secret to be secretive." Is *Psycho* Hitchcock's last time? Is this the last time Hitchcock and we will "meet" like this?

Heard as Hitchcock's own, Norman's words can seem merely facetious. After all, the Bates Motel has hit on hard times, but Hitchcock's business had never been better. But perhaps this line is to be heard as prophesying the loss of the audience first fully assembled by *The Thirty-Nine Steps*. Then again, perhaps even in *Psycho*, commercial blockbuster though it was, Hitchcock had already lost his audience. By winning through to our intimate encounter with Hitchcock, by fulfilling our calling as viewers, have we arrived, by a series of accidents, at a place as far off the beaten path, as privileged, and as treacherously dangerous as Norman Bates's parlor?

Marion enters "Marie Samuels" in Norman's book, but is uncertain about what city to give as her address. At this moment, Marion is framed with the handbag containing the money, out of which juts a folded-up newspaper, the words "OKAY" and "LOS ANGELES" conspicuous (5.33). When Marion momentarily says "Los Angeles," our impression is that she reads it off the page on which her gaze happens to rest. At the moment Marion speaks the name of the city, the camera

5.33

frames Norman, hesitating before making up his mind which cabin to assign his guest (5.34). Marion's opting for Los Angeles catalyzes Norman's decision to hand her the key to cabin 1, as if it were Marion's own guilty lie at this moment that seals her fate. "It's closer in case you want anything," Norman explains. But what does he imagine she might want? Him? Then again, has he already formulated the intention of spying on this woman? Does he know that assigning her to cabin 1 not only condemns her to his unsolicited gaze, but to murder?

5.34

Norman goes outside to get Marion's bag. Their entrance into cabin 1 is pretext for another virtuoso eclipsing. Norman walks behind Marion, who momentarily blocks him from our view (5.35). As he passes her, he is doubled by his shadow (5.36), reversing the earlier effect. Explaining that it is kind of "stuffy" he opens a window (5.37). Then he says, "Well, the, uh, mattress is soft and there's hangers in the closet and stationery with 'Bates Motel' printed on it, in case you want to make your friends back home feel envious."

5.35

Norman's hesitation on the word "mattress" is the first sign of the slight stutter he inherits from the John Dall character in *Rope* and the Robert Walker character in *Strangers on a Train*, and in turn passes on to *Frenzy*'s Rusk. Norman stutters when he is nervous and has to say something he doesn't want to say. His stutter is linked to his habit of starting a sentence, pausing, and then starting it again, leaving it unclear whether the words he speaks are those he initially intended. He hesitates on the word "mattress," I take it, because it embarrasses him to be alone in a bedroom with this attractive woman, and maybe because the word is so close to "matri-

5.36

5.37

5.38

5.39

5.40

5.41

cide." And his next hesitation speaks for itself. "And the, uh, over there," he says, turning on the bathroom light. Marion has to fill in the word he cannot bring himself to say. "The bathroom." "Yeah. Well, if you want anything, I'll be in the office."

Marion says, "Thank you, Mr. Bates," intending to close out the encounter, dismissing Norman. The two stand facing each other as in the motel office, her reflection, contiguous to her handbag, once more framed in a mirror between them (5.38). He invites her to be less formal: "*Norman* Bates." This signals a brief shot/reverse-shot alternation (5.39, 5.40). He smiles. She returns this smile, but it freezes on her face. His smile freezes too. His move toward intimacy, by which he countered her dismissal, precipitates this awkward break, which he in turn takes as a cue. He asks, "Would you have dinner with *me*? I was just about to myself. You know, nothing special, just sandwiches and milk."

Does Norman act as a good samaritan, seeing to it that Marion does not go to bed hungry? He is lonely and hopes to establish some human contact with his guest. Of course, she is not just any guest, but an attractive single woman. We assume that Norman is motivated by a conscious or unconscious fantasy of seduction. With a strained smile, Marion accepts: he has made it difficult for her to decline without offending him; she has no particular wish for his company, but he does not threaten her and she is hungry. Saying "I'll be back as soon as it's ready," he goes to the door and closes it behind him. The camera reframes with his movement, so that we are afforded a view of his face that Marion does not share (5.41). We are taken aback by his smug expression, which might be viewed as innocent pleasure in this glamorous woman's acceptance of his humble invitation but can also be viewed as revealing that he has secret designs on her. His intentions may not be so innocent after all. In any case, this look reveals that, however wrapped in fantasy he may be, he is not entranced like her, but alert. And in presenting to us this revelation that is withheld—Norman also withholds it—from Marion, the camera drives a wedge between her and us. Is Norman in complicity with the camera's disclosure of his alertness? If so, he gives no sign of it. But what *is* the secret design inscribed in his smile?

We might read Norman's expression as resentful. Indeed, several of his remarks may be heard as expressing and veiling a wish for vengeance. For example, the line "You know, nothing special, just milk and sandwiches" can be heard as defensive. *Shadow of a Doubt* prepares us to scan these words in a way that brings out their resentful aspect. These words immediately follow "Would you have dinner with *me*? I was just about to myself," with the word "myself" and the words "You know, nothing special" separated by a cut from Marion to Norman that invites us to read "nothing special" as referring to "myself." Not just Norman's milk and sandwiches, but Norman himself must seem nothing special to this big-city woman. Yet Marion is too wrapped up in her own private thoughts, too sure of her superiority, too confident of her security in Norman's presence, to notice his possibly ironic self-deprecation (this woman to whom Norman is nothing special is nothing special to him, as she is nothing special to Hitchcock; she is unable even to recognize disdain).

On the sound of the door closing behind Norman, the camera cuts to Marion in a frontal framing that contrasts with the shots in this sequence that framed her in profile (5.42). This cut marks the break effected by Norman's exit, registering that she is again alone. (The break is marked on the soundtrack as well, as Herrmann's music, for a spell quiescent, starts up.) But the frontal framing also positions the camera at the door through which Norman just exited. This is the view that would now be his, had he not left. Nonetheless, his gaze haunts the remainder of this passage, the way Charles's gaze

5.42

haunts Graham's tour of the Newton home and his encounter with Charlie in the garage. This framing declares the camera's presence and links it to the gaze of the absent Norman. Even when Marion is alone, she has no privacy.

Marion puts her handbag and suitcase on the bed and looks for a

5.43

5.44

5.45

5.46

place to put the money. She wraps the envelope in the newspaper and places it on top of a night table, in plain view (5.43) (note the lamp in the center of the frame). Just before she puts it down, Hitchcock cuts to her hands (5.44). At the precise moment they lay the paper down, we hear a woman's voice, loud but muffled by distance. "No!" Then he cuts back to the longer, objective setup of (5.43). Marion is riveted. "I tell you no!" The simultaneity of the intrusion of this voice and Marion's guilty gesture is uncanny, as though the voice emanated from Marion's imagination. But whether or not this voice belongs to her private film, it presents itself to her as real, out of her control, coming to her from the old house out back. The camera reframes as she goes to the window, the voice continuing, "Bring girls in for supper . . ." A cut to a profile shot of Marion listening and staring out the window (5.45) ("By candlelight, I suppose"). Then to her view (5.46): the house, the light still burning in the window ("In the cheap erotic fashion of cheap erotic minds").

This last shot appears to confirm that the voice is real and emanates from the house. But it does not fully settle the question of its status. Like the master shot of *Murder!*'s prison-visit sequence, which it echoes, this framing also declares the presence and agency of the camera, hence invokes the film frame itself and posits *Psycho*'s world as unreal, its being a mystery. The old house, light burning in the window, like the theater in *Stage Fright*, is an emblem for the unfathomable bond between the camera and its subject. Within *Psycho*'s world, these voices are real, but this does not mean that they are not also Marion's projections. And this view may itself be a projection of Marion's subjectivity, a vision. Later, we learn—or think we learn—that this scene is actually conjured within Norman's imagination, scripted, directed, and acted by Norman, who plays both parts. Or is it that Norman is literally possessed by his mother's spirit, so that he becomes the medium for her performance? Then, too, there is another possibility: that Norman intends this scene to be overheard by Marion and indeed stages it for her. After all, it is Norman's opening of the window that allows these voices to be heard.

We next hear Norman's voice ("Mother, *please!*"—that is, please don't make a scene: someone may be listening). But the mother is relentless ("And then what? After supper, music? whispering?"). Her words uncannily echo Sam's "And then after the steak, do we turn mother's picture to the wall?" And Norman's insistence that his invitation is perfectly innocent ("Mother, she's just a stranger. She's hungry and it's raining out") in turn recalls Marion's own announcement that from now on all of their meetings are to be respectable. Perhaps it is because this argument resonates so disturbingly with her own life that Marion turns away from the window (5.47), as Norman's mother mocks her son ("'Mother, she's just a stranger,' As if men don't desire strangers. As if . . ."). Only when the mother finds herself unwilling to go on ("No. I refuse to think of

5.47

disgusting things") does Hitchcock cut back, indicating that Marion has again been drawn into this private scene *and wills it to go on.* (Marion's hesitation and its overcoming link this scene to the camera's entrance into Marion's life and to Norman's decision to assign her cabin 1.)

This last cut is synchronized with the mother's invocation of the revolting image of Norman consumed by Marion. The mother makes a specific threat: "Go on, go tell her that she'll not be appeasing her ugly appetite with *my* food or my son. Or do *I* have to tell her because you don't have the guts?" The reprise of Marion's view of the old house suggests that, at this moment, the erotic violence that surfaced in Marion's imagining of Cassidy's impotent rage surfaces in this "real" scene between Norman and his mother. Indeed, the scene of Marion's consumption of Norman invoked by the mother is a companion piece to the scene Cassidy invoked when he vowed to replace his missing money with Marion's fine soft flesh. If Norman goes ahead and defies his mother, she will unleash her vengeful wrath. (It turns out that this is no idle threat.) And this scene, overheard by Marion and by us, threatens to turn violent. The mother goads her son mercilessly, pushing him to the edge of an uncontrollable, murderous rage. As if dreading a turn to violence, Marion once again looks away. By averting her gaze from the house, she does not break the spell of the voices. She remains enthralled, unable either to give in fully to her fascination with the scene or to relinquish her access to it. She does not act to forestall violence but forswears intervention in this scene whose privacy she continues to violate. Only when she hears the door slam does she look back. Norman is on his way to the motel. The moment of truth has been deferred, the issues unresolved.

Seeing Norman coming down the stairs carrying a tray—he has chosen to defy his mother after all—Marion goes out to meet him. In a shot that specifically reverses the framing of their first ex-

5.48

5.49

change in the office, Marion, back to the camera, is in the foreground, while Norman advances from the background (5.48). Again Marion "possesses" the frame like the lodger enthralled by Daisy's laugh, and Norman becomes her mirror image. He hesitates before stepping closer. The following shot sustains the invocation of the earlier exchange in the office (5.49). If (5.48) reverses (5.31), (5.49) reverses (5.30). Norman and Marion again "face off," but their positions are interchanged, and it is now he who is doubled in the "mirror" occupying the center of the frame.

Marion speaks first. "I've caused you some trouble." Norman begins, "No, I . . ." but starts over. "Mother . . ." Then he begins a third time, and finally completes one of the film's most celebrated lines. "My mother is . . . What is the phrase? She isn't quite herself today." Marion says, "You shouldn't have bothered. I really don't have that much of an appetite." Now she denies she is hungry, but she had told Norman that if there is anything she wants more than sleep, it is food. When Norman replies, "Oh, I am sorry. I wish you could . . ." he pauses. Does his continuation ("Apologize for other people") represent what he originally intended to say? Is his real wish that Marion might hunger for him?

Marion replies, "Don't worry about it. As long as you've fixed the supper, we may as well eat it." This is hardly an enthusiastic invitation. Her words say, in effect, "Let's go on as if nothing happened." But her formality suggests that the mother has come between them. As Marion leans against a post watching Norman, the camera reframes slightly, allowing us to glimpse the double bed through the doorway (5.50). (This reframing also displaces Norman's reflection from the center of the frame. The center is now occupied by a lamp: a link with the window in the old house viewed in the schematic framing of (5.24), and hence an invocation of the film frame and the camera, and of the figure of the mother. Again and again, a lamp will be associated with the mother, becoming her

surrogate in the frame and—like the ceiling lamp in *The Lodger*—the emblem of her mystery.) Norman steps forward but then draws back, perhaps embarrassed by the prospect of again being alone in a bedroom with this woman. From Marion's point of view, we see him lower his gaze bashfully.

5.50

The camera reverses to Marion, who stands arms crossed, head tilted, looking right at Norman, watching him as he withdraws and beckons her to follow (5.51). His eyes still lowered, he struggles to find words or courage. Then he looks up, smiling shyly. "It might be nicer and warmer in the office."

Amused by his self-consciousness, she follows him to the office. When Marion steps forward, she turns toward the camera, her face bathed in darkness (5.52). Norman says, "It stopped raining." After a pause, he adds, "Eating in an office is just, just too officious. Stuttering from the effort to appear casual and spontaneous, he adds, "I-I-I-I-'ve got the parlor back here." We take it that he intended all along to invite Marion to the more intimate parlor.

5.51

As Norman enters the parlor, the frame is engulfed in darkness. He turns on a light, the illumination revealing that the room is dominated by stuffed birds on the walls. Marion—framed be-

5.52

5.53

5.54

5.55

5.56

side a dark curtain—blinks as if to convince herself that she is not dreaming (5.53). She looks off, and there is a cut to her view of a large stuffed owl (5.54). (This cut is accompanied by a strange clinking sound, one of Hitchcock's aural symbols, which is to be reprised later in the sequence and then again later in the film.) The camera cuts back to Marion, then to her view of a stuffed raven on a perch. Norman's head bobs into his frame from below, momentarily turning the oval frame-within-a-frame into an eye, a familiar Hitchcock trick (5.55). Then it bobs below the frame line again, as we once more hear the clinking sound. A cut to Norman follows. He rises and invites his guest to be seated (5.56). Marion's "Thank you" opens a bracket that will be closed only at the end of their fateful dialogue.

The camera reframes with Marion; its movement, synchronized with Norman's movement as well, brings him into the frame. Again she eclipses him, as the two sit once more in synchronization, a candle placed schematically in the center of the frame (5.57, 5.58). Norman says, "It's all for you. I'm not hungry. Go ahead." He means: All of this food is for you (although he had told Marion that he was just about to eat when she arrived). But the words can also be heard as referring to this whole show. That is, Norman's remark addressed to Marion can also be heard as Hitchcock's remark addressed to us. Indeed, it is crucial to my understanding of this part of *Psycho* that the entire encounter between Marion and Norman stands in for the viewer's encounter with the film's author. In this dialogue, Hitchcock is really talking about us—who we are, what

we are doing when we view this film
—and about himself. The stuffed birds
on the walls are part of Hitchcock's
"show," their presence charged with
irony. This irony derives in part from
the withheld revelation that Norman
has killed and stuffed his own mother,
and in part from the fact that Norman's
hobby ("stuffing things") is an analogue
of Hitchcock's hobby that is more than a
hobby (fixing human subjects with his
camera, then projecting them on the
screen to grant them the illusion of life).

5.57

Marion begins to slice something on
her plate. Grinning, Norman attends to
her every move. When the first piece
enters her mouth, he laughs and leans
forward. The camera cuts to (5.59), as he
says, simply, "You eat like a bird," then
reverses (5.60). The most extraordinary
of all Hitchcock's shot/reverse-shot sequences has begun.

5.58

This cut from Norman speaking to
Marion listening establishes a pattern
the first few alternations between (5.59)
and (5.60) will sustain. She assumes a
passive role, allows him to take the initiative and then reacts when he does.
For example, when Norman equates
Marion with a bird, she reacts by looking around the room at the stuffed birds
and saying, "Of course you'd know."
(This reply is not without a note of condescension. "You may know about
birds," it suggests, "but what do you
know about a *woman's* appetite?") Norman demurs. "No not really. Anyway, I
hear the expression 'eats like a bird' is
really a fal-fal-falsity." (Is Norman's inability to say "fallacy" a Freudian joke?)
"Because birds really eat a tremendous
lot." In silence, Marion picks up a piece
of bread and holds it in her hand as she
listens, her attention divided between

5.59

5.60

these words and the task of buttering her bread. She looks up, signaling Norman to go on. He shrugs and resumes.

But I don't really know anything about birds. My hobby is stuffing things. You know, taxidermy. I guess I'd just rather stuff birds because I hate the look of *beasts* when they're stuffed. You know, foxes and chimps. Some people even stuff dogs and cats but, oh, I can't do that. I think only birds look well stuffed because, well, because they're kind of passive to begin with.

On the word "passive," Marion tears the piece of bread in her hands (5.61).[8]

Marion speaks. "Strange hobby. Curious." This patronizing comment, spoken on camera, disrupts the prevailing pattern of framing Marion listening and in turn motivates

5.61

an immediate cut that registers Norman's effort to regain the initiative. He says, "Uncommon too," and there is a cut back to Marion for her reply ("Oh, I imagine so"), then back to Norman. The pattern is reestablished: he speaks, there is a cut, she responds. Norman adds, "And it's not as expensive as you might think. It's cheap, really. You know, needles, thread, sawdust. The chemicals are the only things that cost anything."

(This is a joking comment about the link between Norman's stuffing things and Hitchcock's acts of filming.) Holding the buttered bread up in the air, deferring her first bite, Marion chimes in with, "A man should have a hobby." Norman confesses that he lives for his acts of stuffing things. "It's more than a hobby. A hobby is supposed to pass the time, not fill it." Then she asks a question that

5.62

takes him aback. "Is your time so empty?" As Norman gives his response, his hand is touching the stuffed bird on the bureau at his side (5.62). "No. Well, I run the office and, uh, tend the cabins and grounds and do the, uh, little errands for my mother—the, uh, ones she allows I might be capable of doing." He speaks these last words with a grin, as if there were some particular errand his mother performs for herself, the thought of which makes him laugh. Marion presses her interrogation. "Do you go out with friends?" Self-conscious, he takes his hand from the bird and puts it in his lap (5.63). After an uneasy pause, he looks directly at his interlocutor and an-

swers evasively. "Well, a boy's best
friend is his mother." After this lame
reply, striking for this grown man's reference to himself as a boy, Hitchcock
cuts immediately to Marion, who looks
down. Embarrassed, she passes up her
turn to speak, and her silence allows
Norman to regain the initiative. A broad
grin on his face, he turns the tables.
"You've never had an empty moment
in, in your entire life, have you?" In the

5.63

middle of Norman's question, a cut to Marion, whose face freezes,
establishes the return to the editing pattern, but now Marion's passivity is not merely an act.

Marion's response ("Only my share") echoes her guarded "Not
inordinately" when Cassidy asked her whether she was unhappy.
Like Cassidy, Norman presses the attack. "Where are you going?"
Marion does not answer, pointedly passing up an opportunity to
make reference to Sam. In the face of this pained silence, Norman
withdraws his question. "I didn't mean to pry." The pressure removed, she gives an answer, if a deliberately cryptic one. "Trying
to flee to a private island." Norman leans forward. In a firm voice,
he asks an even more disquieting question. "What are you running
away from?" Marion looks right at him as she asks, "Wh-why do
you ask that?" Now it is Norman's turn to be cryptic. "People never
run away from anything." (Does he mean that people always run to,
never simply from, something; or that people never admit they are
running away? Does Norman direct his remark to Marion, ex-
pecting her to acknowledge his perception? Or is Norman addressing, to no one in particular, a remark that takes Marion as its
subject? She is like all the rest, these words may imply; she is not
really addressing *me*.) While Norman speaks there is a cut to
Marion. She looks down and says nothing. He too falls silent. This
is the closest this man and woman will come to an authentic com-
munion.

Acknowledging the shift of mood, Norman says, in a haunting,
gentle voice, "The rain didn't last long, did it?" Then he levels
Marion in his gaze—disconcertingly, she has begun to chew her
food, paying him only divided attention—and launches into his
great monologue on private traps, a fit companion piece to
Charles's speeches in *Shadow of a Doubt*. As Norman speaks,
Marion listens more and more intently, comprehension beginning
to dawn in her eyes.

Do you know what I think? I think that we're all in our private traps.
Clamped in them. And none of us can ever get out. We scratch and claw,

but only at the air, only at each other. And for all of it, we never budge an inch.

Marion looks up, then down, and breathes out slowly, responsive to the poetry in Norman's voice. She is visibly moved. As if endorsing Norman's words and affirming the intimacy of their meeting of minds, she says, "Sometimes we deliberately step into those traps." But this line really undercuts Norman's monologue, denies its authority (although Marion appears oblivious of this). For Norman pictures entrapment as a universal condition of human existence, while Marion's conviction is that she trapped herself. In his reply ("I was born in mine; I don't mind it any more") Norman's skepticism about his chances of becoming free comes through clearly. For him, if not for everyone, freedom was never a possibility, and it is not a possibility now. A cut to Marion for her earnest reply, "Oh, but you should . . ."

Up to this point, the cutting has alternated between a pattern in which there is a cut for each new utterance and one in which there is a cut from Norman speaking to Marion listening. Now Marion fully asserts herself. Her insistence that Norman should mind his trap, that he also is free to be free, pushes Norman into the passive role. Hitchcock registers this reversal of roles by cutting from Marion speaking to Norman listening. "You *should* mind it." (Hitchcock's pun on the word "mind" gives this whole exchange an added edge.) Norman replies, with a little boy's bashfulness, "Oh, I do." Then he laughs and shrugs his shoulders sadly. "But I say I don't." Marion's assertion challenges Norman to admit that freedom could be his and challenges the form their dialogue has taken. It motivates Hitchcock to break with the formal patterns of editing that have prevailed to this point. Norman's mother had challenged him to prove himself a man by rejecting Marion; Marion now challenges him to prove himself a man by breaking with his mother. But what if defiance of his mother calls for him to declare desire for Marion? Is Marion prepared to accept Norman as a man?

Marion lowers her eyes (tactfully? with trepidation?). She breaks

an unwritten rule and refers directly to Norman's mother. "You know that if anyone ever talked to me the way I heard . . ." This remark precipitates a new framing of Norman (5.64), and in turn a new framing of Marion (5.65), and effects a transition to a new phase of the shot/reverse-shot sequence. The new shot of Norman is dominated by a stuffed owl, an extension of his own figure in the frame: this predatory night

5.64

bird is Norman's double or agent or
guardian. (That the nude in the painting
on the wall is Marion's stand-in in this
frame will be confirmed when Marion
strikes that figure's exact pose.) The grin
vanishes from his face as her voice continues offscreen. "The way she spoke to
you." Then the first cut to the new framing of Marion (5.65), which abstracts her
from the detailed setting of (5.60) and
isolates her against the bare wall, joined

5.65

in the frame only by the bottom of an oval painting and the handle
of the milk pitcher. When she falls silent, Norman says, "Sometimes, when she talks to me like that, I feel I'd like to go up there
and curse her and leave her forever, or at least defy her." Marion
lowers her eyes and distractedly raises the bread to her mouth as

she looks back up. Norman leans back,
easing the tension. But this movement
also unveils a second picture on the
wall, previously eclipsed by Norman: a
classical painting of a rape (5.66). Later
we learn that this painting covers a
peephole cut into the wall. "But I know
I can't. She's ill."

Looking directly at Norman, Marion
says, in measured tones, "She sounded
strong." Like Hannay in his encounter
with Margaret, she has taken it upon

5.66

herself to offer instruction and encouragement, so that he may take
his destiny into his own hands, may escape his entrapment. Norman looks up at Marion. "No, I mean, *ill.*" He means by this repetition that his mother's illness is not physical but mental. Marion
does not visibly react. Her silent look solicits his continuation.

She had to raise me all by herself after my father died. I was only five and it
must have been quite a strain for her. She didn't have to work or anything
like that. He left a little money. Anyway, a few years ago, mother met this
man and, and he talked her into building this motel. He could have talked
her into anything. And when he died too it was . . . just too great a shock
for her. And, and the *way* he died!

On these last words, Norman breaks into a broad grin, then lowers
his head, trying to compose himself. "I guess it's nothing to talk
about while you're eating." Presumably, what makes him laugh is
his recollection of the man's death. Marion looks down at the bread
in her hand, as he goes on. "It was just too great a loss for her. She
had nothing left." Taking another bite of bread, Marion says, "Ex-

cept you," putting the period on Norman's story. Then she asks, "Why don't you go away?"

Norman responds to Marion's question first by challenging her assumption that she is fit to judge him. With authority he says, "To a private island, like you?" reiterating his conviction that no attempt to escape imprisonment can succeed. There is no private island where one may be free from one's burdens, one's responsibilities, one's self. Marion has no reply. When she remains silent,

5.67

relaxing her pressure on Norman, he goes on to answer her question. "I couldn't do that. Who would look after her?" Marion has stopped eating and is listening intently, rubbing her arm distractedly: this is when she mirrors the woman in the painting (5.67). "She'd be alone up there. Her fire would go out. It would be cold and damp like the grave." These last words are spoken as if to no one. But now Norman once again addresses Marion directly. He speaks as though from the heart. "If you love someone, you don't do that to them, even if you hate them." Marion looks up. (The Tippi Hedren figure in *The Birds* and *Marnie* would know exactly what Norman means by this remark and its sequel, as do we. But does Marion Crane know the language of love?) "Understand, I don't hate her. I hate what she's become. I hate the *illness*." (What has Norman's mother become? What is her "illness"? In retrospect, we might say that what she has really become is dead. Is it death, then, that fills Norman with hatred? But we might also say that what she has really become is Norman. Does Norman above all hate himself, what he has become, his own illness?)

Marion takes a fateful step. "Wouldn't it be better if you put her . . . someplace?" She cannot bring herself to name the "place" she has in mind but lowers her eyes tactfully, hoping in

5.68

this way to communicate her meaning. The specific irony in Marion's lowering her eyes in avoidance of saying what she means, of course, is that the only "someplace" Norman *could* really consider putting his mother is the "someplace" from which he took her, the grave. At this tense moment, Hitchcock initiates another phase of this complex shot/reverse-shot sequence. In (5.68), Norman is at the right of the frame. A wreath is near the center—it is, after all, almost Christmas, but the wreath also sustains the funereal mood. To the left of the wreath, and counterposed with Norman in this schematic composition, is a sharp-beaked bird and immediately to his left, contiguous with it, is a candle. (The candle and bird, like the gun and globe in the Professor's study in *The Thirty-Nine Steps*, form a "composite," a thing with two faces.) And in (5.69), Marion is framed more tightly and more nearly frontally than before, creating a sense of isolation.

5.69

Norman leans forward, eclipsing the wreath and allowing the bird's beak to come into close proximity to his widened eyes. "Do you mean an *institution? A madhouse?*" Hatred and bitterness have entered Norman's voice. Somber music begins, registering the shift of mood that signals the end of Marion's brief respite from anxiety. She looks deeply troubled, as when she drove through the rainy night, her private film unreeling. She says nothing, as Norman's voice continues offscreen. "People always call a madhouse 'someplace,' don't they? Put her in '*some place.*'" These words, spoken as if to no one present, once again imply that Marion is just like all the rest, not prepared to acknowledge him. She senses that she has said the wrong thing. "I'm sorry, I didn't mean it to sound uncaring." His face is blank when he hears these words, but then it flashes a sardonic grin. "What do you know about caring?" A cut to Marion, as Norman's speech continues: "Have you ever seen the inside of one of those places? The laughing and the tears, and the cruel eyes studying you?" This last line—and indeed, the whole speech—will be echoed, ostensibly by the mother's own "inner voice," at the end of the film. Then the analogy will be explicitly drawn between the condition of living within an institution and the condition of existing within the world of a film. Even now, *our* cruel eyes are studying Norman, in a room filled with the laughing and the tears.

The camera cuts from Marion, spellbound, to Norman, who appears to be on the verge of breaking down. "But she's harmless! She's as harmless as one of those stuffed birds!" Treading carefully, Marion says, "I *am* sorry." Yet she presses on. "I only felt . . . It seems she's *hurting* you. I meant well." This occasions Norman's bitterest indictment against "people" as represented by the likes of Marion, its language barbed with his most explicit identification of people and birds. "People always mean well. They cluck their thick tongues and shake their heads and suggest, oh so very delicately."

Marion again says nothing. (Is her impression at this moment that Norman is a little mad?) But now her silence is awkward and reveals that she has abandoned her attempt to convince him that freedom is within his grasp. The tension deflated by Marion's silent concession, he leans back and quietly makes a concession in turn. "Of course, I've suggested it myself. But I hate even to think about it. She needs *me*." He again leans forward and speaks earnestly. "It's not as if she were a maniac, a raving thing." His eyes glaze. "She just goes a little *mad* sometimes . . ." Norman's words resonate with Graham's summation of the meaning of Uncle Charles's death. But Norman's understanding is deeper than Graham's and closer to Hitchcock's own. He adds, "We all go a little mad sometimes." Leaning back, he grins and asks Marion, "Haven't you?" (His grin may also be amusement at a secret picture of his mother's death. That is, it may register another ghoulish private joke.) But Marion is relieved by Norman's question. She answers, "Yes. Sometimes just one time can be enough." Marion has come to understand that going through with the project she initiated by stealing the $40,000 would be madness. When she adds, "Thank you," she is thanking Norman for more than his food and company. She is also expressing gratitude for the lesson she feels she has learned. Her "Thank you" echoes the words that opened this conversation, closing a bracket, and resonates with the "Thank you, Mr. Bates" with which she undertook to bring their earlier meeting to an end. This could mark the start of a real friendship, or a romance. But Marion is satisfied. She has had her fill of Norman, and declares this encounter, and indeed their entire relationship, closed.

In the warm glow of her pity, Marion feels beholden to this hopeless case, edified by this example of the resilience of the human spirit. She does not regard Norman as her equal. For example, she does not view Norman as a man she could desire or who could desire her. Even as she thanks him for imparting a lesson in humanity, she summarily dismisses him. Norman looks incredulous, then grins again. Is he astounded by Marion's transparency and her foolishness for not being able to recognize that he can perceive her condescension? This grin is a conjunction of resentment and the disdain that was on his face at the end of their earlier meeting. Or does Norman grin in anticipation of the conclusion of a secret scenario? Earlier, Norman replied to Marion's "Thank you, Mr. Bates" by saying "*Norman* Bates," his invitation to informality prefacing his offer of food. When he now says, "Thank you, *Norman*," we can hear him as attempting to consolidate their hard-won intimacy. But in his voice can also be heard disdain for this woman who is oblivious of her own hypocrisy, and oblivious as well of his intelligence. Obligingly repeating "Norman," Marion stands, and the camera tilts up. Her head rises up through the oval frame until she looms statuesque, like a goddess (but there is a bird's beak at her throat) (5.70). This shot and its reversal—a high-angle shot that looks down on Norman from Marion's elevated perspective (5.71)—initiates the final phase of the shot/reverse-shot sequence.

Norman says, "You're not going back to your room already?" There is condescension in his voice: he is not really trying to persuade her to stay longer. Smiling, she says, "I'm very tired, and I have a long drive tomorrow, all the way back to Phoenix." With this remark, Marion announces her decision—she credits it to Norman, although she assumes he does not know what her decision is. Even more incredulous, Norman says, "Really?" When she "explains" her remark ("I stepped into a private trap back there, and I'd like to go back and try to pull myself out of it") Norman says, with a condescension he knows she will not perceive, "Are you sure you wouldn't like to stay just a little while longer, just for talk?" She answers, "I do, but . . ." "All right. I'll see you in the morning. I'll bring you some breakfast, all right?" But she replies, "I'll be getting up very early. Dawn." "All right, Miss, uh . . ." When she says "Crane,"

5.70

5.71

5.72

Norman repeats the name with a trace of a smile on his lips (is he amused by her bird's name? by this confirmation that she signed a false name in the register?).

At this moment, Hitchcock introduces a framing completely unprecedented in the sequence, Marion viewed in profile (5.72). The camera reframes to the right with her as she begins to walk toward the door. As she leaves the frame, the camera pauses, centering the rape painting, which is flanked by the two owls, the nude and the bird/candle (5.73). This schematically composed frame remains devoid of any human subject until Norman rises up into view. Then the camera resumes its original movement, but now reframing with Norman. At the end of this tour de force—it plays a function com-

5.73

5.74

5.75

5.76

parable to that of the shot in *Shadow of a Doubt* which reverses the positions of Charles and Charlie in the frame—Norman is framed in profile, as Marion was at the beginning of the shot (5.74). What follows represents Norman's point of view. From his vantage we watch Marion as she goes out the door, rounds a corner, and disappears from sight, her footfalls still echoing (5.75). The shot/reverse-shot sequence has terminated with this virtuoso transition from Marion's to Norman's consciousness.

Framed frontally—behind him, again in the center of the frame, is the rape painting; directly behind his head, contiguous with his figure, is a stuffed raven—Norman puts a piece of food into his mouth and begins to chew. He steps forward into the outer office and looks through the register, perhaps to confirm that the name she signed was false. He goes back into the parlor. At the sound of a closing door, he looks toward the house so that he is viewed in profile. Still listening, he turns back to face the camera. Then there comes an extraordinary shot in which Norman is framed back to the camera (5.76), standing before the painting as if absorbed in the scene it represents, as if that scene were one with his private fantasy. After a moment, he removes the painting from the wall, revealing a large, jagged hole with a pinpoint of light in its center (5.77). This hole resonates deeply in Hitchcock's work. For example, in its jaggedness—it looks to have been torn from the plaster—it is linked to the hole Alice tears in the clown painting in *Blackmail*. In its schematic division into black region and white region, it is linked to the images that dominate *The Lodger*'s flashback and to a number of charged frames in *Murder!*. The dot of

light in the center, which will soon
project a white circle onto Norman's
face, marking it, is linked to the circle
cut in the wall in *The Saboteur*. And so
on. This hole-within-a-hole is charged
symbolically: it is an eye, and it is an
emblem of female sexuality.[9]

The camera cuts to Norman, viewed
from the side, as he leans forward to
look through the peephole (5.78). This
shot withholds Norman's view from us,
allowing us to recognize our wish for it.
When finally we are given the deferred
view, eerily accompanied by muted
high violins, we are gratified even as we
experience a sense of foreboding (5.79).
What we see along with Norman is
Marion undressing, framed by the bathroom door. This shot is masked to underscore the identity of our view with
Norman's through the peephole, the
mask also declaring that our view is one
with Hitchcock's through the viewfinder of his camera. Still, Norman is
also a subject of the camera, a creature
who may be framed in a view. This is affirmed by the following shot, an extreme
closeup of Norman's viewing eye,
viewed objectively from the side (5.80).
But if this is Norman's eye, it equally
stands in for our eye and Hitchcock's
eye, for any eye intently engaged in the
act of viewing.[10]

There follows a cut back to this eye's
view. Marion, now robed, leaves the
frame (5.81). Hitchcock has played a
trick on us: the cut to the viewing eye
coincided with the moment Marion was
completely naked. While we were viewing this eye, it was viewing Marion
naked, a view of which we were de-
prived. There is a cut to a longer view of
Norman, his face marked with the circle
of light projected through the peephole
(5.82). He replaces the picture on the

5.77

5.78

5.79

5.80

5.81

5.82

5.83

5.84

wall and walks forward, thinking. Then he looks toward the house and turns his profile to the camera, his thoughts opaque (5.83). The camera reframes with Norman as he goes to the door. When he opens the door, the white curtain momentarily dominates the frame, creating a Hitchcockian white flash. This in turn accentuates the darkness of the next shot, framed from the other side of the door, so that when Norman comes through this door, his figure emerges out of blackness. Again he faces the camera and turns toward the house; again full face and profile are schematically alternated. Outside, the camera twists clockwise with Norman as he goes toward the stairs leading up to the house. He exits the frame, leaving it almost completely black.

From a vantage point within the house, we view his entrance. Apparently, his intention is to go upstairs (will he blame his mother for the premature termination of his encounter with Marion? will he concede that his mother was right all along?). But he stops at the foot of the stairs, hand on the bannister post, back to the camera, his figure framed by the staircase rising behind him (5.84), like the lodger riveted by Daisy's laugh. Then Norman slumps down, takes his hand off the post, and walks through the corridor to the kitchen in back, his hands in his pockets, his figure half in light and half in darkness. Then Hitchcock cuts to one of his tunnel shots, looking down the corridor to the kitchen. Norman enters this frame and walks into its depths. In the kitchen, he sits hunched in a strange, angular posture that makes him look like a vulture. On a reprise of the clinking sound, he looks right at the camera (5.85).

This look brings home to us that we do not really know Norman. We do not know his feelings or thoughts or intentions, his powers or the limits of those powers. For one thing, it suggests that he knows he is being viewed. But also, when the camera now cuts directly to Marion writing at her desk, unaware of being viewed (5.86), the suggestion is that Norman's gaze magically possesses, perhaps even conjures, this view. Norman's subjectivity, hovering over this shot, is invoked in part by the mirror in which Marion casts no reflection. His power to penetrate Marion's privacy links his gaze to the camera. Hence this cut develops the suggestion implicit in the cut that concluded their initial meeting, the cut to Marion from the vantage just relinquished by Norman.

5.85

5.86

There is a cut to a column of figures. Marion is trying to work out how she might return the money, making up for what she has spent. She puts her pen down, rests her chin in her hand and pauses, lost in thought. Then she removes the page from her notebook and tears it up. She is about to throw it in the waste-paper basket when a better idea occurs to her. She looks around, first at her handbag—at this moment, her face, viewed in profile, is contiguous with the mirror in which she still casts no reflection (5.87)—and then rises. The camera reframes with her as she goes to the bathroom (momentarily, she is doubled in the mirror, but she is turned away from her reflection, oblivious of its dogging of her path).

Marion enters the bathroom and tosses the shreds of paper into the toilet bowl (5.88). The music, which has kept up a constant low-key, somber accom-

5.87

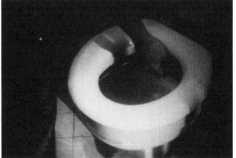

5.88

paniment, falls silent, underscoring the intimate sound of flushing water. She closes the bathroom door to secure her privacy, slips off her robe, drapes it over the toilet bowl, steps into the bath, and closes the shower curtain behind her, filling the frame with a flash

5.89

of white (5.89). The most famous shower in the history of cinema is about to begin.

Although the shower murder is perhaps the most celebrated sequence in all of Hitchcock's work, it has never, to my knowledge, been subjected to more than rudimentary analysis. Most critics have gone little beyond expressions of astonishment at the number of shots crammed into its minute or so of screen time, failing to note the basic facts about its structure and significance. I will divide the sequence into three parts: the shower itself, up to the entrance of the murderer; the murder; the camera's gesture of pulling out from Marion's dead eye to sum up the momentous event that has taken place.

The shower. From Marion viewed through the translucent shower curtain, Hitchcock cuts to (5.90), framed from within the

5.90

space bounded by the curtain. At the top center of this frame, overseeing this space like Hitchcock's camera itself, is the shower head.[11] This shot announces the two main aspects of the symbolic role the shower head is to play in the sequence. Marion's shower is a love scene, with the shower head her imaginary partner, inhumanly calm and poised, and the shower head is also an eye. Marion's murder is a rape, and it is also a blinding.

Marion rises into the frame, as Norman rose into the frame to terminate the shot/reverse-shot dialogue in the parlor. Water begins to stream from the shower head, its sound echoing the rain that accompanied the violent climax of Marion's private film. She looks up into the stream of water and begins to wash her neck and arms. Her expression is ecstatic as the water brings her body to life (5.91). At this point, there is a cut to Marion's vision of the shower head, water radiating from it in all directions like a sunburst (5.92). This shot answers the question, "What does Marion see when she looks up?" But viewed head on, the shower head is the double of Nor-

man's peephole; it is an eye staring into
the camera. Hence this cut retroactively
discloses that (5.91) invoked this eye's
point of view. And it announces that the
following views of Marion, astonishing
in their intimacy and eroticism, likewise
have their source in this eye (as the
views comprising the opening of *Murder!* have their source in the clock-
face/eye framed in that film's first shot).
This is the peephole through which our
gaze penetrates the shower curtain and
through which Norman's gaze continues to possess the frame. This is the lens
of Hitchcock's camera and the projector
that casts its beam of light onto the
screen.

5.91

When Marion looks into the shower
head, there is no sign that she suspects
that she is being viewed. If she envisions the shower head as an eye, it is a
sightless eye, subject to her control like

5.92

the figures in her private film. Do *we* acknowledge the gaze of this
shower head/eye? Viewed from Marion's perspective, it is masked
in our vision as in hers, but we can see through this mask as she
cannot. At least we can recognize it as our eye, secretly subjecting
her to its gaze; as Norman's, continuing
its haunting; as the source of the intimate views that follow. And the shot
that terminates and sums up this series
of erotically charged views will return
us to the reality of the gaze that penetrates her privacy: Hitchcock cuts to the
shower head viewed from the side (5.93)
at the precise moment Marion turns her
naked back to the stream of water. This
echoes (5.80), the closeup of the viewing eye, whose gaze, like the shower

5.93

head's stream, crosses the frame from left to right. But it is only
when the sunburst shot is reprised after the murder, directly cued
by Marion's dead eye—the effect of that climactic cut is enhanced
by the deliberate exclusion of the shower head from all of the literally dozens of shots that make up the montage of the murder—that
the shower head is fully unmasked. Then it is declared that there is
a being separate from ourselves, to whose presence we have been

blind, as Marion has been blind to ours. Even after this unmasking, however, we do not know who or what this being really is: we do not know whether to call this being "Hitchcock" or Norman," or whether—with Norman—to call this figure "mother." This being

5.94

presides over Marion's shower and her murder and rules sovereign over our views, possessing us as we possess Marion in our gaze. Marion sees the shower head only as the source of her pleasure, while we see this "eye" only as the source of views that arouse our appetite and promise satisfaction of our desire. We allow such views as (5.94) to flow over us, as if the camera had no appetite of its own, as if it lived only to satisfy our desire. We take pleasure in this series of sensual images, precisely as Marion takes pleasure in the stream of water emanating from the shower head.

Before Marion begins her shower, her mood is reflective, even melancholy. After all, she has just resigned herself to the oppressive conditions of her existence. She does not anticipate that the water coursing over her body will make her feel alive. It has been said that Marion's shower is a ritual in which her guilt is symbolically washed away. But it is important to keep in mind that, if this is a baptism, it is specifically her body that is born again; and as her body receives the purifying stream emanating from the shower head, she comes alive sexually. Then a fundamental question about this shower is whether Marion's pleasure is in anticipation of her reentry into the world, her rebirth; or whether her ecstasy is in abandonment to the fantasy of finding a private island after all: a privileged place cut off from the world where she can be fulfilled. More specifically, is Marion's pleasure her anticipation of a union with a human sexual partner in the world, or does Marion imagine no one in the world with the power to make her feel this alive, no one to whom she might offer herself this freely and passionately?[12]

Enclosed within this shower curtain, bathed by the shower head's stream, the world drops away from Marion. In this shower, she can imagine herself once again a virgin, unsullied by any man. Indeed, she can imagine herself completely undefiled by the world, as if there were no world outside or as if she had never been born into it. But does Marion wish to be isolated from the world or wish for her isolation to be overcome? Does she wish to attain perfect purity, perfect privacy, perfect self-enclosure? Or does she wish to be reborn, purified, into the world and to enter into a union in which her longing for love is fulfilled? We have no answers to these questions. We can view Marion as longing for love, and we can view her as embracing a self-absorption that is narcissistic in Freud's sense. We can view Marion as taking pleasure in the fantasy of receiving a longed-for lover or in the fantasy that she is complete unto herself, self-enclosed, in need of no one.

Insofar as Marion's pleasure is narcissistic, it bears a violent aspect. Her pleasure is in the denial of the world, and specifically in the denial of men: in withholding herself sexually from men and in denying them the views they desire. She takes pleasure in imagining men as impotent and blind: this is the other face of her pleasure in imagining herself, and the shower curtain that encloses her, as intact and inviolable. On the other hand, insofar as Marion's pleasure is a manifestation of her longing for love in the world, her pleasure is in the fantasy that the being represented by the shower head, the source of her pleasure, might step forward to declare desire.

Our views of Marion have a sensuality unprecedented in the movies. It is not that they escape censorship: they are carefully cropped, for example, to allow no glimpse of her genitals or her nipples (the masking of certain frames makes this censorship all the more apparent). Yet our impression is that, were this shower to continue, Marion's pleasure would be consummated and no view we desire would be withheld. This passage promises an end to all censorship. Our involvement with Marion's story—the story of her relationships with others in her world and with herself—is suspended. We possess Marion in a succession of erotically charged views that invoke the prospect of the consummation of Marion's pleasure and our own as well.

Yet a crucial ambiguity must be registered. On the one hand, no film sequence more compellingly declares the camera's power to let the viewer identify with its subject. We can all but feel the water coursing over our bodies, awakening and arousing us, all but feel Marion's own pleasure, all but become Marion. The shower head's stream and the views of Marion that flow over us are all but one. One consummation this passage invokes is the possibility that the separation of her body from ours will be completely overcome in the simultaneous consummation of her pleasure and ours. On the other hand, no film sequence so compellingly declares the camera's placement outside its subject, who appears to us as an "other." Our views of Marion constitute her as a sexual object. We imagine ourselves being in her erotic proximity, all but feeling the touch of her "fine soft flesh." We are all but able to caress and be caressed by her, even to penetrate her body. Our views of Marion awaken an appetite that cannot be satisfied by more views, but only by transcending the limits of the act of viewing as such. (One of its limits is precisely that viewing allows no consummation.) Our pleasure in viewing Marion cannot be separated from our fantasy that we are about to possess her sexually. (If this is a male fantasy, it is not one that only the men in Hitchcock's audience may indulge. For men and women among the film's viewers, the act of viewing possesses both active and passive aspects, call them "masculine" and "feminine.")

Insofar as we take Marion to be aroused by the prospect of a lover's stepping forward, we may imagine ourselves stepping forward, declaring our desire and being acknowledged as her dream lover. But insofar as we take Marion's pleasure to be in denying the world, we must imagine her as denying that she desires us, as resisting us, as wishing for us to be blind and impotent. Then our fantasy is of overcoming her denial of us, forcing her to accept our advance and acknowledge that she desires us after all. Ours is a fantasy of rape. An aspect of this "rape" fantasy is its disavowal of our own desire. We imagine that Marion is nothing to us: we don't care if she is complete, self-contained, whole. We take pleasure in denying her denial of us not because we desire her, but because she serves our fantasy that the world wishes us to violate it. If we can view Marion as taking narcissistic pleasure in her intactness, our pleasure too has a narcissistic aspect.

We are viewing a film. This means, for one thing, that the barrier separating us from Marion cannot be broached like a shower curtain (a barrier that cannot be broached, perhaps, is not really a barrier at all). We can only "all but feel" the warm water coursing over our bodies, "all but feel" Marion's fine soft flesh. That her body is separate from our own is a fact that joins her with all those who are "others" to us in the world. But she is different—different ontologically—from all real others by virtue of this fact that it is not possible for us to touch her, meet her gaze, make love to her, subject her to violence, or be subjected to violence by her. Our separation from Marion can neither be fully crystallized nor overcome: she is, after all, projected from within us even as she is projected outside us. However long her shower may last, her pleasure can never be consummated, nor can our pleasure in viewing her. Were Marion to finish her shower, she would have to return, unfulfilled, to a world in which she is imprisoned, and we would have to return to her story, and after that to our own. We would fall back into the circumscribed relationship mandated by the camera's familiar role. But Marion never finishes her shower. A monstrous being cruelly cuts her pleasure short. And our pleasure too is abrogated with a sickening finality.

The murder. From the side view of the shower head, Hitchcock cuts back to Marion, still ecstatic (5.95). Then he cuts to a setup that places the camera where the tile wall of the shower "really" is (5.96). This is one of the most important shots in the film. The shower curtain, to which Marion's back is turned, hangs from a bar at the top of the screen, and forms a frame-within-a-frame that almost completely fills the screen. This frame, like the window in *Murder!*'s prison-visit sequence, may be viewed as standing in for the film frame to declare that the world we are viewing is framed, that what we are viewing is a film.[13]

5.95

The camera begins to move forward, until the bar at the top becomes excluded from the screen. Synchronized with this movement of the camera, Marion slides out of the frame, so that the shower curtain completely fills the screen (5.97, 5.98). This movement is closely related to the camera movements that end *The Lodger*, *Murder!*, and *The Thirty-Nine Steps*. When the frame-within-a-frame of the shower curtain comes to engulf the entire frame, it is as if we have crossed a barrier. The camera's gesture deepens its declaration that what we are viewing is a film. At the same time, paradoxically, it asserts the identity of the shower curtain—an object enclosed within the world of *Psycho*, however it may symbolize the film frame—and the real movie screen on which our views have been projected. This gesture of the camera at the same time declares that the world of *Psycho* is not fully real and denies that there is a real separation between that world and reality. In this curtain, the camera's gesture rhetorically declares, our world and the world of *Psycho* come together; or it declares that they have never really been apart.

5.96

5.97

Precisely synchronized with the movement of the camera and with Marion's exit from the frame, a shadowy

5.98

5.99

5.100

5.101

figure, barely visible through the shower curtain, enters the door that can just be made out in the background. It steps forward toward the camera, its form doubled by and blending into its shadow cast on the translucent curtain (5.99). We sense that this figure is coiled, poised to strike, and that it is monstrous. We are shocked, but not caught completely by surprise, when the curtain is suddenly wrenched open and a silhouetted knife-wielding figure is revealed (5.100, 5.101).

Much of the shattering impact of this moment derives from Bernard Herrmann's score. Hitchcock's original intention was to release the shower-murder sequence with no musical accompaniment at all, but Herrmann prevailed on him to try it out with music. Something is lost by this fiendishly effective addition, which creates an obstacle to fully comprehending of the sequence, to grasping its logic and meaning. But something is assuredly gained. The actual unveiling of the silhouetted figure in (5.101), like the deferred first view of the lodger, is intended to be as much anticlimactic as climactic. It is above all the sudden high-pitched shriek of violins, so compellingly suggestive of an attacking birdlike creature, that creates the shock that constitutes Psycho's best-known effect. We are prepared for Marion to scream at the sudden entrance of an intruder. Our tension is at such a pitch that the shriek of violins affects us the way a mischievously shuffled shoe affects a cat intently readying to pounce. Even when we know what is coming, the fact that the silhouetted figure freezes in a tableau makes it impossible for us to anticipate the exact moment of the shriek. All of our efforts to gird ourselves for it only increase our tension and prime us to be unnerved by the shriek when it occurs.

As always in Hitchcock, when the curtain opens, theater is invoked. The intruder's entrance is specifically dramatic, and we are the only audience for this theatrical entrance; Marion is turned away. Someone is revealed to us in this menacing posture, some-one wielding a knife, ready to unleash a murderous assault. This moment is authentically terrifying because it succeeds in provok-ing us to the nightmarish fantasy that the scene of murder now commencing is real, and that we are the murderer's intended vic-tim. We are face to face with our own murderer, confronting the imminent prospect of our own death.

This figure's menacing pose reveals its murderous intention. And the theatricality of the pose reveals the further intention of compelling us to recognize the murderousness and to acknowledge that we are the object of murderous rage. The identification of the shower curtain with the movie screen—that "safety curtain" we as-sumed would separate us from the world of the film—makes this dramatic gesture even more terrifying. For it presents the mon-strous figure not simply as a denizen of a world safely cut off from our own, but as real. Paradoxically, (5.101) also conveys the unreal-ity of this figure: what we see when the curtain is pulled open is not a horrible face but a mere apparition, an incorporeal shadow, a projection on a screen. In addition, the silhouetted figure is sym-metrically flanked by the raised knife on the one side and the light bulb on the other, this balanced composition complemented by the containment of the silhouette within the frame-within-a-frame of the doorway (the background of flowery wallpaper also links this frame-within-a-frame to the mirror in (5.86)—the mirror in which Marion cast no reflection). This shot, so conspicuously composed, represents a vision.

We are not yet prepared to address all the ambiguities and para-doxes that attend this theatrical demonstration directed to us. We are not yet prepared to speculate, for example, on whether to regard this monstrous figure as Norman or his mother. But it has to be clear that this figure stands in for Hitchcock. In this theatrical ges-ture, the camera and the creature that unveils itself by drawing back the curtain are in complicity. Someone real presents to us the views that constitute *Psycho*, and at this moment that "someone" confronts us with his unfulfilled appe-tite and his wish to avenge himself on us. Yet if the being unveiled in this ges-ture declares its reality, its separateness from us, it is also no creature of flesh and blood but a projection from within ourselves that appears before us. We are confronting ourselves.

When the camera reverses field to Marion, turned away (5.102), her figure displaces the silhouette in (5.101), as

5.102

5.103

5.104

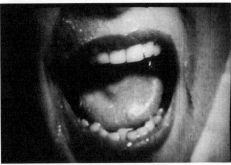

5.105

5.106

though this cut presents us not with views of two separate beings, but two faces of one being, or one face that undergoes a metamorphosis. But also it is through the silhouetted figure's eyes that we now view Marion, as she turns around clockwise until she looks right into the camera (5.103). What she sees makes her open her mouth to scream.

Astonishingly, we are not now presented with the view that is the source of Marion's horror (that is, of (5.101)). Rather, there is a jump cut to a closer view of Marion's face (5.104), then a second jump cut to an extreme closeup of her wide-open mouth (5.105). Only then are we given Marion's point of view, framing the silhouetted figure striking out violently with its knife (5.106).

These jump cuts make palpable Marion's scream, nearly drowned out by the shrieking violins that muffle it. But they can also be seen as registering the attention of the figure standing menacingly before Marion. To this being Marion *is* an open mouth. The jump cuts relate this passage closely to the series of jump cuts in *The Birds* which culminate in the mother's view of her dead friend's pecked-out eye and to their common ancestor, the quick track in to Frank's view of the dead artist's eye in *Blackmail*. These connections help us to recognize, in retrospect, that (5.105) anticipates the image of Marion's dead eye which will be the keystone of the shower-murder sequence as a whole. Imaged in (5.105), Marion's open mouth is also an eye; Marion's murder is a blinding. But this open mouth also encompasses a nightmare vision of a woman as possessing, or being, a mouth that devours whatever is drawn into it.

If this were the conventional horror-film scene of a vulnerable woman attacked by a monster, we would expect Marion's first view of her attacker to be simultaneous with our own, so that our moments of terror would coincide. But Hitchcock's treatment divides our identification. We identify with Marion, who must now confront the vision that was ours. But we are also implicated in this visitation and cannot separate ourselves from the being whose sudden intrusion frightens Marion. We view Marion through this creature's eyes, as she turns to possess it in her gaze. And Marion too is implicated in this presentation. Our impression is that, were she never to turn around, no attack would take place. It is her turning to possess this being in her gaze that brings it fully to life.

Furthermore, it can be said that the intruder intends to teach Marion a lesson, at one level a lesson about her responsibility for her own fate. To this end, he/she compels her to recognize this shadowy, incorporeal figure as a creature of her own imagination, a visitor from her own private film. This is the being she conjured in her ecstasy as she received the shower head's stream, the being whose reality and power she denied. Now this being has violated the "inviolable" shower curtain, the barrier between outside and inside, and stands before her demanding acknowledgment. The visitation demonstrates to Marion that her wish to keep outside and inside separate—this is also her wish to find a private island where she may author her own salvation—will not come true. In her hubris, Marion has denied the world in the person of Norman Bates, denied Hitchcock, and denied us. Now we are joined with Hitchcock in subjecting her to a twofold demonstration. First, she is compelled to acknowledge this apparition as her own projection. Second, she is compelled to acknowledge this nightmare figure also as real, beyond her control. It is not within Marion's power to make the apparition go away. The curtain has really been torn.

But if this is a demonstration addressed to Marion, it is also a theatrical demonstration addressed to us. Just as we are about to unleash an attack, we are also its victim. The author of *Psycho*, a creature of flesh and blood, stands before us threatening vengeance. If we have taken our views of Marion to be solely for the satisfaction of our desires, it is Hitchcock's appetite we have denied, his life's blood—etched in every frame of *Psycho*—we have consumed. In the scene that ensues, we join with Hitchcock in subjecting Marion to a savage assault unprecedented in its violence, while Hitchcock also avenges himself on those who fail to acknowledge him. The author of *Psycho* declares his separateness from us, yet calls upon us to acknowledge that the agency presiding over the camera is within us as well. In the service of this demonstration, poor Marion Crane is cruelly sacrificed.

Let us quickly run through the thirty-four shots that lead up to Marion's death.

1. (5.107). The knife slashes down for the first time.

2. (5.108). The knife slashes through the corner of the screen, effecting a bridge between Marion's and her attacker's separate frames, although the arm and the knife remain silhouetted.

3. In a slightly closer variant of (5.107), the knife is again raised, its blade gleaming in the light.

4. (5.109). This shot frames part of Marion's body along with the intruder's arm, still shadowy in the frame.

5. (5.110). Viewed from overhead, the shower-curtain bar cuts across the screen, graphically defining the boundary between the space inside and the space outside the shower, and forming a perfect ////. This shot declares the reality of the intruder's crossing of the inviolable barrier. As Marion tries to fend it off, the knife strikes three times.

6. (5.111). Marion's face fills the screen, expressing bewilderment and pain.

7. (5.112). Marion holds onto the shadowy arm as it weaves three times in a spiraling movement.

8. Reprise of (5.111).

9. Reprise of (5.112).

10. Another variant of (5.107). The knife again slashes down.

11. Marion turns her face away, her head almost sliding out of the frame.

12. (5.113). The slashing knife creates another //// and echoes the wiper blade that slashed across the windshield at the violent climax of Marion's private film.

13. A shot of Marion recoiling, still bewildered.

14. This shot approximates (5.113), but this time the knife slashes through the center of the frame.

5.107

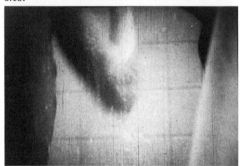

5.108

5.109

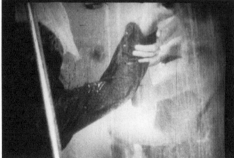

5.110

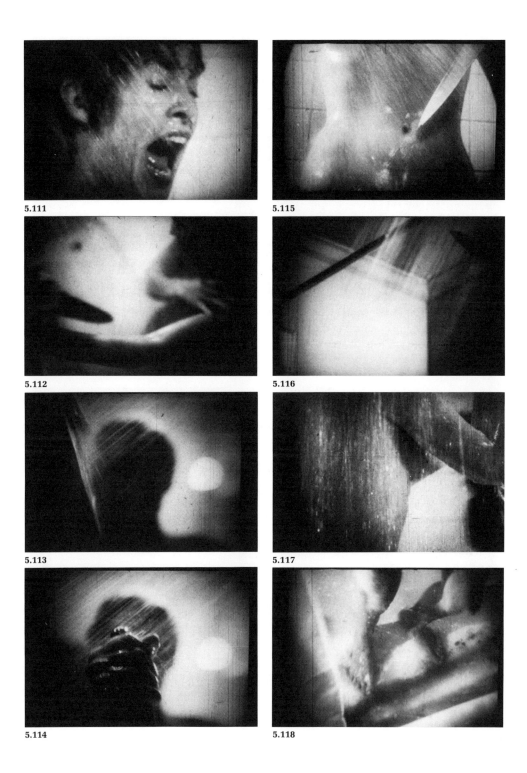

5.111

5.112

5.113

5.114

5.115

5.116

5.117

5.118

15. Marion's bewildered reaction.

16. (5.114). For the first time, the hand and knife come into clear focus and lose their incorporeality. We see the water bounce off the glinting metal of the blade, and see as well that this hand is really made of flesh.

17. (5.115). The climax of the sequence. Within the compass of this shot, Marion's body remains unmarked, immaculate. We see no blood and witness no penetration of knife into flesh. Yet it is this shot's juxtaposition of blade and flesh that announces the fatal wound. By never showing the blade penetrating Marion's flesh, Hitchcock deprives the viewer of a sensually gratifying climax, and also declares that there is no moment when Marion actually feels the knife. The scene of her murder passes before Marion as if she were only dreaming it.

18. Marion recoils, but still looks dazed, entranced. This assault is only a dream, yet she knows she is really dying.

19. (5.116). A low-angle view facing the door. The knife slashes through the frame.

20. (5.117). Marion's back and arms. The intruder's arm again enters the frame.

21. A closeup of Marion's face. She is now clearly in agony.

22. (5.118). Blood drips down Marion's writhing legs. This assault is a rape, a nightmare deflowering. (Compare the shot of Charles's and Charlie's legs intertwined at the climax of *Shadow of a Doubt*.)

23. (5.119). Marion turns her face from the camera.

24. Marion is framed back to the camera in a longer shot. The knife enters the frame.

5.119

5.120

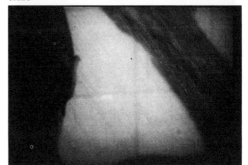

5.121

5.122

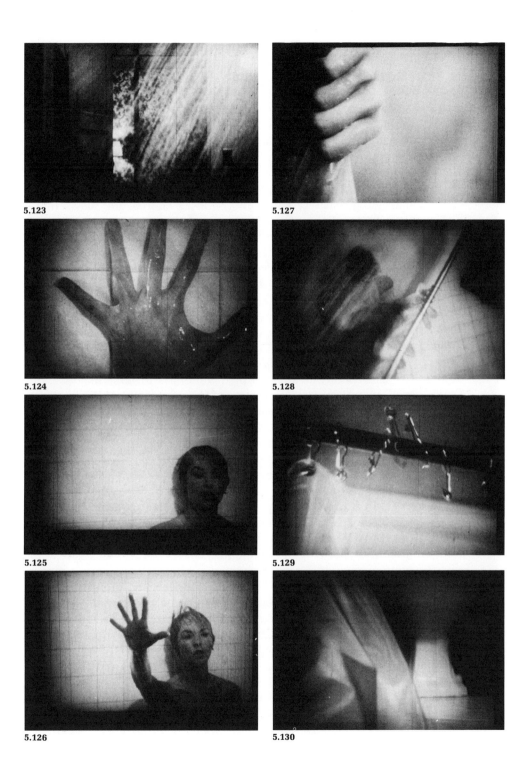

5.123

5.124

5.125

5.126

5.127

5.128

5.129

5.130

25. Reprise of (5.118), with a greater flow of blood.

26. The screen flashes white as the camera momentarily frames only the bare tile wall. Marion's hand, viewed from up close and out of focus, enters and then exits the frame (5.120).

27. (5.121). Marion, turned away from the camera.

28. (5.122, 5.123). The intruder exits as he/she had entered. This shot allows us our clearest view of this figure and apparently shows that it is a woman wearing a long, old-fashioned dress. This view— it is the reverse angle of the view through Norman's peephole—is one Marion does not possess, one to which her back is turned. The harrowing music cadences in a series of chords, and the scene returns to its original silence, broken only by the stream of water emanating from the shower head.

29. (5.124). Marion's hand pressed against the white tile. It slowly slides down the wall, a poignant figure for the loosening of her grip on life.

30. Marion's hand drops out of the frame and her body slowly slides down the wall. She turns to face forward as her back slips down, the camera tilting down with her (5.125). She is alive and conscious, but her eyes are glazed. She is more astonished and bewildered than ever by the nightmarish scene that has just ended, her sense of its unreality coupled with the realization that this "unreal" scene is also the real scene of her own death. At this moment, she looks forward and reaches out, as if to touch someone or something she cannot see (5.126). It is as if Marion were reaching out to touch the screen, to touch the camera, to touch us. But the camera pulls slowly away, reversing the movement by which it earlier allowed the shower curtain to engulf the screen. Then her hand changes its path.

31. In extreme closeup, Marion's hand continues its movement until it grasps the shower curtain in the left foreground of the frame (5.127). Marion's gesture of gripping the furled shower curtain is profoundly moving, if ambiguous. This is the one sensually gratifying moment in the entire sequence. It is satisfying for us—we can all but feel our hand holding the shower curtain in its grip, and we can all but feel Marion's hand holding us in its grip—and it is satisfying for Marion. Gripping the curtain tightly, Marion still feels the life in her body. She holds onto the curtain for dear life. But we can also see Marion's gripping of this shower curtain as her last act of violence; her struggle not to hold herself up, but to pull the curtain down with her, avenging herself.[14]

32. (5.128). This overhead shot is a mirror reversal of (5.110). The shower-curtain bar again demarcates the barrier between inside and outside, and marks this frame with the Hitchcockian ////. From this elevated vantage, we view Marion's dying fall.

33. (5.129). In low angle, from Marion's point of view, we share

her last vision. The shower curtain, unable to bear her weight, pulls away from the supporting bar, as the hooks give way one by one. The popping of the hooks punctuates the stillness left by the cessation of the music, a silence otherwise broken only by the water flowing from the shower head.

34. (5.130). In this schematically composed shot, the shower curtain fills the lefthand region and the toilet bowl the right. Into this evenly divided frame, Marion's arm falls, followed by her head and torso. Her body spills over from within the shower, and lands on the curtain that will be her shroud.[15]

The camera's gesture. From (5.130), there follows a cut to the reprise of the sunburst shot of the shower head viewed frontally. As I have pointed out, the shower head is absent from all the frames that comprise the montage of the murder. This cut reminds us that, in our immersion in the violent scene that has just taken place under the shower head's stream, we have been unmindful of the source of that stream. The shower head remains indifferent to the human tragedy of Marion's death: oblivious of that death and yet sovereign over it. It bears no sign of human passion or appetite. In this frame, the shower head appears no more capable of vengeance than love; it is quiescent, like the masses of birds in *The Birds'* closing tableau. It is just an ordinary shower head, a thing, outside the realm of guilt and innocence. Ours is the very vision that Marion once possessed, the vision that brought her body to life; but Marion has withdrawn. Humanity has departed the scene.

As if directed by the stream emanating from the shower head, the camera cuts to Marion's legs, blood mixing with the water (5.131), and begins to move to the left, following this flow of water and blood. At the moment Marion's legs are about to pass out of the frame, our view becomes masked as when we shared Norman's view through the peephole (5.132). And at this moment, too, the drain comes into view. This simultaneity of entrance and exit suggests that Marion and the drain are interchangeable. The camera reframes to center the drain as it tracks in toward it, so that the blackness within appears about to engulf the screen as when the camera first passed through the hotel window to penetrate, and give birth to, Marion's

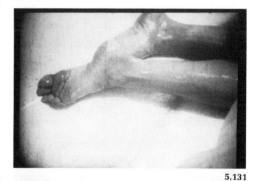

5.131

5.132

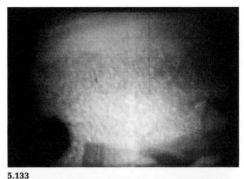

5.133

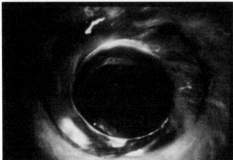

5.134

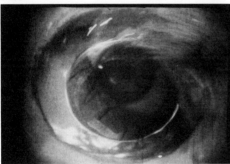

5.135

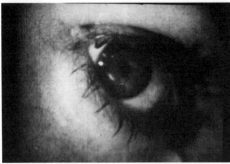

5.136

world (5.133, 5.134). The sound of the shower is simultaneously transmuted into what might be called an "aural closeup" of the water going down the drain. This sound recalls the flushing toilet that preceded Marion's entrance into the shower. The threat of being engulfed by this blackness is the threat of being flushed down with Marion's life's blood. And the spiraling of the water combined with the inward movement of the camera creates a vertiginous effect. The prospect of being sucked into this drain is a nauseating one.[16] We dread to go—we dread even to look—where this blood goes when it is flushed down the drain, our dread combining the fear of death, of intolerable confinement, and of being consumed. But the blackness within the drain also promises release: this drain is the "natural" destination of the shower head's stream, this river's sea. When the water from this shower head, infused with Marion's blood, flows into the drain, will our vision, and the world it frames, be reborn?

At this point, there is an exquisitely slow dissolve from the drain to an eye, viewed in extreme closeup (5.135, 5.136). This eye, which fixes the camera in its gaze, perfectly displaces the drain in the frame, as if they were two aspects of a single thing or as if the drain itself, under the camera's gaze, undergoes a metamorphosis. But this eye also appears to peer out from within the drain; the hole-within-a-hole of this eye is the double of the sunburst and the double of Norman's peephole. And the eye's emergence from within the drain is an image of birth. In this dissolve, the eye, like the eye viewed in profile in (5.80), is born into the world. We might say that this eye is born out of the drain by the shower head, its birth sanctified by

Marion's blood.

When the camera spirals out clockwise as though unscrewing itself, it is disclosed that the eye standing in for our gaze is, within the world of the film, Marion's, and that it is dead (5.137). It emerges stillborn from the drain. The camera keeps spiraling out until we have a full view of Marion's face (5.138). Death has frozen it in inexpressiveness, although there is a tear welled in the corner of her eye.

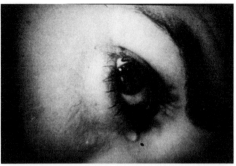

The camera pulls further back, revealing Marion's face to be pressed against the cold white floor. Our view reassumes its mask, once more invoking Norman's gaze (5.139). There follows a cut away to the shower head, viewed from a new, oblique angle (5.140). (Like Diana at the scene of the crime in *Murder!*, the shower head has now been viewed from all points of the compass.) This is the view that would be Marion's were her eye not blinded by death: the shower head, the object of the dead eye's gaze—what this eye is blind to— and the source of our views. But if Marion's gaze is inscribed within our own, it is not that our gaze brings her dead eye to life, but that we too are dead to this world and it dead to us. As if commanded by the shower head, we are returned to our view of Marion in a reprise of (5.139), and the camera begins to move. The movement first reveals Marion's head to be leaning against the toilet bowl; then it altogether excludes Marion from the frame. The screen is momentarily engulfed by whiteness as the door to the bedroom fills the frame, this white flash masking a cut. When the continuing movement causes the door to exit from the frame, the camera is no longer located within the bathroom but has crossed over into the bed-

5.138

5.139

5.140

5.141

5.142

5.143

5.144

room. And the frame is no longer masked. The invocation of Norman's view through the peephole ceases. The camera is on its own.

Autonomously, the camera tracks past the bed, moves in on the night table, and comes to rest on the folded-up newspaper, which still shows its "OKAY" headline (5.141). After a pause, it moves on. It circles the room, skirting the wall, so that the frame momentarily contains nothing but the wallpaper's pattern of branches and leaves (5.142): the view circumscribed by a frame-within-a-frame in (5.86), (5.101), and (5.123) now completely fills the screen. When the camera again comes to rest, it frames a window, within which the old house up the hill in turn is framed (5.143). This echoes Marion's view of the house when she overheard the argument between Norman and his mother. As if cued by the camera's pause, an offscreen voice sounds once again. Norman's voice cries out, "Mother! Oh God! Mother! Blood! Blood!"

Earlier, I spoke of the voices overheard by Marion as also projected from within her, and raised the possibility that the scene overheard may have been staged. But this blood-curdling cry can be uttered by no one within the world of the film whose view we now share. If it is a projection, it can only be from within ourselves. And if this scene is staged, it is a piece of theater whose intended audience only we can be.

Norman leaves the house and runs into the foreground, as a new theme sounds in the strings. He enters the cabin and runs to the bathroom door where he stands frozen, back to the camera (5.144). He turns, holding his mouth as though to stifle a scream or as though

5.145

5.146

5.147

5.148

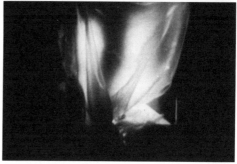

5.149

he might throw up (5.145). A bird picture falls off the wall and lands at his feet. Then he goes to lock the window—this closes yet another bracket—and walks outside to the office to get a pail and mop.

Just before he enters the bathroom, Norman is framed, back to the camera, in the frame-within-a-frame of the doorway (5.146). Then there is a cut to the curtainless shower—the shower head in full view—to all the world a bare and empty stage (5.147). As Marion rose into the frame in (5.90), beginning her shower, Norman rises into this frame and shuts off the water (5.148). He lays the shower curtain beneath Marion's body (momentarily, we view Norman through this curtain in a recreation of our first view of the murderer (5.149), this effect taking its place within the passage's series of echoes and repetitions. And momentarily, Norman turns as if to show the camera his dirty hands (5.150).

Norman goes to the sink to wash the blood from his hands, the sound of water and blood swirling down the drain again heard from up close. He mops the bathtub, towels off the wall, cleans the toilet, goes outside, backs up the car so that the trunk is by the door, and returns to the cabin again. He lifts the body, wrapped in the shower cur-

5.150

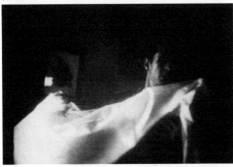

5.151

5.152

5.153

tain, and carries it in his arms over the threshold, a poignant, charged image (5.151). He puts it in the trunk of the car and goes inside yet again. He hangs up the fallen bird picture and packs Marion's things. Then there is a cut to a shot that neither frames Norman nor registers his point of view, but calls attention to something he has missed: the newspaper on the night table (5.152). When he now removes the suitcase and goes back outside, we think he is going to leave the newspaper behind. But he goes inside one last time, at which point (5.152) is reprised, this time from his point of view. Quickly he picks up the newspaper, turns out the bathroom light, goes outside, tosses the newspaper in the trunk with everything else, and closes it. Furtively, he gets in the car and it glides quietly away.

At the edge of a nearby swamp, he gets out and pushes the car into the mud. We hear gurgling sounds as the car begins to sink. There is a cut to Norman, nervously eating something (5.153): he is wishing with all his heart for the car to sink completely out of sight, to be consumed by the blackness of the swamp. The camera cuts back to the car sinking; to Norman, chin on hands, watching with mixed apprehension and satisfaction; to the car almost completely submerged but hesitating in its descent; to Norman, looking around nervously (once again, profile and full face alternate in quick succession). Why isn't the deity that presides over this world obliging? But then a smile crosses Norman's face, and, on a sickening sucking sound, the car sinks without a trace into the depths of this sewer-womb (5.154). From Norman's smiling face, half in light and half in shadow, the camera cuts back to his view. The scene fades out.

An uninitiated viewer would believe that Norman's mother committed the murder; whatever his real feelings about her act, he cleaned up after her like a dutiful son. When he first discovered the dead body, Norman seemed already at least to suspect what he would find, and he seems quite familiar with the steps he has to take to get rid of the evidence: this suggests that Norman all along at least suspected that his mother is a "maniac, a raving thing" and that Marion was in mortal danger. Norman's initial defiance of his mother, coupled with his passivity, allowed Marion to die, as surely as if he had authorized his mother's act himself. Then too we have reason to believe that, knowingly or not, Norman secretly wished for Marion's death. Did his mother then perform "his" murder for him, the murder he lacked the courage to perform himself?

By making us think that Norman will leave the money behind in the room, and then that the car will not be completely swallowed up by the swamp, Hitchcock alerts us to the possibility that Norman will fail to erase all evidence of the crime and will finally be caught and punished. Yet I take it that we wish for him to be spared, to be left alone, even if it means that the mother will be free to kill again. We feel that Norman has suffered enough, and surely Hitchcock does not condemn us for our sympathy. Hitchcock does not condemn us, even for our secret sharing of Norman's wish for Marion's death.

At this juncture, we are completely bewildered. We are at a loss to know how this film could possibly go on, to know how the remaining half of its running time could be filled. Presumably, there will be some sort of investigation, but how could it be of abiding interest to us? It is not that all questions about Marion's murder have been answered, but we believe we know who did it and why, and there is nothing further we wish to know. If there is a compelling mystery in the murderous act at the heart of *Psycho*, it has not yet been revealed to us. Nothing we have viewed makes us wish to be drawn back into this world.

What is next presented to our view is a note being written by Sam, which returns us to the ironic texture of the opening scenes: "Dearest right as always Marion, I'm sitting in this tiny back room which

5.155

5.156

isn't big enough for both of us, and suddenly it *looks* big enough for both of us. So what if we're poor and cramped and miserable, at least we'll be happy. If you haven't come back to your senses and still . . ."

From Sam at his desk in the back room of his hardware store, the camera pulls slowly out in a long tracking movement until the entire space of the store is framed (5.155, 5.156). This declaration of the camera, linked to the camera movement out from the eye, dominates the passage and links it to the murder scene. During the camera's movement, an elderly woman customer complains that they "tell you it's guaranteed to exterminate every insect in the world, but they don't tell you whether it's painless." Killing is an ordinary part of the form of existence we accept as normal.[17] Marion's sister Lila (Vera Miles) arrives in an agitated state, and introduces herself to Sam. "If you two are in this thing together, it's none of my business, but I want *her* to tell me it's none of my business." Then a stranger (Martin Balsam) enters. He introduces himself as Arbogast, a private investigator, and tells Sam about the missing money. Sam angrily insists that he knows nothing, and Lila says that she only wants "to get Marion out of this before she gets into it too deeply."

There follows a montage of Arbogast checking out hotels. Finally he arrives at the Bates Motel. In the ensuing dialogue with Norman, ironies are again embedded, some comprehensible to us ("Do you mind looking at the picture before committing yourself?" "I shouldn't even change the sheets but old habits die hard"), while

5.157

the significance of others remains hidden ("I hate the smell of dampness, don't you? It's such a, I don't know, creepy smell"). Like the earlier exchange in the motel office, this dialogue is filmed in shot/reverse-shot form, with Arbogast's figure doubled in the mirror as Marion's had been (5.157).

When Arbogast shows Marion's photograph to Norman, he is told that no one has stayed at the motel in weeks.

But Norman slips up, letting on that a couple came by last week. As Arbogast looks through the register, Norman is framed in an extraordinary low-angle setup that makes him look disconcertingly like a chicken (5.158). The "Marie Samuels" entry strikes Arbogast's attention, and he shows him the photograph again. Pressed, Norman grows nervous and begins to stutter, but revises his story only slightly. When Arbogast asks

5.158

him about the old woman in the window, Norman's nervousness increases. Perhaps sensing he is onto something, Arbogast tries a different tack, provoking him with the question, "You wouldn't be made a fool of, would you?" Norman almost loses his composure. "I'm not capable of being fooled, not even by a woman. Put it this way: she might have fooled me, but she didn't fool my mother." Then he firmly asks Arbogast to leave and smiles as the detective's car drives off. Arbogast reports to Lila on the phone about the Bates Motel. He doesn't feel entirely satisfied and will go back to speak to the invalid mother. He promises to return to Fairvale within the hour.

The murder of Arbogast is, if anything, even more terrifying than the shower-murder sequence. The passage begins with an extended series of alternations between Arbogast and his views (including a number of Hitchcock's tracking point-of-view shots) as he looks around the motel office and then enters the old house (he removes his hat in deference to the old woman he expects to encounter: Arbogast is a surprisingly courtly man). From his legs approaching the stairs, there is a cut to a high-angle shot that frames his figure against an oriental rug (5.159). This frame-within-a-frame nearly coincides with the borders of the screen, sharpening our awareness of the film frame's delimitation of our vision and in turn the

5.159

limitations of Arbogast's vision. He is not cognizant, for example, that some being might occupy our elevated position. Thus this framing at the same time sustains the camera's identification with Arbogast and invokes a perspective that lies outside the bounds of his awareness, suggesting a trap ready to be sprung.

As Arbogast climbs the stairs, the camera moves up and away, keeping him at a constant distance while the frame-within-a-frame

5.160

5.161

5.162

5.163

contracts, heightening the invocation of a being that fixes him in its gaze. Suddenly, Arbogast starts, and Hitchcock cuts to a door, which opens a crack (5.160). This shot represents what Arbogast is specifically not privileged to see: the cut anticipates the opening of the door by a still unviewed—and presumably murderous—being and attunes us to its presence, driving a wedge between us and Arbogast. When the camera continues moving as Arbogast ascends, we know he is about to be attacked and fear for him; but we also share the exhilaration, the bloodthirsty excitement, of the murderer poised to strike.

At this moment, there is a cut to an extraordinary shot that invokes the perspective of a bird (5.161). Viewed from this perch, Arbogast appears imprisoned, the space of the landing as frighteningly confined as Diana's cell in *Murder!*, Melanie's phone booth in *The Birds*, Blaney's prison cell in *Frenzy*. But this space also resonates with the empty theater in *Stage Fright*, emblematic of Jonathan's interiority. The space in which Arbogast is trapped comes alive, in effect, as an inner space.

The overhead shot sets us up for the sudden entrance of the murderer. Its static framing does not allow us to anticipate the precise instant of the attack. It is a startling shock when the violins again emit their blood-curdling shriek and a knife-wielding figure enters through the open door (5.162). This time, the murderer appears uninterested in theater or instruction: killing alone appears to be on the murderer's mind. There follows a cut to Arbogast, his face already flecked with blood (5.163). His eyes widen and he opens his mouth to cry out. As he falls backward, arms flailing wildly, the floor quickly rises up toward the camera, which keeps a constant distance from him (5.164). The vertiginous effect of this shot expresses Arbogast's frightful sensation of falling, his realization that he is dying, and his terror at the vision of the murderer, which is withheld from us. Part of the shrewdness of the prior cut to the overhead setup is that it allows us to witness the attack without obtaining a clear view of the murderer and yet also without getting the impression that such a view is being withheld deliberately.

5.164

Arbogast falls onto the rug, and what appears to be a woman leaps on him (5.165). A knife slashes down through the frame, and the image quickly fades out. *Psycho*'s central mystery has been revealed. We will not be satisfied until we see for ourselves the vision glimpsed by the dying Arbogast.

5.165

Hitchcock now gives us a series of brief scenes to prepare for his finale.

Sam and Lila express concern that Arbogast has not returned. Sam goes to check out the Bates Motel for himself.

From Lila, backlit and facing the camera (5.166), there is a dissolve to Norman in extreme long shot, contemplating the swamp. (This is the first suggestion of a magical connection between Norman and Lila.) Offscreen, Sam's voice shouts Arbogast's name, and the camera moves in on Norman as he turns (5.167). Then we go from Norman, looking into the camera, to Lila in the store (5.168). (This dissolve resonates with the cut from Norman in the kitchen, looking into the camera, to Marion at the table before she takes her shower.) Lila and Marion are connected in Norman's eyes. And when she steps toward the camera so that she becomes framed

5.166

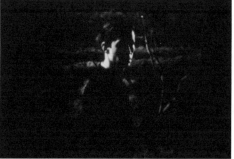

5.167

5.168

5.169

in silhouette (5.169), Lila's link with another figure as well is suggested: (5.169) clearly echoes Marion's view when the murderer pulls open the shower curtain. Through Lila's mediation, we are destined to penetrate Norman's private world. Lila is to play a role in Norman's life related to the role played by the murderer in Marion's life. Although Lila is barely sketched as a character, her role in *Psycho* is of the greatest importance. Otherwise, would Hitchcock have entrusted this part to Vera Miles, *The Wrong Man*'s Rose and Hitchcock's original choice to play Judy/Madeleine in *Vertigo*? It deepens our appreciation of *Psycho* to think of Lila as another incarnation of those figures.

Sam joins Lila, and they resolve to visit Deputy Sheriff Al Chambers.

The ensuing scene at Sheriff Chambers' home provides some comic relief and serves the purposes of exposition. Prodded by Sam and Lila, Chambers calls Norman on the phone and is told that Arbogast came and left. When Lila, disbelieving, asks about the mother, the sheriff drops a bombshell: "Norman Bates's mother has been dead and buried in Greenlawn Cemetery the past ten years. Mrs. Bates poisoned the guy she was . . . involved with . . . when she found out he was married, then took a helping of the same stuff herself. Strychnine. Ugly way to die." The wife adds, confidentially, "Norman found them dead together. *In bed.*" Then who was the old woman Sam saw in the window? And who is buried in Greenlawn Cemetery? (This latter question, posed by the skeptical Sheriff Chambers, is a textbook case of a red herring.)

5.170

We next see Norman going from the office to the house, then up the stairs (5.170). He leaves the frame, and we hear his voice offscreen: "Now, mother, I'm going to . . ." Then the mother's voice: "I am sorry, boy, but you do manage to look ludicrous when you give me orders." Now the camera begins to rise on its own. "Please, mother . . ." "No! I'll not hide in the fruit cellar." "He came after the girl and now someone

will come after him. Mother, please. It's just for a few days." "In
that dark, damp fruit cellar? No!"

The camera has been moving up and circling all this time, so that
we now view the landing from above. It holds this framing, which
exactly reprises (5.161), the framing of the attack on Arbogast.
"Norman, what do you think you're doing? Don't touch me! Don't!
Norman!" Viewed from high above, Norman comes out the door,
his mother slung over his shoulder. "Put me down!" The scene
fades out over the sound of churchbells, which invokes Mrs. Bates's
supposed death, hence the mystery of her continuing life, and provides a lead into the next passage.

Over the sound of bells, there is a fade-in on the front of a church.
Services are letting out. Al Chambers tells Sam that he went out to
the motel earlier in the morning. "I know you're not the seeing-illu-
sions type, but no woman was there and I don't believe in ghosts."
Mrs. Chambers invites them for dinner later. After the Chambers
leave, Sam reluctantly agrees to Lila's suggestion that they go to the
motel. There is a dissolve to Sam and Lila in a car. They will pre-
tend to be husband and wife, register, then nose around.

Norman looks out from a window of the old house. There is a cut
to his view of the motel, then to Lila in front of the motel office, her
back to us. Norman's gaze hovers over this frame; throughout the
next sequence, Norman and Lila are mysteriously coupled, and our
sympathies are divided between them. We have encountered framings like this before: her back to the camera, Lila at the same time
possesses the frame and is the object of the camera's gaze. Again
and again in this sequence, Lila is turned away from the camera in
this way.

Norman joins Lila and Sam, and they
go into the office, where Sam's and
Lila's reflections are framed in the mirror that reflected Arbogast in (5.157) and
Marion in (5.30). This setup is alternated with (5.171), which again frames
Lila, back to the camera. Sam and Lila go
to their room, then sneak out to examine
Marion's cabin. Lila announces her
plan: Sam will keep Norman occupied
in the office as she goes to the house to

5.171

speak to the old woman. Sam is worried that Norman can't be held
if he doesn't want to be, but Lila's unwittingly ironic assurance ("I
can handle a sick old woman") persuades him to go along. The
body of this climactic passage—it takes the form of a parallel-
edited suspense sequence, with Hitchcock cutting back and forth

between the men in the motel office and Lila on her own—now begins.

Hitchcock films Lila's approach to the old house by employing his technique of the traveling point-of-view shot, cutting back and forth between Lila and her views, the first cutaway to the motel office occurring when she enters the house. In the office, Sam leans forward on the counter, eclipsing his own mirror image. He grills Norman mercilessly, asking deliberately embarrassing questions. We feel for Norman and are appalled by Sam's brutal insensitivity. (For one thing, we have little sense that Sam is really acting out of concern for Marion. His cruelty seems primarily a matter of self-gratification, like Cary Grant's cruelty toward Claude Rains at the end of *Notorious*.) Sam says, "You're alone here, aren't you? Drive me crazy." Norman replies, "I think that would be rather an extreme reaction, don't you?" When Sam answers, "Just an expression," the camera cuts to Lila on the stairs. The discoveries Lila is about to make by her penetration of the privacy of Norman's home indeed bear on the theme of aloneness, on the psychic cost of solitude, on the attendant threat of madness.

5.172

5.173

Standing once more with her back to the camera, Lila knocks on Mrs. Bates's door. Receiving no response, she pushes the door open, and the camera cuts to her view of the bedroom (5.172). Then it alternates between Lila and her views, first of an old-fashioned sink then of a fireplace and empty chair. At this point, (5.172) is reprised, but with Lila, back to the camera, now within the frame that had represented her own field of vision (5.173). We have already encountered this device: the suggestion is that Lila has crossed a barrier, as if she has stepped into her own dream. Her back still to the camera, she looks at the old-fashioned dresses hanging in a wardrobe, then at the mother's vanity. She walks toward it, and there is a closer view. A hairbrush—in *The Wrong Man*, Rose attacks Manny with just such a brush—rests on the vanity beside a jewelry box bedecked with a pair of crossed hands cast in bronze (5.174). The camera tracks in quickly, registering these hands' solicitation of Lila's gaze (5.175).

In effect, these hands momentarily come alive, as if Mrs. Bates

were present in this room and these
were her living hands. We feel closer to
Norman's mother than at any other moment in the film. In this hallucinatory
vision, the woman elsewhere invoked as
a monster momentarily appears before
us as human, capable of tenderness and
love, a woman whose illness is a heartbreaking human tragedy. And Lila too,
we take it, is touched. It is as if the tenderness incarnated in these hands
brings Lila back to her own solitude—
there is no indication that Lila even
thinks of marrying. If these hands momentarily bring Mrs. Bates to life, they
also bring home to Lila—and to us—
her deep bond with Marion, almost as if
they appeared to be the hands of her
own mother—that is, the mother of Lila
and Marion. In this vision, the loss of
Marion is inscribed. Now Lila knows in
her heart that Marion is dead, and
mourning may begin.

5.174

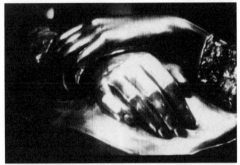

5.175

There is a cut to Lila, back to the camera, looking down as if in meditation
(5.176). Presumably, she is absorbed in
contemplation of the mystery incarnated in these hands: the mystery of the
solitude into which human beings are
born and from which they never escape,
the mystery of love, the mystery of the
continuity of generations. She is oblivious of her own reflection framed in the

5.176

mirror. This reflection is itself doubled: within the mirror, a second
mirror is reflected, and in this mirror there is a second reflection of
Lila. The "real" Lila and her first reflection are face to face, although their lowered gazes do not meet. But the second reflection
is turned away: turned away from the first reflection, from Lila in
the flesh, and from the camera. This makes Lila's second reflection
the perfect double of the real Lila.

At one level, (5.176) registers Lila's trancelike dissociation: as
she contemplates the hands, she is absorbed within herself even as
she stands outside herself. It also registers our separation from Lila,
whose private meditation we cannot penetrate. She is once again
object of our gaze, but, at the same time, this framing identifies us

with her: viewing Lila, it is as if the screen were a mirror and we were viewing ourselves. Indeed, (5.176) creates the specific impression that we are standing behind Lila, viewing her and also viewing, over her shoulder, the mirror reflection she does not see. That is, the first reflection represents Lila and the second reflection represents us.

Suddenly, Lila starts, gasping audibly. She turns—the real Lila and Lila's second reflection turn to face the camera, even as the second reflection turns away (5.177). Then there is a quick cut to the view that just startled her out of her absorption (5.178). Lila sees her own reflection in the mirror. But the apparition that startled her also cannot be separated from Mrs. Bates: Lila's reflection is framed within the mother's mirror, which in the past framed Mrs. Bates's reflection; standing before this mirror and looking into it, Lila occupies the mother's place. In Lila's vision and in her reflection, Mrs. Bates momentarily comes to life, as in Lila's view of the hands. But has Lila taken possession of Mrs. Bates, or has Mrs. Bates taken possession of Lila? We do not know who the being framed in the mirror really is. Nor can we say whether, in this vision, our gaze really represents Lila's or Mrs. Bates's gaze.

5.177

5.178

Furthermore, it is not simply that this is a view of Lila's reflection in the mirror. For the frame is equally divided between the mirror and the large shaded lamp contiguous to it. Indeed, in this frame the lamp and the mirror appear as aspects of a single thing, what I have called a composite. In the transition from (5.177) to (5.178), the lamp displaces the figure of Lila in the frame. The lamp is a surrogate of Lila, of Mrs. Bates, and also of ourselves. It is as if this lamp were looking into the mirror, viewing its own reflection. But of course this lamp may be looking not into the mirror, but out at whoever claims this view. Lila, framed in the mirror, appears as well to be looking out of the camera from within her frame-within-a-frame, yet she is only a reflection, possessed of no real gaze. But if this lamp's gaze is real, what vision does it possess?

Then, too, if we can see this lamp as looking (whether gazing into the mirror or outward from the frame), we can also see it as projecting the figure of Lila onto the frame-within-a-frame. And we can see the lamp not as looking out at Lila or out at us, but as presenting itself—and this vision of itself—to Lila and to us. That is, we can see this lamp not as a viewer like Lila or like ourselves, but as another incarnation of the source of our views and Lila's, another incarnation of the sovereign agency represented by the shower head.[18]

At this moment, Hitchcock cuts to a side view of Lila, who is relieved that what startled her was only a reflection of herself (5.179). Yet her awakening signals another disquieting apparition. Lila turns to face the camera, which cuts to her view: the mother's bed, a depression —the trace of a body—running down the middle (5.180). What Lila sees, the mark of a single body in a bed made for two, is a poetic image of solitude and absence, of sexuality denied. The camera reframes with Lila as she goes to the bed and feels the depression. When she looks up, there is an abrupt cut back to Sam and Norman (5.181).

5.179

Sam says he doubts that Norman can really be happy alone in "this place." Norman answers, "This place? This place happens to be my only world. I grew up in that house up there. I had a very happy childhood. My mother and I were more than happy." Norman's defense moves us partly because we do not believe that he and his mother were ever happy, not to mention more than happy. Despite everything (for example, despite the fact that Hitchcock can seem to be playing Lila's penetration of Norman's "only world" mostly for chills), the poignancy of Norman's clinging to his wishful fantasy of a happy childhood affects us. And again

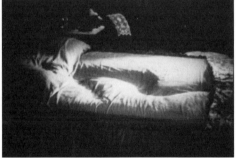

5.180

5.181

we sense that Lila too is attuned, as Sam is not, to this poignancy. What follows illustrates the theme of "this place" as Norman's only world and serves as a comment on the tragedy of human loneliness and on the camera's power to expose, but its powerlessness to overcome, the condition of isolation that is its obsessive fascination.

5.182

5.183

5.184

5.185

When the camera cuts back to Lila, she is opening the door to Norman's bedroom. She sees that the room is empty but enters anyway (5.182). Her penetration of Norman's world has taken on a life of its own. She has become fascinated by Norman's isolation and by this closed-off world into which no stranger has ever entered. From Lila, Hitchcock cuts to her view of a doll, a toy schoolhouse, and a model car, all jumbled in a heap (5.183). We are shocked to see Norman's room: it is a child's room that could be a girl's or a boy's. Then there is a cut from Lila to a stuffed rabbit, which meets her gaze with a slight frown, as if this forlorn creature were slightly ashamed to be seen in a grown man's room (5.184). Just as Lila's glimpse of herself in the mirror signaled her first view of the mother's bed, the stuffed rabbit's embarrassed gaze leads Lila to look at Norman's bed. There follows a slightly different view of the rabbit which places it clearly on a little boy's single bunk (5.185). This shot, I take it, decisively declares Norman's virginity.

Lila next walks toward a phonograph, and we get her view of the record on the turntable (5.186). It is strangely moving that the man/boy to whom this place is the whole world should listen to the Eroica Symphony.[19] We imagine Beethoven's music as animating Norman's fantasy of possessing the world from within the isolation of this place. The next shot sustains this suggestion. Lila picks up a book from Norman's bureau, a globe conspicuously placed in the frame (5.187). This globe links Norman to the Professor in *The Thirty-Nine Steps*. For all Norman's apparent innocence, he dreams the Professor's dream. Lila opens the book and looks inside.

What might this book be? But Hitchcock cuts—maddeningly—to Sam and Norman, withholding from us the view that consummates Lila's penetration of Norman's privacy.

Sam says, "I've been talking about your mother and this motel." Suddenly, Norman is struck by Lila's absence. It dawns on him that he has stepped into a trap. A cut away to Lila, descending the stairs; then back again to Sam and Norman locked in a violent struggle. Norman eclipses Sam in the frame (5.188), knocks him out, and runs toward the house. Through a curtained window, Lila sees him approaching. The moment Hitchcock cuts to the next shot—the downstairs of the house, Lila small in the background—we know there is a region that must beckon her (5.189). As when Melanie tiptoes upstairs in the middle of the night in *The Birds*, we feel like shouting out, warning Lila not to hide in the stairwell appearing in the left foreground of the frame. Of course, in a way we also want her to go there, then to go down into the fruit cellar where Norman's "sick old mother" is hidden.

As we knew she would be, Lila is drawn to these stairs. When Norman first goes upstairs and disappears from view, the camera cuts to her, as it were "behind bars," the framing dominated by the //// (5.190). Perhaps she could escape if she now made a break for the front door. But as soon as we are given her view of the arched doorway to the cellar, we know that Lila will descend the steps to complete her search, at whatever risk (5.191). And the moment she views this door, she knows that Mrs. Bates is in the cellar at the bottom of the stairs. It is as if Norman's mother calls upon her to descend. But it

5.186

5.187

5.188

5.189

5.190

5.191

5.192

5.193

5.194

is also as if the entrance to the fruit cellar were conjured by Lila's imagination.

Lila peers in through the cellar door and sees another door, which leads to an inner chamber. This one opens with a creak, and something catches her eye. Hitchcock cuts to what compels Lila's gaze, a woman in a chair, back to the camera—hence Lila's double in the frame—lit by a bare bulb hanging from the ceiling (5.192). "Mrs. Bates" and this light form yet another composite, one clearly linked to the lamp/mirror in (5.178) and the light bulb/knife in Marion's vision of the murderer in (5.101).

In the reverse back to Lila, the light is at the upper left, bridging these two frames and making them symmetrical (5.193). She has finally come to the end of her search. She steps forward and says hesitantly, "Mrs. Bates . . ." The camera cuts to the woman, framed in medium shot with her back still to the camera, the spiraled bun of her drawn-back hair in the exact center of the frame. From the left, Lila's hand enters, touches the woman's shoulder, then quickly withdraws (5.194). The woman begins to turn around and there is a cut to a closer view (5.195). She completes her turn and her face does a little jiggle, as if to say, "Well, here I am! Your search is over!" (5.196). We are shocked to see a mummy's face; its withered flesh barely covers the bones, and its jaws are locked in a death's head grin.

In the face of this ghoulish apparition, Lila screams and draws her hand violently back, accidently knocking the bulb (5.197). Then there is a cut to the swinging light (5.198). For the remainder of the sequence, the swinging will continue, alternately darkening the frame and lighting it with harsh glare. In the shower-murder sequence, the camera moved in to identify the shower curtain with the movie screen. Now the flickering caused by the swinging bulb makes the inner chamber of the fruit cellar into a movie theater—a stand-in for the room in which, even now, *Psycho* is being screened.

The woman who was going to answer all questions is quite dead. Yet Lila's terror reveals that she is gripped by the illusion that the withered mummy is alive and indeed possesses a power against which, unaided, she cannot hope to prevail. In Lila's nightmarish vision—is it also real?—it is the figure of death who has turned to meet her gaze, in a dramatic gesture kin to the Professor's when he raises his hand into Hannay's view and thereby unmasks himself. Here "Mrs. Bates" unveils herself to Lila. Or is it that death, having claimed both Mrs. Bates and Marion, now steps forward to claim Lila too? Lila thought she penetrated "this place" unobserved, but death was lying in wait for her, knowing she would step into the trap.

There is a cut from the swinging globe to Lila, who is turned away. Momentarily her terror subsides, and she turns again to the mummified face. We can see, in Lila's turning back to look, a return to reason, a breaking of the spell, a realization that this corpse's power is only illusory. But we can also take Lila's

5.195

5.196

5.197

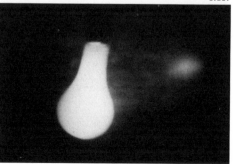

5.198

5.199

5.200

5.201

turning to reveal the depth of her fascination, as though she acknowledges the sovereign gaze of the death's head and subjects herself to its will. This turning suggests the fantastic possibility that an encounter will now take place between the living and the dead. But the moment the light from the swinging bulb falls flush on Lila's open-mouthed face, her eyes fix on another sight (5.199). Hitchcock cuts to the open doorway leading to the outer cellar (5.200). As if cued by the camera or even conjured by it, Norman, dressed as a woman, wearing a woman's wig, makes an entrance, accompanied by shrieking violins (5.201). Or is this figure, brandishing a knife, eyes filled with murder, really not Norman acting the part of his mother but the mother herself, possessed of her son's body? This is the vision that sent Arbogast reeling. But while Arbogast was attacked immediately—his reaction was of no interest to his murderer—Norman/mother pauses dramatically at a distance from Lila and holds a menacing pose. Lila, who undertook to penetrate the most private recesses of this place, has been singled out as audience for this theatrical gesture. If this is to be a scene of murder, it is no ordinary killing. Like Handell Fane when he enters Sir John's view at the circus, and like Charles when he reveals his true face to Charlie on the train, the being standing unmasked before Lila demands acknowledgment. But there is an irreducible ambiguity to the moment. If this is not Norman but the dead mother, who has taken possession of her son, the gesture is Mrs. Bates's demonstration of her power. Then Norman is merely a creature of the mummy, an actor in a piece of theater he has not authored, and which mocks him as it mocks Lila. On the other hand, if this is really Norman acting a role, then he is calling upon Lila to acknowledge that it is he who wields the power of life and death. His gesture, which mocks Lila for believing the dead can live, also mocks his mother, who has no more hold on him.

Hitchcock cuts back to Lila, the swinging bulb making her face flash black and white like Marion's face when she was transfixed by her private film. Then we return to Lila's vision. In a frame that sustains the alternation of shadow and glare, Norman steps forward and Sam suddenly comes through the open door and lunges to take the knife away. The anguish on Norman's face registers, I take it,

5.202

not only the physical exertion and pain of his struggle with Sam, but also a conflict within himself. The wig is almost completely pulled from his head (5.202): before our eyes, Norman/mother undergoes metamorphosis, moults, painfully sheds a skin. But also this is yet another of the film's images of birth: Norman emerges from this wig as from a shell or cocoon or womb. We cannot say whether Norman struggles to keep from being stripped of his costume or to be freed from it. Norman's inner struggle, we might say, is between a part of himself that wishes to be born and a part of himself that wishes to avoid the trauma of birth. Or we might say that we are witnessing a struggle between Norman and the spirit that possesses him.

5.203

The camera cuts away again to Lila, uncomprehending yet spellbound, then to a longer view of the struggle (5.203). Finally, Norman's wig drops to the floor, his whole costume begins to fall away, and Sam decisively gains the upper hand. My impression, however, is that Norman is not vanquished but overcome when he loses the will to continue his struggle. Like the lodger at bay, Norman breaks down.

The next shot is the penultimate one of the sequence: the wig on the floor, flashing white and black (5.204), filling the frame like the drain and eye in

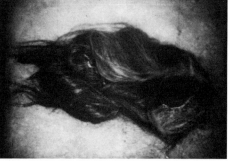

5.204

(5.135). At one level, this shot sums up the mystery of the film, the mystery of Norman/mother. Norman's fetish, nakedly exposed, inscribes a vision of the mother's womanhood that is also a vision of a terrifying threat to Norman's manhood. This shot identifies what inevitably separates Norman from his mother; the wig on the floor proclaims Norman's failure to become his mother or to bring her back to life. Or has Norman after all succeeded in overcoming the separation between this woman and himself? Has he assumed command of death in *Psycho*'s world and succeeded in effecting his own rebirth? Perhaps the wig on the floor proclaims Norman's triumph.

The hypnotic flashing underscores this symbolically charged shot, making its presentation more emphatic. And the flashing, which invokes cinema, is itself symbolically charged. It suggests that the wig-fetish possesses black and white, "bad" and "good," dead and living, destructive and creative aspects, that it represents an irreducible duality. Or is it that this flashing only casts a spell in which what is lifeless appears to come alive, in which an illusion of magic is conjured? The following shot, the final one of the sequence, is a reprise of (5.196)—the grinning death's head—but with the frame flashing black and white and divorced from Lila's point of view. This shot suggests that our view of the wig was from the mummy's perspective. In retrospect, our view of the swinging bulb is likewise disclosed as representing the gaze emanating from these empty eye sockets. "Mrs. Bates," like Marion, like Lila, like us, is a viewer, held spellbound as if by a film. Indeed, (5.198) and (5.204), Mrs. Bates's views, are the very views that hold us in thrall. The mummy's private film and the film that casts its spell over us cannot be separated. This withered corpse is one of Hitchcock's definitive representations of his films' viewers. We are this mother who commands death in the world of *Psycho* and who is possessed by death.

The flickering caused by the swinging lamp alternately fills the eye sockets with light and engulfs them in darkness, creating a dizzying effect. Then is our vertigo in the face of this vision also Mrs. Bates's as she watches her private film? But this dead face also bears a grin. If this death's head represents us, it also represents a being who rules sovereign over this world and to whom the world's fate is no more than a joke. The dead mother is the author of the script that climaxes in Lila's fascination, Norman's theatrical entrance, Sam's intervention, Norman's breakdown, the mummy's grin.

Within the world of the film, the vision of the death's head represents no one's point of view. It is ours and ours alone. Then who or what presents this vision to us? Specifically, does the mummy present itself to the camera, commanding its gaze? Or does the camera frame this death's head without its knowledge or authorization? Do we have the laugh, or are we the butt of the mummy's private joke? *Psycho* gives us no unambiguous answers to these questions about the death's head's relationship to the camera, which are also questions about the dead mother's relationship, and Norman's relationship, to Hitchcock and to us. Is this also Hitchcock's grin, and is it addressed to us?

If this figure framed by the camera presents itself to us as the figure of death, its grin must be announcing that we are about to die. But this grinning death's head—an old chestnut if ever there was one—represents no real threat to us.

The only imaginable fulfillment of this grin's threat would be if the film's author, murder in his eyes, were now to step forward within the space of the theater in which we sit spellbound, were now to cross the barrier between *Psycho*'s world and our own. But the limits of film have been reached. Like a nightmare that has exhausted the dreamer's ability to hold death at bay, the scene can go no further. What follows both is and is not its real continuation. Nothing disavows the finality of this vision of death. And it is not only that *Psycho* declares this vision to be one its ending must not

and cannot disavow; *Psycho* declares that the vision penetrates to the heart of every film that authentically taps the source of film's power. The scene dissolves to the front of the county courthouse, the presence of a television news truck testifying to the publicity that now attends the Bates case (5.205). Of all Hitchcock's meaningful dissolves, this may be the most profound. What Hitchcock superimposes over the death's head, summing up the ambiguous status

5.205

of its murderous gaze, is the //// that is his most cryptic, private symbol for the screen, the barrier that cannot be crossed yet is no real barrier at all.

There is a cut to the office of the chief of police. Lila, Sam, Sheriff Chambers, the district attorney, the police chief, and several other functionaries are in attendance. On Chambers' "If anyone gets any answers, it'll be the psychiatrist," the notable in question enters. He begins to relate what he calls the whole story, which he says he got not from Norman but from Norman's mother.

Now to understand it the way I understood it, hearing it from the mother—that is, from the mother half of Norman's mind—you'd have to go back ten years, to the time Norman murdered his mother and her lover. Now he was already dangerously disturbed, had been ever since his father died. His mother was a clinging, demanding woman, and for years the two of them lived as though there were no one else in the world. Then she met a man, and it seemed to Norman that she threw him over for this man. That pushed him over the line and he killed them both. Matricide is the most unbearable crime of all. Most unbearable to the son who commits it. So he had to erase the crime, at least in his own mind. He stole her corpse. A weighted coffin was buried. He hid the body in the fruit cellar, even treated it so it would keep as well as it would keep. And that still wasn't enough. She was there, but she was a corpse. So he began to think and speak for her, give her half his life so to speak. At times he could be both personalities, carrying on conversations. At other times, the mother half took over completely. He was never all Norman, but he was often only mother. And because he was so pathologically jealous of her, he assumed that she was as jealous of him. Therefore, if he felt a strong attraction to any other woman, the mother side of him would go wild. When he met your sister, he was touched by her, aroused by her. He wanted her. That set off the jealous mother, and *mother* killed the girl. After the murder, Norman covered up all traces of the crime he was convinced his mother had committed. He was simply doing every-thing he could to keep alive the illusion of his mother's being alive. And when reality came too close, when danger or desire threatened that illusion, he dressed up, even to a cheap wig he'd bought. He'd walk around the house, sit in her chair, speak in her voice. He tried to *be* his mother. And, uh, now . . . he *is*. Now that's what I meant when I said I got the story from the mother. You see, when the mind houses two personalities, there's always a conflict. A battle. In Norman's case, the battle is over, and the dominant personality has won. These were crimes of passion, not profit.

This psychiatrist seizes the limelight and plays his act to the hilt. He is an unattractive character, smug and self-satisfied, who ap-pears completely unmoved by the fates of Marion and Norman. Just as we doubt Graham's word when he assures Charlie that he knows, we doubt that the psychiatrist really has the whole story. Indeed, his account cannot be the whole story, any more than "The Inner History of the Baring Case" can be the whole story of the events at the heart of *Murder!*. For it does not acknowledge the camera's presence and agency, to which the film's final images will decisively return us. The psychiatrist's performance sets up *Psy-cho*'s devastating ending, which poses the mystery of the real iden-tity and nature of "Norman Bates," the mystery that the psychiatrist claims to explain away.

The psychiatrist's account must awaken skepticism. He claims authority because he received his story firsthand from "the mother half of Norman." But not having been witnesses to their encounter, we do not know what in the psychiatrist's account comes directly from "mother" and what derives from interpretations by a man whose authority we have neither inclination nor reason to credit. Hence we may entertain doubts about all parts of his story without calling "mother's" own testimony into question. But then too, not having witnessed the encounter, we have only the psychiatrist's own assurance that Mrs. Bates's testimony was sincere. We have no reason to believe that the psychiatrist is "not capable of being made a fool of, not even by a woman." Maybe this woman sold him a bill of goods. But, perhaps more important, we cannot simply take for granted that the psychiatrist is right even about the identity of the being whose testimony he received.

The psychiatrist believes he got the story not from Norman himself (Norman no longer exists, he believes), not from Norman's real mother (who is dead), but from "the mother half of Norman's mind." That is, from a being projected by Norman's imagination in the image of his mother (that is, as he imagines his mother to be, which is compounded of what he wishes her to be and what he dreads she might be), a being Norman takes—and that takes itself —really to be Norman's mother. But in two ways the psychiatrist might be wrong about the source of his testimony. Norman could be possessed from beyond the grave by his real mother. (The psychiatrist assumes that the dead cannot really possess the living, and we do not believe that there are such things as ghosts. But within the world of a film, the opposition between the natural and the supernatural breaks down. For the *camera* represents a supernatural agency to the denizens of the film's world, to whom we and Hitchcock alike are ghosts. And all the camera's subjects, fixed and projected onto the screen, are suspended between death and life.) Also, Norman could be only acting, captive to no illusion, fully aware that "mother" is only a role. The psychiatrist is confident that he can recognize acting when he sees it. But still he might have been taken in by a performance, as were Marion, Arbogast, Sheriff Chambers, Sam, and Lila before him. Perhaps we too have been taken in by Norman and may be about to be deceived one last time.

We are not called upon to accept the psychiatrist's authority. Yet his account does contain revelations with which we must come to terms. The blockbuster among them, of course, is that Norman murdered his mother in a jealous rage and then desperately attempted to deny to himself the reality of his monstrous crime. We cannot simply assume that this "revelation" is true. The sheriff's original story—that Norman's mother killed her lover when she found out he was married, then poisoned herself, with Norman discovering both bodies in bed—cannot summarily be dismissed. For all we know, Norman was unable to accept his mother's guilt and denied her capacity for murder by taking this guilt upon himself. But whether or not Norman poisoned his mother, the real authorship of the scene of her death and the real nature of that scene are issues that remain studded with ambiguities and paradoxes undreamed of by the psychiatrist's philosophy.

For example, *Shadow of a Doubt* and *Strangers on a Train* suggest an alternative picture of the killing. Norman may already have been possessed by "mother." Killing his mother, Norman may have taken himself to be—and may have been—performing his mother's own killing for her; he may have acted as the instrument of her will (as, in *Strangers on a Train*, Bruno acts as Guy's agent). In the face of her husband's death and her lover's treachery, Norman's mother must have felt condemned to unfulfilled longing for satisfaction and love. Then perhaps she called upon Norman—or did he only imagine this?—to grant her the gift of death, to release her from her curse. Or is it that the killing was meant to fulfull her wish to be reborn, to be granted a new life freed from her curse? Was her killing then conceived not as murder but as creation? Was this act intended to bring mother back to life, released from her womanhood, and to allow Norman also to be reborn, freed from the terrifying task of achieving man-hood?

The psychiatrist sees the emergence of the "mother half" as threatening the obliteration, the annihilation, of Norman's self. But perhaps his creation of "mother," which is also the creation of him-self, represents Norman's triumph. The authorship by which he undoes his mother's curse could be "mother's" triumph as well; it could also be his triumph over her, his attainment of vengeance. And if Norman avenges himself on his mother, it may have been for her unforgivable act of "throwing him over" for another man. Or it may have been for possessing desire at all, and thereby betraying the order to which Norman remains dedicated. The psychiatrist as-sumes that Norman wished to possess his mother sexually and killed her in a jealous rage. But Norman's act may also have been an expression of disdain for a woman who disgusted him, who failed to acknowledge his vision, and who could not overcome her sexual-ity. Perhaps in killing his mother, and in allowing "mother" to be reborn within himself, Norman mocks her sexual nature as well as his own.

In the psychiatrist's account, "mother" kills Marion in a fit of jealous rage. This suggests that she remains a creature of desire after all, that she has not fundamentally changed. And indeed we have witnessed scenes in which "mother" goads Norman to the verge of repeating the original act of matricide. Yet what if Norman, not "mother," killed Marion? The psychiatrist asserts that Marion aroused Norman's desire, and we ourselves saw her dismiss him as a potential lover. Then did he kill her in a rage when she aroused his desire and then refused to satisfy it? But we also saw Norman's disdain for Marion. Perhaps Norman killed her as an expression of his disgust for a woman who is, like his mother, only a creature of her appetite. In any case, this line of thought upholds the sugges-tion that if Marion was killed by Norman, she died in "mother's" place, that her killing represents a repetition of the original matricide. Norman's killing of his mother gave rise to a series of killings that threatened to go on forever but now appears to have come to an end.

In a sense, Norman found himself called upon to repeat the killing of his mother again and again. It could be argued that this act had to be repeated because the order of creation to which it was dedicated is an unnatural one, the act representing a necessarily futile attempt to deny a nature that, in the form of uncontrollable desire and revulsion, continually reasserted itself. Every time Norman's appetite awakened, it had to be denied anew. But it could also be argued that Norman repeated the original killing not because it denied his appetite, but because he hungers for these murders that are also acts of creation. Norman has tasted blood, and his hobby of stuffing things is what he lives for, what alone gives him pleasure, fulfills him. His stuffed birds are his trophies, his creations, the natural expression of his form of life, his art. "Mother" was, perhaps, the first and until now the most ambitious of his works, but he has just completed his masterpiece, a work that closes out his authorship. He has created himself. The bird he has stuffed this time is the phoenix.

In *Rope*, the John Dall character—collaborating with Farley Granger, who does his bidding—kills a young man in an act he conceives in purely aesthetic terms. He keeps the body in a trunk until he can properly dispose of it. But the creator is not satisfied that his work of art is complete and conceives of a perfect finish to his masterpiece: he invites his friends, including the boy's own father, to a dinner party and serves dinner from the top of the trunk. This is the artist's signature, the cream of the jest (as a line in *Notorious* would have it). Yet still he is not satisfied. His work remains unrecognized and unappreciated. He invites his old professor (James Stewart), whose theories about the prerogatives of superior men originally inspired him. The professor's arrival at the party sets in motion a chain of events that leads inevitably to the realization of what his student has done and his climactic gesture of opening the trunk.

Marion Crane is totally unable to appreciate Norman's creations. His disdain for her, at one level, is that of an artist for a contemptible critic. Nor is the psychiatrist, for all the pride he takes in his powers of analysis, fit to criticize Norman's work. In my view, he falls for Norman's deception and fails to recognize Norman's triumph. When Dall completes his masterwork, he knows that there is someone in his world capable of acknowledging his creation. But there is no James Stewart character in the world of *Psycho*, no one capable of understanding who Norman is or appreciating what he has achieved. As I have suggested, the scene with the psychiatrist sets up *Psycho*'s ending, which completes its brilliant design. We are called upon to recognize (if we can) and acknowledge (if we dare) the nature of Norman's—and Hitchcock's—creation. But to do so, we have to open the trunk for ourselves.

As the psychiatrist takes out a cigarette, his performance over, a policeman comes in from the hall. "He feels a little chill. Can I

5.206

5.207

5.208

bring him this blanket?" The camera cuts to the hallway, where the policeman with the blanket, accompanied by a second policeman, walks down the corridor, the camera following. The first policeman enters a room at the end of the hall, passing out of our view. The second leaves the scene when his companion reemerges and closes the door behind him. First directing a disgusted look to the camera (5.206), he looks into the room through the window on the door. Then there is a cut to what we take to be his view: Norman wrapped in the blanket, sitting in a chair against a blank wall (5.207). The bottom of this frame is masked to suggest the borders of the window through which the policeman is viewing, the mask also linking this view to Norman's view through the peephole and to the panning movement from Marion's dead body to the drain. This represents the barrier between the space inside, where Norman/"mother" sits, and the space outside, where the policeman watches.

The camera begins to track in (5.208), implying that our view is not literally the guard's, although the mask is retained. His viewing in only a pretext for this declaration of the camera, this invocation of the barrier between the world of the film and the "real" world in which *Psycho* enthralls us. As the camera moves in slowly until it frames Norman in medium closeup (looking miserable, but with no particular expression focused on his/her face), we hear a woman's voice offscreen.

It's sad when a mother has to speak the words that condemn her own son. I couldn't allow them to believe I would commit murder. They'll put him away now as I should have years ago. He was always bad and in the end he intended to tell them *I* killed those girls and that man. As if I could do anything except just stare like one of his stuffed birds. Oh, they know I can't even move a finger and I won't. I'll just sit here and be quiet just in case they *do* suspect me. They're probably watching me. Well, let them. Let them see what kind of a person I am.

If we take the being framed by the camera at this moment to be "mother," then we take this voice—representing "mother's" private thoughts, her inner speech—not to be imagined (like Marion's voices as she sat behind the wheel of her car) but real (like the voices Marion overheard coming from the old house). Then this voice represents "mother's" real thoughts as she reflects on the possibility that even now "they" are viewing and resolves to be passive in the face of "their" gaze. She grants "them" an audience. Of course, within the world of the film, she *is* now being viewed: the revolted policeman, looking in through the window, is the real incarnation of the watchers she conjures in her mind. But the guard's gaze mediates our view. True, she imagines "them" as viewing her, not as having access to her thoughts—but how are we to understand our access to her consciousness? Does it violate "mother's" innermost privacy? (To be sure, what this vantage seems to allow us to discover is "mother's" sincere belief in her own innocence—and her apparently sincere belief that she is separate from Norman, even from what the psychiatrist calls "the mother half of Norman's mind.") Or do we not simply "overhear" this inner voice but listen to words that are addressed to us? She would then be granting us, in effect, audience to her confession.

We may also take the being we are viewing to be not "mother" but Norman. Then this voice would be performing a dramatic monologue, a theatrical speech that constitutes a scene conjured within Norman's imagination. Then Norman—the actor who performs this speech and its secret author—would be sitting as silent spectator within the theater of his own consciousness. In any case, our access to this voice separates us from the revolted policeman. But there is a fundamental ambiguity to our role. We cannot say whether our presence violates Norman's privacy or whether he welcomes us into the audience for this scene projected from within himself.

On the words, "Let them see what kind of person I am," Norman/"mother" looks down at something below the frame line (5.209). As the voice continues ("Why, I'm not even going to swat that fly"), there is a cut to a closeup, from Norman's/"mother's" point of view, of a hand with a fly on it (5.210). This cut sums up the ambiguities attending our access to the inner voice. It breaks

5.209

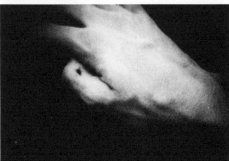

5.210

5.211

5.212

completely with the policeman's point of view and assumes Norman's/"mother's" perspective. And the cut places itself at the service of "mother's" demonstration of her innocence: to be properly swayed by this evidence of her fundamental passivity, they have to see the fortunate fly at issue. The gaze "mother's" words invoke must be granted access to the view framed by the camera in (5.210). Then are we, and not the policeman, really the "them" imagined by "mother"?

When we return to Norman/"mother," the mask at the bottom of the frame is gone (5.211). We have crossed the barrier from outside to inside. Our safety curtain has been removed. We are in this being's presence as the offscreen voice completes its speech: "I hope they *are* watching. They'll see. They'll see and they'll know and they'll say, 'Why, she wouldn't even harm a fly!' " At this moment, Norman/"mother" looks up directly at the camera and smiles (5.212).

If this is "mother's" grin, the joke it registers is at "their" expense. They believe they know what kind of a person she really is. But they are very easy to deceive. Not that this grin reveals that "mother" is murderous by nature. What it reveals is that her nature remains cloaked in a mystery they cannot fathom. And this look to the camera inscribes knowledge of our presence: "mother" possesses our gaze in her own. Then does her grin let us in on her joke, allowing that we know her as they never could? Or is the joke a private one from which we are pointedly excluded? Are we, indeed, its real butt? To take for granted that we are separate from them in "mother's" eyes would be to step into her trap. Such presumption above all must make "mother" laugh.

But if this is Norman's grin, it registers a joke at "mother's" expense. She vows absolute passivity, embraces that nightmarish condition from which Diana recoiled. She believes she can triumph by denying her life to the world. But there is no escape from the death-in-life she embraces. "Mother's" embracing of this condition completes Norman's revenge even as it absolves him of guilt; "mother" has taken her own death upon herself. Norman grins in appreciation of this fiendish twist and at his own brilliance in effecting it. But Norman's grin also inscribes knowledge of our presence. In it, he declares that the last laugh is his. The joke is on "mother," and the joke is also on us.

Whether we attribute this look to Norman or to "mother," then, it incarnates knowledge of our vision, hence a possession of the camera's framings. It declares a bond with the camera, a complicity with its agency. Then the joke this grin registers cannot be separated from the brilliant stroke Hitchcock has just pulled off (the cutaway to the hand and fly that allows the safety curtain to be removed without calling our attention to it). Indeed, this grin registers a joke that cannot be separated from the entire series of views, framed by the camera, that constitute *Psycho*. Whoever this figure projected onto the screen is, it is also a mask for the author of *Psycho*; it is one of Hitchcock's stuffed birds. The grin fixes itself indelibly on our vision of *Psycho*'s author. Again we must ask whether Hitchcock lets us in on *Psycho*'s joke or whether his film is a joke at our expense.

At this moment, Hitchcock superimposes the grinning death's head over Norman's/"mother's" face (5.213). This extraordinary gesture unmasks Norman/"mother," discloses this subject of the camera to be claimed by death, even to represent death. It is death that presides over *Psycho*'s world; it is the film's burden to bring death, at least to wish death, on those who behold it. *Psycho* prophesies our death, announces to us

5.213

what we already know, that we are fated to die. In this unmasking, Hitchcock also asserts his separation from the being who has just claimed the camera's framings for his/her own. He calls upon us to acknowledge our community with him. We too are mortal.

Simultaneous with this superimposition, there is a dissolve to Marion's car being pulled out of the swamp, trunk first, by a clanking chain (5.214, 5.215). Then the graphic pattern of the opening titles is reprised and the image quickly fades out, the film ending abruptly as the music sounds over an empty black frame. I will

5.214

5.215

make only a brief remark on this profound, cryptic final image.

The slow dissolve momentarily superimposes the chain over Norman's/ "mother's" throat, imaging a hanging. It signifies the damnation of this composite. But the dissolve also makes this being dissolve into the swamp. Like the dead eye that emerges from the water mixed with blood which swirls into the blackness of the drain, Marion's car emerges from black waters infused with the substance of this monstrous being. The film's final image, then, echoes the equally cryptic conclusion of the shower-murder sequence. *Psycho* ends with a final disquieting vision of birth or rebirth. Marion is born out of this foul swamp, but she returns to this world already dead. We might also say that it is Norman, or perhaps "mother," who is stillborn. But it is also as if the birth with which *Psycho* ends is that of the film itself.

One myth of art is that the artist who lives for his creations gives a part of his life to each of his works. Through a lifetime of creation, he dies many deaths and is reborn by stages until he is finally recreated as his works' creator. As artist, he is immortal; his art triumphs over human mortality, as it overcomes the human condition of sexuality. But in his acts of creation, the human artist is also brought back to the inevitability of his own death. In the creation of a work of art, the artist takes his own death upon himself. And his art has a murderous aspect as well. How could his impulse to create be separated from his desire to avenge himself on those who, beholding his creations, draw sustenance from them? Norman Bates stands in for every artist whose life is circumscribed by acts singularly composed of murder and creation.

At the conclusion of *Psycho*'s chronicle, the circle of killings initiated by the original matricide has been closed. Norman's rebirth as a creature of his own creations has been achieved. And *Psycho* announces, in my view, that the cycle of Hitchcock films has likewise run its course. Hitchcock has accomplished his recreation of himself as the author of his films. If he had never made another film after *Psycho*, his work would not have been unfinished. The films that Hitchcock did go on to make—*The Birds, Marnie, Torn Cur-*

tain, Topaz, Frenzy, and *Family Plot*—in no way disavow *Psycho*'s finality. *Psycho*'s achievement is to bring Hitchcock's filmmaking project to a successful conclusion. Yet, if *Psycho* confirms the immortality of Hitchcock's authorship, it also acknowledges Hitchcock's own mortality as no earlier Hitchcock film had done. It is as if *Psycho* were the first film he made in clear view of his own death. And in *Psycho,* Hitchcock calls upon us to acknowledge that what brings his films to life is his life's blood on every frame.

If every authentic work of art bears a murderous aspect and calls for its creator's death and allows his rebirth, these conditions, we have seen, are intrinsic to the very medium of film. Every film image is a death mask of the world. The world of every film is past. The camera fixes its living subjects, possesses their life. They are reborn on the screen, creatures of the film's author and ourselves. But life is not fully breathed back into them. They are immortal, but they are always already dead. The beings projected on the screen are condemned to a condition of death-in-life from which they can never escape. What lures us into the world of a film may be a dream of triumphing over death, holding death forever at bay. But *Psycho* decisively demonstrates what Hitchcock's work has always declared: the world of a film is not a private island where we may escape the conditions of our existence. At the heart of every film is a truth we already know: we have been born into the world and we are fated to die.

Postscript

I had just completed the last chapter of this book when Alfred Hitchcock died, at the age of eighty, on April, 29, 1980. Reflecting on the public response to Hitchcock's death, and on my own emotion, I realized that there was a particular postscript that had to be written.

By the time of Hitchcock's death, America had reached a consensus as to who he was and what he had accomplished. The news stories, editorials, and obituaries could have flowed from a single pen. Hitchcock was the Master of Suspense. He was the consummate technician among film directors, as well as the model of the popular entertainer healthily free from artistic pretensions. A typical comment: "The people who paid to see Alfred Hitchcock's movies were infinitely more important to him than the directors and critics who deified him and subjected his films to rigorous scrutiny and high-minded analysis."

Unless one looks closely at Hitchcock's films and reflects seriously on them, this view appears not only plausible but unavoidable. The knowing Hitchcock who emerges in this book is a strikingly different figure. Yet it took Hitchcock's death for me to realize that I would not be satisfied unless I confronted the tyranny of the Hitchcock legend head on.

The language with which Hitchcock's death was reported shows that the press took itself to be at one with the public in its understanding of this man, and also to share with the public the knowledge that they were of one mind on the subject of Hitchcock. Agreement had already been reached and could be taken for granted; no new understanding needed to be attained, no new words found, no new tributes formulated, because Hitchcock had already been acknowledged. There were, for example, the televised tributes to which he lent his presence while he was still alive. These shows, of which the one staged by the American Film Institute in 1979 was the last and most elaborate, presented Hitchcock as the man whose films brought the public together into an audience. The shows pre-

sented themselves as "official" and at the same time as spontaneous public expressions of community. Under the aegis of the insti-
tutions that arranged the productions and wrote their scripts, and
with the underwriting of television, Hitchcock's audience joined in
expressing gratitude for knowing him. He was "one of us."

By repeating the official language of these tributes on the occasion of Hitchcock's death, America commemorated him publicly,
and vowed to remember him privately, in the terms it took to have
received his personal blessing. Hitchcock's death occasioned not
only an expression of community, but a quite extraordinary celebration of society's capacity to acknowledge one of its own. In cele-
brating having known and having acknowledged Hitchcock,
America paid tribute to itself.

When Uncle Charles dies at the end of *Shadow of a Doubt*, all of
Santa Rosa, that microcosm of America, embraces the language of
the minister's eulogy. Only young Charlie knows the truth. Only
she can recognize the irony of this expression of community engendered by the death of the man the town accepted as "one of us" but
did not really know at all (did not know, for example, his disdain
for those incapable of recognizing his longing for acknowledgment
or his murderousness). And only Charlie can view this spectacle in
Charles's spirit and recognize him as its secret author.

Hitchcock, I believe, possessed a secret comparable to Uncle
Charles's. Part of what he knew when he died is that America never
really understood his films. Society's "tributes" were denials of the
meaning of his work. Surely, the spectacle of America paying tribute to itself on the occasion of his death is a Hitchcockian one. I call
it that because it would make a chilling, poignant, and funny scene
in a Hitchcock film, and because his work can teach us to recognize
Hitchcock as its secret author. When Hitchcock authorized the language of his public tributes, and in general appeared to endorse the
official view of who he was, in effect he scripted his own obituary,
assuring that it would be silent on the meaning of his films. All
Hitchcock's public speeches and gestures were also silences. I have
no wish to attempt to reconcile the official Hitchcock and the
knowing figure who emerges in my book, but to convey how the
former may be viewed as the latter's creation, as a perfectly Hitchcockian figure, a projection of Hitchcock's authorship.

Consider one such gesture, one such silence: Hitchcock's designation of John Russell Taylor to write his authorized biography,
Hitch: The Life and Times of Alfred Hitchcock (1978). Taylor begins his project satisfied that Hitchcock's films hold no mysteries.
Unsurprisingly, he arrives at the conclusion that "Hitch" is a primi-
tive with no aspirations to art and no serious intellectual concerns.
"It seems unlikely that Hitchcock, even in the secret places of his

heart, regarded himself as . . . anything other than a practical movie-maker," Taylor writes without marshaling any critical evidence that Hitchcock was no artist or thinker. It is apparent that, from the outset, Taylor's faith in the consensus view conditioned his encounters with the man. He ruled out the possibility of Hitchcock's knowingness, the possibility of conversing seriously with him about his "secret places."

In this respect, *Hitch* may usefully be compared with the Truffaut interviews. Truffaut's book reads like the script of a play or, more exactly, the transcript of a trial. Hitchcock's intelligence can be discerned, but only by reading the dialogue as a scene in a Hitchcock film, imagining Hitchcock as, say, Norman Bates and Truffaut as Marion Crane. The author of *Psycho* could not be oblivious of how Truffaut changes the subject or speaks for him every time a "serious" matter comes up. Viewed in the Hitchcock spirit, Truffaut's obtuseness is often very funny, but the poignancy of Hitchcock's situation is all too real: unable to enter into a serious conversation with a man who thinks he is his intellectual superior but is far from his equal, Hitchcock remains isolated and unacknowledged.

To authorize a man who doesn't know who one is to write the story of one's life is a perfectly Hitchcockian gesture, entirely in the spirit of *North by Northwest*. It is Hitchcockian for the specific risk it takes of remaining altogether unacknowledged even as one is being immortalized as an institution and a monument. By the end of the events chronicled in *Psycho*, Norman Bates despairs of finding a fit critic in his world, one capable of acknowledging his murderous acts of creation. He turns to the camera, challenging us to penetrate his secret. Then is it that Hitchcock despaired of finding a critic who knew the secret places of his work, whom he might have authorized in Taylor's place? Or did Hitchcock wish for a biography that preserved his silence about those secret places? Perhaps the Taylor biography is one of Hitchcock's secret demonstrations of his art, one of his secret triumphs.

Hitchcock's silences mocked those who took for granted that they knew him when they had not penetrated his most elementary secrets, not escaped his simplest traps, not even recognized his disdain or his anguish. But Hitchcock's work can teach us to recognize them also as reminders that his films are the creations of a human being who dedicated his life to his authorship. Hitchcock's silences echoed the silence of his audience in the face of his films' calls for acknowledgment. But if they have a tragic aspect, they are also sublime expressions of his sense of humor. They are summed up in Anthony Perkins' silence as he possesses the camera in his murderous gaze at the end of *Psycho*, but also in Barbara Harris' wink at the end of *Family Plot*, a look whose piquance stands for, and consummates, all the pleasures Hitchcock's films have given us.

Of all Hitchcock's public appearances in his last years, the most moving, and also the most chilling, was the American Film Institute's 1979 show. Several years earlier, Hitchcock had participated in a tribute sponsored by the Film Society of Lincoln Center. That appearance was linked to the release of *Family Plot* and represented a way of keeping in the public eye, of reminding his audience that he was still very much alive. In the AFI tribute, however, what the audience could plainly see was that he was close to death. There would never be another Hitchcock film. Yet on this occasion, the scripted speeches were unusually "official," unusually emphatic in their insistence that Hitchcock's films meant nothing, that the jovial Master of Suspense had nothing serious on his mind. When the show's anonymous director cut away to Hitchcock to remind us of his presence, it was clear that, in effect, Hitchcock was being remembered as though he were already dead; in these cutaways, Hitchcock's face, impassive as always, could just as well have been a memorial bust.

Why did Hitchcock, so near the end of his life, submit silently to such treatment? A number of thoughts come to mind. As a public speaker, Hitchcock, with his mastery of timing, was a performer of genius, and the show provided him with one of his last opportunities to gratify his appetite for displaying his wit on camera. He used this stage to repeat an oft-told anecdote about the time his father arranged with the police for him to spend a night in jail, saying to him, "This is what they do to bad little boys." Having told this story to great effect, Hitchcock looked around at the assembled audience, then directly into the camera, and topped himself. With the flippancy that seemed to assure us that we need not take his words seriously, he added, "And *this* is what they do to *good* little boys." Then too, even if the speeches, taken literally, were affronts rather than acknowledgments, it *was* a real tribute that so many friends and colleagues wished to appear in public to praise him. Surely Hitchcock also participated in the show out of respect and affection for the likes of Ingrid Bergman and Cary Grant and Janet Leigh and Tony Perkins and Tippi Hedren, men and women whose love redeemed the words they were given to speak.

In the show's most privileged moment, Hitchcock ended his own brief speech with a testimonial to the understanding, support, professional collaboration, and love of his wife Alma. This was perhaps the only time in his life when, in public, he set aside irony to speak eloquently from the heart. This speech was also a perfect Hitchcockian gesture, however: what better moment for Hitchcock to present to his audience a telling demonstration of what an authentic tribute is. But whatever pleasures and satisfactions attended this last major public appearance, I could not watch without at every moment wishing for someone to step forward, like Hannay in *The Thirty-Nine Steps*, to stop and unmask the show.

Clearly, in the readings that make up this book, I cast myself as the figure who steps forward to answer Hitchcock's call for acknowledgment. Perhaps it is foolish or arrogant or crazy for me to play such a role. Yet this *is* the role I embrace in these readings, and there is no point in my trying to disavow it. I would not have written this book if I did not believe that I had penetrated some of the secret places of Hitchcock's art.

Charlie knows that her uncle secretly authored his own eulogy; she also knows that he arranged for the way *she* is fated to remember him. When I say that my writing aspires to answer Hitchcock's call for acknowledgment, I also mean that Hitchcock's films call for writing such as this, even call it forth. If Hitchcock is secret author of his own obituary, my readings are equally projections of his authorship; only they are authorized not by his words but by his silences. The Hitchcock who emerges in these readings could well have written them himself. Yet the Hitchcock for whom I speak, who calls forth my words, is also my creation. I am his character and he is mine; the boundary between my identity and his is unfathomable, like that between Norman Bates and "mother." That the voice speaking for Hitchcock's films here is also possessed by them is what is most deeply Hitchcockian about the book, what Hitchcock would most have appreciated, I believe, what might have moved him beyond words.

My role, then, is a Hitchcockian one. In these readings, a struggle for authorship is waged; symbolically, it is a life-and-death struggle. Hence it is a macabre twist that Hitchcock died just as I finished the last chapter, and that his death allowed me to write this postscript which closes out the project that has obsessed me for more years than I care to remember. If the writing of this book had taken place within a Hitchcock film, if Hitchcock and I lived in a world whose author was Hitchcock, it would be a perfect gesture for him to die to allow the book to be completed, the way Handell Fane died to allow the ending of "The Inner History of the Baring Case" to be written. It would be equally perfect, equally macabre, and equally Hitchcockian for him to be sacrificed like Mrs. Bates, to sacrifice himself like Fane, Mr. Memory, or Uncle Charles, or to be murdered by me. The fantasy that my writing, possessed by Hitchcock's films and claiming possession of them, has the power to kill is, again, Hitchcockian. It is akin to the fantasy that runs through Hitchcock's work that his films are murderous. If I step forward to acknowledge Hitchcock, where that calls for discovering his life's blood on every frame of his films (as I put it in the reading of *Psycho*), my gesture would not be fully Hitchcockian if it did not express the fantasy that his blood was also on my hands.

Hitchcock died without reading a word of this book. I sent him no part of it, although for some months several chapters were in virtually final form. It is not that I was afraid of his indifference or rejection; the authority of my claims, such as it is, does not rest on his words and cannot be taken away by them. What I most feared, I now believe, was that he would acknowledge my writing. I was afraid for myself and for him. If Hitchcock's authorship is a call for acknowledgment, it is equally an expression of dread, and avoidance, of acknowledgment. If it would be Hitchcockian for him to die to allow my book to be finished, it would be equally Hitchcockian for him to die to assure that he would never actually have to read it.

Part of what such fantasies mean to me, as I reflect sadly on the fact that Hitchcock will never be able to read my book, is that I was writing, without realizing it, not for Hitchcock but for his audience, which stands in need of instruction in viewing his films. And it is not to claim them for myself that I undertook to speak for Hitchcock's films. It was to free these films from me, to free myself from them, to claim my writing for my own.

Film, in Hitchcock's work, is the medium by which he made himself known, or at least knowable—the bridge between himself and us. But it is also a barrier that stands between Hitchcock and us. It stands for everything that separates Hitchcock from his audience, and indeed for everything that separates any one human being from all others. By dedicating his life to the making of films that are calls for acknowledgment, while doing everything in his power to assure that such acknowledgment would be deferred until after his death, Hitchcock remained true to his art, and true to the medium of film.

Notes

1. The Lodger

1. Opening a film with a hallucinatory fragment of a murder scene is one of Hitchcock's characteristic strategies. He uses it, for example, in *Murder!*, *Young and Innocent*, *Rope*, and *I Confess*.

2. This passage anticipates the more elaborate quasi-documentary framework of *Blackmail*, which details the operations of Scotland Yard. Hitchcock's attitude toward documentary must not be misconstrued, however. A major element of his films of the 1930s is their critique of the British documentary movement led by John Grierson. Films like *Drifters* (1929), *Song of Ceylon* (1935), and *Night Mail* (1936) rhapsodized the mechanisms and processes of society with the aim of furthering social progress. Hitchcock attacks the British documentary for failing to acknowledge the realm of the erotic and for missing the ironies and the poignancy of human existence, which must be lived in private as well as in public and is solitary as well as social. A Grierson-style treatment of the production of the *Evening Standard* would celebrate the smoothly running machinery but ignore the way the newspaper's stories really enter the lives of its readers. It would not even raise the question of who these readers are and what draws them to these stories. It certainly would not reflect on its own attraction, as a film, to the London audience.

3. Daisy's descendants appear in *Blackmail*, *Young and Innocent*, *Suspicion*, *Shadow of a Doubt*, *Stage Fright*, *Vertigo*, *Psycho*, and *Marnie*, among other films.

4. Joe's conflict reappears throughout Hitchcock's work. For example, in *Murder!* Sir John applies his discipline as a playwright to satisfy his duty as a juror and his personal desires, with mixed results. Ingrid Bergman in *Spellbound* bends psychoanalytic discipline to the leanings of her heart, to happy effect. In *The Paradine Case* Gregory Peck plays a lawyer who fatally mixes his official duties and his love for his client, although his fall, unlike Joe's, has something of the weight of tragedy: Peck's failure is not a betrayal of his humanity, but a heroic affirmation of it. *Sabotage*, *Young and Innocent*, *Notorious*, *Rope*, *I Confess*, *Rear Window*, *The Wrong Man*, *Vertigo*, *Torn Curtain*, and *Topaz* are among the other Hitchcock films which take up the implications of Joe's case.

5. The shot specifically alludes to the moment in *The Cabinet of Dr. Caligari* when the somnambulist Cesare opens his eyes at Caligari's bidding and stares into the camera. *The Lodger* incorporates *Caligari's* nightmarish events and places them within a world depicted realistically; this somnambulist makes his entrance into an ordinary home in contemporary London.

6. The novel from which *Suspicion* was adapted specifically breaks with this convention. The heroine's passion is so consuming that, when she discovers that her beloved really is a killer, she embraces him no less rapturously for the knowledge that she will die at his hands.

7. James Naremore, in his useful *Filmguide to Psycho* (Bloomington: Indiana University Press, 1973), suggests that birds have no special significance in Hitchcock's films before the 1950s. Yet *The Lodger's* cuckoo already possesses the symbolic significance birds take on in *Psycho* and *The Birds*. Their significance is partly derived from the idea that birds, with their softness, warmth, and passivity and their knifelike claws and beaks, combine stereotypical masculine and feminine attributes in a dizzying way. Among Hitchcock's British films there are a host of examples, such as the bird in *Blackmail* whose chirping takes on a nightmarish quality; Handell Fane's feather headdress in *Murder!*; the caged birds and the "Who Killed Cock Robin?" episode in *Sabotage*; and the seagulls that preside over murder in *Young and Innocent*.

8. See the discussion of a series of shots of Cary Grant in profile in my "Alfred Hitchcock's *Notorious*," *The Georgia Review*, 29 (Winter 1975), 901.

9. The series of shots (1.29–1.31) gives something of the effect of a zoom in on Daisy's hair. It anticipates the stunning moment in *Blackmail* when the camera moves in quickly to a tight closeup of the face of the man murdered the night before, that movement reflecting Frank's horror and exhilaration at discovering that the dead man is his hated rival for the affections of Alice. It also anticipates the moment in *The Birds* when the mother discovers Mr. Fawcett's corpse and a series of jump cuts ends in a terrifying closeup of the dead man's bloody eye sockets. The sequence also exemplifies Hitchcock's practice of allowing a woman's hair to stand in for her sexuality and the mystery of her identity. When a woman is framed as Daisy is in (1.29–1.31), the focus on her hair is also a mark of her having turned away from the camera.

10. Compare the fireworks in *To Catch a Thief*, a conventional metaphor for a young woman's imagining of the sexual act. See Stanley Cavell, *The World Viewed* (Cambridge: Harvard University Press, 1979), pp. 64–65.

11. Murnau's actors employ this walk in *Nosferatu* and *Sunrise*, for example. The most familiar—and perhaps most memorable—instance is also a kind of parody: Boris Karloff as the monster in *Frankenstein*.

12. An analogous shot appears in *Suspicion*. At the height of our suspicion that Cary Grant is a murderer, Grant looks directly into the camera and smiles. In this shot, Hitchcock compels us to recognize his own

power over us and confronts us with the limits of our knowledge of Grant. I am inclined to distinguish Grant's look from Novello's, however. Novello acknowledges the camera with perfect formality, as though he recognized it as equal in rank to himself, while it is not clear that Grant acknowledges the camera at all. Novello's smile seems knowing; we do not know, but could learn, the secret he shares with Hitchcock. But we do not know whether Grant smiles because he is so alert that he easily penetrates our act of viewing, or because he is in so deep a trance that he can look right into the camera without recognizing it. Grant's thoughts are impenetrable to us. Yet it is not clear that Grant himself—or, for that matter, Hitchcock—possesses a secret knowledge of those thoughts that we lack. Grant's impenetrability, unlike Novello's, is virtually absolute. Grant is impenetrable to Hitchcock, to us, and to himself.

13. Among Hitchcock's early films, *Blackmail* contains the most striking instances of Hitchcock's use of coded sexual references and symbols. Crazed with fear and guilt, Alice wanders through the London night; she has just stabbed to death an artist who tried to seduce her and, when she resisted, tried to rape her. A flashing electric sign, reading "Gordon's gin for purity," catches her eye. The sign is dominated by a cocktail shaker that moves rhythmically up and down. In a subjective shot from Alice's point of view, this phallic cocktail shaker metamorphoses into a knife. Allowing no doubt about the link, in Alice's tortured mind, between the murder weapon she wielded in defense of her "purity" and the sexuality of her attacker/victim, the knife repeatedly stabs at the first half of the word "cocktail." This is not the first time the word "cock" appears on the screen. When the artist slipped Alice a note, written on a page torn from a magazine, to arrange the fatal meeting, a few letters of print from the original page clearly spelled out the words "'Nippy' Cock." Of course, it is one thing to recognize the coded sexual references and symbols in some of Hitchcock's frames, and it is another to account critically for their motivations and significance in particular instances. Revulsion against the excesses of Freudian symbol-hunters must not blind us to the reality of this practice, which is by no means confined to Hitchcock's work. Howard Hawks, for example, regularly employed double entendre and sexual symbolism, both of which became commonplace features of Hollywood films after the Production Code was instituted and enforced in the early thirties.

14. It is illuminating to compare Hitchcock's treatment with the passage in Griffith's *Broken Blossoms* in which the Yellow Man (Richard Barthelmess) advances on Lucy (Lillian Gish), inflamed with desire. Griffith presents us with Lucy's view of the advancing figure, whose gentle face has been transformed into a monstrous mask. In Griffith's films, two male figures are barred from sexual fulfillment. The villain, unmasked, appears inhuman and cannot be loved or desired. The hero, like the villain, has a physical mark that precludes his being desired (Danton's pockmarks, Abraham Lincoln's legendary ugliness, the Yellow Man's skin color), although a good woman must revere him. A villain takes pleasure in imposing himself on women who do not desire him, but the hero

renounces his desire, although doing so fills him, as a title in *Broken Blossoms* puts it, with "all the tears of the ages." The Yellow Man is a Griffith hero; when he sees Lucy's horror, he accepts the necessity of leaving his desire unfulfilled. In the world of a Hitchcock film, however, sexuality is an inalienable aspect of human nature. It is not evil, and its renunciation is not heroic. Indeed, it cannot be renounced. Griffith's titles are his personal pronouncements, emblazoned with his initials and phrased in his flowery diction; they also claim the authority of holy writ. Yet, although Griffith's titles cast their author as God's own spokesman, his camera, like Hitchcock's, has a monstrous aspect; in his own terms, the camera is an instrument of the devil. His last films are extraordinarily moving in their inarticulate groping toward a mode of confession, but he remains anguished, guilty, violent, vengeful, frustrated, desperate even as he claims the voice of God as his own. Hitchcock avoids Griffith's despair, and his hypocrisy, by withholding all personal pronouncements and by invoking no God. Hitchcock claims neither holiness nor unholiness for his work, and within his films there are neither heroes nor villains. There are only the author's agents, knowing or unknowing, obliging or intransigent, innocent or guilty.

15. Such fences appear in film after film throughout Hitchcock's career. I am tempted to say that *this* fence reappears, just as I am tempted to say that *The Lodger*'s staircase, and not just a staircase similar to it, reappears in Hitchcock film after Hitchcock film. Perhaps most notably, the spiked fence reappears in the climactic flashback of *Spellbound*, when Gregory Peck reclaims the traumatic memory of his brother horribly impaled on one of its spikes. That *Spellbound*'s fence and *The Lodger*'s fence are, visually, one and the same makes Peck's reclaiming of his memory coincide with Hitchcock's affirmation of the continuity of his own work. *Spellbound* acknowledges *The Lodger* as its past.

16. In *Hitchcock's British Films* (Hamden: Shoestring Press, 1977), Maurice Yacowar argues that *The Lodger* poses moral tests for its characters and viewers. Only Daisy recognizes that the lodger is not the Avenger, while Joe, Daisy's mother, the bloodthirsty mob, and we all jump to the wrong conclusion, on appearances alone. And when the truth about the lodger is revealed, we fail to recognize that he is, morally, no better than the real Avenger. He is *an* avenger, one who breaks society's laws, who takes God's justice upon himself. But Yacowar assumes that society's law and God's law are one, while Hitchcock makes no such assumption. *The Lodger* declares that there is an author who presides over its world but is silent on the nature of the divinity, if any, that holds sway in our world. If a theology is to be read into the film, it had better have an answer to the question of what, if anything, corresponds in reality to the camera, and a convincing account of what a film is and what it is to make and to view a film. To say that we fail a moral test by jumping to conclusions on the basis of appearances is to fail to acknowledge that *The Lodger* is an author's testimony; the lodger's nature cannot be separated from his relationship to the camera, or from our relationship to Hitchcock. Yacowar's central thesis is that Hitchcock is an ironic artist whose work

does not reveal but masks him. But if this were so, and if his films also pose moral tests, Hitchcock would be compelled to condemn himself for being an avenger. On what grounds can he claim to pass judgment on us? My reading of *The Lodger* pictures him very differently, as stepping forward to declare himself in the medium of film. For a review of *Hitchcock's British Films*, see my "How Much Did Hitchcock Know?", *Quarterly Review of Film Studies*, Summer 1980.

17. Hitchcock's model of a film that undercuts the authority of its own ending is Murnau's *The Last Laugh*. Perhaps the Hitchcock films whose endings most clearly echo that of *The Lodger* are *Suspicion* and *The Wrong Man*. But I am also reminded of his personal appearances at the end of each of his television shows, when he deliberately broke the story's spell by informing us of the innocent's reward, the guilty's punishment, and the sponsor's provenance.

2. Murder!

1. Truffaut sets up his conversation with Hitchcock in such a way that these six films are dismissed almost without comment. My book, regretfully, is guilty of the same offense. However, these films are worthy of detailed, sympathetic study: *Downhill* with its experiments in filming the imaginary and its study of friendship, humiliation, and guilt; *Easy Virtue* with its extraordinary trial sequence that establishes a Hitchcock paradigm and links the camera's eye with the stern gaze of a judge; *The Ring* ("There were all kinds of innovations in it, and I remember that at the premiere an elaborate montage got a round of applause. It was the first time that had ever happened to me." François Truffaut, *Hitchcock* (New York: Simon and Schuster, 1967), p. 37); the beautiful and richly humorous *The Farmer's Wife*; and the deeply moving *The Manxman*. Even the much-maligned *Champagne* has remarkable things in it, although on the whole it falls flat. On these films I can warmly recommend Maurice Yacowar's discussion in *Hitchcock's British Films*, despite my disagreements with his overall understanding of Hitchcock's work.

2. This metaphor is basic to all of Hitchcock's trial sequences. It is implicit in *Easy Virtue*, for example. In *The Paradine Case*, the analogy between the witness box and the film frame is explicitly declared.

3. Staccato knocking is a motif that recurs in all of Hitchcock's sound films. It takes on the status of a symbol—linked to the ////—whose appearance signals the onset of a siege of nightmare anxiety. In *The Saboteur*, for example, a fire extinguisher knocking against the side of a truck triggers the protagonist's recollection of the traumatic scene he witnessed. The sound of shutters knocking in a storm brings terror in *The Paradine Case*. And Marnie's nightmares always begin with this sound. A detailed study of Hitchcock's use of sounds as symbols would be worth undertaking. These motifs include the ringing of a telephone, the sound of a train hurtling down the tracks, the sound of breaking glass, and the sound of ice clinking against the side of a glass. The last attains a singular, almost Proustian power of evocation in Hitchcock's work.

4. Perhaps the greatest of all screen incarnations of unfathomable theatricality are John Barrymore in Howard Hawks's *Twentieth Century* and Jules Berry in Jean Renoir's *The Crime of M. Lange*. The Professor in *The Thirty-Nine Steps*, Uncle Charles in *Shadow of a Doubt*, and Norman Bates in *Psycho* are all instances of this type.

5. In *Stage Fright*, Charlotte (Marlene Dietrich) turns her profile to the camera as she speaks her lament for her husband. The camera assumes the point of view of the innocent Eve (Jane Wyman), who is secretly watching. Charlotte's performance horrifies Eve, who takes it to be a cynical act covering cold, inhuman indifference. But at the same time, as an aspiring actress, Eve is dumbstruck by the power of Charlotte's theatricality.

6. Truffaut, *Hitchcock*, p. 51.

7. In *Notorious*, Captain Prescott authorizes Alicia to enter Sebastian's home for the first time, and she too becomes our eyes and ears.

8. *Rear Window* elaborates on windows as a metaphor for the film frame. This effect in *Murder!* also anticipates *North by Northwest*'s opening, which likewise images the projection of a world onto an empty screen. Lines cut across the frame, creating a crisscross pattern that is transformed before our eyes into a screen on which a view of midtown Manhattan at rush hour is projected, and at the same time this screen becomes the wall of a glass skyscraper. The view of the world comes into sharp relief precisely as the screen completes its metamorphosis into a mirror with the world reflected in it. From this wall and mirror reflection, there is a dissolve to the world of the film itself. This world, conjured in the likeness of its reflection, comes to life, and the events of the film begin.

9. The couple's dialogue illustrates some of Hitchcock's strategies for handling speech. For example, Markham's "Why can't they make *quiet* scenes?" is a nest of jokes and ironies. It reminds us that there is a scene the presiding eye has not brought into view, hence raises the issue of that eye's powers and motives. Also, this man assumes that what is taking place is only an ordinary marital row. Hitchcock is jokingly comparing a married couple's bedroom with a battlefield and with a theater. Perhaps this line is also one of *Murder!*'s quips about "talkies." In the days of silent film, after all, "they" only made quiet scenes.

10. In *The Farmer's Wife, Suspicion, The Paradine Case,* and *North by Northwest,* a pair of chairs likewise stands in for a marriage.

11. Among the noteworthy examples that might be cited are the racetrack sequence in *Notorious*, the ride in the car in *Stage Fright* in the course of which Eve comes to realize that she is in love with Smith, the initial encounter between Bruno and Guy in *Strangers on a Train*, the dialogue over dinner between Thornhill and Eve in *North by Northwest*, the moving exchange between Tippi Hedren and Rod Taylor at the birthday party in *The Birds*, and the scene in *Torn Curtain* in which Paul Newman breaks the news to Julie Andrews that he has to leave for Stockholm. In my reading of *Psycho*, I analyze at length one of the most complex of all

shot/reverse-shot sequences, the dialogue in the parlor between Norman Bates and Marion Crane.

12. Diana's nightmare visions of imprisonment as death-in-life recall Carl Dreyer's *The Passion of Joan of Arc*. I take it that this accounts for *Murder!*'s compelling evocation of the atmosphere and visual surface of Dreyer's great film.

13. Rose in *The Wrong Man* is a Hitchcock figure who comes into full awareness that existence within her world is presided over by a god that bears an inhuman face. At this realization, she breaks into laughter, compounded by her knowledge that no one else is going to get the joke. Others deem her mad, and she is confined to an institution. Hitchcock films this hospital in images that chillingly recall these views of Diana's prison.

14. *The Paradine Case* is an exploration of this possibility.

15. Truffaut, *Hitchcock*, p. 53.

16. Ibid.

17. The culmination of Hitchcock's experiments with what might be called the "reframing mode" is *Rope* (1948), the film made, in effect, with no cuts at all.

18. In its opposition between two forms of theater, *Murder!* anticipates *Stage Fright*, which opposes the art of acting as taught by the Royal Academy of Dramatic Art to the conception of theater personified by Marlene Dietrich.

19. This shot exemplifies a mode of symbolic representation important in Hitchcock's work. The presentation of Sebastian's discovery of Alicia's betrayal in *Notorious* is one of the most prominent examples of this mode. The camera pans across the floor of the wine cellar until it frames the telltale sign of the stained drain. Our view represents Alex's literal one, but it is also a vision, charged symbolically. Through its veiled sexual references, it invokes a scene of lovemaking between Alicia and Devlin that has not actually taken place, but which Alex imagines or fantasizes or dreams. The climax of *Vertigo*, with Judy/Madeleine's vision of the black-robed nun, is another example.

20. This further complication may be registered. Fane's suicide provides "The Inner History of the Baring Case" with a climax that transcends Sir John's powers of imagination, and his letter fills in the murder scene with perfect respect for the spirit of melodrama. But we do not know that the story Fane's letter tells is true. Fane could have known all along, but without Diana's knowledge, that she knew his secret. Fane's account of himself partakes of his mystery, which it leaves intact. But Sir John knows nothing of Fane's mystery.

21. Truffaut, *Hitchcock*, p. 40.

22. The distinction between looks and poses that do and those that do not appear camera-conscious, in both still photography and in film, is not merely conventional. That we make this distinction is an important fact,

itself rooted in basic facts about the form of life we call human: for example, the fact that people have eyes with which they view and through which they reveal themselves.

23. Part of what makes the ending of *Murder!* so disquieting, I have suggested, is our wish for Sir John to be punished for his failure to acknowledge Handell Fane, who is Hitchcock's real surrogate. Is it to right this wrong that Hitchcock casts Herbert Marshall in the villain's role in *Foreign Correspondent?* I can think of no other comparable reversal of casting in all of Hitchcock's work.

24. For a fuller discussion of the problems inherent in cinéma vérité, see my "Alfred Guzzetti's *Family Portrait Sittings*," *Quarterly Review of Film Studies*, Winter 1977.

25. There are those who take the making and praising of what they call "materialist self-reflexive films" to be an anti-metaphysical gesture. Wittgenstein teaches us that metaphysics is not overcome by turning spiritualism on its head. *Murder!* stands opposed to the idea that a film's "self" can be identified with its material, if that material is taken to be the celluloid and emulsion of the film strip. The term "self-reflexive" can only be rescued from grammatical redundancy if one assumes, like a Pavlovian — in the history of film, this means Eisenstein — that the self is a reflex. This is not a philosophical position I take seriously.

3. The Thirty-Nine Steps

1. Cavell's ideas about the significance of such comedies helped me to understand the Hitchcock thriller and its relation to other film genres. See Stanley Cavell, *Pursuits of Happiness: The Hollywood Comedy of Remarriage* (Cambridge: Harvard University Press, 1981).

2. Yacowar reads Hannay's stance as expressing bored indifference (*Hitchcock's British Films*, p. 184), but such a judgment cannot really be made. Hannay has not, so far, expressed himself at all. We do not know what thoughts or feelings to read into his impassivity.

3. There is a close relationship between Hannay/Donat and Buster Keaton. Keaton's gravity and poise, like Hannay's grace, mark him as unselfconscious within the frame and the world of the film. Keaton's world, like Hannay's, is designed to catch him unaware and compel him to act. We might say that Keaton's wish for repose is also a wish to be exempt from the condition of authorship and from having a self. Where Keaton's situation differs from Hannay's is that the author of the reminders addressed to Keaton, the author of the design of his world, is Keaton himself. Keaton is director and star of his films; like Chaplin, he is his own camera's subject. The irony in Keaton's comedy is that he must play his unselfconsciousness with a straight face because he is his own perfect straight man.

4. Robin Wood, *Hitchcock's Films* (New York: Paperback Library, 1970), pp. 109–110.

5. For a complementary discussion of Cary Grant's screen persona, see Marian Keane, "The Design of Authorship," *Wide Angle*, 3.4 (1980).

6. Compare the presentation of Alice's hallucinations in *Blackmail*. Wherever she looks, she sees the dead artist's outstretched arm.

7. John Smith, "Conservative Individualism: A Selection of English Hitchcock," in *Screen*, 13.3 (1972), pp. 65–66.

8. Perhaps the most chilling instance of this type is Claude Rains's mother in *Notorious*. This connection supports the suggestion that the Professor presents his wife as an overbearing mother. This suggestion is also supported and illuminated by the formal link between our view of the Professor's wife and an important shot in *Marnie*, in which Hitchcock presents Tippi Hedren's view of her mother going down the stairs, the mother's steps uncannily echoing the knocking that initiated the nightmare from which Marnie has just awakened.

9. This breathtaking effect is reprised in, for example, *The Wrong Man* and *North by Northwest*. It might be noted that in later Hitchcock films such a shot would probably be framed from above. It becomes a characteristic Hitchcock gesture to cut to high angle when someone's fate is sealed.

10. This aura of necrophilia resonates with a number of passages, comic and not so comic, in Hitchcock's work. Its humor is taken up, for example, in *Mr. and Mrs. Smith*, *The Trouble with Harry*, and, in a darker mood, *Psycho* and *Frenzy*. And it is closely related to one of the most disturbing passages in *Marnie*: Mark's "rape" of Marnie (no longer able to hold him off and unable to accept his advances, she effectively denies life to her body and allows him to do with it as he pleases).

11. An obvious hole in the plot is that no one considers the possibility that the plans could have been photographed, as indeed occurs in *North by Northwest* and *Topaz*. Pointing this out at least underscores the sense in which Mr. Memory's "prodigious feats" make him a kind of camera and allow him to serve as the instrument of a will not his own.

12. This finale is also closely related to such other dramatic scenes within theaters as *Murder!*'s circus scene, *Sabotage*'s "Who Killed Cock Robin?" number, the several theatrical setpieces in *Stage Fright*, the tennis match in *Strangers on a Train*, the *Hamlet*-inspired play scene in *North by Northwest*, the ballet sequence in *Torn Curtain*, and the church service in *Family Plot*.

13. Is Sir John responsible for Handell Fane's death? Charlie for Uncle Charles's death in *Shadow of a Doubt*? Devlin for Sebastian's in *Notorious*? Scottie for Judy/Madeleine's in *Vertigo*? Norman Bates for Marion Crane's in *Psycho*? And is Hannay responsible for Margaret's suffering? We cannot take it for granted that all these questions call for the same answer, or that any of them admits an unambiguous answer.

14. A number of Hitchcock villains are finally confronted in this way with a vision of damnation. In *Stage Fright*, for example, Jonathan is cast by Eve onto a theater's empty stage. He can't see the policemen searching for him, but the cavernous space of the auditorium reverberates with their shouts. This haunted theater is a powerful metaphor for Jonathan's consciousness. Bewildered, unprotected by the ordinary barriers between theater and reality, between the imaginary and the real, between what is

inside and what is outside himself—for he has transgressed these barriers —he looks up, only to see the heavy safety curtain hurtling down to dismember and kill him. The theater itself exacts vengeance.

15. In the melancholy aspect of its ending, as in the flamboyant theatricality of the finale whose aftermath is tinged with melancholy, *The Thirty-Nine Steps* establishes itself as a model. *Shadow of a Doubt*, *Notorious*, *Rope*, *Stage Fright*, *Strangers on a Train*, *I Confess*, *Dial 'M' for Murder*, *The Wrong Man*, *Vertigo*, *Psycho*, *The Birds*, and *Marnie* are among the Hitchcock films whose endings are indebted for their mood to *The Thirty-Nine Steps*.

16. Hitchcock's films consistently declare that, in their worlds, society has no right to judge the union of true lovers and that the institution of marriage has no authority to legitimize love. This position, already staked out in such silent films as *Easy Virtue* and *The Manxman*, allies Hitchcock with Howard Hawks, whose work effects a related transformation of the conventions of romance and comedy. The ending of *To Have and Have Not* affirms the union of Bogart and Bacall although there is no promise of a wedding. Society holds no more authority over Hawks's lovers than Hitchcock's. Yet in the world of *To Have and Have Not*, unlike the world of *The Thirty-Nine Steps*, there is a community that we and the lovers acknowledge. Eddie and Cricket and Frenchy, acting for all freedom fighters, give their blessing to the lovers' union. But this community is not sanctioned by society at large and does not recognize society, as presently constituted, as having authority over it. Perhaps it is in acknowledgment of this situation that Hawks's community does not call upon the lovers to speak any vows. His community is one that would welcome Margaret and Mr. Memory and the nice old innkeepers and Hannay and Pamela and Hitchcock and at least you and me among Hitchcock's viewers. Wouldn't we all gladly accept membership in such a community? By picturing an authentic human community as tangible, Hawks does not break with Hitchcock, but makes a film that is a fantasy in a way *The Thirty-Nine Steps*—a different kind of fantasy—is not. *To Have and Have Not*'s companion piece, *The Big Sleep*, adopts a strain of anti-fantasy similar to Hitchcock's in *The Thirty-Nine Steps*. And one of Hitchcock's favorites among his own films, *The Trouble with Harry*, shows him indulging a fantasy very close to Hawks's.

4. Shadow of a Doubt

1. Hitchcock's attention to flatness and depth culminates in *Dial 'M' for Murder*, made in 3-D. In that film, shot after shot frames bottles, glasses, books, lamps, and so on, in the foreground, creating the effect of a screen separating us from the world that recedes into deep space. This makes it all the more dramatic when a sentence of death is passed on Grace Kelly, and Hitchcock places her against a bare background that defines the plane of the film screen and turns her into an incorporeal figure floating within the space of the theater.

2. In *Strangers on a Train*, Hitchcock films the encounter between the murderous Bruno and his intended victim, Guy's wife, in this way. There

it is a cigarette lighter that enters the frame first, followed by the simultaneous entrance, from opposite sides, of the two human figures. The lighter sparks this woman's desire: she takes her pursuer to be a determined seducer and is thrilled to find herself, at last, near him.

3. Compare, in *North by Northwest*, the reunion in the woods of Cary Grant and Eva Marie Saint.

4. For Hitchcock, green is the color of dreams, fantasies, and memories. The perfect love not attainable in today's world is infused with green in its imagining. When Judy turns into Madeleine before Scottie's eyes in *Vertigo*, she is bathed in a soft green light. Green is the color of a world from which the Hitchcockian red and black and white and brown are banished. Like Hitchcock's practice of employing a set of what I have called aural symbols, his consistent color symbolism—red, green, silver-white, black, and brown play the major roles—is worthy of detailed study. Two brief points.

First, this symbolism is already adumbrated in his black and white films. Even in the silent *Downhill*, fantasy/memory sequences are tinted green. And Hitchcock regularly alludes to symbolically charged colors by the names he gives characters and places. Hence the asylum in *Spellbound* is called Green Manors, and Charles and Emma, in *Shadow of a Doubt*, grew up together on Vernon Street. (The naming of the reprehensible Mr. Green is a private joke.)

Second, Hitchcock at times casts colors against type, as it were. In the case of green, the deepest instance occurs in *The Birds*. Hitchcock concludes the nightmarish passage in which the mother makes her discovery at the Fawcett farm by cutting to a frame dominated by the green of a pickup truck that occupies the extreme foreground of the frame. In *Torn Curtain*, he casts red—usually associated with sexual tension—against type by making it, in the guise of a fire exit at a ballet theater, the signpost for the route of escape from East Germany, a world devoid of color. (*Torn Curtain* uses the //// in a similar way. In *Spellbound*, it triggers Gregory Peck to lose control, but in *Torn Curtain* it is, in the form of the Greek letter pi, the insignia of the underground freedom fighters.)

5. A textbook example of this strategy occurs in *Marnie*. When Marnie first assumes her job at Rutland's, she spills a drop of red ink on her white blouse, the spreading stain shown in a closeup that suggests both her literal point of view and her subjective state. Her momentary breakdown is anticipated by the previous shot of her pen dipping into a bottle of ink whose label dominates the frame, the camera positioned so it reads not "Red Ink" but "Ink Red." Something "incredible" is about to happen.

6. Collinge's performance, like Teresa Wright's, is technically all but indistinguishable from her performance in William Wyler's *The Little Foxes*. But Hitchcock gives Collinge's creation a frame that puts in a deeper perspective her deadpan black humor and subtle explorations of aspects of the American experience that cut painfully deep.

7. In Hitchcock's films, a woman's purse is an emblem of her sexuality. Consider, for example, the moment in *Suspicion* when Joan Fontaine cuts short her would-be lover's advance by snapping her handbag shut, Ray

Milland's theft of the contents of his wife's handbag in *Dial 'M' for Murder*, and the opening of *Marnie*.

8. We have encountered this device before—for example, at the end of *Murder!*, when Sir John meets Diana by the prison gate.

9. The camera's capacity to cross real and symbolic barriers receives its most systematic treatment in Hitchcock's work in the films of the late forties, such as *Rope* and *Under Capricorn*, and also in *The Wrong Man*.

10. Closely related is the racetrack sequence in *Notorious*. When we discover that the intimate encounter between Devlin and Alicia was viewed by Sebastian, we are provoked to speculate on the relationship between our "privileged" views and those secretly possessed by this menacing figure within the world of the film. See my article, "Alfred Hitchcock's *Notorious*."

11. Hitchcock never tired of accusing proponents of "the method" of precisely this failing. Perhaps I might make the observation, however, that we cannot take at face value his celebrated remark that actors are cattle. Certainly it must not blind us to the brilliance of his casting and direction of performers. The flawless individual and ensemble playing in *Shadow of a Doubt* is typical.

12. The crisscross shadows in Graham's but not Charlie's frames recall the differentiation between Sir John's and Diana's setups in the shot/reverse-shot sequence at the heart of *Murder!*'s prison-visit scene.

13. This framing resonates with the ending of *The Lodger*. Also compare, in *North by Northwest*, Cary Grant's initial encounter with Eva Marie Saint.

14. This shot elaborates on, and deepens, the overhead view of the mother on the stairs, burdened with her knowledge, in *The Lodger*. In turn, it is transfigured in *Notorious'* famous camera movement that ends on the key clasped in Ingrid Bergman's hand.

15. This is not all Saint Paul said; he also spoke of marriage as being marginally preferable to burning in hell. Saint Paul enters the script by this reference, and also by virtue of the fact that Charles and Emma grew up together in the city of Saint Paul. The synchronization of the reference to Saint Paul with Charles's momentary occupation of the exact center of the frame underscores the allusion, I take it. It also exemplifies Hitchcock's practice of paying strict attention to whom or what the camera places center-frame.

16. This is, of course, the trick Hitchcock used in *Blackmail*, with the imaginary knife pointing to the first half of the word "cocktail" and the scrap of paper with "'Nippy' Cock" written on it.

17. The sailors in the lounge represent one of the film's few direct acknowledgments that this is 1943 and the United States is at war.

18. Saunders' role as go-between links *Shadow of a Doubt* and the silent *The Manxman*.

19. Alternating shots of a walker and the walker's point of view, with

the camera moving to keep up with the walker and also moving in the point-of-view shots to suggest the walker's movement, are a staple of Hitchcock's technique.

20. Is this an allusion to *The Thirty-Nine Steps* and its Portland Place Murderer? They *could* have caught up with him in Bangor.

21. A number of major Hitchcock moments are closely related to this. For example, in *Young and Innocent*, the breathtaking camera movement that ends by framing a drummer's eye, the camera holding that framing until the "bloke what twitches," stared down by the camera, gives himself away by blinking. Or the arrival of Strutt in *Marnie*: as if in answer to Marnie's anguished "Oh God, somebody help me!" Hitchcock dissolves to an extreme long shot of the hallway of the Rutland home and the camera slowly cranes down until it frames the front door, which finally opens to reveal the threatening figure of Strutt.

22. The silent *The Farmer's Wife* illuminates this reading. That film tells the story of a widower's efforts to find a woman to sit in the chair left empty by the death of his first wife. He is assisted in a series of comically ill-starred courtships by Minta, his lovely young servant. In his imagination, he pictures each woman in this chair, but the picture always falls short of his dream. We know that Minta wants him to propose to her and also that she knows him better than he knows himself, knows that he does not yet know that he loves her. Finally, the time comes when she can wait no longer and must compel him to recognize her. In his full view, she deliberately sits in the symbolic chair. In the vision of Minta in his wife's place, he recognizes his love at last. Guests unexpectedly arrive and she goes upstairs to change. It is the moment of her appearance on the stairs, radiant, that the present passage in *Shadow of a Doubt* echoes: in the face of this vision, and witnessed by the assembled guests, the farmer makes a toast, at the same time a proposal, to the woman he has chosen as his bride, and *The Farmer's Wife* ends as a true comedy.

23. A closely related moment occurs in *Vertigo*. Judy steps forward to assume her place in Scottie's vision and he sees that she is wearing Madeleine's necklace, hence recognizes that Judy and Madeleine are one.

24. In Hitchcock's work as a whole, this tunnel image takes on great resonance. The shot looking down the stairwell in *Vertigo*, for example, is a variant of it. So too are the opening and closing shots of *The Wrong Man* and the second and closing shots of *Notorious*. This framing provides the setting for the erotically charged first meeting of Cary Grant and Eva Marie Saint on the train in *North by Northwest*, and for Sean Connery's desperate shipboard search for his bride in *Marnie*. In *The Birds*, Jessica Tandy must pass twice through such a frame when she comes upon the horrifying spectacle of her neighbor's pecked-out eyes (in a conjunction of Hitchcockian signs, she drops her purse as she runs). And the lyrical image of door after door opening, superimposed over Ingrid Bergman's ecstatic face as Gregory Peck kisses her, is an important occurrence in *Spellbound*. Hitchcock's tunnel image relates to his //// motif and his flashes of black, white, and red. All participate in a system of references to, and invocations of, sexuality, and in a system of self-reference.

25. In *Spellbound*, too, a view from a train window becomes a terrifying vision of nothingness. When Gregory Peck, uneasy in the company of the woman who loves him and also wishes to cure him, looks out onto the blurred lines of the tracks, he becomes possessed by the memory he is not yet prepared to acknowledge. The wife's fainting spell in the early version of *The Man Who Knew Too Much* is closely related to this, as is the structurally central moment early in the later version when the young son, suffering oedipal pangs on board a bus, immerses himself in the view of the Moroccan landscape and then precipitates the narrative by accidentally pulling the veil from a Moslem woman's face.

26. In his conversation with Truffaut, Hitchcock speaks of Charlie's pushing Charles to his death as "accidental." But this must not be taken to mean that her act is not intentional, that she does not mean it (whatever her conscious thoughts or feelings may be). That she looks away when she pushes Charles only shows she has no need and no desire to look, not that she does not mean to push him.

27. *Stage Fright*'s ending is complicated by the fact that the central romantic couple is, in a sense, neither Eve and Jonathan nor Eve and Smith, but rather Eve's father (Alastair Sim) and the star whose presence on stage rivets him (Marlene Dietrich). The young lovers are joined as at the ending of a traditional comedy, but they do not spark the film's passion.

5. Psycho

1. For a detailed analysis of *Notorious*, see my "Alfred Hitchcock's *Notorious*," *The Georgia Review*, Fall 1975.

2. André Bazin, *What Is Cinema?* (Berkeley: University of California Press, 1967), p. 50.

3. The camera's capacity to inflict vertigo on its subjects is perhaps most decisively declared in *The Wrong Man*. Having thrust itself through the narrow opening in Manny's cell door, the camera frames his anguished face, then begins spiraling, so that our view of Manny spirals as well. What gives Manny vertigo is the realization that he has been singled out by the agency that presides over the world, that his world has been created in the image of his innermost fears. Our vertigo is in the face of the camera's demonstration that we cannot take for granted that there are safe, known boundaries between what is inside and outside us, between our selves and the world, between the world of *The Wrong Man* and reality.

4. This line links *Psycho* to *Rear Window*, which opens on a thermometer risen into the nineties (in *Torn Curtain*'s opening, a thermometer plunges below freezing). A natural danger point has been passed. As in *The Birds*, nature helps to trigger the narrative.

5. This moment recalls the scene made by Charles at Joe's bank. The figure of $40,000 seems a deliberate allusion to *Shadow of a Doubt*.

6. A study for this passage is "Breakdown," a teleplay broadcast in late 1955, which consists largely of a series of views of a completely immobile Joseph Cotten—he has been paralysed in an automobile accident and

finds himself taken for dead—accompanied by a voice-over narration that represents his thoughts. Cotten's interior monologue dramatizes the process by which the gravity of the situation impresses itself on him and climaxes in a cry of despair when he thinks that all his efforts to prove he is still alive are doomed to fail. But unlike Cotten (or Sir John in *Murder!*'s shaving-mirror scene, for that matter), Marion does not think in her own voice but imagines a scene in which she remains silent. In this respect, the passage in *Psycho* resembles *Murder!*'s appropriation of Diana's fantasy as she sits in her cell and imagines herself on stage. Marion imagines stepping forward to be viewed like the Avenger at the opening of *The Lodger*. Sam's view of Marion, invoked but withheld, like the victim's view of the Avenger, is at the heart of this scene.

7. The sign, I take it, is a Hitchcockian joke. There is a moment in *The Wrong Man* at which Manny's lawyer stands in front of a window. His figure blocks part of our view of the grocery store across the street, making the sign on its awning read "Center Gore." This alerts us to the possibility of reading "Gorman" as "Gore Man."

8. Compare the dough-heart scene in *The Lodger* and also Charles's tearing his toast as Emma tells the story of his accident in *Shadow of a Doubt*.

9. *Marnie*'s opening—a handbag is framed so as to suggest an eye even as it stands in for the sexuality of the woman who is carrying it—echoes this image of Norman's peephole.

10. This series of shots contrasts in at least two ways with the passage in *Murder!* in which we view Diana through her cell-door window. First, Diana knows she is being viewed and escapes into the private world of her imagination, while Marion appears oblivious of this eye. Second, the being whose view we share in *Murder!* remains unviewed, except for the hand, but in *Psycho* the viewing eye is itself on view.

11. In the Albert Hall sequence of the later version of *The Man Who Knew Too Much*, we are given a view of the auditorium seen through the gap between a pair of cymbals poised to clash. These cymbals, as it were, rule over the scene. Music, the art that holds the concert audience in thrall, is an analogue of Hitchcock's art, the art of film. The shower-murder sequence invokes Hitchcock's art directly, while the Albert Hall sequence alludes to it.

12. In *The Lodger*, Daisy's pleasure in her bath is a manifestation of her desire and cannot be separated from her wish for the lodger to appear and make love to her. Then again, Daisy's desire is focused on no particular object, as Marion's is focused on the shower head.

13. This shot may be compared to the last shot of *The Birds*, which frames the world "outside" into which the Brenners and Melanie must now perilously venture, in a frame-within-a-frame that makes it appear projected on a screen. In the world of *The Birds*, this "screen" is real, like the movie screen on which all our views have been projected. *The Birds* is a film; its world is separate from the real world in which we are viewers. Yet this ending suggests that there is no essential difference between the

outside in which we are fated to live and the outside projected on this frame-within-a-frame. Hitchcock wanted no final title to announce the end of *The Birds*, in part to underscore the suggestion that, when we leave the theater, our condition will not fundamentally change. Our world too is threatened by forces that may be quiescent but may go mad at any time. The world of a film is outside us while it is also our projection; *The Birds* ends with a vision of reality as outside but also projected from within.

14. I think of the hand gripping the shower curtain as, at one level, an allusion to Eisenstein: specifically, to the moment in *Potemkin*'s Odessa Steps sequence when the young mother, pregnant with another child, is shot in the stomach and grips her belt, emblazoned with the insignia of Russia, her hands running dark with blood. This is her blood and the blood of her unborn child, representing all the children of Mother Russia who are being tragically consumed by the enemies of revolution. Hitchcock's allusion here turns on the idea that the shower curtain encloses a womb that has been defiled, a womb that represents both Marion's body and the "private island" of which she dreamed. But Hitchcock also alludes to Eisenstein here, I take it, because the shower-murder sequence is a testimonial to the power of montage. (That film's power derives in part from the possibilities of cutting was the point of Hitchcock's one-sentence speech at the 1976 Lincoln Center tribute. Following an elaborate compilation of his most famous murder scenes, conspicuously including the killing of Swann in *Dial 'M' for Murder*—he is stabbed in the back by a pair of scissors—Hitchcock rose slowly and simply said, "As you can see, scissors are the best way.") Yet while Hitchcock's homage to Eisenstein is sincere, his films are fundamentally opposed to those of the Soviet director. Eisentein assumes a clear separation of guilty and innocent and takes his own innocence, and that of the revolution he serves, for granted. Such an attitude is anathema to Hitchcock. *Potemkin* never acknowledges the possibility that the revolution could also be capable of devouring Mother Russia's children. And Eisenstein, at least in his early films, takes for granted that he has the right to subject his viewers to violence.

15. In "*Psycho!*" (*Hammer's House of Horrors*, March 1978, pp. 36–39), Tony Crawley claims that it was Saul Bass (the designer of *Psycho*'s title credits) who composed the shower-murder sequence and directed it "on a closed set with Hitchcock in close and constant attendance." Given the nature of Hitchcock's work, there is no clear difference between "directing" and "supervising" the shooting. If Bass really did compose the sequence, however, he would be its author, as Crawley implies, not Hitchcock. For evidence, Crawley presents the story board Bass submitted, in which he sketched each shot as he conceived it. The truth, though, is that the sequence in *Psycho* owes nothing essential to this blueprint. In Bass's story board, for example, no special role is given the shower head. Bass does not envision the camera movement that identifies shower curtain and movie screen. Bass's murderer does not address a theatrical demonstration to Marion and to us. In his sketches, there are no jump cuts and no overhead shot in which the barrier between inside and outside inscribes a

//// in the frame; the intruder's hand does not turn to flesh before our eyes; no shot declares the murder to be a rape or a blinding; there is no with-drawal of the camera from Marion's outstretched hand; and so on. Indeed, nothing that makes the sequence a summation of Hitchcock's art derives from Bass's design. Hitchcock, not Saul Bass, is the author of the shower-murder sequence.

16. This swirling blackness, *Psycho*'s central vision of nothingness, is linked to *Vertigo*'s views down the stairwell and also to the spiraling camera movement in *The Wrong Man*.

17. The most inspired example of this mode of irony occurs in the cafe scene of *The Birds*. In the midst of general consternation about the vulnerability of the human species in any war against birds, two orders of southern fried chicken are shouted in.

18. The shot of Lila framed in the mirror is closely related to the shot in *Shadow of a Doubt* that presents Charles's view of Charlie at the foot of the stairs, possessing him in her gaze. Lila has assumed Charles's place in the frame and Charlie's as well.

19. Typically, Hitchcock's musical references are to Beethoven, Wagner, and Mozart, as his literary references are to Shakespeare.

Index

1814